Megatrends and Air Transport

Ruwantissa Abeyratne

Megatrends and Air Transport

Legal, Ethical and Economic Issues

Springer

Ruwantissa Abeyratne
Cote Saint-Luc, Québec
Canada

ISBN 978-3-319-61123-5 ISBN 978-3-319-61124-2 (eBook)
DOI 10.1007/978-3-319-61124-2

Library of Congress Control Number: 2017943003

Printed on acid-free paper

This Springer imprint is published by Springer Nature
The registered company is Springer International Publishing AG
The registered company address is: Gewerbestrasse 11, 6330 Cham, Switzerland

Preface

I commenced writing this book in February 2017, inspired by my lead role on megatrends, in Aviation Strategies International—a global aviation consultancy firm headquartered in Montreal. At this time, the travel and tourism industry was the largest industry in the world where 1 in 10 people across the globe was working in the industry and the industry was contributing US$ 7.6 trillion to the global economy. The industry was growing steadily at an annual rate of 3.5%, and it was thought that the trend would continue for some time. Also at the time, Donald Trump was new in the White House; the vote on Brexit had just been passed in the British House of Commons and was headed for the House of Lords; elections were looming in the Netherlands, France and Germany; the credibility of the European Union was in serious question with Guy Verhofstadt—the European Parliament's Brexit Negotiator—calling for a drastic review of the philosophy of the EU; and, to add to the excitement, North Korea had tested a missile capable of carrying a nuclear warhead, to the chagrin of the United Nations Security Council, and China was still flexing its muscle in the South China Sea.

Whilst all this was going on, new concepts of state sovereignty were being introduced. In international affairs, the preeminent consideration was the sovereignty of states, which was introduced after the 30-year war by the Peace of Westphalia of 1648—which recognized the immutable and inalienable sovereignty and right of states (countries) to charter their own independence and existence without interference from other states or persons. Over the few centuries that lapsed, the pristine concept of sovereignty evolved from a purely domestic application of government prerogative over governance to include responsibility towards people. A more recent concept is called R2P—Responsibility to Protect—pioneered by Canada, where the responsibility of a government to protect its own people is extended to people of other states who might be in need of protection from acts of their own governments and others. In recent times, the way things have gone around the world has brought to bear a further extension of this responsibility, introduced as *sovereign obligation* by Richard Haas, President of the Council on Foreign Relations, in his essay in the January/February 2017 issue of *Foreign*

Affairs called *World Order 2.0—The Case for Sovereign Obligation*: Haas said "[S]uch a concept of sovereign obligation, it is worth pointing out, differs from the notion of sovereign responsibility. . .It stems from a need to expand and adapt the traditional principles of international order for a highly interconnected world. Sovereign obligation thus retains a respect for borders and an opposition to their being changed through coercion or force".

Contemporaneously, a parallel dimension was taking place in the shape of megatrends—large, transformative, global forces that affect everyone in the world—which are emerging as compelling drivers of our existential world, affecting, among many other human endeavours, the development of air transport. To begin with, global balance of power as a megatrend is the first to be addressed in the context of aviation. Climate change and the scarcity of resources, hyperconnectivity, accommodating growing individuality and individual empowerment, harnessing technology, the exponential rise of the middle class, social mobility and decreasing inequality, big data analysis and privacy, digitization, globalized public demand for better services, technological innovation, medical advances, artificial intelligence and super computers and game changers are other megatrends that would affect aviation.

Particular to the aviation industry (and the world) would be that by 2020 the global middle class will number 3 billion people, and we (including the aviation industry) will be able to connect with them all through the smart devices in their pockets. By 2020, 21 billion network devices will be in use—up from 2 billion just a decade ago. Mobile technology, cloud computing, data analytics, biotech and genomics and artificial intelligence are all advancing rapidly. Consequently, one could expect growth opportunities related to aircraft digitization and new high-performance materials, as well as for hybrid engines and 3-D printing. The aerospace industry is probably the slowest cycle industry of any; however, aerospace programs will need to advance much more quickly to respond to advances in technology. Examples include satellite technology, cybersecurity, directed energy, nanotechnology, urbanization, wireless intelligence and smart city concepts.

Intrinsically linked to these developments would be another megatrend—the continued rise of Generation Y (25–35-year-olds) which would constitute 34% of the global population in 2020. Generation Y will be the most adaptive to change, ready to experiment with new technologies and a high level of purchasing power in 2020. Generation Y is identified as the pioneers of another powerful megatrend called the *global code*—which is a new culture of universal values that is reshaping business and marketing. These values are those of what is called the *global tribe* (another term for millennials) who will be responsible for two sub trends that would directly impact aviation. These are the *Gypsy complex*, where the global tribe will associate with each other through international travel (with no permanent home), and *reverse brain drain* which is a massive reversal of highly educated and skilled workers back to their homeland in 2020. This movement of labour force will have a huge impact on the economy and industry, particularly for aviation.

Also important as a megatrend that would impact aviation are the *next game changers* who are the next big emerging markets which are identified as the *Next 11*, or the future economic engines of growth—signalling a shift in economic power in 2020 from BRIC countries to nations of Bangladesh, Egypt, Indonesia, Iran, Mexico, Nigeria, Pakistan, the Philippines, South Korea, Turkey and Vietnam.

Next-generation business models in 2020 will redefine future business propositions and influence technology and product development. Some of these evolving models are *personalization*, *car sharing* and *pay by the hour*, and their impact on changing trends in aviation (beacons at airports, check-in and locating places in airports) would be an interesting development.

Technology is fast changing the way we work and the air transport world is no exception. A megatrend that would be exclusively aviation specific would be the application of the Internet (Internet of Things, *IoT*) to inflight entertainment and communications. Additionally, pilots are already accessing Wi-Fi cabin networks for weather information and flight planning. *IoT* is also being used for flight tracking and real-time flight status. This has now morphed to the Internet of Everything (IOE) which will connect almost all goods and services we use, ostensibly to make our lives easier and communications fluid and seamless. From the airport perspective too, technology has brought forth a compelling megatrend that focuses on the passenger as the priority. It is called Airport Service Quality (ASQ), which Airports Council International (ACI)—the international association of airports—defines as the world-renowned and globally established global benchmarking programme measuring passengers' satisfaction whilst they are travelling through an airport. Essentially, this boils down to the type of services offered and their nature which would earn approval and satisfaction of the passenger. In this context, there are many airports, both international and domestic, that provide special services to passengers in need. One particularly prominent hub airport categorizes those in need of special services as accompanied babies and children, unaccompanied children, pregnant women and sick or disabled passengers. In the case of the mentally incompetent, such as a passenger suffering from dementia, he/she would come under the last category of a sick or disabled person. However, when one reads the array of services offered by this particular airport, they are all physical assistance such as wheelchairs, accessible ramps, crosswalk warning bumps indicating direction, semi-dome-shaped warning spots on the ground and easy access to special phones and service areas enabled by the warning bumps.

When megatrends are analysed against developments in aviation, one would need to conceptualize change in an unprecedented manner, based on contextual and strategic thinking, taking into consideration global technical, political, economic, legal and demographic trends. In this sense, "strategy" is defined by the *Harvard Business Review* as "the creation of a unique and valuable position, involving a different set of activities from your competitors". The leadership of any air transport enterprise in this area would require exposure to new forms of intellectual openness and curiosity and, above all, an enduring capacity to identify and analyse the effects of such trends on aviation. Megatrends and aviation would essentially entail a palpable transition from best practices to strategic analysis in the context of the new global business order and global risks facing global trends.

This book analyses some of the key areas of air transport that could be affected by megatrends and the legal issues that accompany them.

Cote Saint-Luc, Québec, Canada
March 2017

Ruwantissa Abeyratne

Contents

Table of Cases

A

B

C

D

E

F

G

H

I

J

L

M

N

O

P

Q

R

S

T

U

V

W

Chapter 1
Megatrends and Air Transport: An Overview

1.1 Future of Aerospace Transport

Megatrends and air transport means different things to different people. While some think of trends that are emerging, others think long term and this treatise would be incomplete if it did not start with the long term perspective first and then get onto what is emerging right now. On 24 November 2016 there was a luncheon presentation entitled *The Next 100 Years of Aviation* convened by The International Aviation Club of Montreal and McGill University. It was an event well attended by the aviation intelligentsia of Montreal. The presentation was well thought through and eloquently delivered. One of the prognostications presented for the next century was that Mars would be colonized and we would be growing vegetables and other produce for our consumption on the planet. This is not difficult to imagine since at present the Mars One project has developed plans to send humans to Mars, although much has to be accomplished in the nature of making the planet habitable for human existence. It is said though, that "establishing a permanent settlement is very complex, but it is far less complex and requires much less infrastructure that is sent to Mars than on return missions".

Already, Mars One—a not-for-profit foundation that works at establishing permanent human life on Mars—has commenced discussions with established aerospace companies with a view to developing the systems needed for sustaining human life and establishing human colonies. Although such systems require complex designing, construction, and testing, it is said that no scientific breakthroughs are required to sustain human life on Mars as existing technology is sophisticated enough to ensure living conditions on the planet. Perhaps the most encouraging statement issued by Mars One is that there will already be a habitable environment waiting for the first human crew to land on the Planet.

Doubtless, this news is music to the years of the next generation of aviation professionals who occupied two tables at the luncheon—youngsters from both the International Civil Aviation Organization and McGill University. How exciting for

R. Abeyratne, *Megatrends and Air Transport*, DOI 10.1007/978-3-319-61124-2_1

them to be at the cusp of outer space travel, let alone be faced with the long term prospect of being able to have an extra terrestrial abode for their children and grand children!

However, there seem to be a couple of snags here: At the presentation, it was forecast that by 2116, there could be at least one flight a day from Earth to Mars presumably carrying tourists and settlers. But before then, well, way before then, humans would have landed on Mars and in fact settled there permanently. Sarah Knapton, Science Editor for *The Telegraph* in her article entitled *Nasa planning 'Earth Independent' Mars colony by 2030s* quotes NASA as having claimed that humans will be living and working on Mars in colonies entirely independent of Earth by the 2030s. In fact, NASA is purported to have released a plan for establishing permanent settlements on Mars on the basis of creating 'deep-space habitation facilities' which will act as stepping stones to Mars.

If humans were to settle on Mars in just 15–20 years' time, how is this conceivable when we still do not have a global understanding or agreement on at what altitude air space ends and at what point outer space begins? What are the laws that would govern travel from airspace to outer space? Air law and space law are closely inter-related in some areas and both these disciplines have to be viewed in the twenty-first century within the changing face of international law and politics. Both air law and space law are disciplines that are grounded on principles of public international law, which is increasingly becoming different from what it was a few decades ago. We no longer think of this area of the law as a set of fixed rules, even if such rules have always been a snapshot of the law as it stands at a given period of time. The issue of air space and outer space is looming over the aerospace community, particularly with the prospect of space travel on a commercial basis which is already a reality. Currently, the aerospace community is considering such issues as sub-orbital flights and space tourism, both of which could further blur the boundaries between air space and outer space, while raising issues of topical interest. So far, there has not been a universally accepted definition distinguishing air space and outer space. Some years ago, when the legalities of an aerospace plane, which is a hypersonic single stage to orbit reusable vehicle that horizontally takes off and lands on a conventional runway were considered, it was thought that the transit through near space which is involved is incidental to the main transit which takes place within the airspace. Generally, the aerospace plane, which will be constructed with the use of aeronautical and space technologies and would be capable, and, indeed, required to fly both in airspace and outer space, would bring to bear the need to consider the applicability of and appropriateness of laws relating to the space plane's activities. It will be subject to the sovereignty of the State whose airspace it is in. This is an incontrovertible fact which need not be stated since any object within the airspace of a territorial State would indeed be subject to that State's sovereignty.

Recently, the official launch of space tourism, where paying customers travelled beyond Earth's atmosphere, gave rise to an entirely different dimension, where the different issue of sub-orbital flights has emerged as requiring some consideration, particularly on the question as to whether such flights travel to outer space or whether they are deemed to be considered as not leaving the Earth's atmosphere. Unlike the aerospace plane which would leave the territory of one State as an aircraft, enter outer space and travel in outer space until it descends to a destination State, sub-orbital flights would not usually travel between two States but would ascend to an altitude sufficient for the persons on board to view the Earth as a whole globe, a phenomenon not available to aircraft passengers. The vehicle would descent to the State from which it took off. This activity is called "sub-orbital flying" and is gaining increasing popularity in the realm of space tourism. One of the issues that sub orbital flights raise is whether, at the height the flights are conducted, the vehicle is deemed to be in air space or outer space. Therefore, sub orbital flights inevitably call for a determination as to what might be air space, as against outer space This question is particularly relevant when one considers liability arising from death or injury to passengers while travelling in outer space. Although there are established treaty provisions regarding air travel under the Montreal Convention of 1999 there is no such treaty governing travel in a spacecraft in outer space.

Once the travel issue is settled, the other question that would emerge would be what laws would govern human conduct in outer space. Who would be the governing authority? Article 1 of the Outer Space Treaty provides that the exploration and use of outer space, including the moon and other celestial bodies, shall be carried out for the benefit and in the interests of all countries, irrespective of their degree of economic or scientific development, and shall be the province of all mankind. It goes on to say that outer space, including the moon and other celestial bodies, shall be free for exploration and use by all States without discrimination of any kind, on a basis of equality and in accordance with international law, and there shall be free access to all areas of celestial bodies.

Finally, Article 1 provides that there shall be freedom of scientific investigation in outer space, including the moon and other celestial bodies, and States shall facilitate and encourage international co-operation in such investigation.

The more challenging provision in the Treaty is Article 2 which prescribes that outer space, including the moon and other celestial bodies, is not subject to national appropriation by claim of sovereignty, by means of use or occupation, or by any other means. This precludes a State from appropriating a celestial body *inter alia* by use.

Garold Larson, Alternate Representative to the First Committee of the 64th Session of the United Nations Assembly held on 19 October 2009, succinctly outlined the policy of the United States on space exploration. The foremost principle outlined by Larson was that the United States will continue to uphold the principles of the 1967 Outer Space Treaty, which the United States recognized as providing fundamental guidelines required for the free access to and use of outer space by all nations for peaceful purposes. He went on to say that the United States will continue to take an active role in identifying and implementing cooperative efforts with established and emerging members of the international spacefaring community to ensure the safety of the space assets of all nations and also expand cooperation with other like-minded spacefaring nations and with the private sector to identify and protect against intentional and unintentional threats to its space capabilities.

The European Union, in 2008, published a draft Code of Conduct for Outer Space Activities, which it later revised in September 2010. The fundamental postulate of this code is that member states should establish policies and procedures to minimize the possibility of accidents . . . or any form of harmful interference with other States' right to the peaceful exploration and use of outer space. The Code applies three basic principles in pursuance of its overall objective: freedom of access to space for peaceful purposes; preservation of the security and integrity of space objects in orbit; and due consideration for the legitimate defence interests of states. The code is not a legislative instrument and therefore has no legally binding effect on member States. It remains a voluntary agreement among states with no formal enforcement mechanisms. On 4 April 2011 the European Commission published a space strategy for Europe whereby the European Union seeks to identify and support the development of essential technologies for exploration, in particular in the fields of energy, health and recycling (support for life in isolated environments). These matters are not necessarily dealt with in the space sector itself and cross-fertilisation should be promoted with other sectors in order to benefit the citizens directly.

Answers can always be found but the key principle is that technology and space exploration must go on for the benefit of humanity. In the ultimate analysis, a joint space programme between key players of North America, Europe and Asia could greatly stabilize international space exploration. Growing spinach on Mars is one thing, but getting the laws in place within the next 15 years is an entirely different prospect.

1.2 The Future of Air Transport Law

Having discussed the aerospace connection in the next 100 years, one has to consider what an overview of the law would be like in air transport leading on to the megatrends of the present and the future. Half the world is living in cities. It is not probable that globalization will stop and, with exponential development, this city population will only grow globally. An ageing population, many with disposable incomes, is another irreversible trend. Against this backdrop, increasing urbanisation; expanding middle class; and rise in migration, tourism and international students are current and future trends. Development and international cooperation is a buzz word in many developed and developing countries.

Air travel will double in 2020 as against today's figure. It is forecast that, between 2009 and 2028 there will be a demand for 24,951 passenger and freighter aircraft worth USD 3.1 trillion, and that, by 2028 there will be 32,000 aircraft in service compared with 15,750 in 2009. In January 2015, ongoing projects for airport construction amounted to the value of US$543 billion globally. These facts and figures incontrovertibly spell out the future of air transport and the inevitable fact that liberalization of air transport is a compelling need to meet demand. However, protectionism of market access is looming its head, taking us back to the frustrating 70s and 80s.

Additionally, technology and development resonate the fact that in the near future, commercial space travel will take off, posing a challenge to tenets of air transport law. Regrettably, in all these areas, initiatives in air transport law have been insouciant at best. This article looks at the state of the world today in the context of air transport law and inquires into its future in five key areas that have been selected for discussion.

At a time when the world celebrates over 70 years of regulated air transport and *Air and Space Law* celebrates 40 years of publication, it is appropriate to envision the shape public international law pertaining to air transport should take in the years to come.

At the outset a seminal point of nomenclature has to be clarified. The law pertaining to air transport has been quoted, and often misquoted, with the use of various terms, the first being "air law". *Milde* asserts that the term is "controversial and imprecise", saying that it is possibly influenced by the French term "*droit et aerostats*"[1] and that it is misleading in that it wrongfully implies a separate branch of law. He asserts that the term "aeronautical law" would be more to the point although the sustained use of the term "air law" should be respected.[2] According to *Milde,* there is no autonomy that could be ascribed to the term "air law" which he claims is composed of various principles that applies to social relations (physical persons, corporate bodies and sovereign States) regulated by law. Although one cannot question this premise, one could certainly question whether the term "aeronautical law" as suggested by *Milde* is consistent with his argument about social relations, since aeronautical law is essentially the law relating to "aeronautics" which is defined as "a science that deals with airplanes and flying" or the science dealing with the operations of aircraft.[3]

Dempsey, on the other hand is seemingly comfortable with the term "air law" when he says that that international air law or aviation law is composed of public and private categories[4] and that the *Magna Carta* of air law is the Chicago Convention of 1944.[5] Be that as it may, the author prefers to use the term "air transport law" for purposes of this article.

Another disturbing trend that has been consistent throughout the past 70 years is that the meaning and purpose of law as it applies to air transport has been upended, in that the law has inflexibly dictated to changing economic and social circumstances instead of the other way around, where the law, as a management and social

---

[1]Milde (2012), p. 1.

[2]*Ibid.*

[3]http://www.merriam-webster.com/dictionary/aeronautics.

[4]Dempsey (2015), p. 215.

[5]Convention on International Civil Aviation, signed at Chicago on 7 December 1944. See ICAO Doc 7300/8:2006.

tool, should adapt to changing circumstances and be changed accordingly. At the forefront of this inequity are two key influences or drivers—international law and politics—and their treatment of sovereignty of States and air traffic rights which concepts have not overcome the antiquated notions of market share and protectionism that belie modern exigencies of market economics. Generally under legal theory, each State is sovereign and equal and the term *sovereignty* may be used as a synonym for independence. However, in modern parlance, with the rapid growth in telecommunications and global competition and rivalries, no State can be entirely sovereign to the exclusion of others.

Inextricably connected to this phenomenon is the awareness of the international community that, within the progression of air law are two main issues concerning the evolving role of air law. The first is that that the distinction between air law and space law is continuing to blur. The second is that principles of air law are getting increasingly involved in activities related to military warfare. With regard to the threat envisioned in the use of military warfare on civil aviation activity, the same players, i.e. international law and politics, play the same role. Although airspace is common and States have sovereignty over the airspace above their territories, this does not enable them to use such air space arbitrarily. There are strict principles with regard to aerial military activity and prohibition of the use of military warfare on civilian populations and properties. These must be strictly adhered to in the basis of political consensus.

Air law and space law are closely inter-related in some areas and both these disciplines have to be viewed in the twenty-first century within the changing face of international law and politics. Both air law and space law are disciplines that are grounded on principles of public international law, which is increasingly becoming different from what it was a few decades ago. We no longer think of this area of the law as a set of fixed rules, even if such rules have always been a snapshot of the law as it stands at a given moment.

With changing technology, old political dogma and economic theory are no longer viable and today's challenges demand that we look at the world in a new way. With changing political philosophy, where governments are increasingly asserting their sovereignty, a whole new compromise in air transport law becomes necessary. Although one speaks of globalization, in practice, when one looks at cross border integration of markets, the world is only semi-globalized with barriers that effectively preclude air transport's full potential. Air transport, more than any other industry, demonstrates that a borderless world is still a theoretical concept where State interest still takes prominence over the consumer.

New and emerging threats to civil aviation will continue to be a cause for concern to the aviation community. Grave threats such as those posed by the carriage of dangerous pathogens on board, the use of cyber technology calculated to interfere with air navigation systems, and the misuse of man portable air defence systems will remain real and will have to be addressed with vigour and regularity.

Another area that requires attention is the reactive and ineffective manner the legal regime applicable to air transport was put to work over 2014, where several air disasters took the world by surprise. The regulators scrambled to set things rights, and it was as though they had not imagined that such disasters were possible.[6]

It is submitted that the enduring weakness of air transport law is the disconnect between where the world is headed and the role to be played by air transport as a product that should be a more efficient engine for growth.

1.3 Where Is the World Headed?

For the next few years at least, the global order portends a disturbing uncertainty. Economic power is shifting across the globe to emerging markets in the far east. Technology is changing rapidly, affecting the way air transport is being conducted around the world. Globalization and deregulation are no longer intrinsically linked to each other. Although the prevailing cross border flow of people will increase, the quantum of cross border investment of foreign direct investment would probably remain at the current rate of around 10%, thus attracting continued protectionism in air transport.[7] The World Bank, in its January 2015 Report,[8] expects overall, global growth to rise moderately, to 3.0% in 2015, and average about 3.3% through 2017. The Report posits that a growth rate of 2.2% will be seen in high income countries in 2015–17, which would be an increase of 1.8% as against 2014, on the back of gradually recovering labour markets, ebbing fiscal consolidation, and still low financing costs. Growth is projected to gradually accelerate in developing countries, rising from 4.4% in 2014 to 4.8% in 2015 and 5.4% by 2017.

A significant gap in the shape of things to come and existing air transport law is the disconnect between where the world is heading, both politically and technologically, and the laws needed to steer air transport in line with shifting trends while offering a safer, more secure and more efficient product. The power shift to the east, where consumer spending in China is $2.2. trillion in 2015 and Middle Eastern countries such as Saudi Arabia, Qatar UAE, Kuwait and Bahrain have $1 trillion in investment, are harbingers of the direction the world economy is taking. These figures have to be read in conjunction with some basic facts on the direction air transport is headed. Covering the years 1980 to 2013 a study[9] was conducted by the OECD,[10] which reflects that the airline sector is continuing to grow exponentially.

---

[6]see Abeyratne (2014a). Also by the same author, Flight MH 17: The Legal and Regulatory Fallout (2014b), pp. 329–342. Flight MH 370 and Global Flight Tracking – The ICAO Reaction (2014c), pp. 544–558.

[7]Ghemawat (2011), p. 29.

[8]*Global Economic Prospects: Having Fiscal Space and Using it*, January 2015, at 21.

[9]AIRLINE COMPETITION—Background Paper by the Secretariat, Directorate for Financial and Enterprise Affairs Competition Committee, 18–19 June 2014, DAF/COMP(2014)14.

[10]Organisation for Economic Co-operation and Development (OECD), established in 1961, promotes policies that are calculated to improve the economic and social well-being of people around the world. The OECD provides a forum in which governments can work together to share

Another compelling fact The OECD Report brings to bear is that by 2026, air transport will contribute $1 trillion to world's GDP.[11] The International Civil Aviation Organisation (ICAO)[12] posits that passenger trips increased from 4.028 billion in 1980 to 19.125 billion in 2012. and that International scheduled passenger traffic grew by 5.2% in 2013 in comparison to 2012 and is expected to reach over 6.4 billion passenger by 2030.[13] According to ICAO's forecast , there will be an average annual growth rate of 4.5% by 2030 in passenger traffic (of both scheduled and unscheduled services).[14]

The key drivers of air transport, according to an *Airbus Industrie* forecast, of economic growth will be: increasing urbanisation; expanding middle class; and rise in migration, tourism and international students.[15] This forecast predicts that emerging countries-regions (Asia and the Pacific, Africa, Middle East and South America) will overtake the developed countries-regions in terms of economic growth with a 10% increase in growth in passenger travel.

There are three areas that would be crucial in the years to come if we are to avoid self- induced stagnation. They are: competition for growth; international intervention to secure the welfare of people; and investment in a balanced education and healthcare for the people. As for competition for growth, this is not a new measure of economic proactivity.

The World Economic Forum reports in its Global Agenda[16] that geostrategic competition is a compelling sign of future global trends and that recent developments have led to tectonic shifts in state interaction, bringing to centre stage geopolitics and realpolitik causing wide ranging effects on the world economy. Air transport, which has remained a political tool in view of the legal recognition of sovereignty in air space, would undoubtedly be affected by this trend.

---

experiences and seek solutions to common problems. The Organization works with governments to understand what drives economic, social and environmental change.

[11] AIRLINE COMPETITION, *Supra*, note 9, *Background Note* at 3. The Report goes on to say that worldwide, aviation and related tourism generate over 56 million jobs, of which 8.36 million are directly linked to the aviation sector. Around 35% of international tourists travel by air.

[12] The International Civil Aviation Organization is the United Nations specialized agency dealing with international civil aviation. ICAO was established by the Convention on International Civil Aviation (Chicago Convention), signed at Chicago on 7 December 1944. See ICAO Doc 7300/8: 2006. The main objectives of ICAO are to develop the principles and techniques of international air navigation and to foster the planning and development of air transport. ICAO has 191 Contracting States.

[13] ICAO Press Release, 16 December 2013. The OECD Report also notes that the number of travellers has increased because, among many other things, prices have decreased significantly in response to increasing competition in the air transport market. For example, in 1974 the cheapest round-trip New York–Los Angeles flight (in inflation-adjusted dollars) that regulators would allow: $1442. Today one can fly that same route for $268.

[14] Global Air Transport Outlook to 2030, *Circ.333, AT/190*: 2012, at 59.

[15] Airbus Industrie, Global Market Forecast: Flying on Demand 2014–2033, at 16.

[16] World Economic Forum: outlook on the Global Agenda 2015, http://www.weforum.org/reports/outlook-global-agenda-2015.

In view of the above, when one applies the trajectory of the global economy and its direction in the coming years to the market economics of the air transport industry, it becomes eminently clear that the economic forces that are shaping the global economy will affect the progress of aviation. The World Energy Council (WEC) has reported that fuel demand in the transport sector in the next 40 years will come mainly from developing countries such as China and India, where demand will grow by 200% to 300%. In contrast, the WEC is of the view that the transport fuel demand for the developed countries will drop by up to 20%, mainly due to increased efficiencies. The demand of the developing countries is expected to surpass that of the developed countries by the year 2025.

The report also forecasts that oil may still fuel more than 80% of the global transport sector for the next 40 years due to strong demand growth from the heavy duty sector, shipping and air traffic. WEC projects that by 2050 global fuel demand in all transport modes could increase by 30–82% compared to 2010 levels. This portend the inevitability that fossil fuels, the reserves of which are still being discovered, will retain its heavy influence over the coming years and therefore global efforts would have to be concentrated on market based measures as well as the development of alternative fuel technology.

Against this backdrop, and in view of the air transport forecasts discussed above, an IATA forecast which predicts that air travel will double over the next 20 years[17] becomes extremely relevant, inevitably bringing to bear a dichotomy—that in the absence of a more liberalized air transport regime than what prevails currently, this exponentially increased air travel market could be stultified.

1.4 Challenges Facing Air Transport Law

1.4.1 Nationalism and Sovereignty

With regard to the direction in which the world is headed and the impact it has on air transport, arguably, the most significant future challenge to air transport law would be rising nationalism and sovereignty in air space, where the latter has been misunderstood by many States to confer to them absolute immunity against their domestic decisions and actions. This misconception has been exacerbated by Article 1 of the Chicago Convention which recognizes that States have complete and exclusive sovereignty over the airspace above their territory. In light of this lack of clarity in air transport law, many States still believe that air transport services should be subservient to their parochial national interests of protectionism.

The Economist states that it would become necessary in 2015 to recognize that nationalism is back. The trend in politicians' agenda would be to claim that they are

[17]*The Shape of Air Travel Markets Over the Next 20 Years*, https://www.iata.org/publications/economics/Pages/index.aspx.

standing up for their own countries and this would cut across Europe, Asia and the Americas. The political ambition behind this strategy would be popularity that would enable politicians to grow in power. *The Economist* is of the view that there will be an increase in international tensions and an "unpromising background for efforts at multilateral co-operation, whether on climate, trade, taxation or development[18]".

Nationalism, when merged with sovereignty of air space forms a dangerous combination that presents a misconception that ascribes primacy to protectionism. This would be detrimental to the "fair and equal opportunity" for carriers to operate air services that is provided for in the Preamble to the Chicago Convention. Moreover, it would form an ominous cocktail with both Article 1 and Article 6 of the Convention, the latter of which requires an airline operating scheduled air services to obtain permission from a grantor state to fly in and out of its territory, and would undermine the spirit of globalization and its very purpose of economic efficiency.

Steinberger in 2000 observed that numerous and varied legal obligations of States prescribed by international legal instruments would essentially preclude them from exercising the puritanical concept of sovereignty, thus constraining their actions. It was *Steinberger's* view that such international responsibility would endorse a State's sovereignty rather than diminish it.[19] *Amitai Etzioni*, in a compelling article speaks of the new idea of sovereignty which was endorsed by UN Secretary General Kofi Annan, that there is a radical turnaround from the concept of sovereignty (absolute and exclusive rights of States within their borders which no other State could question or interfere with) of the Peace of Westphalia of 1648, to where sovereignty is not absolute but conditional, where a State could only maintain its sovereignty on condition that it met with its national and international obligations.[20]

Etzioni's compelling argument can be traced to UN Secretary General *Kofi Annan*'s statement before the United Nations General Assembly in 1999 where he said that State sovereignty was being redefined in its most basic sense by the forces of globalization and international cooperation. Annan said that the State was "widely understood to be the servant of its people, and not *vice versa*".[21] In similar vein, *Starke* is inclined to stretch the principle of sovereignty to accommodate external involvement by a State in the affairs of another in special circumstances:

---

[18]Nationalism is back: Bad news for international co-operation, *The Economist: The World in 2015*, at 92. See the web version of Nov 20th, 2014 at http://www.economist.com/news/21631966-bad-news-international-co-operation-nationalism-back.

[19]Steinberger (2000), p. 501.

[20]Etzioni (2005–2006), p. 35.

[21]Secretary-General Presents his Annual Report to General Assembly, 20 September 1999, Press Release, SG/SM/7136, GA/9596. See http://www.un.org/press/en/1999/19990920.sgsm7136.html.

> ..."Sovereignty" has a much more restricted meaning today than in the eighteenth and nineteenth centuries when, with the emergence of powerful highly nationalized States, few limits on State autonomy were acknowledged. At the present time there is hardly a State which, in the interests of the international community, has not accepted restrictions on its liberty of action.[22]

If, as the foregoing discussion reflects, air travel will double by 2020 and several thousands of new aircraft are placed in the market, ICAO will have to attempt a definition of sovereignty or in the least offer an interpretation that would be consistent with modern exigencies of market economics in air transport. This could be accommodated in a Repertory Guidance to the Chicago Convention that is long overdue.[23]

1.4.2 Market Access

The ambiguity brought about by the concepts of sovereignty in air space as well as the restriction imposed by Article 6 of the Chicago Convention has given rise to some confusion between open skies on the on hand and protectionism on the other. This has impacted on the financing of airlines, which the Chicago Convention has nothing to do with. The recent spat between the carriers of the United States and the carriers of the UAE and Qatar are a case in point. The term "subsidy" is not defined precisely in economic terms although the *Oxford English Dictionary* defines the word as "a sum of money granted from public funds to help an industry or business keep the price of a commodity or service low". In broad terms therefore, a subsidy can be considered indirect protectionism. Under the WTO *Agreement on Subsidies and Countervailing Measures* (SCM Agreement),[24] a subsidy is recognized as a financial contribution by a government|| which confers a benefit.[25] A financial contribution is either money or anything else of value provided to a manufacturer or exporter (which could be construed as an international air service originating in a country) at a cost less than would have been charged in a commercial transaction. This could include indirect support from a government.[26]

It is quite obvious that the air transport industry stands at the crossroads of two major influences—globalization and the information revolution—which have revolutionized the trading world by driving competition. The fact that the UAE carriers (as well as Qatar Airways and Turkish Airlines) have the geographic advantage of

[22]Starke (1977), p. 106.

[23]In the 1970s ICAO made a half hearted attempt at developing a Repertory Guide to the Chicago Convention and has done nothing since toward explaining the legal and regulatory interpretation of the various provisions of the Convention. A commentary of the Convention was developed in 2013. See Abeyratne (2013a), Chapter 1.

[24]https://www.wto.org/english/tratop_e/scm_e/subs_e.htm.

[25]Article 1.1.

[26]Cunningham (1999), p. 6.

being in the centre of the long air routes of the world should not be taken as an argument supporting competitive distortion or disadvantage to other carriers which would in turn unduly curb the operations of the four carriers. The Air Transport Association (IATA)[27] has recognized that US$ 4.2 trillion is needed over the next two decades to properly offer connectivity to a travelling public who are creating an exponential demand for air transport.[28]

IATA's Director General Tony Tyler has said that what is needed is smart regulation from governments around the world in order to maximize the economic benefits of connectivity—jobs and growth.

The World Trade Organization has clear rules on subsidies as a trade barrier but market access in air transport is not included within the purview of the WTO. This creates a challenge for both ICAO and air transport law, to introduce either guidelines or rules on this subject. As the discussion below suggests, ICAO, being itself confused on its role in air transport, may not be of much help unless it straightens out its own act in the field of air transport.

1.4.3 The Role of ICAO in Air Transport

The role of ICAO in the field of air transport is at best ambivalent and ICAO has been recognized for what it is rather than what it has done. Although one of ICAO's strategic objectives is *Economic Development of Air Transport* which is to foster the development of a sound and economically viable civil aviation system, ICAO goes on to say that the Strategic Objective reflects the need for ICAO's leadership in harmonizing the air transport framework focused on economic policies and supporting activities. It does not take a legal expert to say that this entire statement is fundamentally flawed, convoluted and meaningless. Firstly it says that ICAO fosters the sound and economical a civil aviation system. "Civil aviation system" encompasses the entirety of civil aviation (not merely air transport) including aircraft engine and frame manufacturers and component manufacturers. It then goes on to say that there is a need for ICAO's "leadership" in harmonizing (not "fostering" this time) of the air transport framework (with no mention of the civil aviation system). It is no surprise that the ICAO Council, which doubtless was prompted by the Secretariat to adopt these words, has maundered through confusion worse confounded. This unsatisfactory state of affairs has been documented in depth elsewhere.[29]

---

[27]The International Air Transport Association is a trade association of the world's airlines. These 250 airlines, primarily major carriers, carry approximately 84% of total available air traffic.

[28]Schaal (2015). See http://skift.com/2013/07/01/the-airline-business-is-a-terrible-one-says-leading-airline-industry-group/.

[29]Abeyratne (2013b), pp. 9–29. Also by the same author, The Air Transport Conference of ICAO – A Critical Analysis (2013c), pp. 297–332.

Over the next few years, ICAO would, as a matter of necessity, have to address the issue of the role of air transport law as it should apply globally, even if such were to end up in a lesser compelling code of conduct. In the least, the prevailing ambivalence would have to be clarified with a way forward for ICAO to assert its much vaunted and claimed "leadership" role in harmonizing the air transport framework which is now relegated to a regime of serf serving fragmentation. When everything is said and done, ICAO's role in this area amounts to much said and nothing done.

1.4.4 Commercial Space Transport

It would not be incorrect to say that air transport stands at the threshold of crossing over to the realm of commercial space transport, particularly since the latter is designed to use aerospace craft which begin their journey from ground through the atmosphere. Thus, air transport law will come under careful scrutiny in the future. Also, the question as to whether the Annexes to the Chicago Convention would have to be adapted would become relevant. There seems to be no doubt that some ICAO involvement will be necessary, in view of the inevitable overlap between the air transport and space transport segments of a journey, particularly in the field of air traffic management, and analogous principles may have to be attenuated from the Annexes to the Chicago Convention on subjects such as licensing, documentation to be carried on board, and rules of outer space travel.

There are a number of provisions of the Chicago Convention that could be adapted to apply to commercial space transport. For example, Article 37 which calls for State cooperation in ensuring harmonization of their regulations with those of the Annexes to the Convention can, in a space law context, provide that each State undertakes to collaborate in securing the highest practicable degree of uniformity in regulations, standards, procedures, and organization in relation to spacecraft personnel, space paths and auxiliary services in all matters in which such uniformity will facilitate and improve commercial space transportation. The exception to this requirement as contained in Article 38 can also be adapted to afford some flexibility to any State which finds it impracticable to comply in all respects with any such international standard or procedure, or to bring its own regulations or practices into full accord with any international standard or procedure after amendment of the latter, or which deems it necessary to adopt regulations or practices differing in any particular respect from those established by an international standard. In such an instance a State could give immediate notification to the organization empowered with the regulatory direction to be provided to States of the differences between its own practice and that established by the international standard. In the case of amendments to international standards, any State which does not make the appropriate amendments to its own regulations or practices could be required to give notice to the monitoring body within 60 days of the adoption of the amendment to the international standard, or indicate the action which it proposes to take. Another provision that can be meaningfully adapted is Article 34 which could provide that in respect of every spacecraft engaged in commercial space transport a journey log book in which shall be entered particulars of the spacecraft, its crew and of each journey, in such form as may be prescribed from time to time pursuant to the legal instrument covering commercial space transport. In any such case, the monitoring body could be empowered to make immediate notification to all other States of the difference which exists between one or more features of an international standard and the corresponding national practice of that State.[30]

1.4.5 Rights of the Passenger

Of all the key areas that affect the future of air transport law, the rights of the passenger on a global scale are the most contentious, purely because there simply are no globally recognized legal rights of the passenger. Curiously, the legal constitution of air transport—the Chicago Convention—is all about States and air carriers with no mention of the consumer of the air transport product except in a few isolated instances that are linked to the functions of a State and an air carrier.[31] The European Union leads the way with its passenger rights policy. The EU passenger rights policy is quite equitable and protects the passenger well. Under this policy, a passenger may not be charged a higher price for a ticket because of his nationality or where he buys the ticket from. Secondly, he has certain rights in case things go wrong. This concerns delays, cancellations and overbooking that prevent him from boarding if he is departing from any airport situated in the EU, or arriving in the EU with an EU carrier or one from Iceland, Norway or Switzerland. There are obligations cast upon the carrier in instances of denied boarding or cancelation of flight or overbooking. In such instances the passenger is entitled to either: transport to the passenger's final destination using comparable alternative means, or having his ticket refunded and, where relevant, being returned free of charge to his initial departure point. If the flight is delayed by 5 h or more, the passenger is also entitled to a refund. The airline must inform the passenger about his rights and the reason for being denied boarding, or any cancellations or long delays (over 2 h, although this may be up to 4 h for flights in excess of 3500 km). With regard to compensation for denied boarding, or if the flight is cancelled or arrives more than 3 h late on arrival at the final destination stated on the passenger's ticket, he may be entitled to compensation of €250–600, depending on the distance of the flight, if it is within the EU for an amount of €250 involving 1500 km or less, and €400 for a trip over 1500 km. This amount differs if the carriage was to be between an EU airport and a

[30]For an extensive discussion on this subject, see generally Abeyratne (2014d).

[31]For a discussion on the rights of the passenger see Abeyratne (2015a), pp. 159–275.

non-EU airport which is €250 for a trip involving 1500 km or less; €400 for a trip of 1500–3500 km; and €600 for over 3500 km.[32]

However, mostly in the rest of the world it has been left to individual States with their policies on consumer protection to look after air passengers who are often not aware of their rights (if there are any) in a particular jurisdiction.[33] The preeminent fundamental human right of a passenger is the right not to be wronged. His rights, when taken collectively, act as the fundamental postulate of any constitutional democracy. Not only must a right remedy a wrong that has been committed or obviate a wrong that ought to be prevented, but a right must be contrived according to circumstance and formally recognized.

ICAO is just beginning to focus some attention to what it calls consumer protection and will conduct a seminar later in 2015 on the subject. It would be counter intuitive and counter-productive if what comes out of this event are merely some recommendations or conclusions. A serious discussion on globally accepted rules and a code of conduct for air carriers and States is warranted.

1.4.6 Conclusion

It is unfortunate that, in the twenty-first century and after 70 years of regulated air transport, there is no such thing as a globally accepted set of air transport laws. What exists is a sporadic discussion of isolated issues in a global forum which is confused about its own role in air transport. It is time that this fragmented discussion crystallized into global acceptance by States of at least the key aspects of air transport that have been the subject of this discussion. For this to happen, two key elements are necessary. The first would be the conduct by the Council of ICAO under Article 55 c) of the Chicago Convention[34] of a study of the future of air transport and the laws which could address problems that are looming. An example of an ominous threat to air transport was recently reported where a cyber security consultant had hacked into computer systems aboard airliners up to 20 times and managed to control an aircraft engine during a flight. The consultant, apparently with the good intention of alerting authorities against the threat of hackers manipulating aircraft's flight pattern, had also hacked into in-flight entertainment systems aboard aircraft. He claimed to have done so 15–20 times from 2011 to 2014. He had also revealed an alarming fact—that he had once hacked into the systems and then overwrote code, enabling him to issue a "CLB," or climb, command.[35]

[32]http://europa.eu/youreurope/citizens/travel/passenger-rights/air/index_en.htm.

[33]http://www.cbc.ca/news/politics/airline-passengers-in-dark-about-rights-advocate-says-1.2489336.

[34]Article 55 c) contains one of the permissive functions of the Council of ICAO which provides that the Council may conduct research into all aspects of air transport and air navigation which are of international importance and communicate such to member States of ICAO while facilitating the exchange of information between the States.

[35]http://venturebeat.com/2015/05/17/fbi-says-this-hacker-took-over-a-plane-through-its-in-flight-entertainment-system/.

The second step would be to extend the study of the Council to an inquiry into the feasibility of submitting compelling rules of a globally acceptable nature or codes of conduct (COCs) with regard to issues that may have consequences for air transport from a global perspective. The incorporation of such rules or COCs into local laws would be the final accomplishment. As per Lord Atkin:

> International law has no validity except in so as its principles are accepted and adopted by our own domestic law. . .The courts acknowledge the existence of a body of rules which nations accept among themselves. On any judicial issue they seek to ascertain what the relevant rule is, and having found it they will treat it as incorporated into the domestic law, so far as it is not inconsistent with rules enacted by statutes or finally declared by their tribunals.[36]

The key to meeting the challenges posed by air transport in the future is development and international cooperation. For these two accomplishments to attain fruition, a robust and dynamic set of air transport laws would be essential.

1.5 Digital Transformation of Air Transport

Exponential developments in digital technologies have enabled airlines to offer enhance customer service while increasing their profit margins. Yet, digital transformation of the airline business has brought with it its own challenges, mainly through regulatory reform and an enduring need to protect the interest of the passenger. With the aid of digital information, airlines have enhanced their hub and spoke operations and planning processes, maximising operating profits and forging connectivity. However, these systems have the proclivity, though not often, for going down, in a manner that would disrupt worldwide operations of an airline as in the early August 2016 systems outage faced by Delta Airlines.[37] Such an event would cause concern among both States and the travelling public—that digital databases maintained by airlines may be open to hacking and that the privacy of passengers could be eroded.[38] This concern is compounded by the fact that the vast

[36] *Chung Chi Cheung* v. *R*, [1939] AC 160; 9 AD, p. 264. See also *Commercial and Estates Co. of Egypt* v. *Board of Trade* [1925] 1 KB 271, 295; 2 AD, at 423.

[37] On 8 August 2016 the media reported in breaking news that at least 451 of Delta Airlines flights were stranded around the world, cancelled for nearly 6 h and nearly half a million passengers were facing delays on Delta Airlines flights due to what a spokesman for the airline called "a major systems collapse worldwide affecting passengers trying to check-in/board. See Delta computer system completely down. Flight operation at stillstand, *eTN Global Travel Industry News*, http://www.eturbonews.com/73542/delta-computer-system-completely-down-flight-operation-stillstan.

[38] See Abeyratne (2011a). Also by the same author, Cyberterrorism – The Next Great Threat to Aviation (2011b), pp. 4–8 and 13.

array of information which airlines store digitally are vastly de-centralized and stored in an unstructured and unconnected silo system.[39]

With regard to States responsibility in protecting information of passengers, Annex 9 to The Convention on International Civil Aviation (Chicago Convention)[40] on facilitation[41] has distinct provisions. Standard 3.7 of the Annex requires Contracting States (to the Chicago Convention) to regularly update security features in new versions of their travel documents, to guard against their misuse and to facilitate detection of cases where such documents have been unlawfully altered, replicated or issued. There is a recommendation[42] in the Annex that Contracting States should incorporate biometric data in their machine readable passports, visas and other official travel documents, using one or more optional data storage technologies to supplement the machine readable zone, as specified in Doc 9303, Machine Readable Travel Documents. The required data stored on the integrated circuit chip is the same as that printed on the data page, that is, the data contained in the machine-readable zone plus the digitized photographic image. Fingerprint image(s) and/or iris image(s) are optional biometrics for Contracting States wishing to supplement the facial image with another biometric in the passport. Contracting States incorporating biometric data in their Machine Readable Passports are to store the data in a contactless integrated circuit chip complying with ISO/IEC 14443 and programmed according to the Logical Data Structure as specified by ICAO.[43]

One of the significant issues in passenger data storage is the advance passenger information (API) requirement imposed by some States who wish to check the desirability of the passenger crossing their borders. Annex 9 establishes the principle of API and its usage by saying that, where appropriate, Contracting States should introduce a system of advance passenger information which involves the capture of certain passport or visa details prior to departure, the transmission of the details by electronic means to their public authorities, and the analysis of such data for risk management purposes prior to arrival in order to expedite clearance.[44]

The Annex also states that each Contracting State that introduces an Advance Passenger Information (API)[45] system under its national legislation is required to

---

[39]See Digital Transformation of the Airline Business, August 2016, *Airline Leader*, Issue 35. See http://www.airlineleader.com/categories/opinion/digital-transformation-of-the-airline-business-295085.

[40]*Supra*, note 5.

[41]Annex 9 to the Convention on International Civil Aviation, Thirteenth Edition: July 2011.

[42]Recommended Practice 3.9.

[43]*Infra*, note 18.

[44]Recommended Practice 3.34.

[45]API involves the capture of a passenger's or crew member's biographic data and flight details by the aircraft operator prior to departure. This information is electronically transmitted to the border control agencies in the destination or departure country. Thus, passenger and/or crew details are received in advance of the departure or arrival of the flight. See Abeyratne (2001), pp. 91–121.

adhere to international recognized standards (in accordance with the UN/EDIFACT PAXLST system[46]) for the transmission of API.[47] There are two Recommended Practices in Annex 9 which suggest that Contracting States and aircraft operators should, where appropriate and, as applicable, on a 24/7 (continuous) basis, provide operational and technical support to analyse and respond to any system outage or failure in order to return to standard operations as soon as practicable,[48] and that Contracting States and aircraft operators should establish and implement appropriate notification and recovery procedures for both scheduled maintenance of information systems and non-scheduled system outages or failures.[49]

The other issue in the context of passenger data is the Passenger Name Record (PNR)[50] which is also addressed in Annex 9 which recommends that Contracting States requiring PNR access should align their data requirements and their handling of such data with the guidelines contained in ICAO Doc 9944,[51] Guidelines on Passenger Name Record (PNR) Data, and in PNRGOV[52] message implementation guidance materials published by the World Customs Organization (WCO) and

[46]The UN/EDIFACT PAXLST message is a standard electronic message developed specifically, as a subset of UN/EDIFACT, to handle passenger manifest (electronic) transmissions. UN/EDIFACT stands for "United Nations rules for Electronic Data Interchange for Administration, Commerce and Transport." The rules comprise a set of internationally agreed standards, directories and guidelines for the electronic interchange of structured data, and in particular that related to trade in goods and services between independent, computerized information systems. The WCO, IATA and ICAO have jointly agreed on the maximum set of API data that should be incorporated in the PAXLST message to be used for the transmission of such data by aircraft operators to the border control agencies in the destination or departure country. It is to be expected that the UN/EDIFACT standard may be supplemented by modern message techniques, such as international xml standards or web-based applications.

[47]Standard 3.46.

[48]Recommended Practice 3.46.10.

[49]Recommended Practice 3.46.11.

[50]A passenger name record in the air transport industry is the generic name given to records created by aircraft operators or their authorized agents for each journey booked by or on behalf of any passenger. The data are used by operators for their own commercial and operational purposes in providing air transport services. Industry standards related to PNR creation are detailed in IATA's Passenger Services Conference Resolution Manual and in the ATA/IATA Reservations Interline Message Procedures—Passenger (AIRIMP). See ICAO Guidelines on Passenger Name Record (PNR) Data, *Doc 9944*, First Edition:2010, at 2.1.1.

[51]ICAO DOC 9944—Guidelines on Passenger Name Record (PNR) Data. This circular was developed subsequent to a recommendation that ICAO develop guidance material for States that may require access to Passenger Name Record (PNR) data to supplement identification data received through an advance passenger information (API) system, including guidelines for distribution, use and storage of data and a composite list of data elements that may be transferred between the operator and the receiving State. The first Edition was released in 2010. See Abeyratne (2005), pp. 170–174.

[52]The PNRGOV message is a standard electronic message endorsed jointly by WCO/ICAO/IATA. Depending on the specific aircraft operator's Reservation and Departure Control Systems, specific data elements can be provided.

endorsed by the International Civil Aviation Organization (ICAO)[53] and The International Air Transport Association (IATA).[54] PNR data are captured in many ways. Reservations may be created by international sales organizations—global distribution systems (GDS) or computer reservation systems (CRS)—with pertinent details of the PNR then transmitted to the operating carrier(s). Reservations may be accepted directly by the aircraft operator and the complete PNR stored in the operator's automated reservations systems.

A number of States consider that PNR data are critically important for the threat assessment value that can be derived from the analysis of such data, particularly in relation to the fight against terrorism and serious crime. They have thus legislated or are planning to legislate for aircraft operators to provide their public authorities with PNR data. In addition, a number of States consider PNR data important for the prevention, investigation or prosecution of a terrorist offence or serious crime.[55] The requirement for PNR data transfer should be governed by explicit legal provisions. The reasons for requiring PNR data should be clearly expressed in the appropriate laws or regulations of the State or in explanatory material accompanying such laws or regulations, as appropriate.[56] States should ensure that their public authorities have the appropriate legal authority to process the PNR data requested from aircraft operators, in a manner that observes these guidelines. States are invited to forward the full text of such legislation to ICAO for online dissemination to other States for information. All queries arising from such legislation should be addressed to the State and not to ICAO.[57]

[53]ICAO is the specialized agency of the United Nations which addresses the subject of international civil aviation. The formation and purpose of The International Civil Aviation Organization (ICAO) is given in the Proceedings of the International Civil Aviation Conference (Chicago, Illinois, November1–December 7, 1944) as follows:

"On November 1944, representatives of 52 nations came together at Chicago, to create a framework for the growth anticipated in world civil aviation. The Convention on International Civil Aviation, also known as the Chicago Convention, provided the establishment of the International Civil Aviation Organization (ICAO)—an international body to guide and regulate international civil aviation. ICAO came into existence on 4 April 1947, after 26 states had ratified the convention. Between 1944 and 1947 a provisional organization (PICAO) operated, the purpose of which was to be of a technical and advisory nature of sovereign States for the purpose of collaboration in the field of international civil aviation and to lay down the foundation for a new international organization to be headquartered in Montreal, Canada." Today, ICAO has 191 member States and is comprised of an Assembly, a Council and a Secretariat.

[54]The International Air Transport Association (IATA) is the trade association for the world's airlines, representing some 265 airlines or 83% of total air traffic. IATA supports many areas of aviation activity and help formulate industry policy on critical aviation issues.

[55]ICAO Doc 9944, *supra*, notes 50 and 51 at 2.2.1.

[56]*Id.* 2.4.1.

[57]*Id.* 2.4.2.

An aircraft operator is obliged to observe the laws of both the State from which it transports passengers (State of departure) and the State to which these passengers are transported (destination State).[58]

An aircraft operator or its agent should provide adequate notice to passengers (for example at the time of booking of a flight or purchase of the ticket) that the operator might be required, by law, to provide the public authorities of a State with any or all of the passenger PNR data held by the operator in relation to a flight to, from, or in transit through an airport within the territory of the State and that the information might be passed to other authorities when necessary to satisfy the State's purpose for acquiring the information. This notice should also include the specified purpose for obtaining the information as well as appropriate guidance to passengers on how they might access their data and seek redress.[59]

States should acknowledge that PNR data collected by aircraft operators cannot be verified for accuracy or completeness. Therefore, neither should action be taken against an operator nor should an operator be held legally, financially or otherwise responsible for transferring PNR data that have been collected in good faith, but which are later found to be false, misleading or otherwise incorrect.[60] When an aircraft operator has not transferred PNR data for a diverted flight, States should take the circumstances surrounding the diversion into account.[61] When penalties and sanctions are imposed for not supplying PNR data, States should impose them only on aircraft operators who directly operate flights that enter, depart or transit through airports situated in their territories.[62]

1.5.1 Technology and Air Transport

The proliferation of technological advancements and breakthroughs that affect businesses worldwide also affect air transport not only from a technical sense but also in its legal context. The major tech-megatrends that could affect the legal regime applicable to air transport are: deep learning; artificial intelligence (that would assist air traffic control) and super computers (that would assist airline pilots and perhaps replace them); unmanned aerial systems (drones); internet of things; and robotics. There are also other tech trends such as virtual reality and augmented reality (used in pilot training). Intrinsically connected to these megatrends are hyper-connectivity; accommodating growing individuality and individual empowerment; harnessing technology; the exponential rise of the middle class; social mobility and decreasing inequality; big data analysis and privacy; digitization; and globalized public demand for better services. The megatrends mentioned

[58] *Id.* 2.4.3.

[59] *Id.* 2.14.1.

[60] *Id.* 2.16.1.

[61] *Id.* 2.16.2.

[62] *Id.* 2.16.3.

above portend consequences to the key players in the air transport equation, particularly in the context of air crew and passengers. The ubiquity of mobile equipment and the advance intelligence of super computers would not only affect the value of business intelligence in the air transport industry but also pose issues for existing treaty law, ethics and State responsibility. This chapter examines some of these issues.

1.5.1.1 Drones

Drones—as a megatrend in aviation—deserves some mention. *The Economist* in its article on 18 April 2016 records that a British Airways aircraft coming in to London had reported that it believed that one of its planes had hit a drone as it came into land at London's Heathrow airport. "Although not confirmed, the incident, which involved an A320 en route from Geneva with 137 passengers and crew on board, is thought to have been the first of its kind in Britain. Few think it will be the last. There have been seven 'category A' near misses—those of a serious nature—in Britain in the past year". *Time* also reported this incident on the same day quoting Steve Landells, of the British Airline Pilots Association, who had reportedly said such an incident was "only a matter of time".

The concern voiced in *The Economist* article is that a drone, which is now commonly seen as an unmanned aerial vehicle with a small payload, could one day be used by incendiaries to pack explosives that could cause serious damage and destruction to an aircraft on contact.

The thirty-sixth Session of the Legal Committee of the International Civil Aviation Organization (ICAO) was held from 30 November–3 December 2015. One of the items under discussion was on legal issues pertaining to Remotely Piloted Aircraft Systems (RPAS) as a new component of the civil aviation system. The item had been placed on the agenda by the Council of ICAO—the governing body of the Legal Committee—pursuant to a discussion that emanated from the thirty-eighth Session of the ICAO Assembly held in 2013.

At the thirty-eighth Session of the ICAO Assembly in 2013, the Republic of Korea submitted a working paper on Remotely Piloted Aircraft Systems (RPAS), claiming that between the first official instance of discussion of RPAS in ICAO—which was at the first meeting of the 169th session of ICAO Council on 12 April 2005—to discussions in 2011, liability for RPAS accidents had not been discussed. In this context, it must be noted that in early 2011, as a result of sustained work carried out on RPAS by ICAO, the Organization released a Manual the purposes of which were to: apprise States of the emerging ICAO perspective on the integration of RPAS into non-segregated airspace and at aerodromes; consider the fundamental differences from manned aviation that such integration will involve; and encourage States to help with the development of ICAO policy on RPAS by providing information on their own experiences associated with RPAS. The fundamental premise that ICAO follows in this regard is that, since unmanned aircraft fall within the definition of 'aircraft' all Standards and Recommended Practices (SARPs) of the Annexes to the Chicago Convention applicable to aircraft would apply to RPAS as well.

The ICAO RPAS Manual recognizes a State in which hazards and risks to safety are reduced and alludes to safety management systems as systematic approaches to managing safety, including the necessary organizational structures infrastructure, formalities and procedures. One of the main issues addressed by the Manual is that aircraft operating without a pilot on board present a wide array of hazards to the civil aviation system. These hazards must be identified and the safety risks mitigated, just as with introduction of an airspace redesign, new equipment or procedures. In this regard, States are required to establish a State Security Programme (SSP) to include safety rulemaking, policy development and oversight. The operation of RPAS in desegregated airspace would not only affect operations carried by commercial air carriers but would also affect general aviation. The International Council of Aircraft Owner and Pilot Association (IAOPA) has commented on the issue of RPAS saying that operating rules for RPAS must take into account their potential impact on general aviation aircraft operating in un-segregated airspace.

The answer to this burgeoning issue and serious potential problem can initially be found in a philosophy of rigid rulemaking as IAOPA suggests. Essentially, rule making is the process where governments convert the broad policy embodied in the bilateral or multilateral treaties they ratify into rules that are applicable to their people, thus providing direction and purpose to the governance process. Rules define the mission of a government and bind people to certain conduct that accord with international and internal policy.

The most fundamental principle in rulemaking is that the genesis of the rule should be authoritative. The most common form of rulemaking in air transport is the adaptation of an international treaty provision or a derivative thereof to a domestic or local regulatory regime. For example, the principles contained in the fundamental postulate of air transport law—The Convention on International Civil Aviation (Chicago Convention)—being the genesis of rules and regulations on the subject, and its derivatives—mainly the 19 Annexes to the Chicago Convention—are generally transposed into the local laws of a contracting State to the Convention, firstly by recognition of its legislature and secondly by executive order or regulation.

Rules are not legislation. They are the results of deliberations of the people in their constituent assemblies that have passed a vote. As Justice Oliver Wendell Holmes put it aptly, rules are the skin of a living policy that crystallizes an inchoate normative policy into hard words that are clear and intelligible to the ordinary person. Of course, the living policy has its genesis either in ratified treaties or enacted local laws, or even decisions of the legal hierarchy of a land. Rulemaking is intrinsically linked with the perceived inadequacy of international law, the sources of which should be the genesis of rulemaking by a State. While on the one hand the entrenched principle of sovereignty of States enable a State to make its own rules and laws, on the other hand, the Sate may be circumscribed by the ambivalence of international law.

To a large extent the issue rests with ICAO as the global forum for issues of international civil aviation. For example, there is a distinct division between the work of the Legal Committee and the Remotely Controlled Aircraft Systems Panel (RPAS Panel) of ICAO, in that the Legal Committee was engaged at its last meeting in a theoretical exercise of sifting through statements and interpretations of treaty provisions regarding liability issues of RPAS while the RPAS Panel was seeking a practical outcome to ICAO's work on RPAS. For example, The RPAS Panel, at its meeting on 15 March 2015, clearly indicated that the overall objective of the Panel was to facilitate the safe, secure and efficient integration of RPA into non-segregated airspace and aerodromes by: maintaining existing level of safety for manned aviation; developing SARPs, procedures and guidance; and being the focal point and coordinator of all ICAO RPAS related work. To develop SARPs on RPAS, ICAO would need clear interpretive guidance on liability issues as well as procedural issues from the Legal Committee so that a Standard could be designed in a compelling manner that would lead to accountability.

1.5.1.2 Robotic Pilots

Arguably, the most contentious trend that is emerging is the possible replacement of the pilot with a robot in the flight deck. With an acute shortage of pilots looming ahead, the robot pilot becomes an attractive proposition. A new development called Aircrew Labor In-Cockpit Automation System, or ALIAS, would enable a robot in the pilot's seat to instantaneously look at multiple to see all the instruments and the gauges in the flight deck and read them all at once. Within a millisecond it could read, analyze and manipulate instruments and gauges reacting faster than a human pilot and instantaneously calling up every emergency checklist for a possible situation. This co-pilot genius would be like "having a human pilot with 600,000 hours of experience."[63]

With the already existing autopilot doing a multitude of tasks, ALIAS is not an unimaginable tool that could be used in the future. The snag would be whether a robot-pilot would match a human in a time of crisis in the flight deck. This can be illustrated with two real life situations. The first was when, on 15 January 2009, Captain Chesley Sullenberger and First Officer Jeffrey Skiles operated US Airways Flight 1549 (AWE1549) with an Airbus A320-214 from New York's LaGuardia Airport to Charlotte Douglas International. A few minutes after takeoff, a flock of Canada geese hit the aircraft rendering both engines incapacitated, necessitating an emergency landing. There being no engine thrust to return to LaGuardia Airport, the captain decided to make an emergency water landing on the Hudson River. The two pilots safely glided the plane to ditch in the river. All 155 passengers on board

[63]Lowy (2016). See http://bigstory.ap.org/article/9f8b7a3237f64bbda73c2f470394b55a/pilot-cockpit-may-someday-be-robot.

were saved.[64] The question here would be whether a robot pilot could have shown the decision making acumen shown by the captain, and more importantly whether a robot pilot could or would have gone several times up and down the cabin to make sure all passengers and crew were out of the aircraft before it sank.

The second example was on 4 November 2010, when an engine on a Qantas Airbus A380 aircraft with 450 people on board blew up, firing shrapnel that damaged multiple other critical aircraft systems and the plane's landing gear. It was found that a turbine disc in the aircraft's Rolls Royce Trent 900 engine had disintegrated. There were a series of emergency messages emanating from the plane's overloaded flight management system which gave the flight crew no time to respond. There were five experienced pilots on board -- including three captains -- who, working together, were able to land the plane. It has been questioned whether a "co-pilot genius" in the form of a robot could have displayed the professional integrity and discretion shown by the human pilots.[65] The basic underlying premise is that people are neither machines nor are they numbers or symbols in an algorithm. Laws are made for legal persons, be it humans or corporations, not to mention States, which lay down their legal liability for acts committed or omitted.

1.5.2 Human-Robot Interface and The Law: The Pilot

Commercial airline pilots operate in a highly complex environment. The tenets of international aviation law attribute to the pilot of an aircraft absolute responsibility for the safe operation of his aircraft. Often, this principle is seen to defeat its purpose in the determination of a single instance of professional conduct of the pilot when such is considered to have endangered the safety of the aircraft, its passengers and property. The main reason for this confusion is the clear dichotomy which exists between statutory provisions and international conventions on the one hand which unequivocally lay down the fact of absolute responsibility of the pilot and the treatment of single instances of negligent professional conduct of the pilot in their isolation, on the other. So far, no attempt has been made either by international law and local statute or by judicial decisions to recognize that the conduct of the pilot in the aircraft should be viewed in its entirety, due regard being given to fundamental principles of law, the conduct of the pilot as a professional in whose hands lie the lives of hundreds of passengers and who takes on his job assuring his employer that his special skills and expertise would transport the

[64]US Airways Flight 1549 Full Cockpit Recording, https://www.youtube.com/watch?v=mLFZTzR5u84. The entire crew of Flight 1549 was awarded the Master's Medal of the Guild of Air Pilots and Air Navigators. The award citations read, "This emergency ditching and evacuation, with the loss of no lives, is a heroic and unique aviation achievement".

[65]Lowy.

passengers and their property safely under normal circumstances and any special circumstance which would render the effect of that assurance nugatory.

The law as it exists lays down a presumption of absolute responsibility of the pilot.[66] In sharp contrast, the adjudication of instances of professional conduct of the pilot shows a clear demarcation between good airmanship and bad airmanship. Of these, the latter shows clear evidence of having been decided on individual merits and not on a general criterion or principle of recognizing the elements of law, special circumstances and the human factor as a composite whole. Therein lies the problem.

The basis of liability in negligence is founded on the principle that when a person owes a duty of care to another, a breach of such duty grounds an action in negligence against the offender. The elements of negligence relevant in the case of a pilot is the duty or standard of care he owes and whether that duty has been breached. While the law imposes an objective test of how the "reasonable man" would execute that duty of care in ordinary circumstances which do not require of him some special skill, in the case of a pilot the standard applicable would be that of the reasonable professional pilot. In the words of Mc Nair J.:

> Where you get a situation which involves the use of some special skill or competence then the test as to whether there has been negligence or not is not the test of the reasonable man because he has not this special skill; a man need not possess the highest of expert skill; it is well established law that it is sufficient if he exercises the ordinary skill of an ordinary competent man exercising that particular art.[67]

The degree of negligent conduct required of a person in charge of transporting passengers and cargo has been set out in clear terms both in cases concerned with the responsibility of a captain at sea and a pilot in command of an aircraft. Brett L.J. delivering judgment on a captain of a ship said:

> Captains of ships are bound to show such skills as persons of their position with ordinary nerve ought to show under the circumstances.[68]

In the 1976 case of *Taylor* v. *Alidair,*[69] Bristow J. held that:

> [there] are activities in which the degree of professional skill which must be required is so high and the potential consequences of the smallest departure from that high standard are so serious that one failure to perform in accordance with those standards is enough to justify dismissal. The passenger-carrying airline pilot, the scientist operating the nuclear reactor, the chemist in charge of research into possible effect of, for example, thalidomide, the driver of the Manchester to London express, the driver of an articulated lorry full of sulphuric acid, are all in the situation in which one failure to maintain the proper standard of professional skill can bring about a major disaster.[70]

---

[66]See Abeyratne (1987), pp. 3–10. Also by the same author, Negligence of the Airline Pilot (1998), pp. 219–231.

[67]*Bolam* v. *Friern Hospital Management Company* [1957} 1 *WLR* 582.

[68]The Bywell Castle (1879) 4 P.D. 219 at 226.

[69](1976) *IRLR* 423.

[70]*Id.* 423. See also generally, *Australia National Airlines Commission* v. *The Commonwealth of Australia and Canadian Pacific Airlines* (1974–75) 132 *CLR* 582.

The position of the pilot in command of an aircraft therefore seems to be governed by the application of three presumptions. They are: the special skill and expertise the pilot is presumed to possess; the enhanced duty of care expected of the pilot in view of such special skill and expertise, and the magnitude of the damage that may be caused in the eventuality of a breach of the duty by the pilot.

1.5.3 Cognitive Computing

Cognitive computing has been considered a trend that could assist humans in precision transportation by providing super intelligence. The advent of IBMs Watson—the super computer which beat two world champions at the TV game *Jeopardy*[71] has been largely acclaimed as a super co-pilot. There have also been views that ultimately super computers could replace humans in the flight deck of an aircraft completely.[72] The issue that brings to bear the legal reality of associating cognitive computing with the professional skill of the airline pilot (as discussed above) and the latter's judgment and human interaction leads to an interesting legal discussion.

Although the issue of both pilots being replaced by AI and super computers is theoretical at present, one cannot deny that discussions are currently taking place regarding such intelligence replacing the first officer on the flight deck. In this context one is faced with the possibility of considering what would happen in an instance when the pilot (in command) dies or is incapacitated during the flight.[73] A flight is operated by the captain and first officer on deck. Both the captain and first officer are usually equally qualified and both could fly all segments of a flight. When a captain dies or is otherwise incapacitated the first officer usually takes charge and would be the pilot in command for the rest of the flight. Annex 6 (Operations of Aircraft) to the Chicago Convention[74] states that the pilot in command is responsible for the operation and safety of the aircraft and for the safety of all persons on board, during flight time.[75] A dereliction of this fundamental duty may entail liability for bad airmanship.

The most important factor in air transport is safety of the aircraft and persons and property on board. The general rule is that the pilot in command of an aircraft is directly responsible for, and is the final authority as to, the operation of that aircraft

[71]See generally, Kelly III and Ham (2013).

[72]See Wilson (2000), pp. 51–53.

[73]In October 2015 the captain of an American Airlines jet bound from Phoenix to Boston passed away during flight. The first officer took command and landed the Airbus A320 in Syracuse, NY. This is just one such recorded incident. See When a Pilot Dies in Flight, http://www.askthepilot.com/pilot-dies-in-flight/.

[74]Convention on International Civil Aviation, signed at Chicago on 7 December 1944. See ICAO Doc 7300, 9th edition:2006.

[75]Annex 6, at 4.5.1.

and, being the ultimate authority in flight the pilot in command can exercise prerogative an in-flight emergency requiring immediate action, to deviate from any rule for the safety of persons and property in order to meet the emergency. Inevitably, in such an instance the pilot in command is required to send a written report of that deviation to the authorities as required. Some questions that may arise in the event of a human pilot in command being assisted by a "super first officer" (computer endowed with AI) are: would the pilot in command be responsible when a qualified and capable second in command commits an error? Can the manufacturer of the computer be held liable for a defective product?[76]

From a security standpoint, Article 6 of The Tokyo Convention of 1963[77] provides that the aircraft commander may, when he has *reasonable grounds* (my emphasis) to believe that a person has committed, or is about to commit, on board the aircraft, an offence or act contemplated in Art. 1, para. 1,[78] impose upon such person *reasonable measures* (again, my emphasis) including restraint which are necessary: (a) to protect the safety of the aircraft, or of persons or property therein; or (b) to maintain good order and discipline on board; or (c) to enable him to deliver such person to competent authorities or to disembark him in accordance with the provisions set out in the Convention. The provision also states that the aircraft commander may require or authorize the assistance of other crew members and may request or authorize, but not require, the assistance of passengers to restrain any person whom he is entitled to restrain. Any crew member or passenger may also take reasonable preventive measures without such authorization when he has reasonable grounds to believe that such action is immediately necessary to protect the safety of the aircraft, or of persons or property therein.

The question would be whether artificial intelligence or a super computer could be taken to have the capacity to arrive at "reasonable grounds" *proprio motu* in an emergency as envisioned in the Convention and accordingly take "reasonable measures". In this context a pilot would have reasonable grounds if a set of facts or circumstances would satisfy an ordinary cautious and prudent person that there is reason to believe and which goes beyond mere suspicion. The law has, from 1763, ascribed to a legal requirement associated with "reasonable grounds to believe" the need for existence of a probable cause that would impel a person to go beyond

---

[76]See Speciale and Venhuizen (2007), pp. 817–836.

[77]Convention on Offences and Certain Other Acts Committed on Board Aircraft, signed at Tokyo, on 14 Sep. 1963 See ICAO Doc 8364.

[78]Article 1.1 provides that the Convention applies in respect of: (a) offences against penal law; (b) acts which, whether or not they are offences, may or do jeopardize the safety of the aircraft or of persons or property therein or which jeopardize good order and discipline on board.

suspicion and arrive at "reasonable grounds".[79] Probable cause is "sufficient reason based upon known facts to believe a crime has been committed or that certain property is connected with a crime. Probable cause must exist for a law enforcement officer to make an arrest without a warrant, search without a warrant, or seize property in the belief the items were evidence of a crime".[80]

The question is whether artificial intelligence or a super computer could be identified with having the ontological capability of reason. One commentator says correctly:

> computers are obnoxiously, pedantically, and mechanically literal. The machine does not know or care what you want it to do: it does only what it has been told. This is an important notion when talking about machine intelligence.[81]

Therefore, it could easily confuse the conventional judicial mind, particularly in the context of the cautionary note sounded by futuristic minds of such persons as Stephen Hawking and Elon Musk of the concept of "*singularity*" where we would reach a stage when humans would be incapable of understanding the conduct of artificial intelligence and the runaway direction toward which it would take human civilization.[82]

A contrary view has been given in a commentary by Jerry Kaplan in the MIT Technology Review where he says:

> The Committee on Legal Affairs of the European Parliament recently issued a report calling on the EU to require intelligent robots to be registered, in part so their ethical character can be assessed. The "Stop Killer Robots" movement, opposed to the use of so-called autonomous weapons in war, is influencing both United Nations and U.S. Defense Department policy.
>
> Artificial intelligence, it seems, has a PR problem. While it's true that today's machines can credibly perform many tasks (playing chess, driving cars) that were once reserved for humans, that doesn't mean that the machines are growing more intelligent and ambitious. It just means they're doing what we built them to do[83]

---

[79] *Wilkes v. Woods*, 98 Eng. Rep. 489 (C.P. 1763). Two years after the Wilkes case the issue of probable cause to have reason to believe was again addressed where the Court, in a case addressing trespass of personal property, held that a person must have probable cause to enter a premises without permission and if he did not have reason to believe that he was within the law when the act was committed he would be presumed to be guilty of the offence of trespass. See *Entick* v *Carrington* (1765), 19 St Tr 1029.

[80] http://dictionary.law.com/Default.aspx?selected=1618.

[81] Infante (2004). See http://www.makeuseof.com/tag/heres-scientists-think-worried-artificial-intelligence/.

[82] *Ibid.* Singularity is the hypothesis that the invention of artificial superintelligence will abruptly trigger runaway technological growth, resulting in unfathomable changes to human civilization. See also, Watson (2012), pp. 40–62 at 44.

[83] Kaplan (2017). See https://www.technologyreview.com/s/603761/ais-pr-problem/?set=603799&utm_source=Fareed%27s+Global+Briefing&utm_campaign=707c0ca4f9-EMAIL_CAMPAIGN_2017_03_07&utm_medium=email&utm_term=0_6f2e93382a-707c0ca4f9-83414677.

1.6 Empowerment and Connectivity of the Passenger

The defining force in techno-megatrends is the empowerment of the individual through connectivity that is driven by information technology. The airline passenger is no exception. Global airline passenger communications systems are aiding the passenger to remain connected both at the airport and on board the aircraft. Four basic trends in this regard have been identified as: emergence of agile and smart airport concepts; investments in assistive technologies for differently abled passengers; role of social media; and airports developing into a proactive source of information during disruption.[84] The agile airport[85] thrives on flexibility, the drivers of which are advanced operational efficiencies, offer of quicker turnaround times for airlines, effectively enabling of faster set-up times for concessioners and tenants, and improved passenger experience; the last of which leads to the smart airport concept. Smart airports depend almost entirely for their progress on emerging and maturing technologies. According to a report, smart airports usually employ:

> advanced and pervasively deployed sense-analyze respond capabilities. Systems are built around a "digital grid": a single, converged, often carrier-class IP network that enables high-speed broadband traffic throughout the entire ecosystem, including the airport, airport city, airlines, seaport, logistics, authorities, and other parties. The digital grid is the airport's nervous system, touching and managing every point of interaction.[86]

Emergence of smart airports have come about mainly through their digital transformation. SITA[87] claims that 72% of airports plan to check-in more than half of passengers through a kiosk by 2017 and 65% of passengers are interested in self-service bag drop.[88] In the same report the claim is made that 92% of passengers would like to receive a message on their phones if there is a flight disruption and 70% of passengers want to keep connected from gate to gate. It must be remembered that there is an intrinsic relationship between the airport and the airline in all this process and this is particularly seen in the case of making things easier for

---

[84]Airline Passenger Communications System—Market Trends and Forecasts: *Technavio, Business Wire*, December 08, 2016. See http://www.businesswire.com/news/home/20161108006112/en/Airline-Passenger-Communications-System-%E2%80%93-Market-Trends.

[85]Examples of the agile airport include Toronto Pearson International Airport, London Heathrow Airport, Singapore Changi International Airport, Hong Kong International Airport, and McCarron International Airport (Las Vegas). See Dr. Amir Fattah Howard Lock William Buller Shaun Kirby, Smart Airports: Transforming Passenger Experience To Thrive in the New Economy, Cisco Internet Business Solutions Group (IBSG), 2009 Cisco Systems, Inc.

[86]*Id.* at 3.

[87]*Société Internationale de Télécommunications Aéronautiques*, was founded in February 1949 by 11 airlines in order to bring about shared infrastructure cost efficiency by combining their communications networks. SITA was the first company to handle data traffic in real time via a packet switched network over common carrier leased lines.

[88]Smart Technology for Smarter Airports, http://www.sita.aero/resources/type/infographics/smart-technology-for-smarter-airports.

passengers with disabilities. In August 2016 London's Heathrow Airport committed to becoming the world's first dementia friendly airport. The airport authorities announced that Heathrow was working with the Alzheimer's Society to change global attitudes towards dementia as part of the charity's Dementia Friendly Communities Programme. The airport has pledged to make all 76,000 people that work at the airport dementia aware through the provision of 'Dementia Friends' sessions.[89] The airport is considered an agent of the airline in the context of the contract of carriage between the airline and the passenger.[90]

The creation of seamless travel by smart airports has given rise to location based technology being used by airports to make the travel experience easier and more efficient for the traveler. Location based services (LBS) use instantaneous geo data on a real time basis that is extracted from either a mobile device or smartphone to provide information, entertainment or security. Among the services LBS offers are those which enable the users to reserve their seats at restaurants, coffee shops, stores, concerts, and other places or events. LBS have been defined as:

> software application for a IP-capable mobile device that requires knowledge about where the mobile device is located. Location-based services can be query-based and provide the end user with useful information such as "Where is the nearest ATM?" or they can be push-based and deliver coupons or other marketing information to customers who are in a specific geographical area.[91]

Another tool used by airports to enhance the travel experience is the airport terminal beacon which is a device that uses a short range blue tooth signal to broadcast to apps on a mobile device that are particularly designed for passengers and airport staff information from a database on such important considerations as location of airport areas including airline gates. Beacons transmit information to apps used by the passenger or staff but do not receive information back. Miami International Airport became one of the first to introduce a localized app based on beacon technology with its upgraded app "MIA Airport Official 2.0" which will function as a personalized travel assistant. This app enables passengers to know precisely the estimated walk times, real-time flight updates, and suggestions for nearby shopping and dining, based on a customizable personal profile.[92] Another airport that successfully uses *ibeacon* technology is Côte d'Azur Airport at Nice which introduced the technology in its newly refurbished Terminal 1 retail area. At this airport several beacons installed across the terminal building send contextual retail information and promotions to passengers, based on their location in the terminal. While *ibeacon* information particularly helps passengers in transit by telling them where they are, where they need to go for their next flight, and the

---

[89]Heathrow Commits to Becoming World's First Dementia Friendly Airport, Airports International 16 August 2016. See http://www.airportsinternational.com/2016/08/heathrow-commits-to-becoming-worlds-first-dementSia-friendly-airport/17925. See also Abeyratne.

[90]See *Vumbaca* v. *Terminal One Grp. Ass'n L.P.*, 859 F.Supp.2d 343 (E.D.N.Y. 2012).

[91]http://searchnetworking.techtarget.com/definition/location-based-service-LBS.

[92]See Garcia 2016.

fastest way to get there, thereby effectively precluding the hassle of wandering aimlessly in search of the monorail to the next terminal, this technology also enables privilege gold club members to access fast track security.[93] Other information provided by this technology range from baggage arrival information; boarding information; flight check in notification; the nearest available staff; and security queue information.[94]

Airport World, in its December/January 2017 gives an example of beacons as a communication tool as well as a trend that is becoming important to both airports—in facilitating traffic flows and locating staff who could be deployed to problems in their nearest locations—to passengers who could be saved the bother of walking to the wrong gate in instances of sudden gate changes:

> As an example, say traveler John Smith lands in Atlanta with two hours before his connecting flight takes off. As he gets off the first plane, the app on his phone pings the beacon in that part of the terminal, and he is instantly sent the details of where he is, where he needs to go for his next flight, and the fastest way to get there – all while avoiding a crowded monitor or having to wander aimlessly in search of the tram to the next terminal.[95]

Although admittedly the benefits of the use of *ibeacon* technology at airport terminals outweigh the risks it poses, nonetheless there are risks to be considered. Signal disruption is one, where too many beacons installed at wrong points in the building could interfere with signals and scramble Wi-Fi signals. Another risk would be excessive use of smartphones all at once by passengers which could adversely affect the available spectrum. Communication systems of airlines could also be affected.[96]

This brings one to the human factor. The intelligence, which is intangible and is conveyed only one-way, lies in the app and not in the beacon. A proliferation of use that would cause disturbance of the infrastructure would be presumed to be caused by the user of the app. However, it is the airport which provides the user with the beacon transmitting the information. Therefore, it is arguable that responsibility devolves upon airports to ensure that beacon infrastructure does not interfere with other wireless infrastructure. As an occupier of the premises the airport would also have to ensure that the airport and its shops adopt standardized infrastructure. Beacons could also affect smart phones carried by a passenger in the terminal and therefore liability could lie both with regard to the airport as well as the manufacturer who owes a duty of care to the user. Incorrect information provided through *ibeacon* technology which would cause damage or inconvenience to the user could also entail liability for the airport.[97] Another litigious aspect would be privacy which would definitely become an issue where the user would not have

---

[93]Babu (2016).

[94]See ACI/IATA Airport Terminal Beacons Recommended Practice, p. 10. This document can be accessed at http://www.airport-world.com/features/it/5983-the-benefits-of-beacons.html.

[95]Kohli (2016–2017), pp. 36–37 at 36.

[96]https://www.tnooz.com/article/ibeancons-airport-real-world-test/.

[97]See Abeyratne (2012), pp. 363–372.

been given a clear understanding of the legal implication of the use of the app concerned and the assurance that privacy would be protected.

1.7 The Overview

Whether it is deep learning (which is a new area of research on machine learning which would lead us to the application of artificial intelligence in its full format), augmented or virtual reality or *ibeacon* technology, it is incontrovertible that at least conceptually, we have reached an inflection point between law and ethics. We have already seen how artificial intelligence (AI) has boomed with such innovations as Google's DeepMind and Tesla's self-driving and self-navigating cars. If DeepMind could beat any human being at Go (a more complicated game than Chess) one could wonder how AI could recommend better procedures for surgeries than human medical specialist and technologists can ever concoct with their collective minds. IBM's Watson (a super computer which could read millions of academic articles in a few minutes and synthesize solutions) came into the limelight in 2016, bringing to bear the immense possibilities that technology would offer in the future.

Although we are years away from the use of deep learning and artificial intelligence tools being applied instead of humans in air transport the overriding fact would remain that although AI would operate on superior algorithms that could beat humans in intelligence, they are not capable of human capabilities such as emotion, ethical considerations and empathy. Already, the manufacturers of driverless cars are faced with the compelling distinction between consequentialism[98] and the categorical imperative[99] where the dilemma of whom to save -the driver who probably would be the customer of the manufacturer—or 14 persons on the sidewalk that the car could veer to in saving the driver's life.[100] An aircraft driven solely by algorithms would be faced with the difficulty of offering a guarantee of ethical behavior to solve unforeseen problems. Artificial intelligence systems have no moral status.

[98]The eighteenth century British philosopher Jeremy Bentham propounded the concept of utilitarianism based on the need for commands and sanctions where he claimed that the "fundamental axiom" of his philosophy carried the principle that it is the greatest happiness of the greatest number that is the measure of right and wrong.

[99]The eighteenth century German philosopher Emmanuel Kant posited the principle of the categorical imperative where Kant argued that the human mind creates the structure of human experience, that reason is the source of morality.

[100]In comments published in October 2015 Mercedes-Benz executive Christoph von Hugo has said that the carmaker's future autonomous cars will save the car's driver and passengers, even if that means sacrificing the lives of pedestrians, in a situation where those are the only two options. See Morris (2016).

With regard to empowering the passenger at the airport there would be two issues. From the passenger's point of view the issue would be the possible erosion of the right to privacy and safe data storage. From an airport perspective it could be liability for defects in the infrastructure that would compromise the air transport system and the transmission of erroneous information to the recipient. When artificial intelligence is eventually used in flight deck technology and the use of beacons reach the sophistication that would justify global use with consistency, there will be a compelling need for local rulemaking authorities such as the Federal Aviation Administration of the United States and European Aviation Safety Agency of the European Union to take a hard look at existing rules. In the ultimate analysis, it is a cardinal principle of State responsibility at treaty law that the State is responsible for the dissemination of air navigation and allied information and communication standards pertaining to air transport.[101] It would therefore be interesting to see how potential interferences with this preeminent law could be caused by *ibeacon* information technology provided at an airport run by a private entity that could disrupt communications on aircraft.

1.8 The United Nations Megatrend

The International Civil Aviation Organization[102] was established in December 1944, some months before the United Nations was established on 24 October 1945. Consequently, the former became a specialized agency of The UN by virtue

[101]Article 28 of the Convention on International Civil Aviation prescribes that each contracting State undertakes, so far as it may find practicable, to:

a) Provide, in its territory, airports, radio services, meteorological services and other air navigation facilities to facilitate international air navigation, in accordance with the standards and practices recommended or established from time to time, pursuant to this Convention;
b) Adopt and put into operation the appropriate standard systems of communications procedure, codes, markings, signals, lighting and other operational practices and rules which may be recommended or established from time to time, pursuant to this Convention;
c) Collaborate in international measures to secure the publication of aeronautical maps and charts in accordance with standards which may be recommended or established from time to time, pursuant to this Convention

[102]The International Civil Aviation Organization is the United Nations specialized agency dealing with international civil aviation. ICAO was established by the Convention on International Civil Aviation (Chicago Convention), signed at Chicago on 7 December 1944. Fifty-two States signed the Chicago Convention on 7 December 1944. The Convention came into force on 4 April 1947, on the thirtieth day after deposit with the Government of the United States. Article 43 of the Convention states that an Organization to be named the International Civil Aviation Organization is formed by the Convention. ICAO is made up of an Assembly, which is the sovereign body of the Organization composed of the entirety of ICAO member (Contracting) States, and a Council which elects its own president. The Assembly, which meets at least once every 3 years, is convened by the Council. The Council is a permanent organ responsible to the Assembly,

of the United Nations Charter[103] and abides by the provisions of the agreement it signed with the United Nations.[104] According to this agreement, ICAO supports the work of the United Nations through its constitutional document—The Chicago Convention[105]—and is obligated to render support to The UN's Sustainable Development Goals from the perspective of international civil aviation. In particular, Article 5.2 of the Agreement provides that ICAO agrees to enter into consultation with the United Nations upon request, with respect to recommendations of the United Nations, and in due course to report to the United Nations on the action taken by the Organization or by its members to give effect to such recommendations, or on the other results of their consideration. Article 5.3 follows through by saying that ICAO affirms its intention of cooperating in whatever measures may be necessary to make coordination of the activities of specialized agencies and those of the United Nations fully effective. In particular, it agrees to participate in, and to cooperate with any body or bodies which the Economic and Social Council may establish for the purpose of facilitating such co-ordination, and to furnish such information as may be required for the carrying out of this purpose.

ICAO works with the 191 of the 196 signatory States of the UN as well as industry and aviation groups to develop international Standards and Recommended Practices (SARPs) contained in the 19 Annexes to the Chicago Convention, which are then used by States when they develop their legally-binding national civil aviation regulations. As its Mission Statement mentions, ICAO is a global forum that works in collaboration with its Member States, and has set over 10,000 standards, covering issues such as air traffic services, operation of flights, environmental protection and safety in the air.

One could say that the United Nations Sustainable Development Goals (SDGs),[106] adopted in 2015 to be implemented over 15 years, is a global megatrend that affects air transport. The SDGs are an extension of the UN Millennium Development Goals[107] which were adopted in 2000 to be implemented through to 2015. The Millennium Development Goals had, as their targets, extreme poverty in its many dimensions-income poverty, hunger, disease, lack of adequate shelter, and

---

composed of 36 Contracting States. See Convention on International Civil Aviation, ICAO Doc 7300: 9th Edition, 2006, Articles 43 and 44.

[103]Article 57 of The Charter provides inter alia that the various specialized agencies, established by intergovernmental agreement and having wide international responsibilities, as defined in their basic instruments, in economic, social, cultural, educational, health, and related fields, shall be brought into relationship with the United Nations and are referred to as specialized agencies.

[104]At the first ICAO Assembly held in May 1947, The Assembly adopted Resolution A1-2, which approved the agreement of relationship with the United Nations (UN) and authorized the President of the ICAO Council to sign a protocol bringing into force the agreement concerning such a relationship between the UN and ICAO.

[105]Convention on International Civil Aviation, signed at Chicago on 7 December 1944. See ICAO Doc 7300/9: 2006.

[106]https://www.globalgiving.org/sdg/?rf=ggad_15&gclid=CNvq5ZaSvdECFUSewAodJTsKlQ.

[107]http://www.un.org/millenniumgoals/bkgd.shtml.

exclusion-while promoting gender equality, education, and environmental sustainability, linking poverty to the other grave disadvantages mentioned above. The Sustainable Development goals are 17 in number[108] which have 169 targets, where the first five goals are the same as those embodied in their predecessors. If one creates a link between the goals and aviation, the lead players can be identified as The United Nations as well as ICAO, which is the specialized UN agency taking care of standardizing and harmonizing global principles of civil aviation on behalf of its parent body which is the UN.

ICAO claims that its five Strategic Objectives (enhance global civil aviation safety; increase the capacity and improve the efficiency of the global civil aviation system; enhance global civil aviation security and facilitation; foster the development of a sound and economically-viable civil aviation system; and minimize the adverse environmental effects of civil aviation activities) are strongly linked to 13[109] of the 17 UN SDGs and it is fully committed to working in close cooperation with ICAO member States and other UN Bodies to support related targets. In furtherance of these aims ICAO supports the SDGs in its capacity as an official observer on the UN Inter-agency and Expert Group on Sustainable Development Goal Indicators.

ICAO's current overarching philosophy is anchored on two commitments, the first being supporting the SDGs and the second being aligning its work so that no country is left behind. The latter essentially involves assistance to needy States in

---

[108]The 17 SDGs are: end poverty in all its forms everywhere; end hunger, achieve food security and improved nutrition and promote sustainable agriculture; ensure healthy lives and promote well-being for all at all ages; ensure inclusive and equitable quality education and promote lifelong learning opportunities for all; achieve gender equality and empower all women and girls; ensure availability and sustainable management of water and sanitation for all; ensure access to affordable, reliable, sustainable and modern energy for all; promote sustained, inclusive and sustainable economic growth, full and productive employment and decent work for all; build resilient infrastructure, promote inclusive and sustainable industrialization and foster innovation; reduce inequality within and among countries; make cities and human settlements inclusive, safe, resilient and sustainable; ensure sustainable consumption and production patterns; take urgent action to combat climate change and its impacts; conserve and sustainably use the oceans, seas and marine resources for sustainable development; protect, restore and promote sustainable use of terrestrial ecosystems, sustainably manage forests, combat desertification, and halt and reverse land degradation and halt biodiversity loss; promote peaceful and inclusive societies for sustainable development, provide access to justice for all and build effective, accountable and inclusive institutions at all levels; strengthen the means of implementation and revitalize the global partnership for sustainable development.

[109]See http://www.icao.int/about-icao/aviation-development/Pages/SDG.aspx. ICAO has not identified the 4 SDGs that are not directly relevant to the mission and vision of IC AO. The author believes that the following 6 SDGs are not within the purview of ICAO: end poverty in all its forms everywhere; no hunger; ensure availability and sustainable management of water and sanitation for all; conserve and sustainably use the oceans, seas and marine resources for sustainable development; protect, restore and promote sustainable use of terrestrial ecosystems, sustainably manage forests, combat desertification, and halt and reverse land degradation and halt biodiversity loss; and promote peaceful and inclusive societies for sustainable development, provide access to justice for all and build effective, accountable and inclusive institutions at all levels.

bringing them up to speed in the areas of safety, security, environment protection in the aviation context, capacity building and sound economic policy in air transport. This is a straightforward objective although there is no clear path so far identified as to how the "no country left behind" plan can be implemented. However, it remains a laudable goal which requires the support of member States which could enable ICAO to achieve its goal.

In pursuance of the "no country left behind" aim, ICAO is stepping up its technical cooperation program which is conducted by ICAO's Technical Cooperation Bureau (TCB) under the supervisory eye and policy guidance of the ICAO Assembly and of the Council with a view to "providing advice and assistance in the development and implementation of projects across the full spectrum of civil aviation aimed at the safety, security, environmental protection and sustainable development of national and international civil aviation". ICAO claims that: "since its establishment in 1952, TCB has implemented civil aviation projects with an accumulated value in excess of US$ 2 billion. With an average annual program size of over US$ 120 million, it is involved in approximately 250 projects each year with individual project budgets ranging from less than US$ 20 000 to over US$ 120 million. To date, TCB has provided assistance to over 115 countries, deploying annually approximately 1200 international and national experts".

Member States adopted, at ICAO's 39th session of the triennial Assembly held from 27 September to 7 2016, Assembly Resolution A 39-23—*No Country Left Behind (NCLB) Initiative*[110] which in its preambular clause recognized *inter alia* that that the successful implementation of the NCLB initiative will enhance States' air transport systems and align with the achievement of the United Nations (UN) SDGs and, in pursuance of this recognition *inter alia* encouraged Member States to include within their aviation infrastructure development projects elements of training and capacity building aimed at strengthening their civil aviation authorities to enable an effective oversight of such infrastructure; and to establish partnerships with other Member States, industry, financial institutions, donors and other stakeholders through ICAO to enhance their civil aviation systems and oversight capabilities;

The Resolution also calls upon all member States and relevant partners able to do so to provide States in need with financial and technical resources to assist them in enhancing their civil aviation systems by implementing Standards and Recommended Practices (SARPs) contained in the Annexes to the Chicago Convention which is the constitutive multilateral instrument setting global standardization and harmonization of civil aviation, by fulfilling their oversight responsibilities.

The Assembly also adopted Resolution A39-25—*Aviation's contribution towards the United Nations 2030 Agenda for Sustainable Development*[111] which recognized that air transport is a catalyst for sustainable development and that it

[110]Resolutions Adopted by the Assembly, Provisional Edition, October 2015, at 104.
[111]*Id.*, at 108.

represents an essential lifeline for least developed countries (LDCs),[112] and especially for landlocked developing countries (LLDCs)[113] and small island developing States (SIDS[114]) to connect to the world; and that air transport connectivity is of utmost importance for the economic, social and territorial cohesion of Member States and their populations.

The Resolution goes on to recognize that the benefits enabled by air transportation can only materialize if States have a safe, efficient, secure, economically viable and environmentally sound air transport system and that to this end the NCLB initiative aims at assisting States in effectively implementing ICAO SARPs, plans, policies and programs, as well as addressing Significant Safety and Security Concerns so as to ensure that all States have access to the significant socio-economic benefits of air transport.

In this context ICAO links in the Resolution the 2030 Agenda for Sustainable Development that balance the economic, social and environmental dimensions of sustainable development. Resolution A39-25 further recognizes that a global partnership comprising governments, the private sector, civil society, the United Nations system and other actors would be collectively needed to mobilize all available resources for the implementation of the SDGs which are quite extensive in the scale and ambition of the SDG 2030 Agenda for Sustainable Development. It is also said in the Resolution that ICAO Strategic Objectives contribute to the attainment of the SDGs.

As for action, The Resolution *inter alia* urges Member States to enhance their air transport systems by effectively implementing SARPs and policies while at the same time including and elevating the priority of the aviation sector into their national development plans supported by robust air transport sector strategic plans and civil aviation master plans, thereby leading to the attainment of the SDGs. It directs the Secretary General of ICAO to continue monitoring and reviewing, when applicable, the contributions made towards the attainment of the SDGs through the implementation of ICAO Strategic Objectives and work programs and to ensure that ICAO participate, when applicable and in alignment with its Strategic Objectives, in appropriate mechanisms put in place to support the implementation of the 2030 Agenda for Sustainable Development so that aviation is recognized and prioritized as such by Member States in their development plans.

[112]The least developed countries (LDCs) are a group of countries that have been classified by the UN as "least developed" in terms of their low gross national income (GNI), their weak human assets and their high degree of economic vulnerability.

[113]Landlocked Developing Countries. UNCTAD reports that Currently, 31 countries belong to the Group of landlocked developing countries (LLDCs): 15 are located in Africa, 12 in Asia, 2 in Latin America and 2 in Central and Eastern Europe.

[114]Small Island Developing States (SIDS) are low-lying coastal countries that tend to share similar sustainable development challenges, including small but growing populations, limited resources, remoteness, susceptibility to natural disasters, vulnerability to external shocks, and excessive dependence on international trade.

The Secretary General is also requested to enhance existing and establish new partnerships with Member States, the aviation industry, the United Nations system, international and regional organizations, financial institutions, donors and other actors to assist Member States in enhancing their air transport systems with a view to contributing, consequently, to the attainment of the SDGs.

ICAO has shown that it is, as a UN organization quite sincere and adept at implementing actions prescribed by its Assembly Resolutions. However, there are two considerations that need to be ironed out for this to happen.

1.9 The Eleven SDG'S Relevant to Aviation

1.9.1 Good Health

Aviation, through medical and relief flights could provide urgent medical supplies and medical staff to States that are stricken by man-made and natural disasters. There is a specific provision in Annex 9 to the Chicago Convention for provision by State of relief flights. Contracting States are required, by Standard 8.8 of Chapter 8 of the Annex, to facilitate the entry into, departure from and transit through their territories of aircraft engaged in relief flights performed by or on behalf of international organizations recognized by the United Nations or by or on behalf of States themselves and to take all possible measures to ensure their safe operation.[115] The relief flights referred to should be undertaken to respond to natural and man-made disasters which seriously endanger human health or the environment. An

[115]Standard 8.8 States: "Contracting States shall facilitate the entry into, departure from and transit through their territories of aircraft engaged in relief flights performed by or on behalf of international organizations recognized by the UN or by or on behalf of States themselves and shall take all possible measures to ensure their safe operation. Such relief flights are those undertaken in response to natural and man-made disasters which seriously endanger human health or the environment, as well as similar emergency situations where UN assistance is required. Such flights shall be commenced as quickly as possible after obtaining agreement with the recipient State.

Note 1.—According to its Internationally Agreed Glossary of Basic Terms, the United Nations Department of

Humanitarian Affairs considers an emergency to be "a sudden and usually unforeseen event that calls for immediate

measures to minimize its adverse consequences", and a disaster to be "a serious disruption of the functioning of society, causing widespread human, material or environmental losses which exceed the ability of the affected society to cope using only its own resources".

Note 2. — With respect to the application of measures to ensure the safe operation of relief flights, attention is drawn to Annex 11 — Air Traffic Services, *the* Manual Concerning Safety Measures Relating to Military Activities Potentially Hazardous to Civil Aircraft Operations *(Doc 9554) and the* Manual concerning Interception of Civil Aircraft *(Doc 9433)*".

Standard 8.9 States: "Contracting States shall ensure that personnel and articles arriving on relief flights referred to in 8.8 are cleared without delay".

emergency is acknowledged in the Annex as "a sudden and usually unforeseen event that calls for immediate measures to minimize its adverse consequences". A disaster is described in the Annex as "a serious disruption of the functioning of society, causing wide spread human, material or environmental losses which exceed the ability of the affected society to cope using its own resources[116]".

The United Nations Charter lists the achievement of international cooperation in solving international problems of an economic, social, cultural or humanitarian character, as one of the purposes of the United Nations.[117] The problems that the United Nations is mandated by its Charter to solve should therefore be necessarily of an international nature. Article 2(7) of the Charter expands the scope of this philosophy further when it provides that the United Nations is not authorized to intervene in matters which are essentially within the domestic jurisdiction of any State, without prejudice to the right of the United Nations to intervene in matters which are within the domestic jurisdiction of any State, and apply enforcement measures where there is an occurrence of acts of aggression, a threat to the peace or breach thereof.[118] Therefore *stricto sensu*, the United Nations cannot intervene in instances where natural disasters such as famine, drought or earthquakes render the citizens of a State homeless, destitute and dying of starvation unless invited by the States concerned. The principle however cannot be too strictly interpreted; as natural disasters may usually lead to breaches of the peace. In such instances the United Nations Security Council may take such actions by air, sea or land as may be necessary to maintain or restore international peace and security.[119] For such instances, Article 43 of the Charter provides:

> All members of the United Nations, in order to contribute to the maintenance of international peace and security, undertake to make available to the Security Council, on its call and in accordance with a special agreement or agreements, armed forces assistance and facilities, including rights of passage necessary for the purpose of maintaining international peace and security.

Here again, action can only be taken for the maintenance of international peace, effectively precluding any direct intervention in a domestic issue.

Resolutions adopted by the United Nations Security Council relating to Somalia[120] and Bosnia and Herzegovina[121] clearly demonstrate the parameters of the scope of United Nations' intervention under its Charter.[122] In the case of Somalia,

---

[116] Annex 9, Facilitation, Thirteenth Edition—July 2011, Chapter 8, C, Standard 8.8, note 1 *Ibid.*

[117] *Charter of the United Nations and Statute of the International Court of Justice*, United Nations: New York, Article 1.3.

[118] *Id.* Chapter VII Articles 39, 41 and 42.

[119] *Id.* Article 42.

[120] *S/RES/794* (1992) 3 December 1992.

[121] *S/RES/770* (1992) 13 August 1992.

[122] See also the earlier Security Council Resolution 688 (1991), 5 April 1991 whereby the Security Council expressed grave concern at the repression of the Iraqi civilian population in parts of Iraq and insisted that Iraq allow immediate access by international humanitarian organizations to all parts of Iraq.

the United Nations Security Council recognized the unique character of the situation in the country, where conflict and violence demanded that all concerned take all necessary measures to facilitate the measures of the United Nations, its specialised agencies and humanitarian organizations to provide humanitarian assistance to the affected population in Somalia. In the case of Bosnia and Herzegovina the Security Council recognized in its Resolution that the situation in the two States constituted a threat to international peace and security. In both Resolutions, the Security Council had to function within its mandate of intervention only in instances of conflict and breaches of the peace.

The Geneva Conventions of 12 August 1949 for the Amelioration of the Wounded and Sick in Armed Forces in the Field contain provisions for facilitation of aircraft for the removal of the wounded and sick and for the transport of medical personnel and equipment.[123] The thrust of the Conventions is that relief operations by air in the case of removing wounded and sick soldiers and civilians in instances of armed conflict are protected from attack and facilitated through. The Conventions also provide that medical aircraft of parties to the conflict may fly over the territories of neutral powers, land thereon in case of necessity, or use them as ports of call.[124] Medical aircraft are required by the Conventions to give neutral States previous notice of their passage through such States.

Humanitarian assistance *per se* is by no means contrary to the principles of international law. In *Nicaragua* v. *USA (Merits)*[125] the International Court of Justice (ICJ) held:

> there can be no doubt that the provisions of strictly humanitarian aid to persons or forces in another country, whatever the political obligations or objectives, cannot be regarded as unlawful intervention, or in any way contrary to international law.[126]

When the recipient State however, does not grant permission to a State or organization to operate relief flights into its territory, the *status quo* becomes different, and the legality of the relief flight becomes *prima facie* questionable. In such an instance, a relief flight would *ipso facto* be an intervention. The fact that such a flight does not obtain the permission to fly over or into the recipient State would clearly tantamount to a forcible entry. The question which emerges in this scenario is, when, if at all, does a unilateral humanitarian intervention such as a relief flight operated unilaterally, become legally justifiable?

[123]Geneva Conventions for the Amelioration of the Wounded and Sick in Armed Forces in the Field, *Geneva Conventions of August 12 1949*, International Committee of the Red Cross, Geneva: 1970, Article 36.

[124]*Id.* Article 37.

[125]*Military and Para Military Activities in and Against Nicaragua* (*Nicaragua* v. *US*) Merits *I.C.J. Rep.* 1986 at 14.

[126]*Id.* para 242.

1.9.2 Quality Education

Curiously from an aviation specific standpoint The 39th ICAO Assembly re-hashed Resolution A39-11: *Consolidated Statement of Continuing ICAO Policies in the Legal Field* which in its Appendices have such subjects as general policy; procedure for approval of draft conventions on international air law; ratification of ICAO international instruments; adoption of national legislation on certain offences committed on board civil aircraft (unruly/disruptive passengers); model legislation on certain offences committed on board civil aircraft section; assault and other acts of interference against a crew member on board a civil aircraft; and other offences committed on board a civil aircraft. The most awkward of subjects is in Appendix D: *Teaching of air law*, for the simple reason that this is an ancient Resolution that has been moribund for decades with no meaningful action taken by the Council. The Appendix *inter alia* has such strong words as: The Assembly, "considering the *undoubted* (my emphasis) importance for the Organization and the States of the specialized teaching of air law and the desirability of fostering knowledge of this important subject: invites the Council to take all possible action to promote the teaching of air law in those States where it is not yet available; and urges States to adopt appropriate measures which would further the achievement of the above objective". No action has been taken in this regard (except when, occasionally, a State funds a few ICAO legal officers to talk about the Chicago Convention and ICAO's work, which by no means covers public and private international law). The teaching of air law should constitute such subjects as air carrier liability (with a discussion on case law); treaty law; aviation insurance law and general principles of public international law as applicable to aviation and air transport.

1.9.3 Gender Equality

Gender equality in aviation is a very important subject—an area in which ICAO has taken robust initiatives. With the objective of enhancing the career development of women in aviation, ICAO, in conjunction with the International Aviation Women's Association (IAWA), offers women all over the world the opportunity to apply for an aviation scholarship. This scholarship affords women opportunities to work in aviation organizations and entities involved with aviation. At the 39th Session of the ICAO Assembly the Assembly adopted Resolution A39-30: *ICAO Gender Equality Programme promoting the participation of women in the global aviation sector* whereby The Assembly reaffirmed its commitment to enhancing gender equality and the advancement of women's development by supporting UN Sustainable Development Goal 5: Achieve gender equality and empower all women and girls—including by aiming to achieve an aspirational goal of 50-50 (women-men) by 2030 at all professional and higher levels of employment in the global aviation sector.

The Assembly urged States, regional and international aviation organizations and the international aviation industry to demonstrate strong, determined leadership and commitment to advance women's rights and to take the necessary measures to strengthen gender equality by supporting policies, as well as the establishment and improvement of programmes and projects, to further women's careers within ICAO's governing and technical bodies, the ICAO Secretariat and the global aviation sector.

Furthermore, The Assembly urged States, as part of national commitments to gender equality, to work cooperatively with ICAO by sharing best practices and working in partnership with ICAO on programmes and projects aimed at increasing the pool of women in the aviation sector and encouraging women to further develop their aviation careers, including through the promotion of women in aviation careers by State Ministries responsible for higher education;

Finally, The Assembly instructed the Secretary General to establish an ICAO Gender Equality Programme by mid-2017 with the primary aim of facilitating and coordinating targeted programmes and projects to enable and make regular reports on progress toward the goal of gender equality by 2030, especially in professional and higher levels of employment, within ICAO, and within States and the global aviation sector.

1.9.4 The Climate Change Equation

Renewable Energy, sustainable development of cities and communities, life on land, and climate action are four SDGs which have the same theme for aviation. The 39th Assembly of ICAO, held from 27 September to 7 October 2016, adopted by consensus a Resolution on a Global Market Based Measure (GMBM) to address and mitigate the effects of aircraft engine emissions on the environment. According to the Resolution (which replaces Assembly Resolution A38-18 and which had some reservations of States attached to it), a GMBM scheme would be implemented in the form of a Carbon Offsetting and Reduction Scheme for International Aviation (CORSIA) to address any annual increase in total CO_2 emissions from international civil aviation (i.e. civil aviation flights that depart in one country and arrive in a different country) above 2020 levels, taking into account Special Circumstances and Respective Capabilities (SCRC) of States.

The Council of ICAO is charged with a periodic review of the CORSIA which would be up for consideration by the Assembly, every 3 years from 2022, which would consist of assessment of: progress towards achieving ICAO's global aspirational goal; the scheme's market and cost impact on States and aircraft operators and on international aviation; and the functioning of the scheme's design elements; consideration of the scheme's improvements that would support the purpose of the Paris Agreement, in particular its long-term temperature goals; and update the scheme's design elements to improve implementation, increase effectiveness, and minimize market distortion, taking into account the consequential impact of changing the scheme's design elements, e.g., to Monitoring, Reporting and Verification (MRV) requirements; and a special review by the end of 2032 on termination of the scheme, its extension or any other improvements of the scheme beyond 2035, including consideration of the contribution made by aircraft technologies, operational improvements and sustainable alternative fuels towards achieving the ICAO's environmental objectives.

The ICAO Conference on Aviation and Alternative Fuels in November 2009 (CAAF/09) endorsed the use of sustainable alternative fuels for aviation, particularly the use of drop-in fuels in the short to mid-term, as an important means of reducing aviation emissions. In its Resolution A39-2—*Consolidated statement of ICAO policies and practices related to environmental protection—climate change* also adopted at the 39th Session of the ICAO Assembly, it was resolved that ICAO and its member States with relevant organizations will work together to strive to achieve a collective medium term global aspirational goal of keeping the global net carbon emissions from international aviation from 2020 at the same level, taking into account: the special circumstances and respective capabilities of States, in particular developing countries; the maturity of aviation markets; the sustainable growth of the international aviation industry; and that emissions may increase due to the expected growth in international air traffic until lower emitting technologies and fuels and other mitigating measures are developed and deployed. This Resolution requested States, *inter alia* to consider the use of incentives to encourage the deployment of clean and renewable energies sources for aviation, including sustainable alternative fuels.

CORSIA would be implemented in three phases while accommodating SCRC, in particular of developing States, while at the same time minimizing market distortion. The Resolution was in response to a specification in Resolution A38-18 adopted at the Assembly 3 years earlier which required the Assembly in 2016 to develop a GMBM scheme. It took 6 years, from the 37th Assembly in 2010 (which required the Council to explore the feasibility and modalities of an GMBM scheme) to the 39th Session in 2016 for ICAO to come up with a scheme, which, until 2024 would be a voluntary pilot scheme that would not be an active GMBM. Thereafter, through 2027 the scheme would still be semi experimental. In the meanwhile, pollution caused by engine emissions would exponentially grow over the next 10 years.

Aviation and climate change has a long history as long as the history of environmental law itself. ICAO[127] Assembly Resolution 18-11, adopted at the 18th ICAO Assembly (which took place in Vienna from 15 June to 7 July 1971)—an year before the seminal United Nations Conference on the Human Environment took place in Stockholm in 1972—recognized that aircraft activity

[127]The International Civil Aviation Organization, a specialized agency of the United Nations, was established by Article 43 of the *Convention on International Civil Aviation* (Chicago Convention), signed at Chicago on 7 December 1944 (ICAO Doc 7300/9, Ninth Edition, 2006). The main objectives of ICAO are to develop the principles and techniques of international air navigation and to foster the planning and development of air transport. ICAO has 191 Contracting States.

has an impact on the human environment and that a balance should be struck between the impact and the safe and orderly development of air transport. This resolution was followed by Resolution A18-12 which encouraged ICAO and other relevant Organizations to work diligently toward developing Standards, Recommended Practices and Procedures and/or guidance material addressing the quality of the human environment. Since then, ICAO has had a steady and progressive succession of events which have pronounced on aviation and the environment, leading up to its 39th Session of the Assembly which took place at its headquarters from 27 September to 7 October 2016.[128]

Despite its perceived enthusiasm and diligence sustained over the years, ICAO has been accused of kicking the can down the road and dragging its feet in its quest to find an acceptable global market based measure (GMBM) scheme for some 16 years, only to come up with a request in 2013 from the international community to work at it for another 3 years, where a GMBM scheme could be presented at the 39th Session of the ICAO Assembly in 2016. Such a scheme would start being implemented only in 2020.[129] As discussions to follow will show, even in 2020, what will be put into effect would be a pilot project that States could participate on a voluntary basis for yet another 3 years, thus pushing the commencement of the actual implementation schedule to 2024.

The dilemma faced by ICAO, in all fairness to the Organization, was a polarization between two groups in the ICAO Council, where a majority of Council members of emerging markets and developing States refused to entertain the notion of having to curb their development in air transport called for by the introduction of a substantial burden of any measure, fiscal or otherwise, on aircraft emissions, to offset pollution already caused by the industrial and developed world. The fundamental argument of the objecting States was based on the Pareto principle[130] also known as the 80/20 rule, which is a theory maintaining that 80% of the output from a given situation or system is determined by 20% of the input. The principle doesn't stipulate that all situations will demonstrate that precise ratio—it refers to a typical distribution. More generally, the principle can be interpreted to say that a minority of inputs results in the majority of outputs. When applied to aviation and climate change this principle translates to the fact that 80% of emissions (output) was caused by 20% of air transport carried out by airlines of developed States.

Faced with this conundrum, where the ICAO Council had to come up with an MBM scheme that would not affect any of its 191 States adversely, while at the same time introducing a just and equitable measure, the Council started from

[128]For a detailed discussion on the historical development of ICAO's work on aviation and the environment and challenges faced, see Abeyratne (2007), pp. 99–106 and by the same author, *Aviation and Climate Change—In Search of a Global Market Based Measure* (2014e), pp. 69–150. The two books address ICAO's work up to 2013 and this article discusses work carried out by ICAO from 2013 to 2016 when the 39th Session of the ICAO Assembly took place.

[129]See Abeyratne (2014e), *Id.* 98.

[130]The Pareto principle is a principle, named after economist Vilfredo Pareto, that specifies an unequal relationship between inputs and outputs.

scratch by resorting to the *Strawman model.*[131] The first step toward this approach was for the Council to temporarily abandon the actual focus of the MBM discussions in ICAO by ignoring any debate and adopt a distorted, exaggerated or misrepresented version of the debate which was then falsified to reach a conclusion that could be acceptable to all parties concerned[132] . At its 202nd Session The ICAO Council, remanded the matter to its Committee on Aviation Environment Protection (CAEP)[133] to conduct the first round of technical analyses on the Strawman of MBM, the initial construction of which was carried out by the Environment Advisory Group (EAG). The process went on for some time and was abandoned in desperation as the Council could not make any headway.[134]

Another challenge faced by ICAO, leading up to 2016 was that whatever measure that was proposed, it had to be enforceable and implementable. It had to be precise and clear, if it were to replace the decision taken by the European Union to include aircraft engine emissions in its Emissions Trading Scheme (ETS).[135] The inclusion of aircraft engine emissions in the overall European ETS was opposed by the international aviation community on the ground that it was extraterritorial in application[136] and instead the responsibility devolved upon ICAO to develop a globally applicable MBM scheme. With international pressure mounting, The

[131] A straw-man proposal is a brainstormed simple draft proposal intended to generate discussion of its disadvantages and to provoke the generation of new and better proposals. Often, a straw man document will be prepared by one or two people prior to kicking off a larger project. In this way, the team can jump start their discussions with a document that is likely to contain many, but not all the key aspects to be discussed. As the document is revised, it may be given other edition names such as the more solid-sounding "stone-man", "iron-man", and so on. For example, under the *Strawman* approach taken by ICAO if one were to suggest that the best way to go is to impose a tax on fuel, the EAG would have to falsify this premise, perhaps taking into consideration arguments against it.

[132] Taking a scientific analogy, this approach can be related to the theory of falsification propounded by scientist and philosopher Karl Popper who stated that falsifiability is a criterion for deciding whether or not a theoretical system belongs to empirical science.

[133] The Committee on Aviation Environmental Protection (CAEP) is a technical committee of the ICAO Council established in 1983. CAEP assists the Council in formulating new policies and adopting new Standards and Recommended Practices (SARPs) related to aircraft noise and emissions, and more generally to aviation environmental impact.

[134] For an in-depth discussion on ICAO's Strawman approach see Abeyratne (2015b), pp. 102–107.

[135] The European Parliament, on 8 July 2008, voted to expand the European Union's Emissions Trading Scheme to cover aviation engine emissions by requiring that all airlines leaving from or landing at airports in the EU will have to buy pollution credits commencing in 2012. According to this requirement, 85% of the emissions certificates will be allocated for free and 15% will be auctioned. The reduction target will be calculated on the basis of airlines' annual emissions between 2004 and 2006. In the first period (2012) the cut in airlines emissions would be 3% and in the period to follow commencing 2013 the emissions would be cut by 5%. Research flights and small airlines producing low emissions would be excluded.

[136] See Abeyratne (2008), pp. 155–160.

European Union had to suspend its decision to include aircraft engine emissions in its ETS scheme until such time as ICAO produced its results.

1.9.5 Work Leading Up to the 39th ICAO Assembly

One presumes that ICAO took upon its task as assigned to it by the 38th Session of its Assembly with the full realization that there were two reasons for coming up with a global market based measure scheme. One was obviously to bring some degree of control on a worldwide basis over climate change caused by aviation. The other, which has not been the subject of any ICAO discussion or debate over the years is the deleterious effect global warming would have on aviation itself. Effects such as heat damage to runway and taxiway surfaces; the effect of heat on aircraft performance on takeoffs and flight safety; and changes in wind patterns with increased crosswinds, have been identified as real threats to the efficiency and safety of air transport.[137] Added to this factor are the statistics themselves where passenger numbers are scheduled to double by 2034.[138] Increasing demand for air transport with a supply of aircraft capacity to meet that demand would impact the current output of global aviation of 2% of global CO_2 emissions as stated in the 4th Assessment Report of the Inter-Governmental Panel on Climate Change (IPCC), released in 2007, which says that 65% of total CO_2 emissions by aircraft (or 1.3% of the global CO_2 emissions by aircraft) are from international operations.[139]

Responding to this realization, The ICAO Council established in March 2015 its Environmental Action Group (EAG) which comprised 17 Council Representatives to act as monitor and supervisor of work that would be carried out from 2013 to 2016 on the development of a GMBM scheme. After 15 meetings of the EAG, culminating in its final meeting in January 2016, The Council summarized its analyses and results of discussions both in the Council and at CAEP (Committee on Aviation Environmental Protection—the technical arm of the Council responsible for developing technical standards of a GMBM) through a monitoring, reporting and verification (MRV) process using emissions unit criteria (EUC) and registry.[140]

The ICAO Council at this juncture ought to have realized that one of the biggest challenges in the GMBM equation was the balance between the exponential growth of air transport which would make aviation emissions double over the next 15 years,

[137]Thompson (2016), pp. 105–112 at 106. See http://cclr.lexxion.eu/article/CCLR/2016/2/6.

[138]Ritchie (2016), p. 91. See http://cclr.lexxion.eu/article/CCLR/2016/2/3.

[139]ICAO Environment Report 2016, at 99. See http://www.icao.int/environmental-protection/Documents/ICAO%20Environmental%20Report%202016.pdf.

[140]The tenth meeting of CAEP in February 2016, after a review of all its findings, reported to the Council its recommendations. See generally, *ICAO Environment Report id.* Chapter 4: Global Emissions.

in the same lines as it had doubled over the past 15 years, and an element of control that a GMBM could introduce. In this context, there has been the incontrovertible and unchallengeable argument that any MBM scheme, particularly one that would advocate a carbon offsetting scheme is just a "grappling measure that make people feel good without really changing the fundamental dynamics of the industry".[141] According to this view the fundamental dynamics of the industry calls for acceptance of the fact that the current rate of growth in air transport is unsustainable and that demand must be discouraged or lessened by changing the behavioural pattern by being discerning customers, using air transport when absolutely necessary, coupled with curbing the proliferation of low fare (but not low cost) air transport.[142]

In January 2016, The ICAO Council received an impetus from the Paris Agreement[143] resulting from the 21st meeting of the Conference of the Parties (COP) of the United Nations Framework Convention on Climate Change (UNFCCC) held in December 2015 which sought to limit the global average temperature to well below 2 °C and to proceed toward limiting that increase to 1.5 °C,[144] which impels international aviation to go below the baseline imposed for 2020. Arguably, the most imposing challenge for the ICAO Council in its quest of developing a GMBM was to agree (among its 36 members) on an implementation plan and mechanism. A GMBM would only be effective as its implementation and enforcement. One way to ensure enforcement is by making the GMBM scheme mandatory,[145] as recommended by the IATA At the 39th Session of the ICAO Assembly, IATA drew attention to the danger of different carbon pricing instruments being applied in the world, which would eventually result in an unsustainable patchwork of measures for States as well as operators. IATA has claimed: "in our view, there is a significant risk that policy makers will use the absence of agreement in ICAO as a justification for the introduction of unilateral measures. Similarly, a scheme under ICAO which is implemented on a voluntary rather than a mandatory basis could have the same result".[146]

---

[141]Gelain (2016). See http://aviationweek.com/commercial-aviation/opinion-uncomfortable-truth-about-aviation-emissions.

[142]*Ibid*. See also, Monbiot (2007), p. 198.

[143]The Paris Agreement is an agreement within the United Nations Framework Convention on Climate Change (UNFCCC) dealing with greenhouse gases emissions mitigation, adaptation and finance starting in the year 2020. The language of the agreement was negotiated by representatives of 195 countries at the 21st Conference of the Parties of the UNFCCC in Paris and adopted by consensus on 12 December 2015. It was opened for signature on 22 April 2016 (Earth Day) in a ceremony in New York City.

[144]Decision 1/CP21, Adoption of The Paris Agreement, Annex, UNDOC FCCC/CP2-15/10/Add.1, January 2016.

[145]IATA AGM Urges Governments to Adopt a Global Carbon Offsetting Scheme, https://www.highbeam.com/doc/1G1-454220351.html.

[146]Comments on the Cost Impact of a Global Carbon Offsetting Mechanism, *A39-WP/153*, Ex/57, 9/8/16.

In the above context, it is assumed that the ICAO Council took into consideration four institutional requirements that have been recommended for mandatory compliance: (1) A mandatory system for timely, accurate and transparent reporting of emissions data and emissions units surrendered; (2) An entity or entities responsible for reviewing emissions and surrendered emissions unit data that has the legal, financial and human resources needed to hold participants accountable for compliance; (3) A venue for resolving disputes over compliance; and (4) Financial penalties that exceed the cost of compliance with the MBM, including enhancements for false or fraudulent data reporting.[147]

ICAO's offsetting mechanism, at its developmental stage, had two approaches: The first was called the "individual" approach which was based on the difference between the airlines' emissions in a green year and its projected emissions in 2020. This measure is calculated to ensure the ultimate objective of the GMBM—which is to achieve net zero growth in emissions in 2020. One of the disadvantages of this approach has been identified with the example of an airline operating an aged, inefficient fleet which would retire that fleet, going into a new fleet of efficient aircraft leading up to 2020 which would consequently gain substantial gains under the individual approach, while another airline which is already operating new efficient aircraft would not get the benefit as there would be no improvements in its emission levels.[148]

The second approach was called the "collective" approach which is based on an airline's emissions calculated against its offset obligations and its growth. The collective approach is based on generalization calculated with a multiplier of growth for all airlines. The downside of this method is that it would stultify an airline's growth by offering a disincentive for growth.[149] Both these approaches were applied to the "strawman" experiment by ICAO which has already been referred to. They were considered on the basis that States could seek to purchase offsets based on an average of the two approaches, which again was found to produce a slowing down of fast growing carriers.

It must be mentioned that ICAO worked assiduously between 2013 and 2016 to fulfil its obligation imposed by Assembly Resolution A38-18 to develop a GMBM scheme. One of its efforts was to conduct seminars and workshops which ICAO called Global Aviation Dialogues (GLADs) conducted in two rounds. GLADs were designed to offer transparency of ICAO's work in the context of the development of a GMBM as well as provide States with information sharing opportunities and to receive feedback from States and relevant organizations that would assist ICAO's work.[150]

As a result of a Council decision taken at its 206th Session in November 2015, ICAO convened its High Level Meeting on a Global Market Based Measure

[147]See, e.g., Petsonk et al. (1998), p. 5, cited by Campos (2016), p. 156.

[148]Vaishnav (2016), pp. 120–126 at 121. See http://cclr.lexxion.eu/article/CCLR/2016/2/9.

[149]*Id.* 122.

[150]ICAO Global Aviation Dialogues (GLADs), *HLM-GMBM—WP/3*, 26/04/16.

(HLM-GMBM) in Montreal from 11 to 13 May 2016, mainly to discuss a draft Assembly Resolution, the text of which had been developed in the preceding months, and to seek a way forward towards giving the upcoming Assembly later in the year. 65 member States and 17 international organizations participated in the meeting. The meeting noted that the salient features of the draft resolution were: the need to recognize that the global offsetting scheme proposed in the resolution will enable States to reach the aspirational goals regarding aircraft engine emissions; the importance of factoring in Special Circumstances and Respective Capabilities (SCRC) of States, but at the same time recognizing the need to obviate market distortions; the application of aviation related metrics in implementing the scheme; the significance of a route based approach to ensure equality of opportunity for all States and their carriers; the importance of taking into consideration relevant technical aspects; and the compelling requirement that no country was left behind in the implementation of the offsetting scheme.[151] At this stage it was clear that conclusively, the GMBM scheme proposed would be a Carbon Offsetting and Reduction Scheme for International Aviation (CORSIA) that was calculated to address any annual increase in total CO_2 emissions from international aviation with regard to civil aviation flights that depart from one country and arrive at another country[152] above the aspirational limits set for 2020 levels, while factoring in the SCRC of States.

At the HLM-GMBM a joint statement was issued by several States[153] that voiced concern that the draft proposal on GMBM may impose adverse economic impacts on developing countries where the aviation market was still evolving and maturing. They called for consistency of the proposal with the Paris Agreement of 2015[154] and principles of Common but Differentiated Responsibilities (CBDR) and

[151]Report on the Results of the High Level Meeting on a Global Market Based Measure Scheme (HLM-GMBM), HLM-GMBM Oral Report, 24/05/16 at 1–2.

[152]It is interesting to note that both the Warsaw Convention of 1929 and the Montreal Convention of 1999 (which replaced the Warsaw Convention) on private air carrier liability consider "international carriage" as carriage of persons, mail and freight from a point in one country to a point in another country or between two points in the same country where there in agreed stopping place in another country.

[153]Argentina, Brazil, India, Panama, Russian Federation and Saudi Arabia.

[154]The Paris Agreement decided the following: reaffirm the goal of limiting global temperature increase well below 2 °C, while urging efforts to limit the increase to 1.5°; establish binding commitments by all parties to make "nationally determined contributions" (NDCs), and to pursue domestic measures aimed at achieving them; commit all countries to report regularly on their emissions and "progress made in implementing and achieving" their NDCs, and to undergo international review; commit all countries to submit new NDCs every 5 years, with the clear expectation that they will "represent a progression" beyond previous ones; reaffirm the binding obligations of developed countries under the UNFCCC to support the efforts of developing countries, while for the first time encouraging voluntary contributions by developing countries too; extend the current goal of mobilizing $100 billion a year in support by 2020 through 2025, with a new, higher goal to be set for the period after 2025; extend a mechanism to address "loss and damage" resulting from climate change, which explicitly will not "involve or provide a basis for any liability or compensation;" require parties engaging in international emissions trading to avoid

SCRC. The International Coalition for Sustainable Aviation (ICSA) submitted that keeping to the principles of the Paris Agreement was essential and that the proposed ICAO resolution should have, as a binding goal, carbon neutrality in 2020 with a clear roadmap for an increased and progressive ambition which had to be reviewed every 3 years.[155] The ICSA expressed its concern that a draft resolution showed differentiation by exempting a large number of States which compromised the environmental integrity of the GMBM and suggested, as a correctional measure, a regional route grouping approach whereby proportionality would be achieved through a system where each geographic region's share of the global offset obligation could be commensurate with its share of global traffic.[156]

The International Emission Trading Association (IETA), while acknowledging that the draft resolution established a single market for the aviation sector—which was a good thing—stated that Green House Gas (GHG) programs should meet ICAO's Emissions Unit Criteria (EUC) in the absence of which the integrity of the GMBM would be compromised.[157] Additionally, IETA proposed that a GMBM for aviation should be consistent with long-term science and environmentally based goals in an open and broad market which operated under a sound market infrastructure.[158]

The United States advocated that a GMBM should have a wide reach and widest coverage possible while at the same time taking into consideration States with lower levels of aviation activity. While opposing the proposal that the offsetting of CO_2 emissions should be 100% based on sectoral growth, The United States advocated a balance between fast and slow growing carriers which did not conform to the 100% sectoral growth approach. The United States further insisted that a GMBM put forward by ICAO should be exclusively applicable across the globe to the exclusion of individual and overlapping national implementation schemes on aviation emissions.[159]

China, in its submission, recognized the importance of CBDR and SCRC principles and emphasized that developed countries should take the lead in the post 2020 period by adopting more ambitious, specially quantified aviation emission reduction targets while developing countries should pursue and enhance their "different types of efforts" (my emphasis) to achieve sustainable aviation. At the

"double counting;" and Call for a new mechanism, similar to the Clean Development Mechanism under the Kyoto Protocol, enabling emission reductions in one country to be counted toward another country's NDC. See http://www.c2es.org/international/negotiations/cop21-paris/summary.

[155]Views of ICSA on a Global Market Based Measure for International Civil Aviation, *HLM-GMBM -WP/6,* 26/04/16 at 2.

[156]*Id.*, at 3.

[157]Key Messages from IETA on Global Market Based Measure Design, *HLM-GMBM—WP/7*, 26/04/16.

[158]*Id.* At 5.

[159]Views of the United States on a Global MBM Scheme for International Aviation, *HLM-GMBM-WP/4*, 26/04/16 at 2–3.

same time, China decried the hesitation of developing countries in not taking a lead role in reducing their aircraft emissions drastically, and other groups of countries (referring arguably to the European Union States) which still adhered to a policy of unilateral measures against a global consensus.[160] China suggested inter alia, that any GMBM scheme should on a nationally determined contribution basis from 2020–2025.[161]

As a result of the HLM-GMBM and a subsequent "Friends of the President (of the ICAO Council) Meeting" held in August 2016, the draft Assembly Resolution matured into concrete principles, one of which was that the carbon offsetting scheme should be effected on a phased-implementation basis, to be subject to voluntary participation by States firstly to be on a pilot phase (from 2021 through 2023) to be followed by the first phase (2024 through 2026) and a subsequent second phase (2027 through 2035). With regard to the last phase (2027–2035) all States other than those already participating would also be required to participate, except those exempted.[162]

1.9.6 Considerations of the 39th ICAO Assembly

The ICAO Assembly, was advised by the Council of ICAO of ICAO's work over the past 3 years. Firstly, the Council advised that following 6 years of technical work by ICAO, a recommendation was finalized on an aeroplane CO_2 emissions certification Standard. This new Standard, the first global Standard for CO_2 emissions of any sector, will apply to new aeroplane type designs from 2020 and to aeroplane type designs that are already in-production in 2023.[163] Secondly, the Council detailed work done on the development of a GMBM, which has already been discussed. The broad theme of the proposal by the Council to the Assembly was that the Assembly decides to implement a GMBM scheme in the form of the

---

[160]China's Perspective on a Global Market Based Measure Scheme, *HLM-GMBM—WP/10*, 5/05/16 at 2.

[161]China's proposal in this context was to establish a GMBM scheme in the form of a Carbon Offsetting Scheme for International Aviation (COSIA) for use by Member States on a nationally determined contribution basis from 2021 to 2025. Developed states and other states having an individual share of international aviation activities in RTKs in year 2018 above 0.5% of total RTKs should communicate their nationally determined contributions (the amount of CO_2 emissions to be offset by aircraft operators registered in the country) to GMBM to ICAO for that period (2021–2025)before June 30th, 2020. Those states having an individual share of international aviation activities in RTKs in year 2018 below 0.5% of total RTKs are encouraged to do so. *Id.* At 3.

[162]On the phased implementation basis an Assembly working paper was presented to the 39th Session of the Assembly which took place in Montreal in September/October 2016. See Consolidated Statement of Continuing ICAO Policies and Practices Relating to Environmental Protection—Global Market Based Measures, *A39-WP/52*, Ex/29, 1/09/16 at 3.

[163]Civil Aviation and The Environment, A39-WP/51, EX/28, 30/06/16.

Carbon Offsetting and Reduction Scheme for International Aviation (CORSIA) to address any annual increase in total CO_2 emissions from international civil aviation (i.e. civil aviation flights that depart in one country and arrive in a different country) above the 2020 levels, taking into account special circumstances and respective capabilities.[164]

The Council pointed out that a trend analysis has revealed that international aviation consumed approximately 142 metric tons (Mt) of fuel in 2010. By 2040, it is expected that despite an anticipated increase of 4.2 times in international air traffic, fuel consumption is projected to increase by only 2.8 to 3.9 times over the same period. It was estimated that up to 2% of this fuel consumption could consist of sustainable alternative fuels in 2020. Significant uncertainties exist in predicting the contribution of sustainable alternative fuels in the long-term, however based on the scenarios evaluated by CAEP, it is possible that up to 100% of international aviation jet fuel demand could be met using sustainable alternative fuels in 2050. The future development and use of alternative fuels would highly depend on the policies and incentives in place for such fuels, and also the ecological and economical effectiveness of their use. Based on the analysis assumptions, if enough alternative jet fuel were produced in 2050 to completely replace petroleum-derived jet fuel, the Council opined that it would reduce net CO_2 emissions by 63%. This expansion would represent a large increase in the use of sustainable alternative aviation fuels.[165]

A working paper presented by a group of European States[166] requested the Assembly to endorse and support the development of a broad range of policy measures under a 'comprehensive approach' to effectively address environmental impacts from the aviation sector.[167] These European States were of the view that the adoption of a long term objective should be considered following the initiative taken by the international aviation industry for a 2050 target in the context of the global climate goals. The paper stated that Europe supports the implementation of the ICAO 'basket of measures', including the non-market-based measures as agreed at the 37th ICAO Assembly. Although the current 'basket of measures' on CO_2 as reflected in the proposal before the 39th Session of the Assembly represents a

[164]Resolution A39-XX: Consolidated statement of continuing ICAO policies and practices related to environmental protection—Global Market-based Measure (MBM) scheme, A39-WP/52, EX/29, 1/09/16, Appendix B, clause 4.

[165]Present And Future Aircraft Noise And Emissions Trends, A39-WP/55, EX/32, 17/06/16 at 2–3.

[166]Presented by Slovakia on behalf of the European Union and its Member States (Austria, Belgium, Bulgaria, Croatia, Cyprus, Czech Republic, Denmark, Estonia, Finland, France, Germany, Greece, Hungary, Ireland, Italy, Latvia, Lithuania, Luxemburg, Malta, Netherlands, Poland, Portugal, Romania, Slovakia, Slovenia, Spain, Sweden and United Kingdom), and the other Member States of the European Civil Aviation Conference (Albania, Armenia, Azerbaijan, Bosnia and Herzegovina, Georgia, Iceland, Republic of Moldova, Monaco, Montenegro, Norway, San Marino, Serbia, Switzerland, The former Yugoslav Republic of Macedonia, Turkey and Ukraine).

[167]European Comprehensive Approach to Environmental Protection, *A39-WP/91*, Ex. 42, 18/07/16.

significant start, it will need to be revisited in the light of achievement of present and future targets. In addition, further scientific work should be encouraged in order to gain a better understanding of the climate impact of aviation emissions other than CO_2, particularly in areas where significant uncertainties over their magnitude remain.[168]

The Council of ICAO also informed the Assembly of its "buddy programme"[169] pertaining to the States' Voluntary Action Plans initiative which has become an essential pillar of the Organization's activities on the environment.[170] These action plans were also represented as a vehicle for ICAO to support the United Nations Sustainable Development Goals (SDGs), in particular, SDGs 7, 10, 13, and 17. Substantial efforts in this regard were undertaken by ICAO to engage more States and the industry in this initiative. The Assembly was additionally advised that, as for future work, ICAO would continue to facilitate access to financial resources, through continued partnerships with the EU, the United Nations Development Programme (UNDP) and The Global Environment fund (GEF), and through possible new partnerships. Such projects would contribute to the ICAO *No Country Behind Left Behind*[171] initiative, and helps to identify beneficiaries as potential knowledge-sources in the regions. It was also envisaged that ICAO would be conducting regional hands-on training seminars, in cooperation with Member States and regional organizations, during the next triennium to provide further support to States in the preparation and update of voluntary action plans with quantified data, and to encourage States that already submitted their action plans to build partnerships with other Member States in order to support those States that have not yet prepared their action plans.[172]

Brazil favoured a phase-in implementation using a route-based approach as an essential pre requisite that should take into consideration SCRC, while at the same time minimizing market distortions. Brazil also supported a two-phased approach for the implementation of the GMBM, with a minimum 5-year gap between them. In each phase, Brazil emphasized the necessity of classifying States based primarily on aviation sector criteria such as revenue tonne-kilometre (RTK), air operator

[168] *Id* at 3.

[169] According to the Buddy Programme, States that have submitted action plans are encouraged to build partnerships with Member States that have not yet prepared action plans, in order to provide support and share experiences and knowledge. By June 2016, three such partnerships had been established, multiplying the environmental benefits of States' Action Plans.

[170] States' Voluntary Action Plans On CO_2 Emissions Reduction Activities, A39-WP/54, EX/31, 17/06/1, at 2.

[171] The No Country Left Behind (NCLB) campaign highlights ICAO's efforts to assist States in implementing ICAO Standards and Recommended Practices (SARPs). The main goal of this work is to help ensure that SARP implementation is better harmonized globally so that all States have access to the significant socio-economic benefits of safe and reliable air transport. The NCLB effort also promotes ICAO's efforts to resolve Significant Safety Concerns (SSCs) brought to light through ICAO's safety oversight audits as well as other safety, security and emissions-related objectives. See http://www.icao.int/about-icao/NCLB/Pages/default.asp.

[172] *Id.* at 5.

certificate (AOC), reflecting also different states of development. Brazil also supported the 100% sectoral approach for the distribution of offsetting obligations since it accommodates potential market distortions and balances countries' historical responsibilities with the principle of non-discrimination embodied in the Chicago Convention. Finally, Brazil suggested that the implementation of GMBM must be carried out in response to environmental integrity and consistent with the regime under the United Nations Framework Convention on Climate Change Conference (UNFCCC). Any future work of CAEP on the implementation of a GMBM, in particular on emissions unit criteria, must be guided by consistency with UNFCCC and its Paris Agreement and should not be inconsistent with or in any way duplicate or overlap with the UNFCCC rules and policy on market-based measures. Brazil also insisted that ICAO and UNFCCC, being two intergovernmental organizations, cannot achieve different outcomes on the same subject.

A fortiori, Brazil pointed out that, States must decide that emission reduction units generated under the Clean Development Mechanism of the Kyoto Protocol and the mechanism established under paragraph 4, Article 6 of the Paris Agreement would not be subject to further monitoring, reporting, and verification (MRV) by CAEP/ICAO, i.e. are automatically eligible for complying with GMBM requirements, in order to operationalize this logic in the Assembly resolution.[173]

In its submission to the ICAO Assembly, IATA stated that a global carbon offsetting scheme for international aviation was intended to be a complementary and temporary emissions gap-filler in addition to the basket of measures available to the sector. It was not intended to replace efforts to improve fuel efficiency through new technology and improved operational and infrastructure measures. Nor would the scheme make fuel efficiency any less of a day-to-day priority for operators.[174] IATA also joined several other international organizations in identifying four features that should define a GMBM: It should not be designed or used to raise general revenues or to suppress demand for air travel; it must be global in scope and preserve fair competition; it must avoid adoption of unilateral measures which would create an unsustainable regulatory patchwork, leading to increased complexity, cost and market distortion; and it should be simple to administer, with each operator only reporting its emissions to one State.[175]

---

[173]See generally, Key Design Elements of the Global Market-Based Measures for International Civil Aviation: Brazil's Position, A39-WP/233 EX/92 16/8/16.

[174]Comments On the Cost Impact of a Global Carbon Offsetting Mechanism, *A39-WP/153*, EX/57, 9/8/16, at 1.

[175]Industry Views on a Global Market-Based Measure for International Aviation, presented by the Airports Council International (ACI), the Civil Air Navigation Services Organisation (CANSO), the International Air Transport Association (IATA), the International Business Aviation Council (IBAC) and the International Coordinating Council of Aerospace Industries Associations (ICCAIA), A39-WP/155, EX/59 9/8/16, at 3.

1.9.7 The Assembly Resolution

Three Resolutions were adopted in the context of aviation and the environment. They were: A39-1 *Consolidated statement of continuing ICAO policies and practices related to environmental protection—General provisions, noise and local air quality;* A39-2 *Consolidated statement of continuing ICAO policies and practices related to environmental protection—Climate change*; and A39-3 *Consolidated statement of continuing ICAO policies and practices related to environmental protection—Global Market-based Measure (MBM) Scheme.* Of these A39-3 deserves discussion, particularly because, unlike the other two which again contain re-hashed text from earlier resolutions, the MBM scheme offered in A39-3 was the most contentious issue at the Assembly.

Resolution A 39-3 (which replaces Assembly Resolution A38-18 and which had some reservations of States attached to it), while acknowledging the adoption of the Paris Agreement which came into effect in October 2016[176] under the United Nations Framework Convention on Climate Change (UNFCCC) and recognizing that the work related to a global MBM scheme for international aviation and its implementation will contribute to the achievement of the goals set out in the Paris Agreement, introduces a global market based measures (GMBM) scheme that would be implemented in the form of a Carbon Offsetting and Reduction Scheme for International Aviation (CORSIA) to address any annual increase in total CO_2 emissions from international civil aviation (i.e. civil aviation flights that depart in one country and arrive in a different country) above 2020 levels, taking into account Special Circumstances and Respective Capabilities (SCRC) of States. CORSIA would be implemented in three phases while accommodating SCRC, in particular of developing States, while at the same time minimizing market distortion. The Resolution was in response to a specification in Resolution A38-18 adopted at the Assembly 3 years earlier which required the Assembly in 2016 to develop a GMBM scheme. It took 6 years, from the 37th Assembly in 2010 (which required the Council to explore the feasibility and modalities of an GMBM scheme) to the 39th Session in 2016 for ICAO to come up with a scheme, which, until 2024 would be a voluntary pilot scheme that would not be an active GMBM. Thereafter, through 2027 the scheme would still be semi experimental. In the meanwhile, pollution caused by engine emissions would exponentially grow over the next 10 years.

---

[176]The Paris Agreement's central aim is to strengthen the global response to the threat of climate change by keeping a global temperature rise this century well below 2 °C above pre-industrial levels and to pursue efforts to limit the temperature increase even further to 1.5 °C. Additionally, the agreement aims to strengthen the ability of countries to deal with the impacts of climate change. To reach these ambitious goals, appropriate financial flows, a new technology framework and an enhanced capacity building framework will be put in place, thus supporting action by developing countries and the most vulnerable countries, in line with their own national objectives. The Agreement also provides for enhanced transparency of action and support through a more robust transparency framework.

CORSIA would be implemented in three phases with a view to accommodating SCRC, in particular of developing States, while minimizing market distortion. The first phase would be a pilot phase that would apply from 2021 through 2023 to States that have volunteered to participate in the scheme. States participating in this phase would be given the flexibility of determining the basis of their aircraft operator's offsetting requirements on the basis that from 2021 through 2023, 100% sectoral and 0% individual, though each participating State may choose during the pilot phase whether to apply this to: an aircraft operator's emissions covered by CORSIA in a given year (on a basis to be decided upon by the Assembly based upon a formula on a % basis for sectoral and individual offsetting, not identified in the draft text or an aircraft operator's emissions covered by CORSIA in 2020).

The first phase following the pilot phase would apply from 2024 through 2026 to States that voluntarily participate in the pilot phase, as well as any other States that volunteer to participate in this phase, with the calculation of offsetting requirements. A new entrant (any aircraft operator that commences an aviation activity falling within the scope of the scheme on or after its entry into force and whose activity is not in whole or in part a continuation of an aviation activity previously performed by another aircraft operator) would be exempted from the application of the CORSIA for 3 years or until the year in which its annual emissions exceed 0.1% of total emissions in 2020, whichever occurs earlier. From the subsequent year, the new entrant would be included in the scheme and treated in the same way as the other aircraft operators. Irrespective of any condition in the Resolution CORSIA would not apply to low levels of international aviation activity with a view to avoiding administrative burden: aircraft operators emitting less than 10,000 metric tonnes of CO_2 emissions from international aviation per year; aircraft with less than 5700 kg of Maximum Take Off Mass (MTOM); or humanitarian, medical and firefighting operations. Emissions that are not covered by the scheme, as the results of phased implementation and exemptions, would not be assigned as offsetting requirements of any aircraft operators included in the scheme.

Leaving aside the fact that the Resolution is a consensual result of political compromises and arrangements which has no legal effect, the implementation process of the offsetting scheme appears to be an ambivalent monitoring scheme revolving round a 3 year compliance cycle, starting with the first cycle from 2021 to 2023, for aircraft operators to reconcile their offsetting requirements under the scheme, while they report the required data to the authority designated by the aircraft operator's State of registry every year. The Council of ICAO is charged with a periodic review of the CORSIA which would be up for consideration by the Assembly, every 3 years from 2022, which would consist of assessment of: progress towards achieving ICAO's global aspirational goal; the scheme's market and cost impact on States and aircraft operators and on international aviation; and the functioning of the scheme's design elements; consideration of the scheme's improvements that would support the purpose of the Paris Agreement, in particular its long-term temperature goals; and update the scheme's design elements to improve implementation, increase effectiveness, and minimize market distortion, taking into account the consequential impact of changing the scheme's design elements, e.g., to Monitoring, Reporting and Verification (MRV) requirements; and a special review by the end of 2032 on termination of the scheme, its extension or any other improvements of the scheme beyond 2035, including consideration of the contribution made by aircraft technologies, operational improvements and sustainable alternative fuels towards achieving the ICAO's environmental objectives.

The Resolution requires The Council to develop, with the technical contribution of the Committee on Aviation Environment Protection (CAEP)—a specialized committee of the ICAO Council comprised of experts—the Standards and Recommended Practices (SARPs) of the Annexes to the Chicago Convention and related guidance material for the implementation of the MRV system under the CORSIA, including simplified MRV procedures, for adoption by the Council by 2018 and requires all Member States whose aircraft operator undertakes international flights to develop the necessary arrangements, in accordance with the MRV SARPs, for implementation from 1 January 2019.

It is somewhat disheartening that, despite the original appeal of the International Air Transport Association (IATA) to make the scheme mandatory (where the MRV system would have a similar approach to ICAO's USOAP[177]) and the request of the member States of Europe to have the scheme operative and effective from the start, the political compromise achieved by the Resolution inevitably ended up with SARPs and guidance material where States would have the option of not complying with such SARPs.[178]

---

[177]ICAO's Universal Safety Oversight Audit Programme (USOAP) was initially launched in January 1999, in response to widespread concerns about the adequacy of aviation safety oversight around the world. Initially, USOAP activities consisted in regular and mandatory audits of ICAO Member States' safety oversight systems.

USOAP audits focus on a State's capability in providing safety oversight by assessing whether the State has effectively and consistently implemented the critical elements (CEs) of a safety oversight system, which enable the State to ensure the implementation of ICAO's safety-related Standards and Recommended Practices (SARPs) and associated procedures and guidance material. In 2007 The 36th Session of the ICAO Assembly adopted a Resolution (A36-14) which adopted the new USOAP Continuous Monitoring Approach (CMA which introduced a systematic and more proactive conduct of monitoring activities in would make a more effective and efficient use of ICAO resources and reduced the burden on States caused by repetitive audits.

[178]Article 38 of the Chicago Convention provides: "Any State which finds it impracticable to comply in all respects with any such international standard or procedure, or to bring its own regulations or practices into full accord with any international standard or procedure after amendment of the latter, or which deems it necessary to adopt regulations or practices differing in any particular respect from those established by an international standard, shall give immediate notification to the International Civil Aviation Organization of the differences between its own practice and that established by the international standard. In the case of amendments to international standards, any State which does not make the appropriate amendments to its own regulations or practices shall give notice to the Council within sixty days of the adoption of the amendment to the international standard, or indicate the action which it proposes to take. In any such case, the Council shall make immediate notification to all other states of the difference which exists between one or features of an international standard and the corresponding national practice of that State.

By 2020 it would be 10 years since ICAO embarked on its work on a GMBM and still it would only be at the start of the voluntary pilot phase. The Washington Post reports that by then the climatic tipping point would have started in in Manokwari, Indonesia; by 2023 in Kingston, in the Caribbean; by 2029 in Lagos; by 2047 in Washington; by 2066 in Reykjavik; and by 2071 in Anchorage, Alaska.[179] A Pacific Northwest National Laboratory (PNNL) study reports: "by 2020, human-caused warming will move the Earth's climate system into a regime in terms of multi-decadal rates of change that are unprecedented for at least the past 1000 years".[180] All scientific indications are that climate change would bring significant adverse effects on the world in 2020 onwards and that the rate of climate change, which has risen sharply in recent decades, will soar by the 2020s.

It would only be in 2027 (17 years after ICAO earnestly started working on a GMBM) that a mandatory element would kick in on the carbon offsetting scheme as envisioned in the Resolution. In the meanwhile, some questions would have to be answered. For instance: why wait for another 10 years (from 2017) or more for a mandatory system for timely, accurate and transparent reporting of emissions data and emissions units surrendered to be put in place?; who is the entity or entities responsible for reviewing emissions and surrendered emissions unit data that has the legal, financial and human resources needed to hold participants accountable for compliance; is there a suitable venue for resolving disputes over compliance; and what are the financial penalties that exceed the cost of compliance with the GMBM, including enhancements for false or fraudulent data reporting?

Some have claimed that:

> Offsetting is widely considered a false solution because it does not lead to emission reductions but merey shift emissions from one sector to another and, at best, is a zero-sum game.[181]

Another commentator says:

> ICAO's proposal relies heavily on carbon offsetting. The proposal gives the impression of taking action on climate change but it will do nothing to reduce emissions. Action on climate change means reducing emissions from burning fossil fuels. Carbon offsetting does not reduce emissions. In theory, carbon trading reduces emissions in one place and allows them to continue somewhere else. In practice, the clean development mechanism massively increased production of hydrofluorocarbons (HFC) coolant gases purely to profit from carbon trading and in the process making climate change worse.[182]

---

[179]Earth's climate change tipping point to start in 2020, new model predicts, http://www.japantimes.co.jp/life/2013/10/10/environment/earths-climate-change-tipping-point-to-start-in-2020-new-model-predicts/#.WAkfH4WcFjo.

[180]Romm.

[181]More than 80 NGOs oppose aviation sector's carbon offsetting plans, World Rainforest Movement (2015).

[182]Lang (2016).

The 39th Assembly of ICAO adopted by consensus a modified version of a draft Assembly working paper presented to the Assembly.[183] According to the text of this draft (which, once adopted, was calculated to replace Assembly Resolution A38-18), the Assembly was invite to decide on the implementation of a GMBM scheme in the form of the Carbon Offsetting and Reduction Scheme for International Aviation (CORSIA) to address any annual increase in total CO_2 emissions from international civil aviation (i.e. civil aviation flights that depart in one country and arrive in a different country) above the 2020 levels, taking into account special circumstances and respective capabilities. CORSIA would be implemented in three phases with a view to accommodating SCRC, in particular of developing States, while minimizing market distortion. The first phase would be a pilot phase that would apply from 2021 through 2023 to States that have volunteered to participate in the scheme. States participating in this phase would be given the flexibility of determining the basis of their aircraft operator's offsetting requirements on the basis that from 2021 through 2023, 100% sectoral and 0% individual, though each participating State may choose during the pilot phase whether to apply this to: an aircraft operator's emissions covered by CORSIA in a given year (on a basis to be decided upon by the Assembly based upon a formula on a % basis for sectoral and individual offsetting, not identified in the draft text or an aircraft operator's emissions covered by CORSIA in 2020).

A new entrant (any aircraft operator that commences an aviation activity falling within the scope of the scheme on or after its entry into force and whose activity is not in whole or in part a continuation of an aviation activity previously performed by another aircraft operator) would be exempted from the application of the CORSIA for 3 years or until the year in which its annual emissions exceed 0.1% of total emissions in 2020, whichever occurs earlier. From the subsequent year, the new entrant would be included in the scheme and treated in the same way as the other aircraft operators. Irrespective of any condition in the Resolution CORSIA would not apply to low levels of international aviation activity with a view to avoiding administrative burden: aircraft operators emitting less than 10,000 metric tonnes of CO_2 emissions from international aviation per year; aircraft with less than 5700 kg of Maximum Take Off Mass (MTOM); or humanitarian, medical and firefighting operations. Emissions that are not covered by the scheme, as the results of phased implementation and exemptions, would not be assigned as offsetting requirements of any aircraft operators included in the scheme.

The Resolution that was adopted at the 39th Session of the Assembly had text consistent with the draft text for the most part. The adopted Resolution states that the pilot phase (which all ICAO member States were strongly encouraged to participate in) applies from 2021 through 2023 to States that have volunteered to participate in the scheme. States participating in this phase may determine the basis

[183]Resolution A39-XX: Consolidated statement of continuing ICAO policies and practices related to environmental protection—Global Market-based Measure (MBM) scheme, A39-WP/52 EX/29 Appendix B.

of their aircraft operator's offsetting requirements as follow: where the % Sectoral and % Individual will be applied as follows:

1. from 2021 through 2023, 100% sectoral and 0% individual, though each participating State may choose during this pilot phase whether to apply this to:
   (a) an aircraft operator's emissions covered by CORSIA in a given year, as stated above, or
   (b) an aircraft operator's emissions covered by CORSIA in 2020.

The first phase which would be from 2024 through 2026 includes States that voluntarily participate in the pilot phase, as well as any other States that volunteer to participate in this phase, with the calculation of offsetting requirements that have already been discussed.

The second phase applies from 2027 through 2035 to all States that have an individual share of international aviation activities in RTKs in year 2018 above 0.5% of total RTKs or whose cumulative share in the list of States from the highest to the lowest amount of RTKs reaches 90% of total RTKs, except Least Developed Countries (LDCs), Small Island Developing States (SIDS) and Landlocked Developing Countries (LLDCs) unless they volunteer to participate in this phase.

The pilot phase was a concern to Member States of the European Union and the other Member States of the European Civil Aviation Conference, which, through a working paper submitted through Slovakia, stated that there was a compelling need for a credible, robust and effective global MBM scheme to be decided by the Assembly as a critical element of the "basket of measures" to tackle CO_2 emissions from international aviation and to achieve carbon neutral growth from 2020. Emphasis was laid on the need for key design elements to be clear, credible and agreed upon as a package for the duration of the global MBM scheme, together with a roadmap for implementation from 2020. The EU States also called for the implementation of the scheme from the start, and requested States, who can do so, to declare before the end of the Assembly their commitment to voluntarily participate in the global MBM scheme from the beginning.

India, China and the Russian Federation called for a review of the scheme after the pilot and first phases that would determine the design parameters of the second phase from 2027, such as the RTK threshold for the exemption of States and a specific individual rate in the dynamic approach from 2030. The three States made a strong request that developed States should take the lead in the implementation of the MBM scheme together with a distribution of offsetting requirements on the basis of Nationally Determined Contributions (NDCs) by individual participating States, or by the formula provided in the draft text. A noteworthy requirement submitted by the three States was that different thresholds should be applied in the participation in the scheme between new entrants from developed and developing States. Another request was that Standards and Recommended Practices (SARPs) should not be used for Monitoring, Reporting and Verification (MRV) requirements and that and different timelines should be set for implementation of MRV by States participating in different phases of the scheme.

After pointing out the various negative impacts that CORSIA would inflict, an umbrella scheme was suggested by the Russian Federation which was of the view that an alternative approach to addressing environmental challenges, based on the Clean Development Mechanism for International Civil Aviation (ACDM), as a basis for implementing a global MBM scheme was a better way forward. The Russian proposal intended to establish a mechanism for mobilizing resources available to international aviation, by introducing an environmental fee from States calculated as a flat charge rate per tonne of aviation fuel used for internal flights, in order to fund environmentally efficient aviation projects in developing States.

It is worthy of note that GREENAIRONLINE, an e-journal on aviation and climate change, reported: "Russia, India and Saudi Arabia, along with Argentina and Venezuela announced during the plenary that they would file reservations, or objections, against the carbon-neutral growth from 2020 (CNG2020) goal of the CORSIA scheme. They argued it was inconsistent with the Paris Agreement and had the potential to inhibit the growth of aviation in developing countries. China also said it would file a similar reservation over the goal and offered little open support for the scheme during the Assembly". The same report said that after the resolution was adopted: Aliu (President of the ICAO Council) explained to journalists, "There have been a number of reservations made but that doesn't stop the process moving forward. We have adopted the resolution, so the resolution is in effect."[184] What The President of the ICAO Council perhaps knew (or ought to have known) is that a resolution would not be "in effect" for the States which filed reservations to the Resolution to the extent of such reservations (unless reservations were filed against the entire resolution), and to that extent the Resolution would not be globally applicable and therefore be destitute of effect, if indeed it had any effect.[185]

The above notwithstanding, ICAO has to be lauded for its tireless efforts over the years. Obtaining some form of global consensus on such a contentious issue is indeed a reckonable feat. And perhaps it is never too late.

[184]http://www.greenaironline.com/news.php?viewStory=2294.

[185]The fundamental issue *in limine* is whether resolutions adopted by the United Nations bodies form hard law which States are legally bound to adhere to. *Brownlie* has expressed the view that decisions by international conferences and organizations can in principle only bind those States accepting them. See Brownlie (1990), p. 691. Malcolm Shaw, referring to the binding force of United Nations General Assembly Resolutions states: "...one must be alive to the dangers in ascribing legal value to everything that emanates from the Assembly. Resolutions are often the results of political compromises and arrangements and, comprehended in that sense, never intended to constitute binding norms. Great care must be taken in moving from a plethora of practice to the identification of legal norms" See Shaw (2003), p. 110.

1.9.8 The Climate Change Megatrend: Renewables and Alternative Fuels

What is proposed in Resolution A39-3 in terms of CORSIA is by no means a megatrend. As discussed, it is a reaction to an issue that has confused ICAO and the Member States for more than 10 years. The real megatrend comes in the economic effect of renewables (solar energy to power aircraft) and alternative fuels. ICAO' Environment Report of 2016 states: "[A]lthough not ready for wide-scale application today, the use of solar energy offers promise for aircraft propulsion over the long term. As announced in 2014, ICAO is an Institutional an Aeronautical Partner for the Solar Impulse around-the world flight that is demonstrating the potential of using clean, renewable, solar energy for powering an aircraft in flight. In addition, a number of experimental electrically-powered aircraft demonstrations have been conducted, showing a future where aircraft may no longer be dependent on liquid fuels".[186]

On the subject of alternative fuels Resolution A 39-2 (Consolidated statement of continuing ICAO policies and practices related to environmental protection—Climate change) is prominent, which in one its preambular clause referred to the Conference on Aviation and Alternative Fuels in November 2009 (CAAF/09) which endorsed the use of sustainable alternative fuels for aviation, particularly the use of drop-in fuels in the short to mid-term, as an important means of reducing aviation emissions. The Resolution requests States *inter alia* to consider measures to support research and development as well as processing technology and feedstock production in order to decrease costs and support scale-up of sustainable production pathways up to commercial scale, taking into account the sustainable development of States; recognize existing approaches to assess the sustainability of all alternative fuels in general, including those for use in aviation which should achieve net GHG emissions reduction on a life cycle basis, contribute to local social and economic development; competition with food and water should be avoided; and adopt measures to ensure the sustainability of alternative fuels for aviation, building on existing approaches or combination of approaches, monitor, at a national level, the sustainability of the production of alternative fuels for aviation, and work together through ICAO and other relevant international bodies, to exchange information and best practices, including for the harmonization on the sustainability criteria of aviation alternative fuels.

As for obligations of the Council of ICAO the Resolution requires the Council to continue to maintain the ICAO Global Framework for Aviation Alternative Fuels (GFAAF); continue to give a global view of the future use of alternative jet fuels and to account for changes in life cycle GHG emissions in order to assess progress toward achieving global aspirational goals; work with financial institutions to facilitate access to financing infrastructure development projects dedicated to

[186]http://www.icao.int/environmental-protection/Documents/ICAO%20Environmental%20Report%202016.pdf at page 154.

sustainable aviation alternative fuels and incentives to overcome initial market hurdles; and cooperate with other relevant international initiatives, including the Sustainable Energy for All (SE4ALL) initiative, to facilitate the aviation's access to renewable energy.

GFAAF presents a conundrum in itself as there is no identifiable global framework that ICAO has developed on alternative fuels. There is a website[187] which gives facts and figures but no framework. The closest one can come to a framework is text contained in Resolution A38-18 (Consolidated Statement of continuing ICAO policies and practices related to environmental protection—Climate change) which requires that States set a coordinated approach in their national administrations in order to develop coordinated national policy actions to accelerate the appropriate development, deployment and use of sustainable alternative fuels for aviation, in accordance with their national circumstances; consider measures to support research and development as well as processing technology and feedstock production in order to decrease costs and support scale-up of sustainable production pathways up to commercial scale, taking into account the sustainable development of States; recognize existing approaches to assess the sustainability of all alternative fuels in general, including those for use in aviation which should: achieve net GHG emissions reductions on a life cycle basis; respect areas of high importance for biodiversity, conservation and benefits from ecosystems; contribute to local social and economic development, and avoid competition with food and water; Adopt measures to ensure the sustainability of alternative fuels for aviation, building on existing approaches or combination of approaches, and monitor, at a national level, the sustainability of the production of alternative fuels for aviation; and work together through ICAO and other relevant international bodies, to exchange information and best practices, including on the sustainability of alternative fuels for aviation.

This having been said, the most relevant requirement of Resolution A39-2 in the context of work by the Council is that it should encourage States to cooperate in the development of predictive analytical models for the assessment of aviation impacts; continue evaluating the costs and benefits of the various measures, including existing measures, with the goal of addressing aircraft engine emissions in the most cost-effective manner, taking into account the interests of all parties concerned, including potential impacts on developing world.

These provisions impose an obligation on both States and the ICAO Council to diligently move towards developing alternative fuels through modelling and studies—a permissive function of the Council under Article 55 of the Chicago Convention.[188] This is where the megatrend comes in. Contrary to popular belief, the

---

[187]http://www.icao.int/environmental-protection/GFAAF/Pages/default.aspx.

[188]Article 55 d) identifies as a permissive function (non-mandatory) of the ICAO Council to study any matters affecting the organization and operation of international air transport, including the inter- national ownership and operation of international air services on trunk routes, and submit to the Assembly plans in relation thereto.

megatrend would not be the move towards alternative fuels by itself but its economic consequences and ICAO must be mindful of this eventuality and study it thoroughly.

Photo-voltaic cells and wind turbines are rapidly coming into use and alternative fuels are also gaining ground. ICAO records that 2500 commercial flights have already been flown with the use of alternative fuels pursuant to commercial flights operated by airlines that have signed alternative fuel purchase agreements. Those agreements are: United Airlines and KLM flights departing from Los Angeles (LAX); Lufthansa, SAS, and KLM / KLC flights departing from Oslo (OSL); and SAS, KLM, and BRA flights departing from Arlanda (ARN). At an ICAO Seminar on alternative fuels held in February 2017, an FAA presentation revealed that 1.1 million gallons in 2016 had been produced by one commercial producer.[189] At the same event Virgin Australia announced the programme on alternative fuels it had launched in March 2016 had been successful in that 200 million litres of fuel are projected to be produced in Australia or New Zealand for 10 years from 2020 and that responses from all parts of the supply chain had been received with strong interest from the region and internationally. There had also been strong interest from governments and industry stakeholders. Virgin Australia was in commercial negotiations with short-listed respondents.

British Petroleum (BP) has estimated that in the wake of this growth in renewables, they would account for half of the growth in global energy supply by 2040. However, it would involve an investment of 20 trillion US dollars to achieve this goal and to get rid of the traditional sources of production such a coal power plants which now produce energy. Since green energy is relatively cost free, its introduction would harm its competitors and drastically reduce their profitability, eventually eradicating them altogether. Besides, the development of bio fuels requires the development of low-cost, effective growth systems, efficient and energy saving harvesting techniques, and methods for oil extraction and conversion that are environmentally benign and cost-effective.

Economists are already calling for a revision of the policy to go exclusively to renewables (in terms of solar powered aircraft) and alternative fuels with a view to evaluating the potential of fixing markets and toning down or balancing subsidies.

An MIT report suggests:

> alternative jet fuels are generally superior to petroleum-based fuels in terms of their impacts on air quality when combusted. However, the production of alternative aviation fuels may come at a cost. For example, bio-based fuel production could compete with food production; increased agricultural activity could strain freshwater reservoirs and pollute rivers and oceans. Fuel production may be prohibitively expensive if the biomass yield is insufficient, biomass availability limited, or the conversion technology inefficient or capital-intensive. It could induce alterations in land use, which can increase CO_2 emissions associated with fuel production if, for example, carbon-sinks such as forests are cleared for cropland.[190]

[189]http://www.icao.int/Meetings/altfuels17/Documents/Jim%20Hileman%20-%20FAA.pdf.

[190]Alternative Fuls, The MIT Laboratory for Aviation and the Environment, http://lae.mit.edu/alternative-fuels/.

The report further suggests that:

> alternative jet fuels' greenhouse gas impact must be comprehensively assessed because greenhouse gas emissions differ between pathways and feedstocks, and not all candidate fuels decrease greenhouse gas emissions on a well-to-wake, or lifecycle, basis. The overall sustainability impact of alternative fuels must be addressed using a multicriteria approach that considers technical, environmental, and economic aspects.

Therefore, as committed in the 39th Session of the ICAO Assembly, both member States and ICAO have an international obligation in studying this megatrend comprehensively in all it facets that should include the economic fallout the transition from conventional power to alternative power would bring, if at all.

1.9.9 Economic Issues

Good jobs and economic growth, reduced inequalities, responsible consumption and partnerships for growth are four SDGs which can collectively be addressed by ICAO in the context of aviation. Multilateralism in air transport which ICAO promotes through its Resolution A 39-15—*Consolidated statement of continuing ICAO policies in the air transport field* which also recognizes that the basic principles of sovereignty, fair and equal opportunity, non-discrimination, interdependence, harmonization and cooperation set out in the Convention have served international air transport well and continue to provide the basis for and contribute to its future development, go a long way to conceptualize (from an aviation context) the four SDGs mentioned under the economic field. Another Resolution is A39-23—*No Country Left Behind (NCLB) Initiative* which urges Member States to improve their civil aviation systems by actively participating in ICAO's work and by effectively implementing ICAO Standards and Recommended Practices (SARPs) contained in the 19 Annexes to the Chicago Convention and policies so that they can foster sustainable local and regional prosperity and fully benefit from improved global connectivity. The Resolution also directs the ICAO Council to maintain the focus of the community on the global contribution and value of aviation through support of NCLB efforts and future ICAO World Aviation Forums, while directing the ICAO Secretary General to coordinate, facilitate and implement comprehensive assistance programmes, in partnership with all stakeholders, that will help Member States in enhancing their civil aviation systems and oversight capabilities.

The Resolution urges Member States, the industry, financial institutions, donors and other stakeholders to coordinate and cooperate amongst themselves and through ICAO, and to support the implementation assistance activities in line with the global and regional priorities established by ICAO, thereby avoiding duplication of efforts. An important provision in the Resolution urges Member States to make use of and benefit from the ICAO Air Services Negotiation (ICAN) facility, as a forum for Member States to negotiate and conclude bilateral and/or multilateral air services agreements, which contributes to enhancing air transport connectivity and consequently the development of tourism, trade, and national and global economies, and calls on all Member States and relevant partners able to do so to provide States in need with financial and technical resources to assist them in enhancing their civil aviation systems by implementing SARPs and fulfilling their oversight responsibilities.

1.9.10 Industry Innovation and Infrastructure

Mobile technology, cloud computing, data analytics, biotech and genomics, and artificial intelligence are all advancing rapidly. Consequently, one could expect growth opportunities related to aircraft digitization and new high-performance materials, as well as for hybrid engines and 3-D printing. The aerospace industry is probably the slowest cycle industry of any and therefore aerospace programs will need to advance much more quickly to respond to advances in technology. Examples include satellite technology, cybersecurity, directed energy, nanotechnology, urbanization, wireless intelligence, and smart city concepts.

A megatrend that would be exclusively aviation specific would be the application of the Internet (Internet of Things, *IoT*)[191] to inflight entertainment and communications. Additionally, pilots are already accessing Wi-Fi cabin networks for weather information and flight planning. *IoT* is also being used for flight tracking and real time flight status.

Arguably, the most contentious trend that is emerging is the possible replacement of the pilot with a robot in the flight deck. With an acute shortage of pilots looming ahead, the robot pilot becomes an attractive proposition. A new development called Aircrew Labor In-Cockpit Automation System, or ALIAS, would enable a robot in the pilot's seat to instantaneously look at multiple to see all the instruments and the gauges in the flight deck and read them all at once. Within a millisecond it could read, analyze and manipulate instruments and gauges reacting faster than a human pilot and instantaneously calling up every emergency checklist for a possible situation. This co-pilot genius would be like "having a human pilot with 600,000 hours of experience."[192]

ICAO Resolution A39-12: *ICAO global planning for safety and air navigation* has some provisions regarding industry innovation, although it comes nowhere near the trends discussed above. The Resolution *inter alia* urges Member States to develop sustainable solutions to fully exercise their safety oversight and air navigation responsibilities which can be achieved by sharing resources, utilizing

[191]IoT is part of IBM's bigger bet on investing on newer technologies to offset declines in the company's legacy businesses of servers and the tech that supports them (although it's trying to make a new spin on that, too). In 2014, it committed to invest $3 billion over 4 years to build out that IoT business, which is based around its Watson artificial intelligence business.

[192]Lowy. See http://bigstory.ap.org/article/9f8b7a3237f64bbda73c2f470394b55a/pilot-cockpit-may-someday-be-robot.

internal and/or external resources, such as regional and sub-regional organizations and the expertise of other States. One of the areas where ICAO calls for industry innovation is in halon replacement where the Resolution acknowledges that more needs to be done because the available halon supplies are decreasing and unsure and that the environmental community continues to be concerned that halon alternatives have not been developed for all fire extinguishing systems in civil aircraft. Accordingly, it urges States and their aviation industries to intensify development and implementation of acceptable halon alternatives for fire extinguishing and suppression systems in aircraft cargo compartments.

1.9.11 Obstacles to ICAO Supporting the SDGs

The trouble with ICAO is that, as already discussed, it is guided by jumbled maze of generalized concepts that create a rag tag collection of ideas on cooperation towards supporting the SDGs. Even when one looks at Resolution A39-25: *Aviation's contribution towards the United Nations 2030 Agenda for Sustainable Development* it merely urges Member States to recognize the significant contributions of aviation to sustainable development realized by stimulating employment, trade, tourism and other areas of economic development at the national, regional and global levels, as well as by facilitating humanitarian and disaster response to crises and public health emergencies. The action called for is a watered down direction to the Council and the Secretary General, within their respective competencies, to *demonstrate* that ICAO continues to serve as an advocate for aviation by raising awareness among Member States, including relevant authorities beyond the air transport sector, the United Nations system, the donor community and all relevant stakeholders about aviation's contributions to sustainable development and the attainment of the SDGs. As for Member States, they are requested to *enhance their air transport systems* by effectively implementing SARPs and policies while at the same time including and elevating the priority of the aviation sector into their national development plans supported by robust air transport sector strategic plans and civil aviation master plans, thereby leading to the attainment of the SDGs.

The sum total of the Resolution boils down to directing the Secretary General to *consider* the special needs and characteristics of LDCs, LLDCs and SIDS; to continue monitoring and reviewing, when applicable, the contributions made towards the attainment of the SDGs through the implementation of ICAO Strategic Objectives and work programmes; to ensure that ICAO *participate*, when applicable and in alignment with its Strategic Objectives, in appropriate mechanisms put in place to support the implementation of the 2030 Agenda for Sustainable Development so that aviation is recognized and prioritized as such by Member States in their development plans; and *enhance* existing and *establish* new partnerships with Member States, the aviation industry, the United Nations system, international and regional organizations, financial institutions, donors and other actors to assist Member States in enhancing their air transport systems with a view to contributing, consequently, to the attainment of the SDGs.

A careful review of this Resolution shows that through key words such as "demonstrate", "enhance and establish new partnerships", "consider", and "participate", there are no specific and concrete actions calculated to proactively implement a plan. There is no requirement of the Secretary General to be proactive in establishing a special programme to be reviewed by the ICAO Council that can be put into action over the next 15 years.

Another anomaly is that ICAO has dealt with the SDGs in one Resolution and the No Country Left Behind concept in another separate Resolution. These two should be considered together and not in isolation. ICAO can actively and meaningfully contribute to the attainment of the SDGs through its No Country Left Behind programme. The problem is, that neither is the No Country Left Behind concept a programme nor does it have a plan that can be implemented. Through a timid attempt by the Technical Cooperation Bureau ICAO is trying to muster experts of retirees to provide reactive support with regard to needs that may come up in needy States. This is not sufficient.

It is submitted that a collection of Resolutions will not proactively support the SDGs through aviation. ICAO must be mindful that Assembly Resolutions are results of political compromises and arrangements to which no legal force can be ascribed[193] and therefore ICAO may have an uphill task in implementing the two resolutions. The other is that "no country left behind" has been perceived by many as an ambivalent "concept" that has not shown a sense of direction or purpose so far. ICAO claims that NCLB "highlights ICAO's efforts to assist States in implementing ICAO Standards and Recommended Practices (SARPs). The main goal of this work is to help ensure that SARP implementation is better harmonized globally so that all States have access to the significant socio-economic benefits of safe and reliable air transport". Is there a plan to carry this noble objective through? ICAO goes on to say that it should provide more direct assistance to developing countries by playing a more active coordination role between States and by helping to generate the political will needed for States to pool resources, participate in regional efforts, earmark voluntary funds and build capacity. The question would be: how would this be done?

The reason behind ICAO's impotence in playing an active role in supporting the SDGs with purpose, direction and specificity has two dimensions. The first is that ICAO has shown reluctance in fulfilling its obligations under the Chicago Convention in certain crucial areas, for example, Article 55 d) identifies as a permissive function (non-mandatory) of the ICAO Council to study any matters affecting the organization and operation of international air transport, including the international ownership and operation of international air services on trunk routes, and submit to the Assembly plans in relation thereto. Thus far, no study has been conducted on how Member States could support the SDGs except the adoption of an Assembly resolution. All that one sees on the ICAO website is a grid which identifies the various programmes of ICAO that are relevant to each SDG. A

[193]Brownlie (1990), p. 691.

dedicated study could reflect how exactly the ICAO programmes could be applied by States in supporting the SDGs. Such a study could be in the form of a roadmap such as the safety roadmap developed in the area of safety.

The second dimension is that, when one links the relationship between ICAO and the UN—which has been discussed in the introduction to this article—with its conduct as a toothless tiger, one observes that ICAO has developed no concrete plans on both its initiatives relating to the UN SDGs and its NCLB. It has merely exhorted States to take measures in supporting the SDGs. The reason is clear: ICAO has only aims and objectives as provided by Article 44 of the Chicago Convention, which are to develop principles and techniques of air navigation and foster the development of air transport. This clearly shows that while ICAO has an authoritative role in the technical field, it has absolutely no coercive role in the air transport field[194] The SDGs that are related to ICAO's work are mostly in the air transport field where ICAO is effectively precluded by Article 44 from developing principles that would have a coercive effect on their compliance by Member States. This has led to the unfortunate situation where neither ICAO nor its Member the States can meaningfully contribute to the SDGs in the context of aviation, and they need more purpose and direction from ICAO than mere resolutions which are couched in ambivalent and overarching statements and requests.

It is time a concrete plan is drawn up by ICAO to show a creative way forward for States in the various areas covered by the SDGs which would use innovation and creativity to address the trends that are showing. The sooner this is done the better.

1.10 ICAO'S Approach to Megatrends

ICAO's approach to megatrends—if there was one—can be gleaned only through one source, which is the 39th session of the Organization giving a glimpse of its activities through resolutions adopted mainly in the fields of environment; safety; security; and its cumbersome and slow moving legal work. The 39th Assembly of the International Civil Aviation Organization (ICAO) was held from 27 September to 7 October 2016. A much awaited event, particularly as the global community anxiously looked forward to being presented with a long due economic instrument that would introduce a global market based measure scheme to manage aircraft engine emissions, the Assembly adopted several Resolutions in the safety, security and environmental fields as well as in the legal field. The policy adopted at the Assembly defines the direction that member States as well as ICAO should take in moving forward over the 3 years to follow. Additionally, the 39th Session was flavoured with a new and desirable dimension that couched the Resolutions implicitly within two key concepts that have become the overarching philosophy of the

[194]Of the 19 Annexes to the Chicago Convention only two (Annex 9 on facilitation and Annex 17 on security) are on air transport.

Organization. The first of these concepts is the No Country Left Behind initiative of the ICAO Council and the second represents a concerted effort at supporting the Sustainable Development Goals of the United Nations through aviation.

The ICAO Assembly is the sovereign body of the Organization, triennially convened by the 36 Member Council to set ICAO's policy as adopted by its 191 member States in the form of Resolutions. The Assembly also reviews ICAO's work programme in the technical, economic, legal and technical cooperation fields. Curiously, The ICAO website's description of the Assembly has no mention of its major accomplishment—that of adopting policy through Resolutions, but only goes on to enumerate powers and duties of the Assembly such as election of Member States to be represented on the Council; examination of reports of the Council and taking appropriate action; taking decisions on any matter reported to it by the Council; and approval of the budgets of the Organization. The Assembly can also delegate to Council the powers and authority necessary or desirable for the discharge of the duties of ICAO and revoke and modify the delegations of authority at any time; and "deal with any matter within the sphere of action of ICAO not specifically assigned to the Council", implying that the Assembly would not have jurisdiction to intervene in any matter that is being considered by the Council. It is also worthy of note that The Convention on International Civil Aviation (Chicago Convention)[195] does not make any mention or reference to the Assembly's ability to adopt Resolutions.[196]

The analysis to follow has to be prefaced and highlighted by the fact that the problem with Resolutions adopted within the United Nations system is that their legal legitimacy has been questioned at international law. The record of the United Nations over its seven decades of history is that member States have on occasion, but in a consistent manner, refused to automatically comply with the corporate will of the Organization.[197] *Brownlie* has expressed the view that decisions by international conferences and organizations can in principle only bind those States accepting them.[198] Shaw, referring to the binding force of United Nations General; Assembly Resolutions states:

> ...one must be alive to the dangers in ascribing legal value to everything that emanates from the Assembly. Resolutions are often the results of political compromises and arrangements and, comprehended in that sense, never intended to constitute binding norms. Great care must be taken in moving from a plethora of practice to the identification of legal norms.[199]

With regard to the practice of other international organizations, a little more caution might be required, as a resolution might create a custom. Non-binding

---

[195] *Supra*, note 5.

[196] *Id*. Article 49.

[197] Zoller (1987), p. 32.

[198] Brownlie (1990), p. 691.

[199] Shaw (2003), p. 110.

instruments form a special category that is sometimes referred to as "soft law" which is definitely not law in the sense of enforceability.[200]

ICAO's conferred powers enable the Organization to adopt binding regulations by majority decision (which is usually unnecessary as most of ICAO policy is adopted through consensus). However, States could opt out of these policies or make reservations thereto, usually before such policy enters into force. This is because States have delegated power to ICAO to make decisions on the basis that they accept such decisions on the international plane. In such cases States could contract out and enter into binding agreements outside the purview of ICAO even on subjects on which ICAO has adopted policy. The only exception to this rule lies in the adoption of Standards in Annex 2 to the Chicago Convention on Rules of the Air, in particular navigation over the high seas and other overflight areas where freedom of flight prevails which all Contracting States are bound to follow in order to maintain global safety.

The 39th Assembly of ICAO adopted by consensus a slew of Resolutions—some new and some a rehash or verbatim duplications of existing resolutions—notable among which are three resolutions pertaining to environmental protection in the context of aviation, one of which addresses the thorny issue of carbon offsetting as a market based measure scheme. On a general note, The President of the Council, Dr. Benard Aliu commented at the commencement of the Assembly session: "ICAO has accomplished a tremendous amount in the past three years, most especially in our efforts to drive more targeted and effective assistance for States under our No Country Left Behind initiative, and through new frameworks for cost-effective capacity building such as the ICAO International Programme for Aviation Volunteers... we have also become more forward-looking and responsive and we are well-prepared for the new challenges our 39th Assembly will place before us... [T]his Assembly will be one for bold decisions, and a time to refine our vision for how air transport can be of even greater service to States and regions, businesses and travelers, in the exciting years ahead. I very much look forward to this journey".[201]

One can certainly agree with the statement of the President of the ICAO Council that ICAO has accomplished much over the years. Also evident is the hard work, tenacity and perseverance of ICAO in addressing any issue assigned to it by the Assembly. It is on this positive note that the legal analysis of some Resolutions of the 39th Session of the ICAO Assembly is undertaken.

---

[200] *Id.* 111. See also Tammes (1958), p. 265.

[201] http://www.icao.int/Newsroom/Pages/Landmark-agreement-on-international-aviation-emissions.aspx.

1.10.1 The Assembly Resolutions: The Legal Field

1.10.1.1 Conflict of Interest in Civil Aviation

Apart from a few resolutions in the legal field entreating contracting States to the Chicago Convention to ratify amendments to the Chicago Convention[202] the first substantive Resolution adopted in the legal field at the Assembly was A39-8: *Conflicts of interest in civil aviation.* This Resolution recognizes that conflicts of interest may hamper effective, independent and impartial safety regulation of civil aviation and thereby pose risks to the safety and security of international civil aviation; and acknowledges the need for and the benefits of drawing upon the experience and expertise of qualified industry personnel to help ensure that important regulatory oversight functions can be provided. It therefore urges States which have not done so to consider establishing a formal legal framework to detect, avoid, mitigate and manage conflicts of interest in civil aviation.

The Resolution also invites States to examine at the national level the adequacy of their domestic legal regimes on measures and practices to detect, avoid, mitigate and manage conflicts of interest in civil aviation, with a view to ensuring and improving transparency and accountability in civil aviation regulatory activities and to balancing their particular circumstances and ability to fulfil their oversight obligations with addressing the risks to aviation safety and security posed by conflicts of interest; and where necessary, to enact legislation and establish systems, codes and practices which promote the awareness of potential conflicts of interest in civil aviation.

The Resolution furthermore urges States to ensure the enforcement of rules and measures to detect, avoid, mitigate and manage conflicts of interest relating to safety oversight in civil aviation. It should be noted that this issue came up for discussion in the Legal Committee of ICAO prior to the 37th Session of the Assembly in 2010 where the United States called for reasonably consistent rules across the sector to "establish and preserve a clear separation between civil aviation authorities and the activities that they oversee were desirable".[203] There were three areas of conflict of interest identified: financial interests in regulated entities; the movement of individuals from positions in government to industry and vice versa; and the practice of designating or seconding personnel to carry out oversight functions on behalf of the Civil Aviation Authority. The consideration of these elements was deemed appropriate with a view to fostering the objective, and disinterested exercise of regulatory responsibilities.

[202]A39-4: Amendment to Article 50 (a) of the Convention on International Civil Aviation; A39-5: Ratification of the Protocol amending Article 50 (a) of the Convention on International Civil Aviation; A39-6: Amendment to Article 56 of the Convention on International Civil Aviation; and A39-7: Ratification of the Protocol amending Article 56 of the Convention on International Civil Aviation.

[203]The Topic "Consideration of Guidance On Conflicts Of Interest" Should Be Added To The Work Programme Of The Legal Committee A37-WP/80, LE/6 20/8/10.

6 years later, at the 39th Session of the ICAO Assembly, Canada, Mexico and United States submitted a joint paper[204] which further elaborated that first, through interactions between a department of the Government or its regulatory agencies with operating entities that are subject to regulation (such as air operators, aviation training organizations, approved maintenance organizations, design organizations, production organizations, air navigation service providers and aerodrome operators); and second, through relationships between different organs or entities of the State involved in civil aviation activities, which could include: overlap of functions between regulatory bodies and the government or its other organs such as the military, police, customs and investigative bodies; ownership or control of regulatory and operator entities by the State; and combination of regulatory and service provision functions in the same or related entities.

One example of conflict of interest is enumerated by Transport Canada which defines conflict of interest as any relationship that might influence an approved check dispatcher (ACD) to act, either knowingly or unknowingly, in a manner that does not hold the safety of the travelling public as the primary and highest priority.[205] All ACDs are held to be in a "perceived conflict of interest" in that they are simultaneously employees (regular or contract) of the company and delegates of the Minister when performing their checking duties. To avoid a "real conflict of interest", the Manual states that it is imperative that ACDs strictly adhere to the policy and guidelines contained in the manual as lack of adherence to the manual could result in a suspension or cancellation of an ACD's delegation.[206]

1.10.1.2 Assistance to Victims of Aviation Accidents and Their Families

Although not strictly a Resolution on legal affairs, mention should be made of Resolution *A39-27: Assistance to victims of aviation accidents and their families* which invokes Article 28 of the Montreal Convention of 1999 on the subject of the provision of advance payments, without delay, to aircraft accident victims, and their families, and considers it essential that support be provided to family members of victims of civil aviation accidents, wherever the accident may occur, and any lessons learned from support providers, including effective procedures and policies, be promptly disseminated to other Member States and ICAO to improve States' family support operations.

The Resolution calls upon Member States to establish legislation, regulations and/or policies to support victims of civil aviation accidents and their family members and encourages States that have legislation, regulations and/or policies to support civil aviation accident victims and their families to review such laws.

---

[204]Conflicts of Interest in Civil Aviation, A39-WP/77 LE/3 5/8/16.

[205]*Approved Check Dispatcher Manual*, Section 1.5. http://www.tc.gc.ca/eng/civilaviation/publications/tp14114-chapter1-section1-5-322.htm.

[206]*Id.* 1.5.2.

This Resolution becomes significant and important in the context of certain accidents which occurred over the past few years.[207]

1.10.1.3 The Montreal Convention (1999)

Resolution A39-9: *Promotion of the Montréal Convention of 1999*, which a re-hashing of A38-20, *Promotion of the Montréal Convention of 1999,* brings to bear important significance and connotations to private air carrier law, in the conflicts it represents. The Resolution, with good reason, urges all Contracting States to support and encourage the universal adherence to the Convention for the Unification of Certain Rules for International Carriage by Air, done at Montréal on 28 May 1999 (Montréal Convention of 1999) and entreats all Contracting States that have not done so to become Parties to the Montréal Convention of 1999 as soon as possible. It also directs the ICAO Secretary General to provide assistance, as appropriate, with the ratification process if so requested by a Contracting State.

There are still some States which are under the Warsaw regime which was replaced by the Montreal Convention. A clash between the application of both these systems to a claim arising out of carriage by air of persons, baggage and freight if the country of departure had ratified one system and country of destination had ratified the other would create ambiguity. For example, in the case of the Air Asia flight QZ 8501[208] crash where the flight was between Indonesia and Singapore the former was under the Warsaw system while the latter had ratified the Montreal Convention. The court of adjudication in this instance would have to decide which system would apply (in contrast, the disappearance of Flight MH 370[209] would not pose any difficulties for the judiciary as both countries involved—Malaysia and China—have ratified the Montreal Convention of 1999, and so is the case of Flight MH 17[210] where both the Netherlands and Malaysia have ratified the Montreal Convention).

[207]See Abeyratne (2014a), also by the same author, Flight MH 17: The Legal And Regulatory Fallout (2014b), pp. 329–342. Also, Abeyratne (2014f), pp. 238–249.

[208]On Sunday 28 December of 2014 Air Asia flight QZ 8501 crashed into the Java sea on its way from Surabaya to Singapore, killing all 162 passengers and crew on board. It was later reported that the flight did not have authorization to be operated on the route on Sundays since authorization had been withdrawn by the Indonesian authorities. Later, on 2 January 2015, the Indonesian authorities suspended Air Asia flights departing from Indonesian airport and brought in strict regulations and even stricter monitoring and supervision controls in its air transport system.

[209]A Malaysian Airlines aircraft which took off from Kuala Lumpur for Beijing at 12.41 a.m. on Saturday, 8 March 2014 lost contact with air traffic control two hours into the flight. The Boeing 777-200 carrying 239 people including 12 crew members carried fourteen nationalities (mostly Chinese but Malaysian, Indonesian and Australians as well) on board. At the time of writing the aircraft and passengers on board were still missing.

[210]Malaysian Airlines Flight MH 17, operated by a Boeing 777-200ER aircraft flying from Amsterdam to Kuala Lumpur on 17 July 2014, and carrying 283 passengers and 15 crew, was

In the Canadian case of *Thibodeau* v. *Air Canada*[211] where the Supreme Court of Canada considered three international flights where plaintiffs claimed under the *Official Languages Act* that they had not been served in the French language by the defendant airline (where the Act provided that they be served in French) and decided that the Montreal Convention (which Canada had ratified) held sway over the domestic legislation of Canada. In *Sidhu* v. *British Airways*[212]—a British case—and the US Supreme Court decision in *El Al Israel Airlines Ltd* v *Tseng*[213] the same principle was upheld in both jurisdictions where the Convention's pre-emptive effect on local law was recognized. In *Chubb* v. *Asiana Airlines*[214] where the carriage by air was between South Korea (which had ratified the Warsaw Convention) and the United States (which had not ratified the Warsaw Convention but had ratified the Hague Protocol which amended a portion of the Warsaw Convention) the court held that actions of the United States and South Korea did not create treaty relations with regard to the international carriage of goods by air because the United States and South Korea are not in treaty relations with regard to the international carriage of goods by air. This discussion would arguably lead to the conclusion that if there is a clash between the application of the Warsaw system on the one hand and the application of the Montreal Convention on the other hand where the origin and destination have ratified one or the other exclusively, the two countries would not be in treaty relationship and therefore neither treaty would apply. It is this reason that renders justification for Resolution A39-9 which urges States to ratify the Montreal Convention of 1999 so that there could be a unified application of treaty law.

1.10.1.4 The Beijing Convention and Protocol

Resolution A39-10: *Promotion of the Beijing Convention and the Beijing Protocol of 2010* is a repeat of Resolution A38-19 entitled *Promotion of the Beijing Convention and the Beijing Protocol of 2010* and urges all States to support and encourage the universal adoption of the *Convention on the Suppression of Unlawful Acts Relating to International Civil Aviation* (Beijing Convention of 2010) and the Protocol Supplementary to the *Convention for the Suppression of Unlawful Seizure of Aircraft* (Beijing Protocol of 2010); while urging all States to sign and ratify the Beijing Convention and Beijing Protocol of 2010 as soon as possible.

---

shot down by a BUK surface to air missile over Donetsk Oblast in Eastern Ukraine, while at an altitude of 10,000 meters. All those on board perished.

[211]2014 SCC 67, [2014] 3.

[212][1997] AC 430.

[213]525 US 155 (1999).

[214]Docket No. 99-7617, Decided: June 08 2000. See http://caselaw.findlaw.com/us-2nd-circuit/1013697.html.

After 6 years of its signing, The Beijing Convention has only 32 signatures, 9 ratifications, 6 accessions, 1 acceptance and has yet to enter into force. The ICAO leadership at the time (particularly the Secretariat and its Legal Bureau) showed remarkable ineptitude and ignorance in drafting and presenting the final draft for signature in Beijing. A full delegation of the Secretariat which travelled to Beijing presented a fundamentally flawed document to the Beijing Conference[215] in 2010. For instance, the treaty provides in Article 1d) that an offence is committed when a person destroys or damages air navigation facilities or interferes with their operation, if any such act is likely to endanger the safety of aircraft in flight. This clearly refers, inter alia, to cyber terrorism, but links the offence exclusively to the safety of aircraft in flight. Regrettably the Beijing Convention—the only international attempt at hinting at cybercrime—does not seem to cover the LOT Polish situation.[216]

Just when we thought the manipulation of aircraft in flight by a crazy pilot was scary enough, we are now being disturbed by an even more ominous phenomenon—hacking of aircraft computer systems to control its flight. It was recently reported that a cyber security consultant had informed that he hacked into computer systems aboard airliners up to 20 times and managed to control an aircraft engine during a flight. The consultant, apparently with the good intention of alerting authorities against the threat of hackers manipulating aircraft's flight pattern, had also said he hacked into in-flight entertainment systems aboard aircraft. He claimed to have done so 15–20 times from 2011 to 2014. He had also revealed an alarming fact—that he had once hacked into the systems and then overwrote code, enabling him to issue a "CLB," or climb, command.

One airplane manufacturer is reported to have countered that the entertainment systems on board its aircraft are isolated from flight and navigation systems and that its aircraft have more than one navigational system available to pilots. Furthermore that manufacturer had added: "no changes to the flight plans loaded into the airplane systems can take place without pilot review and approval. In addition, other systems, multiple security measures, and flight deck operating procedures help ensure safe and secure airplane operations."

Whatever the case may be, the importance of cyber security cannot be overstated. Cyber terrorism is with us to stay.

In late November last year, Sony Pictures' computers were hacked. Vlad Savov of *The Verge* reported:

---

[215]The two instruments adopted by the Beijing Conference are the *Convention on the Suppression of Unlawful Acts Relating to International Civil Aviation* (hereinafter 'Beijing Convention' or 'Beijing Treaty') and the *Protocol Supplementary to the Convention for the Suppression of Unlawful Seizure of Aircraft.*

[216]On 21 June 2015, hackers attacked the computer system of LOT Polish Airlines, grounding several aircraft, resulting in the grounding of 10 flights and delay caused to 12 other flights. This caused severe inconvenience to nearly 1500 passengers. For more details, see Abeyratne (2011c), pp. 243–255.

> A successful attack on Sony Pictures' computer systems threw the entire studio into disarray in late November. The hijackers' identity and motivation remain unclear, though in the days following the attack, evidence has surfaced to suggest it originated in North Korea. Rather than attempting to steal money or otherwise profit from the information it obtained, this hack seems to be focused on making life difficult for Sony Pictures employees. They have been subjected to threats from the hacking group, which has posted much of the data it collected from the studio's servers to the web.

Cyberspace, which comprises millions of fibre optic cables enabling servers, computers and routers, is the nervous system of any nation's critically important infrastructures, prominent among which is transportation. Attacks on cyberspace can cause immeasurable harm, particularly by disrupting essential services such as banking and finance, telecommunications, health and health care, transportation, religious places of worship, infrastructures, government services, education centers, power and energy generation and distribution, manufacturing, agriculture and food, electricity and water supply, and military defence. Of these, aerospace activities and air traffic control are significant targets.

The aviation world has taken the issue of cyber terrorism seriously, as cybercrimes and cyber terrorism are becoming increasingly menacing and the latter has been identified as a distinct threat requiring attention. At the 21st Aviation Security Panel Meeting of The International Civil Aviation Organization (ICAO) (AVSECP/21, 22 to 26 March 2010) a new Recommended Practice related to cyber threats was proposed for adoption by the Council as part of amendment 12 to Annex 17 (Security) to the Convention on International Civil Aviation. It was adopted on 17 November 2010, became effective on 26 March 2011 and applicable on 1 July 2011. This Recommended Practice suggests that each Contracting State develop measures in order to protect information and communication technology systems used for civil aviation purposes from interference that may jeopardize the safety of civil aviation. At the 22nd Meeting of the Panel, conducted by ICAO from 21 to 25 March 2011, the Panel noted the value of vulnerability assessments pertaining to cyber security in aviation whose objectives are to evaluate the efficiency of existing mitigation measures and identify any vulnerabilities from a threat-based perspective and further noted that better understanding of residual risks will support a State's efforts to refine its risk response.

Whether conducted by an individual, a corporation or a State, cyber terrorism has the potential to target the electronic systems of companies that design and develop hardware and software used at airports and in air traffic control systems. Such terrorism may also target industries involved in the construction of aircraft and components, whether they are used for civil or military purposes. Stefano Male, in his 2010 article *Cyber Warfare and its Damaging Effects on Citizens*, says: "[h]ere, the objective is that of manipulating, in the design phase, software or hardware which will eventually come to be used in critical environments. The events linked to the theft of designs relating to the American F-35 project are an example of this kind of act".

The consultant who demonstrated ease of hacking into the in-flight system of an aircraft showed that hacking is all about interfering with data. Interception of data is a significant offense that is a precursor to cyber crime and cyber terrorism. The *Cybercrime Convention* defines interception as listening to, monitoring or surveillance of the content of communications, to the procuring of the content of data either directly, through access and use of the computer system, or indirectly, through the use of electronic eavesdropping or tapping devices.

Some countries have legislated against such interception. Australia adopted the *Telecommunications (Interception and Access) Act* in 1979. Section 7(1) provides that a person must not intercept, authorize, suffer or permit another person to intercept or do any act or thing that will enable him or her or another person to intercept a communication passing over a telecommunications system. In Canada, a Bill was introduced in Parliament in 2005 aimed at introducing reforms to the legislative structure concerned with the unlawful interception of documents and communications. In the absence of specific legislation, parallels may be found in Canada's criminal legislation. For example, Section 184(1) of the *Canadian Criminal Code* provides that an agent of the State may intercept, by means of any electromagnetic, acoustic, mechanical or other device, a private communication if either the originator of the private communication or the person intended by the originator to receive it has consented to the interception, or the agent of the State believes on reasonable grounds that there is a risk of bodily harm to the person who consented to the interception and the purpose of the interception is to prevent such bodily harm.

In the United Kingdom, the 2000 *Regulation of Investigatory Powers Act* was a legislative attempt by Parliament to unify in a single legal framework provisions countering the interception of information and communications. This Act does not discriminate between types of communications or the location at which communications are intercepted.

The United States has numerous cyber security legislation among which are *The Cyber Security Research and Development Act,* also enacted in 2002, which established research responsibilities in cyber security for the National Science Foundation (NSF) and National Institute of Science and Technology(NIST). *The E-Government Act of 2002* serves as the primary legislative vehicle to guide federal IT management and initiatives to make information and services available online, and includes various cyber security requirements: *The Federal Information Security Management Act of 2002 (FISMA)* clarified and strengthened NIST and agency cyber security responsibilities, while establishing a central federal incident center.

A particular feature of cyber terrorism is that the threat is enhanced by globalization and the ubiquity of the Internet. Given such a global problem, requiring a global solution, the one forum that can provide a global framework against cyber terrorism in aviation is ICAO. A sustained global process of security risk assessment is the first necessary step.

At its 12th Air Navigation Conference in 2012, ICAO identified some emergent risk factors that may facilitate cyber attacks against aviation, mainly due to the advancement of technology. ICAO opined that there is an increased reliance on a small number of technologies, such as Linux, Windows, IPv6 protocols and Ethernet (AFDX), and these technologies are widely used in the IT industry and as a result there is widespread understanding of these technologies, and of their weaknesses and vulnerabilities. Also systems are becoming more interconnected and security lapses in one system are likely to affect others; and there is greater impact from systems failures due to increased reliance on them.

As a result, vulnerabilities abound. ICAO reported at this conference that an expert had given an unnerving demonstration of weaknesses in the air traffic control systems coming into use. He showed that with just $2000 worth of store-bought electronics an ADS-B beacon could be 'spoofed' to show that a non-existent aircraft was coming in to land. This 'Ghost Plane' presentation was possible because air traffic control systems have no way of verifying where messages are coming from.

1.10.1.5 The Consolidated Statement on Legal Issues

Another re-hashed Resolution is A39-11: *Consolidated Statement of Continuing ICAO Policies in the Legal Field which* in its Appendices have such subjects as general policy; procedure for approval of draft conventions on international air law; ratification of ICAO international instruments; adoption of national legislation on certain offences committed on board civil aircraft (unruly/disruptive passengers); model legislation on certain offences committed on board civil aircraft section; assault and other acts of interference against a crew member on board a civil aircraft; and other offences committed on board a civil aircraft. The most awkward of subjects is in Appendix D: *Teaching of air law*, for the simple reason that this is an ancient Resolution that has been moribund for decades with no meaningful action taken by the Council. The Appendix *inter alia* has such strong words as: The Assembly, "considering the *undoubted* (my emphasis) importance for the Organization and the States of the specialized teaching of air law and the desirability of fostering knowledge of this important subject: invites the Council to take all possible action to promote the teaching of air law in those States where it is not yet available; and urges States to adopt appropriate measures which would further the achievement of the above objective". No action has been taken in this regard (except when, occasionally, a State funds a few legal officers to talk about the Chicago Convention and ICAO's work, which by no means covers public and private international law). The teaching of air law should constitute such subjects as air carrier liability (with a discussion on case law); treaty law; aviation insurance law and general principles of public international law as applicable to aviation and air transport.

1.10.2 *The Assembly Resolutions: Safety And Security*

1.10.2.1 Safety

Resolution A39-12: *ICAO global planning for safety and air navigation* endorses the second edition of the Global Aviation Safety Plan (GASP)[217] and the fifth edition of the Global Air Navigation Plan (GANP)[218] as the global strategic directions for safety and air navigation, respectively. The Resolution also calls upon ICAO to implement and keep current the GASP and the GANP to support the relevant Strategic Objectives of the Organization, while ensuring necessary stability and resolves that these global plans shall be implemented and kept current in close cooperation and coordination with all concerned stakeholders. These global plans provide the frameworks in which regional, sub regional and national implementation plans will be developed and implemented, thus ensuring consistency, harmonization and coordination of efforts aimed at improving international civil aviation safety, capacity and efficiency. With regard to GASP the Resolution Stresses the need for continuous improvement of aviation safety through a reduction in the number of accidents and related fatalities in air transport operations in all parts of the world, particularly in States where safety records are significantly worse than the worldwide average and that limited resources of the international aviation community should be used strategically to support States or regions whose safety oversight maturity is not at an acceptable level. It also urges Member States to support the GASP objectives by implementing the safety initiatives outlined therein; and urges them also, along with regional safety oversight organizations (RSOOs), regional aviation safety groups (RASGs) and international organizations concerned to work with all stakeholders to set priorities, targets and indicators consistent with the GASP objectives with the view to reduce the number and rate of aircraft accidents.

In the context of the GANP, the Resolution *inter alia* urges the Council to provide States with a standardization roadmap, as announced in the GANP, as a basis for the work programme of ICAO and calls upon States, planning and

---

[217]GASP sets out the global air navigation safety objectives including specific milestones and priorities to be addressed by State and regional aviation safety planners. Secondly, it provides a familiar planning framework to assist States and regions to make improvements in safety through the use of the four Safety Performance Enablers: standardization, collaboration, resources and safety information exchange. Finally, it outlines implementation strategies and best practice guidance material to assist States and regions in their efforts to tailor State and regional solutions to address the global objectives and priorities.

[218]At its 12th Air Navigation Conference (AN-Conf/12) held in Montréal, from 19 to 30 November 2012, the International Civil Aviation Organization (ICAO) introduced its Global Air Navigation Capacity and Efficiency Plan (GANP) for the period 2013 to 2028. The Plan is meant to be approved by the ICAO Assembly at its sessions every 3 years. This is the fourth such Plan adopted by ICAO over the years and is based on operational objectives agreed upon by States and the aviation industry. It provides for a rolling15 year strategic methodology and introduces Aviation System Block Upgrades (ASBUs), each of which has a 5-year time scale.

implementation regional groups (PIRGs), and the aviation industry to utilize the guidance provided in the GANP for planning and implementation activities which establish priorities, targets and indicators consistent with globally-harmonized objectives, taking into account operational needs. It also invites States to take into consideration the GANP guidelines as an efficient operational measure for environmental protection and calls upon States, PIRGs, and the aviation industry to provide timely information to ICAO, and to each other, regarding the implementation status of the GANP, including the lessons learned from the implementation of its provisions.

Regional cooperation is key to achieving an acceptable level of safety and Resolution A39-14: *Regional cooperation and assistance to resolve safety deficiencies, establishing priorities and setting measurable targets*, has given the ICAO four major tasks, the first being that the Council, in partnership with all aviation safety partners, implement a comprehensive assistance programme that will help Member States to correct deficiencies identified through USOAP-CMA, with priority given to the resolution of SSCs. The Council has also been tasked with promoting the concepts of regional cooperation, including the strengthening of RSOOs and RASGs, as well as the establishment of objectives, priorities and indicators and the setting of measurable targets to address significant safety concerns (SSCs) and safety-related deficiencies; taking appropriate actions to ensure that the specificities of a regional aviation system established by a group of Member States are recognized and integrated in the ICAO framework; and continuing to partner with Member States, industry and other aviation safety partners for coordinating and facilitating the provision of financial and technical assistance to States and sub regional and regional safety and safety oversight bodies, including RSOOs and RASGs, in order to enhance safety and strengthen safety oversight capabilities.

1.10.2.2 Security

Resolution A39-18: *Consolidated statement of continuing ICAO policies related to aviation security* addresses the importance of aviation security and the compelling need for States to ratify legal instruments of air law that pertain to security. It urges the Council to continue to attach the highest priority to the adoption of effective measures for the prevention of acts of unlawful interference commensurate with the current threat to the security of international civil aviation, to take into account the innovative and evolving nature of that threat, and to keep up to date the provisions of Annex 17 to the Chicago Convention from a threat and risk perspective. The Resolution also recognizes the integral link between Annex 17 on security and Annex 9 on facilitation and urges States to intensify their efforts for the implementation of existing SARPs, and procedures relating to aviation security, to monitor such implementation, to rectify any gaps or deficiencies as a matter of urgency, to take all necessary steps to prevent acts of unlawful interference against international civil aviation and to give appropriate attention to the guidance material contained in the ICAO *Aviation Security Manual* (Doc 8973 Restricted) and other security-related guidance material available on the ICAO restricted website. States are also called upon to cooperate with each other in curbing the conduct of unruly passengers and acts of unlawful interference. Here again cooperation is the key where the Council is requested to take into account the G8 Secure and Facilitated International Travel Initiative (SAFTI) and to continue its collaboration with the group and other relevant groups of States such as the Asia-Pacific Economic Cooperation Secure Trade in the Asia and Pacific Region (STAR) initiative in its work relating to development of countermeasures against the threat posed by man portable air defence systems (MANPADS) and encourage their implementation by all Member States. The Council is directed by the Assembly to continue its cooperation with the United Nations Counter-Terrorism Committee (CTC), in the global effort to combat terrorism.

Special mention must be made of a new resolution—A39-19: *Addressing Cybersecurity in Civil Aviation.* In its preamble the Resolution recognizes that the threat posed by cyber incidents on civil aviation is rapidly and continuously evolving, that threat actors are focused on malicious intent, disruption of business continuity and theft of information for political, financial or other motivations, and that the threat can easily evolve to affect critical civil aviation systems worldwide, (although not all cybersecurity issues affecting the safety of civil aviation are unlawful and/or intentional), and should therefore be addressed through the application of safety management systems. The Resolution reaffirms the importance and urgency of protecting civil aviation's critical infrastructure systems and data against cyber threats. The emphasis is on establishing a culture that robustly addresses cyber security as an issue requiring the full attention of States, and therefore the Resolution calls upon States *inter alia* to identify the threats and risks from possible cyber incidents on civil aviation operations and critical systems, and the serious consequences that can arise from such incidents. It also calls upon States to define the responsibilities of national agencies and industry stakeholders with regard to cybersecurity in civil aviation; encourage the development of a common understanding among Member States of cyber threats and risks, and of common criteria to determine the criticality of the assets and systems that need to be protected; encourage government/industry coordination with regard to aviation cybersecurity strategies, policies, and plans, as well as sharing of information to help identify critical vulnerabilities that need to be addressed; develop and participate in government/industry partnerships and mechanisms, nationally and internationally, for the systematic sharing of information on cyber threats, incidents, trends and mitigation efforts; and adopt a flexible, risk-based approach to protecting critical aviation systems through the implementation of cybersecurity management systems; based on a common understanding of cyber threats and risks.

At the 39th Session of the Assembly, both ICAO and its member States have wrapped their resolutions around two overarching themes: The No Country Left Behind Philosophy and cooperation with the United Nations in achieving the latter's Sustainable Development Goals, with contributions from aviation. As this chapter has discussed, the key areas of safety, security and the environment under the broad umbrella of legal treaties and issues that come through ICAO are coalesced into a central philosophy that all 191 member States will be looked after on an equal basis. In this context it is important to focus on Resolution A39-23: *No Country Left Behind (NCLB) Initiative* which urges Member States to improve their civil aviation systems by actively participating in ICAO's work and by effectively implementing ICAO SARPs and policies so that they can foster sustainable local and regional prosperity and fully benefit from improved global connectivity. The Resolution directs the ICAO Council to maintain the focus of the community on the global contribution and value of aviation through support of NCLB efforts and future ICAO World Aviation Forums. The Resolution requires the Secretary General to coordinate, facilitate and implement comprehensive assistance programmes, in partnership with all stakeholders, that will help Member States in enhancing their civil aviation systems and oversight capabilities. Member States, the industry, financial institutions, donors and other stakeholders are requested to coordinate and cooperate amongst themselves and through ICAO, and to support the implementation of assistance activities in line with the global and regional priorities established by ICAO, thereby avoiding duplication of efforts.

Furthermore, the Secretary General is tasked with enhancing the coordinated and comprehensive implementation and evaluation mechanisms of the initiative to assist States in implementing ICAO SARPs, policies, plans and programmes and coordinating with States, international organizations, industry and donors on the implementation of assistance activities by establishing partnerships through an ICAO network for aviation development. In pursuance of these tasks the Secretary General has to engage States and financial institutions to secure their support for strengthening the safety, security and efficiency of the global aviation system. For their part, industry and financial institutions are requested to develop and present to ICAO their own action plans in support of the full implementation of this resolution.

The other thematic Resolution is A39-25: *Aviation's contribution towards the United Nations 2030 Agenda for Sustainable Development* which seeks to support the United Nations goals in the realization that air transport is a catalyst for sustainable development and that it represents an essential lifeline for least developed countries (LDCs), and especially for landlocked developing countries (LLDCs) and small island developing States (SIDS) to connect to the world. The Resolution recognized that air transport connectivity is of utmost importance for the economic, social and territorial cohesion of Member States and their populations, under the important premise that the benefits enabled by air transportation can only materialize if States have a safe, efficient, secure, economically viable and environmentally sound air transport system. There is also the recognition that the Whereas the NCLB initiative aims at assisting States in effectively implementing ICAO Standards and Recommended Practices (SARPs), plans, policies and programmes, as well as addressing Significant Safety and Security Concerns so as to ensure that all States have access to the significant socio-economic benefits of air transport.

The Resolution urges Member States to recognize the significant contributions of aviation to sustainable development realized by stimulating employment, trade, tourism and other areas of economic development at the national, regional and global levels, as well as by facilitating humanitarian and disaster response to crises and public health emergencies. It therefore directs the Council and the Secretary General, within their respective competencies, to demonstrate that ICAO continues to serve as an advocate for aviation by raising awareness among Member States, including relevant authorities beyond the air transport sector, the United Nations system, the donor community and all relevant stakeholders about aviation's contributions to sustainable development and the attainment of the Sustainable Development Goals. Member States are requested to enhance their air transport systems by effectively implementing SARPs and policies while at the same time including and elevating the priority of the aviation sector into their national development plans supported by robust air transport sector strategic plans and civil aviation master plans, thereby leading to the attainment of the Sustainable Development Goals.

Every ICAO Assembly yields much work to follow, both for member States as well as the Council. This necessitates the formulation of a packed work programme for the coming years. The significant difference in the 39th Assembly is that there are two themes that impel the Resolutions to move forward. This ought to give ICAO a renewed sense of purpose, a more focused sense of direction and an overall sense of achievement.

References

Abeyratne RIR (1987) Negligence of the airline commander and bad airmanship – new frontiers. Air Space Law XII(1):3–10

Abeyratne RIR (1998) Negligence of the airline pilot. Professional Negligence 14(4):219–231

Abeyratne R (2001) The exchange of airline passenger information – issues of privacy. Tolley's Commun Law, pp 91–121

Abeyratne R (2005) The use of information contained in the airline passenger name record – some issues. Commun Law 10(5):170–174

Abeyratne R (2007) Aviation and the carbon trade. Nova Publishers, New York, pp 99–106

Abeyratne R (2008) The new emissions trading scheme: airlines – is it extraterritorial? Environ Policy Law 38(2):155–160

Abeyratne R (2011a) Cyber terrorism and aviation – national and international responses. J Transportation Secur (Published on line 31 May 2011)

Abeyratne R (2011b) Cyberterrorism – the next great threat to aviation. Air Space Lawyer 24(1):4-8 and 13

Abeyratne R (2011c) The Beijing Convention of 2010: an important milestone in the annals of aviation security. Air Space Law 36(3):243–255

Abeyratne R (2012) The airline passenger's right to flight information at airports. Eur Transport Law XLVII(4):363–372

Abeyratne R (2013a) The Convention on International Civil Aviation – a commentary. Springer, Heidelberg

Abeyratne R (2013b) Reinventing ICAO's role in air transport – a compelling need? Issues Aviation Law Policy 13(1):9–29

Abeyratne R (2013c) The air transport conference of ICAO – a critical analysis. Air Space Law XXXVII(4–5):297–332

Abeyratne R (2014a) Flight MH 17 and state responsibility for ensuring safety and security of air transport. J Air Transport Secur. 7:347–357. doi:10.1007/s12198-014-0148-0 (published on line 2 October 2014)
Abeyratne R (2014b) Flight MH 17: the legal and regulatory fallout. Air Space Law 39 (6):329–342
Abeyratne R (2014c) Flight MH 370 and global flight tracking – the ICAO reaction. Zeitschrift Fur Luft-und Weltraumrecht (German J Air and Space Law ZLW) 63:544–558
Abeyratne R (2014d) Regulation of commercial space transport – the astrocizing of ICAO. Springer, Heidelberg
Abeyratne R (2014e) Aviation and climate change – in search of a global market based measure. Springer, Heidelberg, pp 69–150
Abeyratne R (2014f) Integrity of travel documents: the wakeup call from flight MH 370. Zeitschrift fur Luft-und Weltraumrecht (German J Air Space Law ZLW) 63:238–249
Abeyratne R (2015a) Aviation and international cooperation: human and public policy issues. Springer, Heidelberg, pp 159–275
Abeyratne R (2015b) Global market-based measures for aviation emissions. Environ Policy Law 45(3–4):102–107
Abeyratne R. Airport service quality, a new dimension. http://www.slguardian.org/2016/08/airport-service-quality-a-new-dimension/
Babu P (2016) 10 airports using beacons to take passenger experience to the next level. Beaconstac, 16 March 2016. https://blog.beaconstac.com/2016/03/10-airports-using-beacons-to-take-passenger-experience-to-the-next-level/
Brownlie I (1990) Principles of public international law, 4th edn. Clarendon Press, Oxford, p 691
Campos P (2016) Compliance tools for a global market based measure for international aviation. CCLR 2:156
Cunningham RO (1999) Subsidies to large civil aircraft production: new WTO subsidy rules and dispute settlement mechanism alter dynamics of U.S.–E.U. dispute. Air Space Law, p 6
Dempsey PS (2015) The future of air law in the 21st century. Zeitschrift Fur Luft-und Weltraumrecht (German J Air Space Law ZLW) 64(2):215
Etzioni A (2005–2006) From right to responsibility, the definition of sovereignty is changing. Insight, p 35
Garcia M (2016) Miami airport becomes one of the first to connect consumers with beacons. Skift, 9 February 2016. https://skift.com/2016/02/09/miamis-airport-becomes-one-of-the-first-to-connect-consumers-with-beacons/
Gelain A (2016) Opinion: the uncomfortable truth about aviation emissions. Aviation Week and Space Technology, 10 August 2016
Ghemawat P (2011) World 3.0: global prosperity and how to achieve it. Harvard Business Review Press, p 29
Infante A (2004) Here's why scientists think you should be worried about artificial intelligence. Future Tech, 4 August 2004
Kaplan J (2017) AI's PR problem. MIT Technology Review, 3 March 2017
Kelly JE III, Ham S (2013) Smart machines – IBM's Watson and the era of cognitive computing. Columbia University Press
Kohli D (2016–2017) The benefits of beacons. Airport World, p 36
Lang C (2016.) Aviation industry's plan to 'offset' its emissions is crazy. The Ecologist 2016-09-12. See file:///C:/Users/tissaabe/AppData/Local/Microsoft/Windows/INetCache/Content.Outlook/0STBO7DL/Aviation%20industry's%20plan%20to%20'offset'%20its%20emissions%20is%20crazy%20(002).pdf
Lowy J (2016) Robot pilots may someday fly passenger and cargo planes. AP, 18 October 2016
Lowy J. U.S. program aims to replace co-pilots with robots. CTV News. http://www.ctvnews.ca/sci-tech/u-s-program-aims-to-replace-co-pilots-with-robots-1.3119693
Milde M (2012) International Air Law and ICAO. Eleven International Publishing, The Hague, p 1 (Second Edition, Marietta Benko ed.)

Monbiot G (2007) Heat: how to stop the planet from burning. South End Press, London, p 198
Morris DZ (2016) Mercedes-Benz's self-driving cars would choose passenger lives over bystanders. Fortune Tech, 20 October 2016. http://fortune.com/2016/10/15/mercedes-self-driving-car-ethics/
Petsonk A, Dudek DJ, Goffman J (1998) Market mechanisms and global climate change: an analysis of market mechanisms, October 1998. http://www.c2es.org/docUploads/pol_market.pdf. Last accessed 20 July 2016
Ritchie J (2016) The opportunity and challenge of a global market based measure for aviation. CCLR 2:91
Romm J. Rate of climate change to soar by 2020s, with Arctic warming 1°F per decade. https://thinkprogress.org/rate-of-climate-change-to-soar-by-2020s-with-arctic-warming-1-f-per-decade-85db70fb9d1#.8hp0pa58u
Schaal D (2015) The airline business is a lousy one, airline industry study shows. SKIFT: Megatrends Defining Travel in 2015
Shaw MN (2003) International law, 5th edn. Cambridge University Press, p 110
Speciale RC, Venhuizen BD (2007) The pilot in command and the fars: the buck stops here (almost always). North Dakota. Law Rev 83:817
Starke JG (1977) An introduction to international law, 7th edn. Butterworth, London, p 106
Steinberger H (2000) Sovereignty. In: Bernhardt R (ed) Encyclopaedia of public international law, vol IV. Elsevier, Amsterdam, p 501
Tammes AJP (1958) Decisions of international organs as a source of international law. HR 94:265
Thompson TR (2016) Climate change impacts upon the commercial air transport industry: an overview. CCLR 2:106
Vaishnav P (2016) ICAO's market based mechanism: keep it simple. CCLR 2:121
Watson R (2012) Future files: a brief history of the next 50 years. Nicholas Brealey Publishing, Boston, p 44
Wilson J (2000) Miracles of the next 50 years. Popular Mech 177(2):51–53
World Rainforest Movement (2015.) REDD: a collection of conflicts, contradictions and lies. See file:///C:/Users/tissaabe/AppData/Local/Microsoft/Windows/INetCache/Content.Outlook/0STBO7DL/More%20than%2080%20NGOs%20oppose%20aviation%20sector's%20carbon%20offsetting%20pl%20(002).pdf
Zoller E (1987) The corporate will of the United Nations and the rights of the minority contributors. Am J Int Law 81(3):32

Chapter 2
Global Balance of Power and Aviation

2.1 Introduction

2.1.1 The New World Order

The emergence of neo-postmodernism is founded upon the fundamental premise that change is the defining feature of our times. Information technology and development have changed our world and made our lives easier. However, they have facilitated the work of those who intend to pursue their own agendas even at the expense of human life. There are no longer looming superpowers that breed terrorism. Now, it is weaker States that give rise to evil ambition among groups no longer happy with a decaying status quo. A whole new paradigm is required if modern day terrorism is to be effectively restrained. This requires not mere State responsibility but also a global understanding that States need to be held accountable for preventing the spread of terrorism.

There has been a trend to obfuscate the legal legitimacy of State accountability by the misconceived use of the concept of State sovereignty. However, in the context of prevention of threats to national security, a new paradigm can be recognized. The supremacy of State sovereignty now lies in State responsibility and international cooperation aimed at ensuring the safety and security as well as the general welfare of the people, rather than State prerogative. As the then Secretary General of the UN said in 1999: "State sovereignty, in its most basic sense, is being redefined – not least by the forces of globalization and international cooperation". States are now widely understood to be instruments at the services of their peoples and not vice versa.

When one avers to global balance of power one could only look at the political swings of 2016. Most of the commentaries one hears about retrospective looks at 2016 consist of what we have heard over and over: populism has been the trend the world over—Brexit and Donald Trump's victory; The vote by Italians who rejected a referendum which precipitated the exit of the Prime Minister (the reason for

R. Abeyratne, *Megatrends and Air Transport*, DOI 10.1007/978-3-319-61124-2_2

which is wrongly attributed to populism whereas the referendum was perceived by the Italian public as restricting democracy and the democratic institution); the ongoing misery in Syria; Iraq, Libya Yemen and some African States bringing about a refugee crisis not seen since world war 2; and sporadic terror attacks in Europe. Not much is said about the reasons for these trends and occurrences.

Populism grew because of rising inequality which has been identified as the defining feature of our times. This exponential rise in inequality has in turn been attributed to two decades of failed liberal governance where western governments have been boosting the markets instead of developing and pumping money into economies. Italy's crisis was purely a result of the rejection of perceived concentration of power in one individual. The misery in Syria and other places mentioned was because of ineptitude of the West in not nipping off in the bud the autocracy of certain villainous dictators. No doubt the refugee crisis is a corollary of this feckless insouciance. Sporadic terror attacks in Europe were the result of a combination of bad intelligence gathering, inadequate anticipatory intelligence and the displacement of terrorism to soft targets.

Nationalism is another global trend that raised its head during the year where people were in serious search of their national identity and their historical rights viewed against the influx of foreigners who were "taking away" jobs that were rightfully belonging to the former.

The above notwithstanding, hyper-connectivity was the most pervasive agent of change in 2016. The year personified the changing nature of power from the world of big government and commerce to the individual, where individual empowerment was a key driver. This was brought about by a technology revolution which relentlessly bombarded the 12 months of 2016, making education the key factor that kept on increasing the numbers of the middle class. Corollaries of this trend made artificial intelligence (AI) boom with such innovations as Google's DeepMind and Tesla's self-driving and self navigating cars. If DeepMind could beat any human being at Go (a more complicated game than Chess) one could wonder how AI could recommend better procedures for surgeries than human medical specialist and technologists can ever concoct with their collective minds. IBM's Watson (a super computer which could read millions of academic articles in a few minutes and synthesize solutions) came into the limelight in 2016, bringing to bear the immense possibilities that technology would offer in the future.

There were also signs of decreasing inequality in emerging markets coupled with increasing mobility. Big data analysis took a huge leap forward in 2016, an example being applications such as "hopper" which gives the air traveller the best air fares to reach his destination through a search of three billion airfare combinations. However, a Global Economic Forum (GEF) study released in mid 2016 pointed out that individuals are beginning to lose trust in how governments are handling meta data which was seemingly a threat to their privacy rights. The solution put forward by the GEF is to set up "living labs" to test potential new regulations for rights and responsibilities of the individual. This solution portends a dilemma for China as a Rand study pointed out where a dichotomy exists where China's future development depends on global internet connectivity which in turn is stymied by China's own circumscription of the internet. Meanwhile, a McKenzie Study reported that the internet would increase in real GDP per capita of $500 on average in the next 15 years.

2016 also saw massive improvements in medicine, guaranteeing better health and extended longevity. Jobs created in 2016 outnumbered those destroyed and "digitization"—the mass adoption of connected digital services by consumers, enterprises and governments provided billions of dollars to boost world economic output. Greater independence of the individual has resulted through globalization. There were also emergent game changes for the future: the growing possibility of war (particularly regionally); new technologies; the ambiguity presented by global politics that wavered from left to right.

Global environmental protection took a more optimistic turn with the Paris Agreement—an agreement within the United Nations Framework Convention on Climate Change (UNFCCC) dealing with greenhouse gases emissions mitigation, adaptation and finance starting in the year 2020. The language of the agreement was negotiated by representatives of 195 countries at the 21st Conference of the Parties of the UNFCCC in Paris and adopted by consensus on 12 December 2015. It was opened for signature on 22 April 2016 (Earth Day) in a ceremony in New York City. This Agreement, which came into effect in 2016 sought to limit the global average temperature to well below 2 °C and to proceed toward limiting that increase to 1.5 °C. On 5 October 2016, the threshold for entry into force of the Paris Agreement was achieved. The Paris Agreement entered into force on 4 November 2016. The first session of the Conference of the Parties serving as the Meeting of the Parties to the Paris Agreement (CMA 1) took place in Marrakech, Morocco from 15–18 November 2016.

Finally, a political "bombshell" was dropped in the United Nations Security Council on 23 December where the Security Council adopted Resolution 2334 relating to Israeli settlements in "Palestinian territories occupied since 1967, including East Jerusalem". The Resolution, which was passed with the support of 14 of the 15 members of the Council with the United States, which has veto power, abstaining, states that Israel′s settlement activity constitutes a "flagrant violation" of international law and has "no legal validity", and demands that Israel stop such activity and fulfill its obligation as an occupying power under the Fourth Geneva Convention. Israel responded to this condemnation by blaming the United States for failing to block the Council resolution, among other more serious allegations of the Resolution being orchestrated by the United States.

Although the Resolution is non-binding and does not have an immediate compelling effect on Israel, it leaves a strong flavor of political discord among two allies. As Prime Minister Benjamin Netanyahu of Israel said: "friends do not take friends to the Security Council". Legal validity cannot be ascribed to UN Resolutions as they are merely the result of political compromises and arrangements. Above all, this led up to an inauspicious and tense start to 2017. As the age old Chinese curse says: "may you live in interesting times". Viewed in this context 2017 and the years to come might well be "interesting".

The New World Order is a term concocted 25 years ago by both Presidents Bush and Gorbachev to reflect a new trend in US diplomacy bringing with it a new discipline to the world. The term was conceived during the Persian Gulf crisis when Iraq invaded Kuwait, and was calculated to usher in a more harmonious cooperation among states in matters of international interest. Based on the principle of collective security, the New World Order coalesced States into the collective authority of the UN Security Council which adopted and enforced measures against what it perceived as belligerent States. Under the New World Order came the notion of US exceptionalism where the US acted as *de facto* policeman of the world, ensuring a balance between the regions of the world and intervening when necessary, particularly when that balance was threatened.

The New World Disorder is the current state of affairs in the world where the prevailing balance has been fragmented and eroded. Examples are the Saudi Arabian coalition's air strikes in Yemen, the Russian Annexation of Crimea, the shooting down of Flight MH 17 over Donetsk, the Chinese-Japanese spat over the Senkaku Islands and unilateral belligerence by non States such as Al Qaeda, ISIS and Al Shabab which have crossed borders, particularly in the case of ISIS where it has proclamed a caliphate. There is seemingly no global policeman to sustain harmony anymore and disorder is widespread and fragmented.

The new world disorder is also threatening the onward march of globalization which favours competition in air transport. Populism and national fervor seem to be emerging as a megatrend. Generally, this rising political concept is based on the claim that globalization—the free movement of trade, people and assets adversely affects local populations as a result of migration of companies from larger tax bases to lower tax bases, immigration and overall job losses. As for the free movement of people, the vote on BREXIT, the rising popularity of the National Front in France and the claims of the Republican Party Nominee at the next US election all bear evidence to the popularity sweeping across the world against globalization. There are two schools of thought: one view is that globalization and the advancement of information technology has had an overall beneficial effect on the world economy. For example, a report released in 2013 said that the world economy had improved in 2012 by 10% over the previous decade and 40% over the decade of the 1980s. As a continuing trend, these facts have generally been endorsed. For instance, Mike Collins, in a 2015 *Forbes* article says: "There is no question that globalization has been a good thing for many developing countries who now have access to our markets and can export cheap goods. Globalization has also been good for Multinational corporations and Wall Street. But globalization has not been good for working people (blue or white collar) and has led to the continuing deindustrialization of America".

The complaint against globalization is that jobs migrate to low wage cost countries which offers an impetus to the rich (Presidents, CEOs and senior managers) to get richer while the poor get poorer. To counter this argument Fairooz Hamdi in an article written in 2015 entitled *The Impact of Globalization in the Developing Countries* says: "globalization helps developing countries to deal with rest of the world increase their economic growth, solving the poverty problems in their country. In the past, developing countries were not able to tap on the world economy due to trade barriers. They cannot share the same economic growth that developed countries had. However, with globalization the World Bank and International Management encourage developing countries to go through market reforms and radical changes through large loans. Many developing nations began to take steps to open their markets by removing tariffs and free up their economies. The developed countries were able to invest in the developing nations, creating job opportunities for the poor people".

The Economist, in its latest issue (October 1 2016) discourages protectionism and extols the benefits of free trade which is a corollary to globalization: "Protectionism, by contrast (to free trade), hurts consumers and does little for workers. The worst-off benefit far more from trade than the rich. A study of 40 countries found that the richest consumers would lose 28% of their purchasing power if cross-border trade ended; but those in the bottom tenth would lose 63%. The annual cost to American consumers of switching to non-Chinese tyres after Barack Obama slapped on anti-dumping tariffs in 2009 was around $1.1 billion, according to the Peterson Institute for International Economics. That amounts to over $900,000 for each of the 1200 jobs that were saved".

So who is right?

Globalization brings to bear the blatant reality that increasing global connectivity, together with integration and interdependence in the economic, social, technological, cultural, political and ecological spheres, have removed all trade barriers, making a world without boundaries. Encyclopedia Britannica defines globalization as the "process by which the experience of everyday life is becoming standardized around the world.". Globalization reflects the inevitable corollary of the contemporaneous advancement of technology and growing trends toward liberalism in international trade. The information and telecommunications revolution, which really kick started in the 1980s, dramatically lowered the costs of doing business across national borders. The giant strides made by information technology, which took its incipient steps in the 1990s, together with paradigm shifts in trade practices such as outsourcing and off-shoring, have ensured the opening of a world which no longer sees boundaries that inhibit global trade and information exchange. The movement toward outsourcing and subcontracting of services is evident in both developed and developing countries. Provision of information technology is now frequently outsourced to specialized companies. One of the distinctive characteristics of outsourcing in the context of trade is that it is not inhibited by national requirements imposing ownership restrictions, which allows trading services to blend in to the process of globalization. Off-shoring on the other hand allows a business to move its base to a country where human resources are accessible at rates lower than its home base but at the same time are of the same or higher quality than found at home. China is a good example of an attractive off-shore base.

The strongest thrust of globalization in the business world is its ability to generate competition within and between nations to offer the best goods and services at the lowest prices. The quality of services and pricing in China as an off-shore base have encouraged other nations, such as Malaysia, Thailand, Ireland, Vietnam, Brazil and Mexico to vigorously compete as viable off-shore bases.

The World Is Flat: A Brief History of the Twenty-first Century is a best-selling book which analyzes the progress of globalization with a focus on the early twenty first century. It was first released 2 years ago in and was later released as an updated and expanded edition last year in 2006. The author, Thomas L. Friedman uses the metaphor of a flat world suggesting that the competitive playing fields between industrial and emerging market countries are leveling. This is both an interesting and real phenomenon. The book is excellently researched, well written and makes for compelling and interesting reading.

As the book confirms, there is no doubt that two of the greatest catalysts in the globalization equation have been e-information and e-trade, which were individually and collectively spawned by the internet. Downloading and uploading are tools that make the exchange of knowledge instantly accessible throughout the globe. These tools, when viewed in the perspective of the greatest global inhibitors of all—poverty, war and ill health- open a whole new dimension of hope.

There are two basic premises which are incontrovertible. The first is that globalization enhances the wealth of nations, promotes trade and increases the gross domestic product of a country. The second is that at the very core, the primary need of every human being is to be rid of poverty, war and ill health. The question then is, how could globalization assist in eradicating poverty, war and ill health.

As for poverty, it is highly possible to bring an end to poverty through globalization. Jeffrey D. Sachs, Director of the Earth Institute at Columbia University and onetime Special Advisor to former United Nations Secretary General Kofi Annan on the UN Millennium Development Goals and Economic Advisor to Governments around the World, in his book, *The End of Poverty—Economic Possibilities of Our Time*, says it is a distinct and real possibility. Sachs quotes the prescient 1930 book of British economist John Maynard Keynes, Economic Possibilities for Our Grandchildren, where Keynes envisioned that there would be no more poverty by the end of the twentieth century, attributing to the eradication of poverty the relentless march of science and technology resulting in exponential global economic growth.

Sachs follows through without reservation, by invoking the same logic as Keynes, claiming that by 2025, we could be totally poverty-free by using the wealth of the world and the power of unending repositories of knowledge that we have. Of course, as every good news has a caveat, Sachs lays down the condition that our ability to transcend global poverty would depend on our collective wisdom in using our resources prudently and with good judgment. In his book, Sachs shows the way towards charting a wiser path towards global wealth and prosperity.

The key to Sach's claim lies in the sharing of wealth, which is what globalization does best. Sharing of wealth comes from sharing of information and the prudent use of human resources. To do this, governments must enable and empower citizens to learn trades that are needed in today's society, recognize the potential of its people, give them the opportunity to develop meaningful connections with other people in global society, and above all, adopt liberal trade policies that promote trade without boundaries.

The first step is to make a commitment toward ending poverty. This could be done nationally, regionally or globally. To start with, the national dimension would be the initial approach. Secondly, we need a plan, which we already have in the United Nations Millennium Goals. These Goals demand that no individual and no nation must he denied the opportunity to benefit from development. The equal rights and opportunities of women and men must he assured. Global challenges must be managed in a way that distributes the costs and burdens fairly in accordance with basic principles of equity and social justice. Those who suffer or who benefit least deserve help from those who benefit most. The Goals also call for responsibility for managing worldwide economic and social development, as well as threats to international peace and security, to be shared among the nations of the world and be exercised multilaterally. As the most universal and most representative organization in the world, the United Nations must play the central role in this saga.

The poor need to be empowered. The rich nations may not be encouraged to assist in this goal if the poor nations and their citizens are silent. The biggest inhibitor to reducing trade barriers—the political economy—where removal of trade barriers is considered harmful to domestic industry, should be viewed with apprehension. A good approach would be to have better dissemination of information on the benefits to consumers and service providers alike and encouragement of technological innovation. Sachs cites the likes of Mahatma Gandhi and Martin Luther King who did not wait for the rich and powerful but went ahead helping the cause of the poor and downtrodden. Another important and compelling need is to empower the United Nations and strengthen it, along with raising the profiles and standing of such financial institutions as the International Bank for Reconstruction and Development (World Bank) and the International Monetary Fund. We also need to ensure sustainable development by harnessing scientific and technological advancement. The last frontier is of course individuals—all of us as separate beings, contributing to the cause and supporting our governments.

On another front, the reclamation of land from the sea by China in the South China SEA, its claim on the Senkaku Islands, missile tests by North Korea bring to bear aerial problems of overflight; sovereignty of air space and interference by military aircraft in civil air navigation routes. Added to this is the air transport dimension where the wave of populism that swept the world in 2016 was best illustrated by the BREXIT vote which has serious ramifications on air traffic rights and forms a relevant subject of discussion, which will follow.

2.1.2 Stultification and Innovation

Arguably, the key word, (if there is such a thing) in megatrends is openness and innovation. This is particularly so in air transport where openness has led to liberalization of markets in many regions of the world and open skies between many partners ensuring connectivity as well as facilitation of air transport in a burgeoning global market. This has become necessary in the face of such megatrends as an ageing population; the economic and political power shift to the East; and focus on the empowerment of the individual rather than the State and multinational corporations. History has played its part in paving the way as the discussion that follows clearly illustrates.

Nobel laureate Paul Krugman is of the view that while a depression of the nature of the 1930s might not return, what he calls "depression economics" has returned and is with us. Krugman says:

> ...for the first time in two generations, failures, on the demand side of the economy – insufficient private spending to make use of the available productive capacity – have become the clear and present limitation on prosperity for a large part of the world.[1]

This irrefutable principle, when applied to air transport, brings to bear a compelling shortcoming of the industry in government control on foreign private spending. Many airlines in India, such as Kingfisher, are suffering because of this trend. As Michael Spence, Nobel Laureate and Professor of Economics at New York University observes in the example of India:

> India's earlier slow growth was partly attributable to a distrust of foreign investors and a relatively low level of foreign investment by multinational firms. If you look at the data for India and China for example, the differences are dramatic. Of course this is changing now with India's growing options.[2]

Commercially, if this view applies to the industrial world in general, there is no reason it should not apply to air transport. Niall Ferguson, Professor of Business Administration at Harvard University draws the interesting parallel of Marco Polo's visit to China in the 1270s when he was impressed by the volume of traffic in the Yangzi. Polo observed that the quantity of merchandize carried up and down made the Yangzi looked like a sea rather than a river. In comparison to this Ferguson argues that the Thames in the early fifteenth century was the backwater. Ferguson goes on to suggest that one of the reasons for the success of European States in the sixteenth century onwards was its opening out to commerce and competition.[3]

China seemingly underwent, in the 1980s through the 1990s a similar experience to that of Europe with a radical change in the advancement of competition which was spontaneous and speedily executed. The change came in transferring agricultural property from communes to households. Jeffrey Sachs, an internally renowned economic advisor to many countries says this of his experience with China:

---

[1]Krugman (2009), p. 182.

[2]Spence (2011), p. 73.

[3]It was Adam Smith who said: "a country which neglects or distrusts foreign commerce, and which admits the vessels of foreign nations into one or two of its ports only, cannot transact the same quality of business which it might do with different laws and institutions" Adam Smith, *The Wealth of Nations*, (1776) cited in Ferguson (2011), p. 19.

> There was nothing gradual about this change. Around seven hundred million individuals in farm household were suddenly farming on plots assigned to the household rather than to the commune. This new household responsibility gave massive incentives to individual farmers to work harder, apply inputs with more care, and to obtain higher yields.[4]

While China has shown positive growth (of around 9%) throughout the past decades,[5] followed by steady South Korean growth over the past 20 years, Europe is teetering despite a second bailout of 130 billion Euro to Greece with 1 trillion bank loans from the European Central Bank. As stated earlier, it is now on the fence between a pull towards austerity from the Germans and a cry for growth by the French—the two major European powers (with Britain rather comfortably out of the Eurozone). A pullout of Greece from the Eurozone could bring to bear a contagion spreading to countries such as Spain, Portugal, Ireland and Italy. Europe needs a firewall against such a contagion, more investment, a more flexible monetary policy, reforms to inflexible market policies and structural reform.

Although in 2011 Germany's exports increased by 34% and it has expectations of achieving 2 million Euro by 2020, its economy shrank in the first quarter of that year and could suffer a setback if there were to be a contagion following a pullout of Greece and perhaps other States mentioned.

Although out of the Eurozone, Britain's economy was stuttering, where in April 2012 it discovered that in the first quarter of 2012 its GDP had been reduced by 0.2% and that it was still slap bang in a recession. There were palpable drops in household consumption and inflation rose by 3.5%.The World Bank, in its statement in January 2012 stated that developing countries should prepare for further downside risks, as the Euro debt crisis and weakening growth in several big emerging economies were discouraging for global growth prospects.

Despite the encouraging privatization trend in the Western world of the 1970s through the 1990s, the somewhat rash privatization "binge" introduced by Boris Yeltsin in Russia in the 1990s taught that indiscriminate privatization is dangerous to an economy. What is now wildly popular is the Keynesian philosophy of State controlled growth, where economic downturns caused by capitalism and globalization could be mitigated by State support both in the areas of hard infrastructure (such as roads and bridges) and also soft infrastructure involving public and private corporations.

Therefore, from an aviation perspective, this is hardly the time for Europe to engage in trade wars with the rest of the world on its intransigent emissions trading scheme. More so, this is the time to view air transport in a defragmented way and try to solve the puzzle of a fast growing industry amidst finite resources and environmental challenges. Europe will have to interact with the likes of China, Russia, India, the United States and Latin American countries, not to mention the rest of

[4]Sachs (2005), p. 160.

[5]In 1990, China contributed only 2% to the global gross domestic product. At the time of writing, it had a global GDP of 8% and it is estimated by some that China's ec006Fnomy will become the world's largest between 2016 and 2018. See Zakaria (2011), p. xii.

Asia if it were to spur growth and this prospect would be seriously endangered if there were to be conflict between Europe and these countries on what the latter considers an arrogant measure in the nature of including aviation in the ETS and making it applicable to flight sectors outside the territory of the EU countries.[6]

The need for defragmenting air transport with a systemic approach should be considered in the context of conflicting commentaries. The 2011 Report of the World Bank stated:

> The world economy has entered a very difficult phase characterized by significant downside risks and fragility. The financial turmoil generated by the intensification of the fiscal crisis in Europe has spread to both developing and high-income countries, and is generating significant headwinds. Capital flows to developing countries have declined by almost half as compared with last year, Europe appears to have entered recession, and growth in several major developing countries (Brazil, India, and to a lesser extent Russia, South Africa and Turkey) has slowed partly in reaction to domestic policy tightening. As a result, and despite relatively strong activity in the United States and Japan, global growth and world trade have slowed sharply.[7]

This somewhat gloomy picture, however correct it might be, brings to bear an illusory perception which seemingly belies reality in terms of market economics, where development reflects an upward trend. Fareed Zakaria, a respected commentator and leading expert on international affairs and economics says:

> Over the last two decades, about two billion people have entered the world of markets and trade – a world that was, until recently, the province of a small club of western countries. The expansion was spurred by the movement of western capital to Asia and across the globe. As a result, between 1990 and 2010, the global economy grew from $22.1 trillion to $ 62 trillion, and global trade increased by 270 %.[8]

Against this scenario, another distinguished commentator Ruchir Sharma says of the future:

> Over the next decade, growth in the United States, Europe and Japan is likely to slow by a full %age point compared to the post World war II average, owing to the large debt overhang, but that slowdown will pale in comparison to a 3 to 4 %age average slowdown in China.

---

[6]EU carbon rule cuts EU off from growth, *Air Letter*, Monday 28 May 2012 No. 17,492 page 2.

[7]http://siteresources.worldbank.org/INTPROSPECTS/Resources/334934-1322593305595/8287139-1326374900917/GEP_January_2012a_FullReport_FINAL.pdf. The Report also stated that the global economy is now expected to expand 2.5 and 3.1% in 2012 and 2013 (3.4 and 4.0% when calculated using purchasing power parity weights), versus the 3.6% projected in June for both years. High-income country growth is now expected to come in at 1.4% in 2012 (−0.3% for Euro Area countries, and 2.1% for the remainder) and 2.0% in 2013, versus June forecasts of 2.7 and 2.6% for 2012 and 2013 respectively. Developing country growth has been revised down to 5.4 and 6.0% versus 6.2 and 6.3% in the June projections. Reflecting the growth slowdown, world trade, which expanded by an estimated 6.6% in 2011, will grow only 4.7% in 2012, before strengthening to 6.8% in 2013.

[8]Zakaria (2011), p. 21. The author goes on to say: "The so called emerging markets have accounted for over half of this global growth, and they now account for over 47 % of the world economy measured at purchasing power parity (of over 33 % at market exchange rates)." *Ibid.*

> The big story will be that China is too big and too middle-aged to grow so fast. And as it starts buying less from other emerging nations, the average pace of growth in emerging markets is likely to slow from nearly 7 % over the past decade to the 1950s and 1960s pace of around 5 %.[9]

Added to this factor is the contagion effect the Euro debt crisis was having on China and India where the decrease in demand for their goods was being felt worldwide and the effects were being felt as far as Australia which is the only G-20[10] economy that was not affected by the recession of 2008.

The woes of the air transport industry have always centered on the claim of most that aviation is effectively precluded from entering the free market due to government meddling. This seems to go contrary to the Keynesian view of the advantages of some degree of government control of the free market economy. Harsh restrictions on ownership and control of airlines and market access are stringent tools of government control. The argument for deregulation, as against government control, pervaded the economic crisis of 2008 where some argued that the bubble burst because the markets had not been free enough from government meddling and that the US Congress pushed lenders to have unfettered ability to lend to those who could not pay back their loans, leading to a housing bubble. Pankaj Ghemavat, referring to the 2008 bubble says:

> Media magnate Rupert Murdoch blamed the Government for the debacle, stating: "It's very easy to blame the free market but how did we get to the housing bubble? We got it because of Congress pushing Fannie Mae and Freddie Mac into lending money to people who couldn't afford it and blowing up the price of housing....[11]

In the air transport sector this principle is reversed in that governments meddle in fettering the freedom of air carriers by imposing political and economic restrictions. This trend seems to continue, much to the disappointment of the air transport industry. Anne-Marie Slaughter of Princeton University speaks of a new world order where The State will not be the only actor in the international system but will still be the most important actor; the State will not disappear but will disaggregate into its component institutions, which will increasingly interact principally with their foreign counterparts across borders; these institutions will represent distinct national or State interests, even as they also recognize common professional identities; and government networks will exist alongside and sometimes within

---

[9]Sharma (2012), p. 242.

[10]The Group of Twenty Finance Ministers and Central Bank Governors (also known as the G-20, G20, and Group of Twenty) is a group of finance ministers and central bank governors from 20 major economies: 19 countries plus the European Union, which is represented by the President of the European Council and by the European Central Bank Their heads of government or heads of state have also periodically conferred at summits since their initial meeting in 2008. Collectively, the G-20 economies account for more than 80% of the gross world product (GWP), 80% of world trade (including EU intra-trade), and two-thirds of the world population. They furthermore account for 84.1% and 82.2% of the world's economic growth by nominal GDP and GDP (PPP) respectively from the years 2010 to 2016, according to the International Monetary Fund.

[11]Ghemawat (2011), p. 12.

more traditional international Organizations.[12] For air transport this is good news in that The State will not be the only actor in the international system, which hopefully mean that International Organizations may be more empowered and that government networks may exist within international Organizations, promoting interest groups within such Organizations to push liberalization of air transport, the primary such Organization being ICAO.

The answer to the economic slump lies in global growth. And growth comes from innovation. One thing we should be very clear of is that innovation and the "predict and provide" philosophy are antithetical and the former is the only way air transport can meet growing demands of the next two decades. On this, Nobel Laureate Michael Spence has said:

> Innovation, which is sometimes called technological progress, increases the production potential of an economy over time. That means that with the same amounts of capital, labor, raw material and energy, you can produce more – or more valuable – output. You can also think of it as reducing the cost of producing a given amount of output.[13]

Innovation in air transport that could facilitate the megatrends discussed in this book could start with a systematic defragmentation of air transport and market access. fragmentation and "divide and rule" in air transport economics must go, even if it means political and military sacrifices of the United States and the rest of the Atlantic States. This would mean relaxation of national interests and foreign ownership and control restrictions on airlines as well as ensuring the best interests of the consumer of air transport. Aviation should be truly globally shared, with other partners, particularly at a regional level, getting together with the so called world powers and devising a universally applicable market economy for air transport. As one commentator aptly puts it:

> The liberalization of markets, the construction of a globalized economy and the spread of prosperity are defining legacies of the era of Western primacy. The fundamentals of this order are firmly in place, anchored by institutions like the World Bank and the World Trade Organization. But the maintenance of this order faces significant challenges. Due to the West's political and economic troubles, the Atlantic democracies may no longer be up to minding the store. The United States already seems to have lost its traditional enthusiasm for being the engine behind the global liberalization of trade.[14]

After all this discussion on the way the world economy is headed, one has to ask: what of the next few decades? In March 2010, Larry Elliott, writing to the Guardian said of the decade 2010–2020:

> Get ready for the austerity decade. Forget all thoughts that the economic storm of the past 30 months is about to blow over. We've had what Mervyn King once called the NICE period of non-inflationary constant expansion but now we face a long DRAG – deficit reduction, anaemic growth. The lessons of economic history, the current configuration of

[12]Slaughter (2004), p. 18.

[13]Spence (2011), p. 36.

[14]Kupchan (2012), p. 198.

> the economy, and inescapable long-term challenges that have to be faced provide the same message: it's payback time.[15]

Perhaps it is, and if there were to be anemic growth in the years ahead, indubitably the downturn would affect air transport adversely. The problem with air transport is that, while on the one hand it is a product, on the other hand regulations pertaining to this product may constrain its availability to the consumer by depriving him of the various choices of air travel he might have under a liberalized system. In other words, State policy and the protection of national interests take precedence over the interest of the user of air transport. The aviation industry offers only one product to the ultimate consumer and that is the air transport product. One might well ask why this product is precluded from attracting untrammelled foreign direct investment (FDI) like other products such as those in the agriculture, textile manufacture and energy industries. In this context, the next chapter will discuss the course air transport would have to take to cope with the economic trends facing us in order to keep offering services in response to continuing demand.

Someone must take over minding the store, and no State has structured and developed air transport as a vertically integrated public utility that is privatized and open to market forces. China is going to be the biggest economy in the world in 2016. Just as an example, when this equation is applied to aviation one sees a phenomenal trend in China. More than two thirds of the world's new airports are being constructed in China and it is expected that Chinese airlines will triple in fleet size over the next decade, generating phenomenal sales for the world's major aircraft manufacturers—particularly Boeing and Airbus. Better still, China aims to have its own aircraft manufacturers by that time. Of China's current 5 year plan, one commentator, who has researched China's aviation dreams thoroughly, has said:

> The twelfth five year plan, the one that included aerospace as a strategic industry, wouldn't officially begin until later in the year (2011) but at the start of 2011 the steps toward China's ambitious future in the skies kept coming…they paralleled the leaps the country had previously made in electronics, automobiles and many other fields, and the operative principle did seem to be "everything is about to take off" all at once.[16]

In 1950, the western world had 20% of the global population. Now it has only 10%. If China were to be divided into countries along the lines of the European Union in terms of population spread, it would have 99 countries. However, China has to be vigilant and guard against a possible collapse in the future of its "growth targets" in its massive growth impetus that sees what some call "phantom cities and towns" being developed and make sure its managed growth can accommodate this initiative.

The key decisions to be made over the next 20 years are going to be made in the East and not in the West. The rest is going to be stronger than the West in the years

---

[15] http://www.guardian.co.uk/business/2010/mar/01/drag-deficit-reduction-anaemic-growth.

[16] Fallows (2012), p. 32.

to come. There will be a shift in thinking on many issues including the economic future of air transport—one of the most powerful drivers of the world economy. It will be only a matter of time before market economies of the East dominate the world. The time has come.

This begs the question: how does one defragment the market system in air transport? First, we might have to go back to basics and, taking a cue from ICAO's new Strategic Objective of developing the economics of air transport, determine intellectually as to how market economies might head in the next two decades, and carve out a system where economically, Article 44 of the Chicago Convention is fully served with air transport as a trade that would serve the needs of the people of the world—whether be it for business travel or tourism. The IATA "Agenda for Freedom" is an excellent initiative in this regard. Through conferences in Istanbul in 2008[17] and Montebello, Canada, States were exhorted to do away with nationality clauses in their bilateral air services agreements which in turn would open out the air transport industry to transnational markets and enable the airlines to cope better with the challenges posed by market economics. At the Montebello meeting, encouragingly States representing 60% of global air transport committed themselves to accepting the IATA Statement of Policy Principles that advocated reciprocal waivers of the nationality clauses that precluded their airlines from taking advantage of free market economies.

If all this entails bringing in the World Trade Organization into the picture in terms of market access, that discussion should be allowed without being obviated *in limine*. There is much work to be done in re-interpreting Article 6[18] of the Chicago Convention in accordance with things to come. Now seems to be the time to start doing it.

---

[17]At the Istanbul meeting, Giovanni Bisignani, Director General of IATA in his opening address said: "Look at what happened to the banking system. In a week it became a state enterprise in many countries. We have already seen the re-nationalisation of AerolineasArgentinas. This is not the solution that we want. We are not asking for bailouts or more government involvement in our business. Governments have a critical role inregulating safety, security, monopolies and environmental standards. What we were asking for this weekend was simply the ability to act like any other global business".

[18]Article 6 of the Chicago Convention states: "No scheduled international air service may be operated over or into the territory of a contracting State, except with the special permission or other authorization of that State, and in accordance with the terms of such permission or authorization.

2.2 Brexit and Air Transport

Populism and separation from Unions and regional blocks has proved to be a trend that is far reaching. On 23 June 2016 the populace of the United Kingdom[19] voted by referendum to leave the European Union[20] bringing to bear numerous legal issues, among which are some that pertain to air transport in the United Kingdom. The referendum, which reflects the will of the people is "advisory rather than binding",[21] and will not be binding until it enters into force upon ratification by the British Parliament and the invocation of Article 50 of the Lisbon Treaty,[22] which provides *inter alia* that any Member State may decide to withdraw from the Union in accordance with its own constitutional requirements, and if it does so, the State concerned is required to notify the European Council of its intention. In light of the guidelines provided by the European Council, the Union would then negotiate and conclude an agreement with that State, setting out the arrangements for its withdrawal, taking account of the framework for its future relationship with the Union. The legal instruments that are the multilateral treaties governing the United Kingdom's membership of the EU would cease to apply to the UK from the date of entry into force of the withdrawal agreement or, failing that, 2 years after the notification referred to above. In addition to the conditions above, the *European Communities Act* of 1972[23] which gives legal effect to the membership of the UK in the EU, would have to be amended or completely repealed according to Part II of the Act.

In March 2017 the House of Commons voted with a significant majority that Prime Minister Theresa May invoke Article 50 and make way for the 2-year long negotiation process for Brexit. One of the main corollaries to this historic measure is expansion of the British infrastructure to prepare for what the British hope would be a greater Britain. Expanding Heathrow—the nation's hub airport—is considered to be the most critical infrastructure project to secure the long-term prosperity of Britain's economy. A report of March 2017 said:

[19]The United Kingdom of Great Britain consists of England, Wales, Scotland and Northern Ireland.

[20]The European Union (EU) is a politico-economic union of 28 member states that are located primarily in Europe.

[21]See The EU air law consequences of Brexit for the UK, Clyde&Co, *Aviation, June 2016 Update*, at 1.

[22]The Treaty of Lisbon (initially known as the Reform Treaty) is an international agreement which amends the two treaties which form the constitutional basis of the European Union (EU). The Treaty of Lisbon was signed by the EU member states on 13 December 2007, and entered into force on 1 December 2009. It amends the Maastricht Treaty (1993), known in updated form as the Treaty on European Union (2007) or TEU, and the Treaty of Rome (1957), known in updated form as the Treaty on the Functioning of the European Union (2007) or TFEU.

[23]An Act to make provision in connection with the enlargement of the European Communities to include the United Kingdom, together with (for, certain purposes) the Channel Islands, the Isle of an and Gibraltar. [17th October 1972].

> In new polling by ComRes released today, Parliamentary support for expanding Heathrow reached a record high, with 77% of MPs now backing the project which will make Britain the best-connected country in the world, create up to 180,000 new skilled jobs and boost growth by up to £211 billion across the country.
>
> The polling reveals a rare show of Parliamentary unity behind the Government's decision to back an expanded Heathrow. Heathrow expansion is seen by Parliament as the most beneficial infrastructure project for all regions across the UK – ahead projects specifically located outside of London like HS2, HS3 and Hinkley Point C – and enjoys the cross-party support of 83% of Conservative and 74% of Labour MPs.[24]

The European Economic Community, which was an economic union of States, had its genesis in the Treaty of Rome of 25 March 1957,[25] and became the European Union by virtue of the Treaty of Maastricht of February 1992, which was amended by the Treaty of Amsterdam of October 1997. The EU is founded on the basic premise that there is no discrimination based on nationality. The application of this premise to air transport can be translated to the fact that only nationally owned carriers of the EU Member States could be the subject of bilateral air services agreements negotiated by the Union with third countries. As such, individual states members of the EU cannot separately negotiate bilateral air services agreements with third countries on issues of nationality, as Member States have the obligation to honour European Community law when they negotiate air services with third countries.

There are some indications that Britain will ultimately reach a favourable trade agreement with the EU. Britain would however, be subject to the "Most Favourable Nations' Treatment" clause[26] of the World Trade Organization (WTO) which

[24]London Heathrow Airport: Brexit makes Expansion essential, *ETN Global Travel Industry News*, 16 March 2017. http://etn.travel/london-heathrow-airport-brexit-makes-expansion-essential-16037/.

[25]Air transport in the European Community is fundamentally regulated by two treaties, i.e., the Treaty which establishes the European Coal and Steel Community (ECSC Treaty) and the Treaty which establishes the European Economic Community (EEC Treaty, now called the EC Treaty). The former, which was signed in Paris in 1951, addresses issues related to the carriage of coal and steel through the media of rail, road and inland waterways and as such is not directly relevant to aviation. The latter, however, admits of issues relating to all modes of transport in the carriage of persons and goods and is of some relevance to aviation. The EEC Treaty, signed in Rome on 25 March 1957, has at its core a Common Transport Policy (CTP) concept that is calculated to achieve the fundamental purposes of the European Community. One of the most salient features of the EEC Treaty is that the tasks of the Community are set out succinctly in Article 2 of the Treaty, which provides, inter alia, for the adoption of a CTP as provided for in Article 3(1) of the Treaty. This provision is linked to Article 74, which in turn provides that the objectives of the Treaty in relation to issues of transportation would be pursued by State parties within the parameters of the CTP, which is established by the Council of Europe through secondary legislation.

[26]As an integral policy provision of the WTO stands the most favored nation (MFN) whereby a State grants this clause to another State if it is interested in increasing trade with that country. Countries achieving most favored nation status are given specific trade advantages, such as reduced tariffs on imported goods. MFN treatment is synonymous with non-discriminatory trade policy, because it ensures equal rather than exclusive trading privileges between two partners.

Britain would have to revert to as a member of the WTO after its break from the EU. A report on Britain and Brexit[27] opines that this change will not have disastrous results for Britain as many suggest, and that, even in the case of Foreign Direct Investment (FDI) Britain would not lose out as many would suggest for the reason that firms invest in Britain not merely for the reason of gaining advantages under the single European market.[28]

The air carriers of the United Kingdom operate (until the UK steps out of EU formally) within the single European transport market in accordance with the provisions of EU Regulation 1008/2008.[29] The objective of this Regulation is to establish a "community[30] carrier" status for all carriers that have their nationality in members of EU and apply a homogeneous application of Community legislation to EU carriers at Community level. In pursuance of this objective, the Community may adopt measures to sustain the common carrier status and equal rights and privileges for all EU Community carriers. Regulation 1008 lists, as its objective, the regulation of licensing of Community air carriers, the right of Community air carriers to operate intra-Community air services and the pricing of intra-Community air services.[31] Article 15 of the Regulation stipulates that Community air carriers are entitled to operate intra-Community air services and that Member States cannot subject the operation of intra-Community air services by a Community air carrier to any permit or authorisation. Member States are also not entitled to require Community air carriers to provide any documents or information which they have already supplied to the competent licensing authority, provided that the relevant information may be obtained from the competent licensing authority in due time.

---

[27]The Economic Impact of Brexit, A Report by Capital Economics for Woodford Investment Management, February 2016. https://woodfordfunds.com/economic-impact-brexit-report/.

[28]*Id* at 3.

[29]Regulation (EC) No 1008/2008 of The European Parliament and of The Council of 24 September 2008 on common rules for the operation of air services in the Community (Recast), Official Journal of the European Union L 293/3.

[30]The word "Community" alludes to the European Economic Community which is now called the European Community consequent upon the signing of the Treaty of the European Union on 1 November 1993. The European Court of Justice (ECJ) in 1971 decided that the Community has both external competence and internal competence on an intra-Europe basis. This judgment gave implicit external competence to the European Union to take over control of negotiations on behalf of European Member States in matters relating to international air transport agreements. Although this implicit right has not been used by the Union extensively, it was indeed used in the Nineties when the European Community adopted internal rules pertaining to computer reservations systems (CRS) on an intra-Europe basis. This right does not, however, extend to trade in services, on the basis of a 1994 ECJ judgment which decided that trade in services including trade relating to air transport services is beyond the jurisdiction of the Union.

[31]*Id.*, Article 1.

2.2.1 *The Brexit Process*

Although the United Kingdom government went on the assumption that the referendum result was sufficient to trigger Article 50[32] of the Lisbon Treaty[33] The Supreme Court of the UK disagreed, stating that parliamentary authority must be obtained by the Prime Minister to trigger the provision, after which formal notice of Brexit to the EU could be given. On 8 February 2017, this requirement was complied with through an absolute majority in Parliament. The next step would be the obtaining of assent of the second limb of the bicameral process in the UK—The House of Lords—which, at the time of writing was not considered an obstacle to the process. Once Article 50 notification is received by the EU, there will be a 2-year period from March 2017 that will have to lapse until formal exit of the UK takes place.

During the 2-year period exit terms will have to be agreed upon before negotiations could start between the EU and the UK on the future relationship between the two parties. For her part, the Prime Minister of UK has submitted 12 Principles (discussed below) that indicates a framework for negotiation with the EU. The 12 principles would have to be discussed during the interim 2-year period for a meaningful agreement to be reached between the parties that would obviate ambivalence with regard to the positions of the parties. In the meanwhile, the UK airlines would have to await results of the negotiations which could pose difficulties in their planning for the future.

2.2.2 *Air Traffic Rights in Europe*

With regard to the exercise of air traffic rights within the EU, Article 19 provides that the exercise of traffic rights are essentially and exclusively subject to published Community, national, regional and local operational rules relating to safety, security, the protection of the environment and the allocation of slots and that a Member State, after consultation with interested parties including the air carriers and airports concerned, may regulate, without discrimination among destinations inside the Community or on grounds of nationality or identity of air carriers, the distribution

[32]Article 50 provides *inter alia* that any Member State may decide to withdraw from the Union in accordance with its own constitutional requirements; a Member State which decides to withdraw shall notify the European Council of its intention. In the light of the guidelines provided by the European Council, the Union is required to negotiate and conclude an agreement with that State, setting out the arrangements for its withdrawal, taking account of the framework for its future relationship with the Union. That agreement must be negotiated in accordance with Article 218 (3) of the Treaty on the Functioning of the European Union. It will l be concluded on behalf of the Union by the Council, acting by a qualified majority, after obtaining the consent of the European Parliament.

[33]*Supra*, note 22 in this chapter.

of air traffic between airports in accordance with certain conditions. These conditions vary from the airports serving the same city or conurbation; the airports being served by adequate transport infrastructure providing, to the extent possible, a direct connection making it possible to arrive at the airport within 90 min including, where necessary, on a cross-border basis; the airports being linked to one another and to the city or conurbation they serve by frequent, reliable and efficient public transport services; and the airports offering necessary services to air carriers, and do not unduly prejudice their commercial opportunities. Any decision to regulate the distribution of air traffic between the airports concerned would be taken subject to the principles of proportionality and transparency, and would be based on objective criteria.

There are also several other provisions in the Regulation on air operator certificates and their issuance; pricing; registration and leasing that apply commonly to EU carriers.

Another significant line of control for the UK carriers that exists until the coming into force of Brexit is the US-EU Open Skies Agreement[34] which would no longer apply to such carriers when the UK separates from the EU. The Open Skies Agreement allows European carriers to fly without restrictions from any point in the EU to any point in the US and *vice versa*. Consequently, the Agreement saw the emergence of much closer alliance agreements between airlines of both the US and the EU, facilitating competition, particularly between hub carriers. It also forges additional investment and market access opportunities, as well as strengthening the framework of cooperation in regulatory areas such as safety, security and, in particular, the environment, where both sides have agreed on a dedicated Joint Statement on the Environment. These conditions would no longer apply to UK carriers once Brexit is formally effected.

With Brexit entering into force for the UK carriers, and depending upon the ultimate outcome of negotiations between UK and the EU, the aforementioned conditions and instruments may no longer remain in force for them and "Community Carrier" status could be removed. Should this happen, The UK may have to revert to the *status quo ante* existing prior to the UK joining the EU. It is reported that the EU is the single largest air transport market for the UK carriers, involving 49% of passenger traffic and 54% of scheduled carriage of UK carriers being within the EU.[35] These figures could change with Brexit where the UK would have to

[34]The EU-US Air Transport Agreement signed on 25 and 30 April 2007, the main purpose of which is to establish a Trans-Atlantic open aviation area, was provisionally applied from 30 March 2008 for all EU Member States, and Amended by a Protocol, signed and provisionally applied on 24 June 2010. Norway and Iceland accession to the Air Transport Agreement as amended by the Protocol is provisionally applied from 21 June 2011.

[35]EUROCONTROL, which is the European Organisation for Safety of Air Navigation, and is made up of 39 member States of the European Community, forecasts that there will be 16.9 million aircraft movements in Europe in 2030, which is approximately 2% more than the movements in 2009. The number of flights concerned is estimated between 13.1 to 20.9 million flights during 2030.

negotiate separate bilateral air services agreements with the rest of the EU member States. It would follow that under the new circumstances, unless granted within the Brexit negotiations, the UK carriers will lose their inherent right to market access on an intra-Europe basis between cities within the same EU Member State (e.g. Paris/Nice) or between two cities in two different EU member States (e.g. Lisbon/Rome).

2.2.3 How Market Access Is Determined for EU Carriers

As long as the UK carriers remain with the "community carrier" status, they would come within a particular regime of distribution of traffic rights for all carriers of member EU States. This distribution is based on the philosophy of non-discrimination and equality recognized by the decision of the European Court of Justice (ECJ) in 2002 which obviated the "designation" clause that existed in the standard bilateral air services agreements entered into by European States with third countries which had the latter "designating" national carriers with each bilateral. The "designation" of a European carrier entitled to operate air services into a third country was based on the "ownership and effective control" clause in the bilateral air services agreement which gave the third country the right to revoke traffic rights granted if it were not satisfied that a State did not have majority ownership and effective control of its designated carrier under the agreement. The ECJ rejected this discrimination which, in the view of the Court was based on nationality and therefore was repugnant to the freedom of movement enshrined in Article 43 of the Treaty of Rome, which forbade the restrictions on the establishment of freedom of nationals of a member State in the territory of another member State. The effect of the ECJ decision was that all EU carriers should be treated as national carriers among all EU member States without distinction or discrimination, which in turn gave rise to the concept of "community carrier".

With the plethora of bilateral air services existing between EU member States and other States (1500–2000)[36] it was impossible for individual EU States to step up to the task of renegotiating all their bilateral air services agreements. The European Commission was recognized as the entity that could simplify the task on behalf of the EU member States by being the body that would enter into "Horizontal Agreements" with third States that would bring all existing agreements in to conformity with EU law. The effect of this type of agreement was that the national designation clause was removed from all existing bilateral air services agreements to be replaced by a common clause entitling any member of the EU to nominate any carrier which was a national carrier (by registration) of another member State to perform air services under an agreement entered into by the former with a third State. This did not, however, preclude any sovereign State of the EU

[36]See Van Fenema (2006), pp. 172–195 at 172.

from negotiating other aspects of air services between that State and a third country outside the EU.

Operating licenses of airlines, however, remain with the State concerned. In the EU, in keeping with Article 4 of Court Regulation 2407/92, national authorities are vested with the power of granting operating licenses based on the criteria that the principal place of business of the carrier applying for the license must be located in the licensing member State; the carrier must be involved in air transportation as its main occupation; the holder of the license must be under direct or majority ownership nationals of the European Union; and the licensee must be effectively controlled by such nationals. Effective control essentially means the power and ability to exercise a decisive influence on an air transport undertaking, including but not limited to the use, enjoyment and alienation of movable and immovable property of that undertaking. One of the reasons, at least from the perspective of the European Union, of retaining the ownership and control criteria within its territory, is to safeguard the interests of the member States of the Union and to preclude carriers of non EU States from capitalizing on a liberalized European Union Market.

The mechanism of the Horizontal Agreement is explained succinctly and clearly by Van Fenema who says:

> This freedom of the designating Member State *vis-à-vis* the third country extends to all Community carriers whatever the aeropolitical relationship is between the Member State of the carrier and the third country. To give an example: if LOT Polish Airlines obtains a designation from the UK authorities to operate on the London–Santiago de Chile route, Chile would have to accept that designation even if (a) there is no bilateral between Poland and Chile, or (b) Poland has a protectionist policy that prevents the Chilean airline from operating the desired number of frequencies between Chile and Poland, or (c) Chile has imposed restrictions on LOT operations between Poland and Chile.[37]

Such an open ended concept, which could lead to spurious designation where any carrier can be designated by a member State of the EU, has already been envisioned. The solution is a conditional clause called the "Free Rider" clause which gives sufficient flexibility to a non EU partner to an agreement where the former could suspend, revoke or limit authorization for operation of air services by a "purported" EU carrier under a horizontal agreement. This could happen if the Non EU party to the agreement realizes that the carrier so designated is not established in the EU or that the carrier's ownership and effective control is not vested with a EU Member State.[38] In other words, if a designated carrier does not

---

[37]*Id.* 180.

[38]There is no documented definition of, or agreed meaning to the term "substantial ownership and effective control". This *in limine* creates a certain ambivalence in the field of trade and competition in the airline industry, particularly for an airline that is not fully owned and operated by a State or instrumentality of State. See *Ownership and Control, Report of the Think Tank*—World Aviation Regulatory Monitor 2000, IATA, Government and Industry Affairs Department: Geneva, 7 September 2000 at p. 4. The European Union, by Council Regulation No. 2407/92 of 23 July 1992, identifies "effective control" as a relationship constituted by rights, contracts or other means

conform to the requirements of EU law, the non EU party could consider the agreement voidable.

2.2.4 How Market Access Would Be Determined for UK Carriers After Brexit

The most preliminary fact in the context of Brexit for UK carriers is that, unless otherwise determined in the Brexit negotiations between UK and EU (for example where the UK retains certain rights within the EU similar to say, Norway which is within the single aviation market but is not part of the EU), the UK carriers, and indeed the UK authorities, would be free of all the rules, regulations and conditions of the EU pertaining to air transport and market access. It would be an open slate where the UK will renegotiate its bilateral air services agreements with all other States with which it has such agreements. In this event the UK carriers will lose two basic rights they enjoy within the EU, which are seventh freedom and ninth freedom rights (intra European cabotage and same country cabotage respectively, as already discussed). Conversely, EU carriers would also lose the same rights within the territory of the UK.

According to the International Air Transport Association (IATA)—the global association of air carriers—"the UK air market is dominated by outbound traffic, with such traffic accounting for just over two-thirds of total flows (in 2015 there were 53.9 million visits overseas by air by UK residents, compared to 26.2m visits to the UK by overseas residents)".[39] A sizeable portion of this traffic is intra-European, as has already been discussed and therefore, negotiations of the UK with individual EU members, (or if the EU wishes to negotiate as a collective body) would be the most important element for the UK. IATA further opines that as a result of direct effects of Brexit the UK passenger market will descend to 3–5% lower by 2020 than the no Brexit baseline. This would translate to a reduction of air passenger growth by 1.0–1.5 percentage points each year over the near term. The first step for the UK would be to consider the two measures it has to take with regard to trade in general and trading in air traffic rights. The first would be to determine which trade deal the UK is going to negotiate with the EU and the second would be

which, *inter alia*, grants the right to exercise a decisive influence on an undertaking, in particular by the right to use all or part of the assets of an undertaking and determine the composition, voting or decisions relating to the running of the business or undertaking. See Article 2(g). United States law too contains explicit requirements pertaining to nationality in terms of management of airlines, in some contrast to Regulation 2407/92 of the EU which does not expressly address issues regarding nationality of management. Arguably, the EU addresses external control by stockholders of a company, and not particularly, as envisaged by the United States law, management control of the administration and running of the air transport enterprise. See 49 U.S.C. ξ 40102 (a) (15) 1994.

[39] IATA, The impact of 'BREXIT' on UK Air Transport: June 2016, see https://www.iata.org/whatwedo/Documents/economics/impact_of_brexit.pdf.

the nature of the trade deal it would enter into with the rest of the world. Both these measures should be addressed against the backdrop of trends in the European market as well as the global market.

In the field of air transport, The United Kingdom has shown that national prosperity is created, not inherited and that, contrary to popular belief, a commercially successful enterprise within a nation does not necessarily grow because of that nation's natural endowments, its cheap labour force or its currency values, but rather by the capacity of that industry to innovate and upgrade. As the winds of change are sweeping commercial aviation towards the new millennium, European nations have shown that, at least in air transportation, nations have become more, not less important. They have created competitive advantages for themselves through a highly localized process. This is also true of air transport in the United Kingdom.

The UK, when it goes alone in the path to seeking air traffic rights from both the European States and other States (there is a larger outgoing passenger market from the UK than an incoming one) must reconcile with the fact that, unlike large nations such as the United States, Canada and Russia, it is relatively small in size. Geographic magnitude of a country becomes a relevant consideration in air transport both in terms of the volume of traffic generated by a particular country and the negotiating leverage it has in bartering air traffic rights and points of departure and landing. If a country is small, it is usual for that country to have lesser airports than a larger country and the latter would consequently have more opportunity at bargaining. Therefore, incontrovertibly, The UK will have to optimize its collective potential in the air transport industry.

2.2.5 The 12 Options

The 12 Principles put forward by the Prime Minister of the UK are as follow: providing certainty and clarity; taking control of UK's own laws; strengthening the Union; protecting the strong historic ties that the UK has with Ireland and maintaining the Common Travel Area; controlling Immigration; securing rights for EU nationals in the UK and UK nationals in the EU; ensuring free trade with European markets; securing new trade agreements with other countries; ensuring the UK remains the best place for science and innovation; cooperating in the fight against crime and terrorism; and delivering a smooth orderly exit from the EU

Of these principles a handful pertain to air transport: providing certainty and clarity; taking control of UK's own laws; ensuring free trade with European markets; and securing new trade agreements with other countries.

The ambiguity surrounding Brexit haunts air transport as well, and it would be essential for the UK to reach clarity and certainty in the context of market access for UK carriers. In this regard the airlines' position (particularly Ryan Air and EasyJet) has been to maintain existing traffic rights without let or hindrance. Therefore, in terms of trading in air transport services, the UK may wish to go for a bilateral treaty with the EU that ensures accessible and affordable air transport for those in the EU as well as in the UK, given the fact that free trade agreements do not usually include air transport in them. A corollary to such a bilateral agreement could be that UK carriers would continue to have access to European market: but for that to happen, The UK would have to remain within the European Common Aviation Area (ECAA)—which includes nine European countries and Switzerland. However, it must be noted that the white paper presented to the UK Parliament did not have any mention of the UK's membership of the ECAA.

Brexit would present the air transport industry of the UK with some opportunity *vis a vis* the market outside the EU. Aviation authorities in the UK could well capitalize on emerging markets by forging bilateral air services agreements advantageous to the UK with other States without being shackled by restrictive EU laws and rules which bound the UK as an EU member.

Former Secretary of State Henry Kissinger makes the point that in every century, almost as if dictated by natural law, a country emerges with the power, the will and the intellectual and moral persuasion to shape the entire international system in accordance with its own values.[40] If this principle were to apply to the twenty-first century, the political scientist would have to take into consideration the role that might be played by emerging economic giants such as China and India and the threatened single European Union in the overall equation of the United States' retaining its position as the only super power capable of influencing the world community consensually with other key players. This is compelling enough reason that the future structure of the international system might have to restore the fading significance of international law and the evanescence of the international political system.

Undoubtedly, the impact of Brexit on both the UK and the EU would be far reaching and would last for several years, unless a well thought out study and plan, particularly by the UK in terms of air transport is developed to cope with possible effects. One has to remember that Brexit was driven by a certain resentment of globalization and the permeating and often restrictive EU regulations which stultified industries in the UK. Although the average UK voter may not have factored air transport into this equation the overall theme of Brexit was the issue of sovereignty or "getting the country back". In many ways Brexit liberates air transport in the UK and leaves the country to decide its own fate. However, an independent air transport system in the U could still be fettered by and subject to EU regulations when it comes to operating air services from the UK to EU member States. It is for this reason that the UK has to plan the future of its air transport policy and direction carefully against the backdrop of negotiations with the EU.

The circumstances of a Brexit would present the UK with three options to choose from: remain part of the Common Aviation Area (ECAA); negotiate a separate

[40]Kissinger (1994), p. 17. Kissinger identifies France under Cardinal Richelieu in the seventeenth century; Great Britain in the eighteenth century; Maternich's Austria in the nineteenth century and the United States in the twentieth century.

open skies agreement with the EU, regarding the EU as a composite whole entity; and negotiate separate bilateral air services agreements with each country (both within and without the EU). In any one of these options the UK, it should develop and adopt strict legislation in product performance, product safety and environmental impact to promote a competitive advantage and stimulate and upgrade domestic demand. The last element—environmental impact—should be particularly addressed in harmony with global regulations as promulgated through the International Civil Aviation Organization. As a future measure, The UK should also continue limiting direct co-operation in the air transport field among industry rivals in order to obviate anti-competitive conduct. As a supplemental measure, competition should be deregulated and State monopolies should be eschewed. Finally, the UK government should pursue vigorously an open market policy which veers from managed trade that has a tendency to deal with the fallout of national competitiveness.

As for UK airlines, they should continue to seek out pressure and challenge in order to innovate commercially toward more achievements while seeking out their most capable competitors as motivators. More importantly, and as prudent airlines must, airlines of the UK should establish early warning systems which would indicate any hint of change in the air transport market both within and without Europe. Airlines could find and serve passengers and consignors who have the most anticipating needs; find places whose regulations foreshadow emerging regulations elsewhere; bring outside expertise into their management teams if needed and constantly conduct research on market access.

UK airlines should tap selectively into sources of advantage in other nations' airlines. However, airline alliances have to be used only selectively in order to minimize cost bases and obviate relinquishing profits that would accrue to an airline without the alliance concerned. Inevitably, an airline alliance shows the partners mediocrity to an extent, particularly if profits are not optimized and alliances are formed on core activities. The central theme for the UK and its airlines for the future is "leadership" which it currently holds in air transport regulation by being second to none and equal to the best.

2.3 Connecting the Dots

The international liberal order which emerged in 1945 in the aftermath of the war introduced a system of multinational institutions and treaties that advocated free distribution of goods and services. The Chicago Convention of 1944 provided the constitutional basis for the provision of air transport globally. The fundamental premise of the Convention lies in its Preamble (which sets the tone and philosophy of the treaty) which *inter alia* calls for international air transport services to be "established on the basis of "*equality of opportunity*" (my emphasis) and operated soundly and economically" The words "equality of opportunity" represent the first dot that seeks connectivity with other dots. There has been much debate among both academics and professionals as to what equality of opportunity means. Some have opined that the words mean equality of opportunity to operate air services while others have said should represent equality of opportunity to compete in operating air services. The next dot which connects to equality of opportunity is the slew of tech megatrends that proliferate air transport giving certain States and carriers which have the resources to compete in the field of air transport. The third dot is the megatrend that shifts from the international liberal order to the concentration of power in States such as the United States, China, India and developed States in the European Union along with non State actors that may possibly veer towards a certain protectionist and hegemonic trend in market access. The fourth and final dot would be essentially trade and economics related in terms of market access where the term equality of opportunity may lead to the offer by carriers of "connectivity" of people and goods throughout the world. State aid plays a huge part in this shift of power particularly in the field of air transport that would also apply to aircraft and component manufacture.

Just as an example, it was announced on 8 February 2017 that a decision had been taken by the Government of Canada to provide $372.5 million as repayable loans to Bombardier. These funds have been allocated for research and development (R&D) activities for the Global 7000 and CSeries business jet programs. The press release follows a day after the government of Brazil launched a formal complaint against Canada in The World Trade Organization (WTO), saying the loans to Bombardier were contrary to the rules on subsidies of the WTO.

In a similar case, The World Trade Organization (WTO), in its judgment rendered in March 2012 found that Boeing received between $3 billion and $4 billion in U.S. subsidies, and by contrast WTO had said in December 2011 that Airbus received $18 billion in subsidies from European governments. The operative provision under WTO in this context is Article XVI.4 which provides that as from 1 January 1958 or the earliest practicable date thereafter, contracting parties are required not to grant either directly or indirectly any form of subsidy on the export of any product other than a primary product.

A subsidy, which has been a contentious issue in international trade, is defined by the Agreement on Subsidies and Countervailing Measures ("SCM Agreement") of the World Trade Organization (WTO)[41] as the conferring of a benefit by way of a financial contribution by the government or any public body.[42] This would include

[41]The World Trade Organization (WTO) headquartered in Geneva, is the only global international organization dealing with the rules of trade between nations. At its heart are the WTO agreements, negotiated and signed by the bulk of the world's trading nations and ratified in their parliaments. The goal is to help producers of goods and services, exporters, and importers conduct their business. The WTO is run by its member governments. All major decisions are made by the membership as a whole, either by ministers (who usually meet at least once every two years) or by their ambassadors or delegates (who meet regularly in Geneva). WTO has a Dispute Settlement Body which compellingly pronounces on trade disputes including those related to subsidies. See Abeyratne (1997), p. 397.

[42]See https://www.wto.org/english/tratop_e/scm_e/subs_e.htm.

the transfer of funds, such as grants, loans, equity infusion and potential transfer of loan guarantees; forgone government revenue, such as tax credits or any other form of fiscal incentives; government provided goods and services excluding infrastructure or purchases of goods; government sponsored payments to a funding mechanism, or if a government entrusts or directs private bodies to carry out the same functions and practices mentioned in the above three categories; and any form of income or price support. The SCM Agreement, which only applies to goods, does not address nor does it define a subsidy in air transport.

In general terms a subsidy can take many forms and is therefore amorphous in nature. Alan Sykes[43] says that a subsidy is a synonym for government transfer of money to an entity in the private sector and it could also mean the provision of a service or product at a price below its marked price that the entity receiving the subsidy would usually have to pay for it. In other instances, subsidies could even mean governmental policy that act to the advantage of entities in other commercial practices. Overall, however, all the above measures may not mean that they for subsidies at all.[44]

To make matters worse, there is no mention of a subsidy in the Convention on International Civil Aviation (Chicago Convention)[45] which is the preeminent multilateral international treaty containing principles of conduct of States in international aviation. A remote and indirect reference is found in the Preamble to the Convention which provides that the signatory States agree on certain principles and arrangements in order that international civil aviation may be developed in a safe and orderly manner and that international air transport services may be established on the basis of equality of opportunity and operated soundly and economically. One could take it that "equality of opportunity" would encompass the rejection of iniquitous use of subsidies by States to give their national carriers an undue advantage over their competitors. Slightly more to the point, Article 44 f. of The Convention has, as one of ICAO's[46] aims and objectives to foster the planning and

[43]Sykes (2003), pp. 2–3.

[44]*Ibid.*

[45]Convention on International Civil Aviation, signed at Chicago on 7 December 1944. See Doc 7300/9 Ninth Edition:2006.

[46]The formation and purpose of The International Civil Aviation Organization (ICAO) is given in the Proceedings of the International Civil Aviation Conference (Chicago, Illinois, November 1–December 7, 1944) as follows:

"On November 1944, representatives of 52 nations came together at Chicago, to create a framework for the growth anticipated in world civil aviation. The Convention on International Civil Aviation, also known as the Chicago Convention, provided the establishment of the International Civil Aviation Organization (ICAO) – an international body to guide and regulate international civil aviation. ICAO came into existence on 4 April 1947, after 26 states had ratified the convention. Between 1944 and 1947 a provisional organization (PICAO) operated, the purpose of which was to be of a technical and advisory nature of sovereign States for the purpose of collaboration in the field of international civil aviation and to lay down the foundation for a new international organization to be headquartered in Montreal, Canada." Today, ICAO has 191 member States.

development of air transport, by insuring that the rights of contracting States are fully respected and that every contracting State has a fair opportunity to operate international airlines. One way of ensuring that this objective is reached is found in Article 54 i) of the Chicago Convention which imposes on the Council of ICAO the mandatory duty and obligation of requesting, collecting, examining and publishing information of international air services, including information about the costs of operation and particulars of subsidies paid to airlines from public funds. According to one commentator, there is no evidence of the Council having published information pertaining to subsidies as required in Article 54 i).[47]

It is interesting to note that Tim Clark, President, Emirates has said that a common set of transparent financial reporting metrics to measure and apply against all international carriers should be determined by IATA and ICAO on what defines a subsidy. One can certainly agree with this proposition as, if the ICAO Council met its obligation of carrying out its mandatory duty imposed upon it by Article 54 i), the natural corollary would have been for the Council to firstly define what a subsidy was (not merely give examples of subsidies in its guidance material) and its many forms and seek to establish at least a code of conduct with defined rules of conduct that would erode the Preambular concept of the Chicago Convention (as well as subsequent provisions already mentioned) of equality of opportunity for all carriers. Furthermore, in pursuance of Article 54 i) the Council can require States to report finance assistance given to their carriers for purposes of publication. States should be encouraged to use the dispute resolution provisions[48] of ICAO to come before the Council for its decision where restrictive subsidies granted by other States to their carriers adversely affect the carriers of the complaining State.

The ICAO *Manual on The Regulation of International Air Transport* recognizes that State aids/subsidies to air carriers by governments have existed since the beginning of commercial air transport and that they have been provided at all stages of national or aviation development and have taken a wide variety of forms[49] and goes on to say that "State aids/subsidies which confer financial benefits on national air carriers that are not available to competitors in the same international markets could distort trade in international air services and can constitute or

---

[47]Milde (2008), p. 153.

[48]Article 84 of The Chicago Convention provides that if any disagreement between two or more contracting States relating to the interpretation or application of the Convention and its Annexes cannot be settled by negotiation, The Council can and indeed shall decide on the issue on the application of any State concerned in the disagreement. No member of the Council is entitled to vote in the consideration by the Council of any dispute to which it is a party. Any contracting State has the option of subject to Article 85, appealing from the decision of the Council to an ad hoc arbitral tribunal agreed upon with the other parties to the dispute or to the Permanent Court of International Justice. Within 60 days of receipt of notification of the decision of the Council, an appeal will be notified to the Council. Article 85 provides for an arbitration process if the Article 84 process fails to bring about resolution to the issue under dispute.

[49]Manual on The Regulation of International Air Transport, Effects of State Aids and Subsidies, *Doc 9626*, 2nd Edition: 2004 at 2.3.6.

support unfair competitive practices".[50] Some of the undesirable subsidies identified in the ICAO Manual as distorting competition are: the provision of State funds for the purposes of covering operating losses, avoiding insolvency, financing of restructuring or expansion; partial or full cancellation of air carrier debt to the government; the guarantee of loans; the giving of "soft" loans (i.e. at below-market rates of interest or with insufficient collateral); and the assumption of air carrier debt owed to other parties.

The Manual also identifies indirect subsidies that may affect fair and equal competition: preferential tax treatment; funding of unemployment benefits to national air carrier workers whose services are declared redundant; measures in bankruptcy laws which, after a declaration of insolvency, grant legal relief from certain financial obligations for extended periods in order to permit the air carrier to continue operations while attempting to reorganize; and cross-subsidization measures, for example, charging higher airport fees for international than domestic flights, thereby benefiting national air carriers which operate both types of flights.[51] It must be mentioned that *The Manual* is mere guidance material issued by ICAO which does not carry with it compelling obligation to States to adhere to its recommendations nor does it carry any consequences if States do not follow its guidelines.

Sovereign States are entitled to enact their own laws pertaining to fiscal and competition policy and therefore, under the aforementioned parameters, bankruptcy laws that provide solace to companies that are failing and seek protection are not subsidies; nor are employment environments that are free of labour unions. Similarly, an airline that uses an airport as a hub that is subsidized, and derives some benefits therefrom cannot be identified as being subsidized.[52]

There have been several instances where airlines have been found to have enjoyed a subsidy to the detriment of its competitors,[53] with one significant instance of blatant subsidizing.[54] There have also been instances where States have been found guilty of providing anti-competitive subsidies to aircraft manufacturers.[55] In the latter instance WTO, in its judgment rendered in March 2012 found that Boeing received between $3 billion and $4 billion in U.S. subsidies, and by contrast WTO had said in December 2011 that Airbus received $18 billion in subsidies from European governments.[56] The operative provision under WTO in this context is Article XVI.4 which provides that as from 1 January 1958 or the earliest practicable date thereafter, contracting parties are required not to grant either directly or indirectly any form of subsidy on the export of any product other than a primary

[50]*Ibid.*

[51]*Ibid.*

[52]Lumbroso (2015).

[53]See Abeyratne (2015), pp. 119–121.

[54]Abeyratne (2004), pp. 585–601.

[55]Abeyratne (2005), pp. 379–398.

[56]Rooney (2012).

product[57] which subsidy would result in the sale of such product for export at a price lower than the comparable price charged for the like product to buyers in the domestic market. Until 31 December 1957 contracting parties could not extend the scope of any such subsidization beyond that existing on 1 January 1955 by the introduction of new, or the extension of existing, subsidies.

2.4 The US Carriers *vs* the Middle East Carriers

At the centre of the subsidies debate are the "super connected" middle east (Gulf) carriers[58] who have robustly followed a business model capitalizing both on their advantages brought to bear by their geographic locations as well as generous government support and understanding of the inherent advantages that accrue to the economic well being of their States. The passengers of these carriers merely switch planes at hubs in their cities on their way to their ultimate destinations. These carriers—Emirates Airways (hereafter Emirates), Etihad Airways (hereafter, Etihad) and Qatar Airways—along with Turkish Airlines, carried 115 million passengers in 2014 as against 50 million in 2008[59] on more than 700 aircraft.[60] These carriers, with Emirates at the helm, are threatening the market share of the US carriers as well as those of European carriers, particularly to the East (There are four major routes in contention: North America—South Asia; Europe—South Asia; Europe—Southeast Asia; Europe—Australia/NZ). One of the complaints of the allegedly affected carriers of the West is that States in the Middle East are building super airports to encourage hubbing[61] by their carriers to the detriment of the carriers of the West, and that additionally, the airports concerned are applying drastically reduced landing charges for their carriers, which is an anti-competitive practice. Other practices, it is claimed, which act to the unfair advantage of the Middle East carriers are low wage structures and low tax bases in their countries, which the writer believes to be not strictly within the parameters of anti-competitive practices.

[57] A primary product has been defined in The Havana Charter of 1948, Article 56 (1) (which the WTO adopted) which states that a primary product is a product of a farm, forest or fishery or mineral in its natural form.

[58] For purposes of this article, the words "Middle East" and "Gulf" will be used interchangeably.

[59] Super Connecting the World, *The Economist*, 25 April 2015, http://www.economist.com/news/business/21649509-advance-emirates-etihad-and-qatar-latterly-joined-turkish-airlines-looks-set.

[60] Zhang (2015).

[61] Hubbing is a practice by some airlines where airline hubs or hub airports are used by one or more carriers to concentrate passenger traffic and flight operations at a given airport, and in the context of the Middle East, airports such as Dubai for Emirates, Abu Dhabi for Etihad Airways and Doha (Qatar) for Qatar Airways. They serve as transfer (or stop-over) points to get passengers to their final destination.

By far the largest allegation aimed at the Gulf carriers is that these carriers receive State aid in the nature of subsidies which, together with the advantages mentioned above, are robbing the carriers of the West of their "market share" by moving into the American and the European markets with undue and unfair advantages granted to them by their States. A lobby group[62] representing the three major airlines that brought the complaint against the Gulf carriers—American Airlines, Delta and United Airlines—has said that the three carriers of the United Arab Emirates and Qatar have received $42 billion in subsidies and other benefits.[63] The claim goes on to say that, over the past decade, the three Middle East carriers have spent more than $100 billion on acquiring bloated fleets of modern wide body aircraft.[64] The request of the three American carriers was that the "open skies" agreements between The United States and The United Arab Emirates and between The United States and Qatar be "renegotiated" and modified as the alleged subsidies had distorted international trade.[65] It was also claimed that the Gulf carriers have grown their seat capacity (combined) over the U.S. carriers by 1500% and that their daily departures had shot up by 32% from the U.S carriers in 2014.[66] The same lobby group stated that: "The systematic subsidization of Qatar, Etihad and Emirates is part of a closely managed effort by the governments of Qatar and the UAE to direct the flow of international traffic through their own hubs and grow their economies. Qatar, Etihad and Emirates operate as arms of the state carrying out the will of their respective governments—not as independent companies" … and that "the massive government subsidies provided to Qatar, Etihad and Emirates are not only a clear violation of Open Skies policy, but they also pose a direct threat to the U.S. airline industry and thousands of American jobs. These state-owned carriers are using their huge, artificial advantage to rapidly expand their fleets and take over international routes, unfairly capturing U.S. airline market share and shifting U.S. aviation jobs overseas".[67]

The United States airlines claimed that they are the back one of the country's infrastructure and a critical component of the entire infrastructure system, and that the $42 billion of subsidies the Gulf carriers were favoured with would critically impair the ability of the U.S. carriers to service American communities. Another allegation aimed at the Gulf carriers is that the subsidies they receive would drive the U.S. carriers to reduce their fleets, thus threatening the security of The United

[62]Partnership for Fair and Open Skies. See the Deck is Stacked, http://www.openandfairskies.com/subsidies/.

[63]See Zhang (2015), *Ibid.*

[64]*Ibid.*

[65]See Carey (2015). See also, Carey and Jones (2013).

[66]Britton (2015). The author states that Emirates alone links The United States via Dubai with 17 cities in the Middle East; 21 cities in Africa; 86 cities in the South, South East and East Asia and 7 in Australia and New Zealand. India is the largest connecting market where the Gulf carriers have quadrupled capacity from 2008 to 2014. *Ibid.*

[67]Partnership for Fair and Open Skies *supra*, note 62 in this chapter, *ibid.*

States, where commercial carriers in the country are to stand ready to be deployed for military operations.

It is not only subsidies to the tune of $42 billion that the Gulf carriers have apparently enjoyed, the complaint goes. In addition, the U.S. carriers claim that the Gulf Airlines' States made good losses associated with the airlines' hedging fuel contracts and gave them interest free loans—which governments the U.S. carriers claim are the main shareholders of the Gulf carriers. Furthermore, it is alleged that the carriers enjoyed benefits from the use of land at no cost, partial airport revenues and loans guaranteed by the government. Although admittedly, these benefits may be perceived as anti-competitive anomalies calculated to reflect a subsidy,[68] one could only match these measures with the definition of a subsidy as presented at the outset of this article and draw one's own conclusions.

The Europeans have had the same complaint against the Gulf carriers, alleging that Emirates has had €1.9 billion in unquantified subsidies of purchases of goods and services from other companies owned by the Government of the United Arab Emirates, as well as €2.1 billion Euro in government assumption of fuel hedging losses, and another €2.1 billion on subsidized airport infrastructure at Dubai International Airport.[69] As for Etihad, the Europeans claim that the airline benefitted from €5.9 billion in government "loans" with no repayment obligation. The other figures submitted against Etihad are that the airline received €5.6 billion in capital injections by the United Arab Emirates; €3.1 billion additional undisclosed government funding in 2014; €630 million in government grants; and €450 million in airport fee exemptions at Abu Dhabi International Airport. Against Qatar Airways, the European figures are that the airline received €7.5 billion+ in "loans" and "shareholder advances" by the State of Qatar with no obligation for repayment; €6.1 billion in government loan guarantees; €550 million in airport fee exemptions and rebates at Doha International Airport; and €403 million in free land.[70] These figures differ substantially from those provided by the three United States carriers.[71]

One commentator claims that at least one airline—Etihad—has shown a clear case of subsidies in the nature of €14.3 billion in capital from the government that comprised equity of €9.1 billion and €5.2 billion in loans, calling Etihad a "State funded boondoggle".[72] American Airlines, which has a code share agreement with Etihad, has added that it has no objection to Gulf carriers flying into the U.S. but the subsidies issue has made airlines of the US competing with governments and not with airlines.[73] The threat to the U.S. carriers from the Gulf carriers is a relatively

[68]Kingsley (2016), p. 2. See https://mei.nus.edu.sg/themes/site_themes/agile_records/images/uploads/Download_Insight_140_Kingsley.pdf.

[69]It's Time for Europe to Stand Up For Fair Competition, European Commission Executive Summary at http://e4fc.eu/executive-summary/.

[70]*Ibid.*

[71]Clampet and Schaal (2015).

[72]Levine-Weinberg (2013).

[73]Schaal (2013).

new phenomenon, as one commentator has said: "for a while the Gulf carriers" expansion drew only modest complaints from US airlines (they were busy going through massive restructuring after the 9-11 terrorist attacks and a series of deep, long economic upheaval that followed). For the first decade of the twenty-first century the Gulf carriers were viewed almost like experiments in the Petri dish of global airline competition. Emirates was a very small operation when the U.S. and The U.A.E agreed to an open skies treaty in 1999 and Etihad didn't even exist.[74]

The United States carriers allege in specific terms that there are two provisions of the open skies agreement between the United States and the United Arab Emirates are being violated by the conduct of Emirates and Etihad. Article 11 Sections 1 & 2 on Fair Competition is the first provision cited. Section 1 grants each Party the right to allow a fair and equal opportunity for the designated airlines of both Parties to compete in providing the international air transportation governed by the Agreement. Section 2 allows each designated airline to determine the frequency and capacity of the international air transportation it offers based upon commercial considerations in the marketplace. Consistent with this right, neither Party can unilaterally limit the volume of traffic, frequency or regularity of service, or the aircraft type or types operated by the designated airlines of the other Party, except as may be required for customs, technical, operational, or environmental reasons under uniform conditions consistent with Article 15 of the Chicago Convention.[75]

Article 12 Section 1 provides that each Party is obligated to allow prices for air transportation to be established by each designated airline based upon commercial considerations in the marketplace. It must be noted that the term "marketplace" is a significant consideration in the context of the intention of the two parties—The United States and The United Arab Emirates. It is incontrovertible that an open skies agreement would intrinsically refer to exclusive third and fourth freedom traffic rights. Therefore, in this context the "marketplace" is "U.S.-UAE traffic" which makes the position of the United States unconvincing.

Intervention by the Parties shall be limited to: prevention of unreasonably discriminatory prices or practices; protection of consumers from prices that are unreasonably high or restrictive due to the abuse of a dominant position; and

---

[74]Reed (2013).

[75]Article 15 of The Chicago Convention provides inter alia that every airport in a contracting State which is open to public use by its national aircraft shall likewise, subject to the provisions of Article 68, be open under uniform conditions to the aircraft of all the other contracting States. The like uniform conditions shall apply to the use, by aircraft of every contracting State, of all air navigation facilities, including radio and meteorological services, which may be provided for public use for the safety and expedition of air navigation. Any charges that may be imposed or permitted to be imposed by a contracting State for the use of such airports and air navigation facilities by the aircraft of any other contracting installations shall not be higher as to aircraft not engaged in scheduled international air services, than those that would be paid its national aircraft of the same class engaged in similar operations, and as to aircraft engaged in scheduled international air services, than those that would be paid by its national aircraft engaged in similar international air services.

protection of airlines from prices that are artificially low due to direct or indirect governmental subsidy or support.

It is submitted that none of these provisions is linked to the issue of subsidies and there has been no indication that the carriers of the United Arab Emirates prevented the three American carriers (or any other carrier for that matter) from having fair and equal opportunity to compete nor had they resorted to "unreasonably discriminatory prices or practices". Prior to addressing the position of the Gulf carriers which has been documented in response to the complaints of the American and European carriers, it is relevant to discuss a report released by *Oxford Economics* in June 2011 according to which the success of Emirates is the result of strategy formulation and decisions jointly taken by the Dubai government and the airline along with the entire aviation sector of the Dubai government of the importance of developing aviation in Dubai; transparency and openness; consensus in investment policy; and a focus on servicing underserved markets, the last of which is now identified as "disruptive innovation".[76] One commentator, analyzing the European situation vis a vis competition with the Gulf carriers opines that: "All in all, the unlevel playing field is primarily caused by Ricardian comparative advantages of States in the Gulf region. The playing field is further tilted by EU policy measures to the detriment of the European network carriers. The third and least important category of factors that also tilt the playing field emerges from the economic and institutional conditions in the Gulf States. In contrast with the European approach these conditions work in the Gulf carriers' favour. Protectionist measures in Europe are primarily justified by this third and least important category[77]".

Emirates responded to the allegations of the American carriers by saying that the subsidy claim was a "smoke and mirrors" attempt to cover a "professional bid to restrict consumer choice",[78] and that, in the words of Tim Clark, President of Emirates: "all governments should pursue liberalization and open skies with the objective to end the greatest subsidy of all – aero-political protectionism".[79] Emirates further claimed that the world's largest airline group—Star Alliance—composed of 15 carriers, has had nearly half its member airlines receiving subsidies

[76]Explaining Dubai's Aviation Model, A Report for Emirates and Dubai Airports, June 11 at 5. See http://www.dubaiairports.ae/docs/default-source/Publications/oxford-economics_explaining-dubai's-aviation-model_june-2011.pdf?sfvrsn=4 An article on disruptive Innovation in the Harvard Business Review says that disruptive innovation originates in low-end or new-market footholds.: "Disruption" describes a process whereby a smaller company with fewer resources is able to successfully challenge established incumbent businesses. Specifically, as incumbents focus on improving their products and services for their most demanding (and usually most profitable) customers, they exceed the needs of some segments and ignore the needs of others. Entrants that prove disruptive begin by successfully targeting those overlooked segments, gaining a foothold by delivering more-suitable functionality—frequently at a lower price". See Christensen et al. (2015).

[77]de Wit (2013). See https://www.researchgate.net/publication/259519730.

[78]Carp (2015).

[79]Airlines Subsidy: Our Position, Emirates:2015, Preface, at 1. See http://www.emirates.com/english/images/Airlines%20and%20subsidy%20-%20our%20position%20new_tcm233-845771.pdf.

from their governments totaling €6.8 billion,[80] citing inter alia Lufthansa and KLM which have received cash injections from their governments during hard times or prior to privatization.[81] Having said that, Emirates categorically denied that the airline was subsidized, emphasizing that it was completely financially independent of the Government of Dubai and had no access to cheap or free fuel.

Emirates supported its claims that in 1985 the airline started with US$10 million received from the Dubai government as startup capital along with US$88 million for infrastructure development, which paid for two Boeing 727 aircraft and a training school. These amounts, Emirates claimed, had since been repaid through dividend payment to the government of Dubai which has amounted to US$2.5 billion up to 2015, Emirates has also stated that the aviation policy of the Government of Dubai is that the airline should be self-sufficient, self-sustaining and profitable.

Qatar Airways, in its response to the American carriers' claim has said that the United States is one of the few countries in the world that allows bankrupt companies to continue in business and the U.S. carriers have received up to $30 billion in cost savings related to Chapter 11 bankruptcy proceedings. Asserting that the claim against Qatar Airways is a thinly veiled "subsidy" argument against true competition, Qatar Airways claims that American carriers have received several benefits from their government in the nature of access to government funded traffic under the Fly America Scheme and subsidies through the Essential Air Services Programme for the provision of air services to small communities within the United States, along with fuel tax exemptions and rebates.

In a 400-page document, Emirates responded to the allegations of the American carriers claiming that the latter's arguments against Emirates were rife with errors, misstatements and legal distortions. The first legal distortion identified by Emirates was that the WTO Agreement on Subsidies and Countervailing Measures did not apply to air services and that rules against subsidies did not even form part of the Agreement.[82]

As for subsidies, Emirates pointed out in its rebuttal to the United States carriers charges that what it received from the United Arab Emirates government could not be categorized as subsidies as they were only loans and equity infusions and, in any case the only connection between subsidies and the US/UAE open skies agreement was that subsidies (if at all subsidies had been granted to Emirates by its government) should not be linked to price reduction, which was not a practice of Emirates in the United States market. It was also pointed out that United States carriers have

[80] *Id.* Introduction, at 4.

[81] *Id.* At 9. Emirates also cites Air France which was given three capital injections between 1991 and 1994 totaling €5.8 billion.

[82] The WTO Agreement on Subsidies and Countervailing Measures Agreement applies to goods and not services. He only WTO Agreement that apples to air transport in The General Agreement of Trade in Services (GATS) which again does not apply to market access and the provision of air transport services.

had huge U.S. government support of their own at the Federal, state and local government levels.

Etihad, in its response to the United States carriers' allegations regarding subsidies pointed out that, as against the latter's claim that Etihad received US $750 million cash grants from the Abu Dhabi government, The United States carriers had received $70 billion in government benefits.[83]

The Department of Justice of the United States rejected the claims made by the United States carriers against the Gulf carriers, calling their allegations "a call for protectionism that hurts U.S consumers", and that the open skies agreements signed by and between the United States and the United Arab Emirates and Qatar do not preclude financial assistance received by the Gulf carriers inasmuch as they do not preclude financial assistance the United States airlines have received from the United States. Additionally, Emirates claimed that the open skies agreement between the United States and The United Arab Emirates encompassed enhanced competition, more consumer choices and connectivity as well as increased flight frequency, improved service and innovation.[84]

In a meeting convened in July 2016 with the Gulf carriers that discussed the open skies agreement and the complaints of the three American carriers the United States government decided to take no action against the Gulf carriers. The United States government recognized that any action to curb or freeze operations of the Gulf carriers into the United State would put an end to the open skies agreement and that there was no need to do so in the absence of any unfair competitive conduct on the part of the Gulf carriers. It was said that "of the 1,700 routes flown by the Big Three and the Gulf carriers, they compete head-to-head on exactly two... furthermore, according to a comprehensive study by Oxford Economics, only 0.7 per cent of passengers who flew on a Big Three flight to the US could have flown the same route on a Gulf carrier".[85]

2.5 Subsidies in Air Transport Services

The underlying principle that would determine the law of subsidies in air transport is that a State aid in the nature of a subsidy would be unacceptable if it would erode the principle of equality of opportunity for carriers to compete with each other on a level playing field, as required by the Chicago Convention's Preamble and the subsequent provisions—that the operation of international air transport services should meet the needs of the people of the world *inter alia* for economical and efficient air services; unreasonable competition through economic waste be

[83]Etihad: US carriers got $70B in government aid, Reuters, 14 May 2015. http://www.cnbc.com/2015/05/14/.

[84]For a detailed discussion on the debate see Abeyratne (2016), pp. 113–130.

[85]McAuley (2016).

obviated; and every State has an fair opportunity to operate international airlines, as reflected in Article 44 of the Convention. The American carriers failed to prove that any of these principles was eroded by the business practices of the carriers of the United Arab Emirates.

Given the absence of the overarching WTO umbrella on subsidies for air transport services, the laws that would apply in any given jurisdiction would hinge upon anti-competitive conduct of a commercial entity. In the United States the *Sherman Act* of 1890[86] (a law to protect trade and commerce against unlawful restraints and monopolies) starts off in Article 1 by providing that every contract, combination in the form of trust or otherwise, or conspiracy, in restraint of trade or commerce among the several States, or with foreign nations, is illegal. Furthermore, any legal person who conducts business in the United States (which includes foreign carriers operating air services to the United States) is prohibited from monopolizing, or attempting to monopolize, or combining or conspiring with any other person or persons, to monopolize any part of the trade or commerce among the several States, or with foreign nations.

Section 2 of The *Clayton Act* of 1914[87] makes it unlawful for any commercial entity or other person to discriminate on pricing or fix prices that would put a competitor off the market. There are well established anti competitive policies both in the United States and Europe, which are calculated to prevent and punish anti competitive conduct. However, the measures taken against anti-competitive conduct in Europe differ from those of the United States in that while in Europe there is an administrative system for anti-competitive enforcement, where fines are imposed on the offenders, in the United States remedies lie at criminal law with financial penalties as well as custodial measures are imposed on those transgressing the law, where private compensation is offered to victims at rates disproportionate to the actual damage suffered.[88]

The fundamental principle of anti-competitive conduct in European trade was introduced in the Paris Treaty of 1951 which provided inter alia that measures or practices which discriminate between producers, between purchasers or between consumers, especially in prices and delivery terms or transport rates and conditions, and measures or practices which interfere with the purchaser's free choice of supplier were prohibited under the treaty and that subsidies or aids granted by States, or special charges imposed by States, in any form whatsoever were also prohibited.[89] The Treaty of Rome of 1957 establishing the European Common Market has specific anti-competitive provisions. Article 85 of the treaty prohibits and deems null and void the application to parties to transactions of unequal terms

[86] *Sherman Act*, 26 Stat. 209, 15 U.S.C.

[87] *Clayton Act*, 15 U.S.C Section 13.

[88] See Private anti-trust remedies under US law, Kenneth Ewing, Steptoe & Johnson LLP, http://www.steptoe.com/assets/attachments/2804.pdf.

[89] *Treaty Establishing the European Coal And Steel Community And Annexes I-Iii* Paris, 18 April 1951, Article 4 (b) and (c).

in respect of equivalent supplies, thereby placing them at a competitive disadvantage; or the subjecting of the conclusion of a contract to the acceptance by a party of additional supplies which, either by their nature or according to commercial usage, have no connection with the subject of such contract. any agreements or classes of agreements between enterprises, or any decisions or classes of decisions by associations of enterprises, and any concerted practices or classes of concerted practices which contribute to the improvement of the production or distribution of goods or to the promotion of technical or economic progress while reserving to users an equitable share in the profit resulting therefrom, and which: neither impose on the enterprises concerned any restrictions not indispensable to the attainment of the above objectives; nor enable such enterprises to eliminate competition in respect of a substantial proportion of the goods concerned are however exempted from the aforementioned restrictions.

Article 86 of the treaty considers inconsistent of the principles of the treaty which lays down policy for the Common Market, action by one or more enterprises to take improper advantage of a dominant position within the Common Market or within a substantial part of it shall be deemed to be incompatible with the Common Market and shall hereby be prohibited, to the extent to which trade between any Member States may be affected thereby. Some practices that are deemed unacceptable by the prohibition in Article 86 are: (a) the direct or indirect imposition of any inequitable purchase or selling prices or of any other inequitable trading conditions; (b) the limitation of production, markets or technical development to the prejudice of consumers; (c) the application to parties to transactions of unequal terms in respect of equivalent supplies, thereby placing them at a competitive disadvantage; or (d) the subjecting of the conclusion of a contract to the acceptance, by a party, of additional supplies which, either by their nature or according to commercial usage, have no connection with the subject of such contract.

Article 92 of the Treaty of Rome explicitly prohibits State aid in certain circumstances by saying that, except where otherwise provided for in the Treaty, any aid, granted by a Member State or granted by means of State resources, in any manner whatsoever, which distorts or threatens to distort competition by favoring certain enterprises or certain productions shall, to the extent to which it adversely affects trade between Member States, be deemed to be incompatible with the Common Market. There are of course certain practices that are acceptable to Europe. They are aids of a social character granted to individual consumers, provided that such aids are granted without any discrimination based on the origin of the products concerned; aids intended to remedy damage caused by natural calamities or other extraordinary events; and aids granted to the economy of certain regions of the Federal Republic of Germany affected by the division of Germany, to the extent that such aids are necessary in order to compensate for the economic disadvantages caused by such division.

Also compatible with the principles of the treaty are aids intended to promote the economic development of regions where the standard of living is abnormally low or where there exists serious under-employment; aids intended to promote the execution of important projects of common European interest or to remedy a serious disturbance of the economy of a Member State; and aids intended to facilitate the development of certain activities or of certain economic regions, provided that such aids do not change trading conditions to such a degree as would be contrary to the common interest and any other practices of State aid as are permitted on a case by case basis by the European Commission which could submit such practices for approval of the European Council.

Enforcement of the EU competition laws are the purview of national competition authorities by virtue of Regulation 1/2003 (which came into force on 1 May 2004). *The Treaty on the Functioning of the European Union* (TFEU) also contains provisions on anti-competitive practices within the European Union. Article 101 inclusively prohibits certain agreements between undertakings, decisions by associations of undertakings and concerted practices which may affect trade between Member States and which have as their object or effect the prevention, restriction or distortion of competition within the internal market. Some of the prohibited commercial practices under the TFEU which are rendered *null and void ab initio* are those which directly or indirectly fix purchase or selling prices or any other trading conditions; limit or control production, markets, technical development, or investment; share markets or sources of supply; apply dissimilar conditions to equivalent transactions with other trading parties, thereby placing them at a competitive disadvantage; and make the conclusion of contracts subject to acceptance by the other parties of supplementary obligations which, by their nature or according to commercial usage, have no connection with the subject of such contracts.

Article 102 of TFEU follows through with a provision on the abuse of dominant position by stating that any abuse by one or more undertakings of a dominant position within the internal market or in a substantial part of it is prohibited as incompatible with the internal market in so far as it may affect trade between Member States. Again this is an inclusive provision which particularly mentions such practices as those that directly or indirectly impose unfair purchase or selling prices or other unfair trading conditions; limit production, markets or technical development to the prejudice of consumers; apply dissimilar conditions to equivalent transactions with other trading parties, thereby placing them at a competitive disadvantage; and make the conclusion of contracts subject to acceptance by the other parties of supplementary obligations which, by their nature or according to commercial usage, have no connection with the subject of such contracts.

Under a special agreement signed between the United States and The European Communities, both parties have agreed to cooperate in combatting anti-competitive practices. The agreement[90] states that the parties agree to establish cooperative procedures to achieve the most effective and efficient enforcement of competition law, whereby the competition authorities of each Party will normally avoid

[90]*Agreement between the European Communities and the Government of the United States of America on the application of positive comity principles in the enforcement of their competition laws*, signed on 04/06/1998.

allocating enforcement resources to deal with anti-competitive activities that occur principally in and are directed principally towards the other Party's territory, where the competition authorities of the other Party are able and prepared to examine and take effective sanctions under their law to deal with those activities.

The legal justification for prohibiting State aid in certain circumstances where markets are distorted and competitors face dire circumstances as a result of not having access to equality of opportunity to compete with each other is based on the simple theory that if a government only subsidizes a particular entity or company and not its competitors, that entity would gain an undue advantage and an automatic dominant position over its competitors which could lead to abuse of dominant position, monopoly and inequity. Furthermore, the entity at an advantage as a result of receiving exclusive subsidies would be complacent and not compete on merit, thus creating an imbalance in the competition process. Although this problem could be overcome by competitors in an expanding market by aggressively and robustly competing with the subsidy recipient, it would not be possible in a depleting market. Another danger would be the monotonous reliance of the subsidy recipient on State aid which would decrease the efforts of that entity to be more competitive, resulting in a depletion of consumer choices for a product and also a minimizing of quality of the product.

In order to obviate the dangers of subsidies distorting the market there has to be strict rules of transparency and justification, that subsidies are granted to obviate market failure Require demonstration that aid is targeted at market failure and that there was no other alternative for the State to prevent such market failure. Furthermore, subsidies cannot be provided ad infinitum but must be for a limited to sufficient to rectify a situation of failure in the market. Also the subsidy recipient must adhere to proactive conditions imposed by the State to enhance availability and quality of service.

Although there is a great degree of ambivalence on the subject of subsidies for services, and an inherent disadvantage of subsidies for services do not come under the WTO umbrella, many WTO members grant subsidies for services in such sectors as construction services, education and audio visual services as well as for air transport services. One commentator mentions that the airline industry receives state support amounting on average to more than US$7 billion a year.[91] There is implied reference to subsidies in the service sector under the General Agreement on Trade in Services (GATS) in Article XV which provides that members of WTO are cognizant of the fact that, in certain circumstances, subsidies may have distortive effects on trade in services and that members should enter into negotiations with a view to developing the necessary multilateral disciplines to avoid such trade-distortive effects. Special mention has been made in the provision to the role of subsidies in relation to the development programs of developing countries which should take into account the relevant needs of the member countries with flexibility and fluidity.

---

[91] Benitah (2004), p. 3.

This could be a cue to ICAO, which has several provisions in the Chicago Convention that impels the Organization to achieve a level playing field through its Council, as discussed in the introduction to this article, which mandatorily requires the Council to request, collect, examine and publish details pertaining to subsidies paid to airlines from public funds. Along the premise and rationale of the Most Favored Nations Treatment clause contained in GATS the level playing field could be considered on the basis of Article II (1) of the GATS which states: "With respect to any measure covered by this Agreement, each Member shall accord immediately and unconditionally to services and service suppliers of any other Member treatment no less favorable than that it accords to like services and service suppliers of any other country."

Anchoring itself on this philosophy the Council could, as per Article 55 d) of the Chicago which details the permissive functions of the Council submit to the Assembly details of a study on subsidies conducted by ICAO with the assistance of its member States with plans to introduce global principles of conduct on the application of subsidies only in instances where fair competition and equality of opportunity to compete are not eroded by the grant of such subsidies. The study should engage all ICAO member States to arrive at a consensus on what constitutes fair subsidies under the meaning, purpose and spirit of the Chicago Convention. States should report on all subsidies granted to their carriers under the already existing requirement for the Council of ICAO in Article 54 i) of the Convention which mandatorily imposes an obligation on the Council to publish details of subsidies. Given that States would have different criteria and structures relating to aid, States should adhere to the guidelines issued in the ICAO *Manual on the Regulation of International Air Transport*.[92]

Finally, a dispute settlement process under Articles 84 and 85 of the Chicago Convention should enable the Council to decide on any disagreement or complaint arising out of subsidies that may distort competition and adopt a resolution that would in the least impose a moral obligation on an offending State to make reparation to a victim State that has suffered economically as a result of unfair subsidies that disrupts and adversely affects its air transport obligations.

References

Abeyratne RIR (1997) The settlement of international aviation disputes under the GATS and The ICAO Council – a comparative analysis. In: Petersman EU (ed) International Trade Law, The

---

[92]Doc 9626 (Second Edition—2004), In Chapter 2.2—Structure of Bilateral Regulation, section 2 on typical provisions of bilateral air services agreements, description is given to "a fair and equal opportunity article", "a fair competition article", and "a settlement of disputes article" (pages 2.2-2 to 2-4). Some description on the issue of "predatory pricing" can be found in Chapter 4.3—Air Carrier Tariffs (pages 4.3-10 to 4.3-11). These are reproduced in Appendix G.

GATT/WTO Dispute Settlement System, Studies in Transnational Economic Law. Kluwer Law International, Part 11, p 397
Abeyratne R (2004) The decisión in the Ryanair Case – the low cost carrier phenomenon. Eur Transport Law XXXIX(5):585–601
Abeyratne R (2005) The Airbus-Boeing subsidies dispute – some legal issues. Air Space Law XXX(6):379–398
Abeyratne R (2015) Competition and investment in air transport. Springer, Heidelberg, pp 119–121
Abeyratne R (2016) Chapter 6: Competition and innovation in air transport. In: Market access and subsidies in air transport: the US UAE debate and WTO. Springer, Heidelberg, pp 113–130
Benitah M (2004) Subsidies, services and sustainable development. International Centre for trade and Sustainable Development, Issue Paper No 1, p 3
Britton R (2015) The big three: U.S. airlines versus Persian Gulf Carriers. Forbes Magazine, 15 May 2015. http://www.forbes.com/forbes/welcome/
Carey S (2015) U.S. airlines detail claims of subsidies to Persian Gulf Rivals. The Wall Street Journal, 5 March 2015
Carey S, Jones R (2013) DJ – U.S. Airlines Claim to Document Subsidies at Gulf Rivals. IFX – International Foreign Exchange. https://www.internationalfx.com/uk/news/2015042014963/u-s-airlines-claim-to-document-subsidies-at-gulf-rivals
Carp G (2015) Emirates Airline lashes back at U.S. carriers. Chicago Tribune, 30 June 2015. http://www.chicagotribune.com/business/ct-emirates-rebuttal-0701-biz-20150630-story.html
Christensen CM, Raynor ME, McDonald R (2015) What is disruptive innovation? Harverd Business Review. https://hbr.org/2015/12/what-is-disruptive-innovation
Clampet J, Schaal D (2015) U.S. airlines reveal evidence they say proves Gulf Carriers get unfair subsidies. Skift, 05 March 2015. https://skift.com/2015/03/05/u-s-airlines-reveal-evidence-they-say-proves-gulf-carriers-get-unfair-aid/
de Wit J (2013) Unlevel playing field? Ah yes, you mean protectionism? J Air Transport Manag. Abstract
Fallows J (2012) China Airborne. Pantheon Books, New York, p 32
Ferguson N (2011) Civilization – the west and the rest. Penguin Press, New York, p 19
Ghemawat P (2011) World 3.0 – global prosperity and how to achieve it. Harvard Business Review Press, p 12
Kingsley J (2016) Open skies no more. Middle East Insights, Middle East Institute, National University of Singapore, 22 February 2016, p 2
Kissinger H (1994) Diplomacy. Simon and Schuster, New York, p 17
Krugman P (2009) The return of depression economics and the crisis of 2008. Norton, New York, p 182
Kupchan CA (2012) No one's world – the west, the rising rest and the coming global turn. Oxford University Press, New York, p 198
Levine-Weinberg A (2013) At least one middle Eastern Airline giant is fuelled by subsidies. The Motley Fool. http://www.fool.com/investing/general/2015/08/30/at-least-one-middle-eastern-airline-giant-is-fuele.aspx
Lumbroso A (2015) Subsidies in aviation: the elusive flight towards fair competition. OECD Insights: Debate The Issues, 14 August 2015. http://oecdinsights.org/2015/08/24/subsidies-in-aviation-the-elusive-flight-towards-fair-competition/
McAuley A (2016) Victory for Gulf airlines as US government ends Open Skies row with no further action. The National, 27 July 2016. http://www.thenational.ae/business/aviation/victory-for-gulf-airlines-as-us-government-ends-open-skies-row-with-no-further-action#page1
Milde M (2008) International Air Law and ICAO, Essential Air Law Series. Eleven International Publishing, Utrecht, p 153
Reed D (2013) In Debate Vs, Persian Gulf Carriers, U.S's big three airlines can't win – even if they win. Forbes Magazine. http://www.forbes.com/sites/danielreed/2015/03/18/in-debate-vs-persian-gulf-carriers-u-s-s-big-three-airlines-cant-win-even-if-they-win/#89cdb6e35f11

Rooney B (2012) U.S. and EU claim victory in Boeing subsidy case. CNN Money, 12 March 2012. http://money.cnn.com/2012/03/12/markets/boeing-airbus-wto/
Sachs JD. The end of poverty, economic possibilities of our time, The Penguin Press: New York, 2005, at 160
Schaal D (2013) Future of open skies hinges on the definition of the word: subsidy. Skift. https://skift.com/2015/04/28/future-of-open-skies-hinges-on-the-efinition-of-one-word-subsidy/
Sharma R (2012) Breakout nations – in pursuit of the next economic miracles. Norton
Slaughter AM (2004) A new world order. Princeton University Press, p 18
Spence M (2011) The next convergence. Farrar, Straus and Giroux, New York, p 73
Sykes AO (2003) The economics of WTO rules on subsidies and countervailing measures. John M. Olin & economics working paper no. 186 (2D Series), University of Chicago Law School, May 2003, pp 2–3
Van Fenema P (2006) EU horizontal agreements: community designation and the "Free Rider Clause". Air Space Law XXXI:172
Zakaria F (2011) The Post American World (Release 2.0). Norton
Zhang B (2015) The Middle East's 3 best airlines have infuriated their US competitors. Business Insider, 28 July 2015. http://ca.finance.ret1p.global.media.yahoo.com/news/middle-eastern-us-airlines-having-massive-dispute-future-133000846.html

Chapter 3
E-Trends and Air Transport

3.1 Biometric Identification

At the time of writing, KLM and Schiphol Airport had just started a pilot programme that was calculated to be applied in 2018 that involved biometric boarding that would admit a passenger through facial identification that obviated both a passport and a boarding pass. This would be accomplished through a special gate that passengers merely had to pass through just prior to boarding the aircraft. The test, which would be carried out in 3 months involves prior registration of passengers and passage through a special kiosk at the airport.

At the point of registration, the passenger would have to submit his passport for scanning along with the boarding pass and submission to a scan of the passenger's face. Following boarding, all personal data will be erased, and all data stored in the registration kiosk will be erased after 10 h. This initiative ties in with the earlier discussion on digital transformation and the emerging legal issue in Europe of the right of privacy of the passenger. Privacy in Europe is an important legal right where the European Union is riven with regulations.

European law on privacy pertaining to digital records of passenger details could be traced to 2002 Directive 2002/58/EC of the European Parliament and of the Council of 12 July 2002 concerning the processing of personal data and the protection of privacy in the electronic communications sector (Directive on privacy and electronic communications), as amended by Directive 2009/136/EC of the European Parliament and of the Council of 25 November 2009 aimed at—primarily in Article 1(1)—harmonizing the provisions of the Member States required to ensure an equivalent level of protection of fundamental rights and freedoms, and in particular the right to privacy and to confidentiality, with respect to the processing of personal data in the electronic communication sector and to ensure the free movement of such data and of electronic communication equipment and

R. Abeyratne, *Megatrends and Air Transport*, DOI 10.1007/978-3-319-61124-2_3

services in the European Union.[1] Article 1(2) clarifies that provisions of the Directive are calculated to particularizing and complementing Directive 95/46[2] for the purposes mentioned in Article 1(1).[3]

Directive 2002/58/EC abides by the basic principles of its predecessor EC Directive 95/46—that data processing is only lawful if the data subject has unambiguously given his consent; or processing is necessary for the performance of a contract to which the data subject is party; or processing is necessary for compliance with a legal obligation to which the controller is subject; or processing is necessary to protect the vital interests of the data subject; or processing is necessary for the performance of a task carried out in the public interest or in the exercise of official authority vested in the controller or in a third party; or processing is necessary for the purposes of the legitimate interest pursued by the controller or by the third party, except where such interests are overridden by the interests for fundamental rights and freedoms of the data subject which require protection.

The fundamental postulate of both Directives is that personal data must be processed fairly and lawfully, and collected for specified, explicit and legitimate purposes. They must also be adequate, relevant and not excessive, must be accurate and, where necessary, kept up to date. They must not be stored for longer than

[1]The European Union was created as a political and economic community with supranational and inter-governmental features. It is composed of twenty-seven member states primarily located in Europe. The member States which created the EU contemporaneously delegated to the Union the exercise of certain national competencies. In 1963 the European Court of Justice handed down a decision which inter alia confirmed that the EC Treaty which established the Union went beyond the boundaries of an international agreement that confers mutual obligations between States by constituting a new order of international law. Member States have, by this act transferred certain powers to the European Community, thereby creating a community that can legally represent member States in the international scene, having its own institutions and legal capacity. In effect, the member States have limited their sovereign rights in certain fields by creating a body that limits the exercise of their national competencies in particular areas and binds themselves and their nationals. The European Union works through the European Commission which was created by the Treaty of Rome and exercises the competencies of the EU.

[2]European Council Directive 95/46/EC of 24 October 1995 applies to data processed by automated means (e.g. a computer database of customers) and data contained in or intended to be part of non-automated filing systems (traditional paper files). It does not apply to the processing of data: by a natural person in the course of purely personal or household activities; in the course of an activity which falls outside the scope of Community law, such as operations concerning public security, defense or State security. The Directive aims to protect the rights and freedoms of persons with respect to the processing of personal data by laying down the key criteria for making processing lawful and the principles of data quality.

[3]It must be stated that an earlier instrument of 2001 preceded the 2002 Regulation: Regulation (EC) No 45/2001 of the European Parliament and of the Council applies to the processing of personal data by the Union institutions, bodies, offices and agencies. Regulation (EC) No 45/2001 and other Union legal acts applicable to such processing of personal data are still adapted to the principles and rules established in Regulation 2016/679 (see later reference in the text of this article) and applied Regulation. Regulation 2016/679 goes on to say that In order to provide a strong and coherent data protection framework in the Union, the necessary adaptations of Regulation (EC) No 45/2001 should follow after the adoption of Regulation 2016.679.

necessary and stored solely for the purposes for which they were collected. Some special conditions of processing are that: it is forbidden to process personal data revealing racial or ethnic origin, political opinions, religious or philosophical beliefs, trade-union membership, and the processing of data concerning health or sex life. In this context the rights of the data subject are preeminent which include: the right to obtain information[4] and the data subject's right of access to data which every data subject should have the right to obtain from the controller. Another inherent right of the data subject is the right to object to the processing of data[5]:

With regard to the security of data processing, Article 4 of Directive 2002/58 provides that the provider of a publicly available electronic communications service must take appropriate technical and organisational measures to safeguard security of its services, if necessary in conjunction with the provider of the public communications network with respect to network security. These measures, while having regard to the state of the art and the cost of their implementation, ensure a level of security appropriate to the risk presented.

3.1.1 Directive 2006/24/EC

Directive 2006/24/EC was introduced by the European Council 4 years later to seemingly take away some of the restrictive provisions of Directive 2002/58/EC. The 2006 Directive was a corollary to the Declaration on Combating Terrorism adopted by the European Council on 25 March 2004 which instructed the Council to examine measures for establishing rules on the retention of communications traffic data by service providers. The Regulation was developed on the basis of Article 8 of the European Convention for the Protection of Human Rights and Fundamental Freedoms (ECHR)—signed in Rome on 4 November 1950—which recognized that everyone has the right to respect for his private life and his correspondence and that the only exceptional circumstance in which public authorities may interfere with the exercise of that right is in accordance with the law and where necessary in a democratic society, inter alia, in the interests of national security or public safety, for the prevention of disorder or crime, or for the protection of the rights and freedoms of others. Because retention of data has proved to be such a necessary and effective investigative tool for law enforcement

[4]The controller must provide the data subject from whom data are collected with certain information relating to himself/herself (the identity of the controller, the purposes of the processing, recipients of the data etc.).

[5]The data subject should have the right to object, on legitimate grounds, to the processing of data relating to him/her. He/she should also have the right to object, on request and free of charge, to the processing of personal data that the controller anticipates being processed for the purposes of direct marketing. He/she should finally be informed before personal data are disclosed to third parties for the purposes of direct marketing, and be expressly offered the right to object to such disclosures.

in several Member States, and in particular concerning serious matters such as organised crime and terrorism, it is deemed necessary in the Regulation that retained data are made available to law enforcement authorities for a certain period, subject to the conditions provided for in Directive 2006/24/EC.

Article 1 of the Directive clarifies its aim, which is to harmonise Member States' provisions concerning the obligations of the providers of publicly available electronic communications services or of public communications networks with respect to the retention of certain data which are generated or processed by them, in order to ensure that the data are available for the purpose of the investigation, detection and prosecution of serious crime, as defined by each Member State in its national law. Article 5 sets out the modalities of retention of data necessary to trace and identify the source of a communication: concerning fixed network telephony and mobile telephony: the calling telephone number; and the name and address of the subscriber or registered user. With regard to internet access to information of the data subject it is important, according to Article 5; the user ID and telephone number allocated to any communication entering the public telephone network; the name and address of the subscriber or registered user to whom an Internet Protocol (IP) address, user ID or telephone number was allocated at the time of the communication; and data necessary to identify the destination of a communication. With regard to mobile telephones or fixed network telephones the provision identifies the importance of retention of: the number(s) dialled (the telephone number(s) called), and, in cases involving supplementary services such as call forwarding or call transfer, the number or numbers to which the call is routed; the name(s) and address(es) of the subscriber(s) or registered user(s); the user ID or telephone number of the intended recipient(s) of an Internet telephony call; the name(s) and address(es) of the subscriber(s) or registered user(s) and user ID of the intended recipient of the communication; and data necessary to identify the date, time and duration of a communication.

While Article 6 of the Directive limits the period of the retention of the above information to 6 months, Article 8 specifies that the data should be retained in such a manner as not to cause any delay in their relay to competent authorities when such data is called upon for delivery to them. Discretion to appoint supervisory authorities to monitor and ascertain that the retention of data is carried out in accordance with the provisions of Directive 2006/24/EC and is vested in States as per Article 9 of the Directive. Penalties for any infringement of provisions of The Directive are set forth in Article 13 which provides that each member State is required to take necessary measures to ensure that the national measures implementing Directive 95/46/EC that provide for judicial remedies, liability and sanctions are fully implemented with respect to the processing of data under the Directive and that each member State has the legal obligation to take necessary measures to ensure that any intentional access to, or transfer of, data retained in accordance with the Directive that is not permitted under national law adopted pursuant to the Directive is punishable by penalties, including administrative or criminal penalties, that are effective, proportionate and dissuasive.

3.1.2 Case Law

Two cases brought into focus the relevance of Directive 2006/24/EC—Case 293/12[6] decided in 2014 by The European Court of Justice, and Case 594/12.[7] In both of which The Court held that Directive 2006/24/EC of the European Parliament and of the Council of 15 March 2006 on the retention of data generated or processed in connection with the provision of publicly available electronic communications services or of public communications networks and amending Directive 2002/58/EC are invalid. The reasoning of the Court was based on its response to the basic question remanded to it—whether Directive 2006/24/EC was inconsistent with Articles 7 and 8 of the Charter of Fundamental Rights of the European Union.[8] Article 7 of the Charter provides that everyone has the right to respect for his or her private and family life, home and communications. Article 8 states that everyone has a right to the protection of personal data pertaining to him or her and that such data must be protected fairly for specified purposes and on the basis of the consent of the person concerned or some other legitimate basis laid down by law. Everyone has the right of access to data which has been collected concerning him or her and the right to have it rectified. Article 8 goes on to say that compliance with the provisions mentioned would be subject to an independent authority.

The court held that the data considered in the relevant provisions of the Directive i.e. Articles 3, 4 and 5 include data necessary to trace and identify the source of a communication and its destination, to identify the date, time, duration and type of a communication, to identify users' communication equipment, and to identify the location of mobile communication equipment, data which consist, *inter alia*, of the name and address of the subscriber or registered user, the calling telephone number, the number called and an IP address for Internet services. Such data would enable one to determine the identity of the person with whom a subscriber or registered user has communicated and by what means, and to identify the time of the communication as well as the place from which that communication took place. The data envisioned in the Directive would also admit of the possibility of a person's having access to the frequency of the communications of the subscriber or registered user with certain persons during a given period.

The court therefore recognized an inherent danger in the provisions of the Directive 2006/24/EC of allowing very precise conclusions to be drawn concerning the private lives of the persons whose data has been retained—such as the habits of everyday life, permanent or temporary places of residence, daily or other movements, the activities carried out, the social relationships of those persons and the

---

[6]*Digital Rights Ireland Limited* v. *Minister for Communications, Marine and Natural Resources, Minister of Justice, Equality and Reform; Commissioner of the Garda Siochana and Attorney General*, ECLI:EU:2014:238.

[7]*Kärntner Landesregierung, Michael Seitlinger, Christof Tschohl and others, Id.*

[8]Charter of Fundamental Rights of the European Union, 2007/c 303/01, 14, 12, 2007, Official *Journal of the European Union.*

social environments frequented by them. In such circumstances, according to the Court, it was not inconceivable that the retention of the data in question might have an effect on the use, by subscribers or registered users, of the means of communication covered by that directive and, consequently, on their exercise of the freedom of expression guaranteed by Article 11 of the Charter, which states *inter alia* that everyone has the right to freedom of expression, which right would include the freedom to hold opinions and to receive and impart opinions and ideas without interference of public authorities and regardless of frontiers.

The court opined that, by requiring the retention of the data listed in Article 5 of Directive 2006/24 and by allowing the competent national authorities to access those data, Directive 2006/24, derogated from the system of protection of the right to privacy established by Directives 95/46 and 2002/58 with regard to the processing of personal data in the electronic communications sector, directives which provided for the confidentiality of communications and of traffic data as well as the obligation to erase or make those data anonymous where they are no longer needed for the purpose of the transmission of a communication, unless they are necessary for billing purposes and only for as long as so necessary. The court was also of the view that, in similar manner and along the lines of its reasoning above, Directive 2006/24 constituted an interference with the fundamental right to the protection of personal data guaranteed by Article 8 of the Charter, because it provides for the processing of personal data.

3.1.3 A Recent Initiative

On 27 April 2016 The European Parliament and the Council adopted *Regulation (EU) 2016/679*[9] which aims at the protection of natural persons in relation to the processing of personal data which is recognized as a fundamental right. The Regulation, which in its Article 1 provides that it lays down rules relating to the protection of natural persons with regard to the processing of personal data and rules relating to the free movement of personal data[10] while protecting fundamental rights and freedoms of natural persons and in particular their right to the protection of personal data, goes on to say that the free movement of personal data within the Union shall be neither restricted nor prohibited for reasons connected with the protection of natural persons with regard to the processing of personal data.

---

[9]Regulation (EU) 2016/679 Of The European Parliament and of The Council of 27 April 2016. http://data.europa.eu/eli/reg/2016/679/oj.

[10]"Personal data" means any information relating to an identified or identifiable natural person ('data subject'); an identifiable natural person is one who can be identified, directly or indirectly, in particular by reference to an identifier such as a name, an identification number, location data, an online identifier or to one or more factors specific to the physical, physiological, genetic, mental, economic, cultural or social identity of that natural person. See Article 4 of the Regulation.

In its Preamble, and prior to its substantive provisions, the Regulation states that the principles of, and rules on the protection of natural persons with regard to the processing of their personal data should, whatever their nationality or residence, respect their fundamental rights and freedoms, in particular their right to the protection of personal data. The Regulation further states that it is intended to contribute to the accomplishment of an area of freedom, security and justice and of an economic union, to economic and social progress, to the strengthening and the convergence of the economies within the internal market, and to the well-being of natural persons.

Regulation 2016/679 recognizes that rapid technological developments and globalisation have brought new challenges for the protection of personal data and goes on to say that the scale of the collection and sharing of personal data has increased significantly. The fact that technology allows both private companies and public authorities to make use of personal data on an unprecedented scale in order to pursue their activities is considered a significant factor by the Regulation to the extent that natural persons increasingly make personal information available publicly and globally. This notwithstanding, the Regulation recognizes that technology has transformed both the economy and social life, and should further facilitate the free flow of personal data within the Union and the transfer to third countries and international organisations, while ensuring a high level of the protection of personal data.

As a result, it is recognized that the aforementioned developments require a strong and more coherent data protection framework in the Union, backed by strong enforcement, given the importance of creating the trust that will allow the digital economy to develop across the internal market. At the same time, natural persons should have control of their own personal data and be given legal and practical certainty and the involvement of economic operators and public authorities should be enhanced.

The Regulation, which allows for the processing of personal data in the context of the activities of an establishment of a controller or a processor in the Union, regardless of whether the processing takes place in the Union or not, applies to the processing of personal data of data subjects who are in the Union by a controller or processor not established in the Union, where the processing activities are related to: the offering of goods or services, irrespective of whether a payment of the data subject is required, to such data subjects in the Union; or the monitoring of their behaviour as far as their behaviour takes place within the Union. It also applies to the processing of personal data by a controller not established in the Union, but in a place where Member State law applies by virtue of public international law.[11]

The Regulation endorses the fundamental principles enunciated by Directive 95/46/EC and contains provisions in its Preamble regarding genetic data, personal data and children's' data. Genetic data is defined as personal data relating to the inherited or acquired genetic characteristics of a natural person which result from the analysis of a biological sample from the natural person in question, in particular chromosomal, deoxyribonucleic acid (DNA) or ribonucleic acid (RNA) analysis, or

[11]Regulation 2016/679, Article 3.

from the analysis of another element enabling equivalent information to be obtained. Personal data, the collection and retention of which should be lawful and fair, include all data pertaining to the health status of a data subject which reveal information relating to the past, current or future physical or mental health status of the data subject. This includes information about the natural person collected in the course of the registration for, or the provision of, health care services. The Regulation provides that children merit specific protection with regard to their personal data, as they may be less aware of the risks, consequences and safeguards concerned and their rights in relation to the processing of personal data. Such specific protection should, in particular, apply to the use of personal data of children for the purposes of marketing or creating personality or user profiles and the collection of personal data with regard to children when using services offered directly to a child. The consent of the holder of parental responsibility should not be necessary in the context of preventive or counselling services offered directly to a child.

Article 5 lays down rules for collection and processing of personal data by providing that personal data is required to be: processed lawfully, fairly and in a transparent manner in relation to the data subject ('lawfulness, fairness and transparency'); collected for specified, explicit and legitimate purposes and not further processed in a manner that is incompatible with those purposes. It also provides that further processing for archiving purposes in the public interest, scientific or historical research purposes or statistical purposes shall not be considered to be incompatible with the initial purposes ('purpose limitation'); adequate, relevant and limited to what is necessary in relation to the purposes for which they are processed ('data minimization'); accurate and, where necessary, kept up to date. Every reasonable step must be taken to ensure that personal data that are inaccurate, having regard to the purposes for which they are processed, are erased or rectified without delay ('accuracy'); Furthermore, personal data must be kept in a form which permits identification of data subjects for no longer than is necessary for the purposes for which the personal data are processed and may be stored for longer periods insofar as the personal data will be processed solely for archiving purposes in the public interest; and processed in a manner that ensures appropriate security of the personal data, including protection against unauthorized or unlawful processing and against accidental loss, destruction or damage, using appropriate technical or organizational measures ('integrity and confidentiality'). The controller appointed to monitor the provisions and their implementations is accountable for the proper implementation of the Regulation.

3.1.4 Industry Views

IATA[12] has called for a modern legal framework that applies to data protection of the airline passenger in the European Union saying that such a framework should be

[12] *Supra*, note 27 in Chap. 1.

comprised of clear objectives which address real threats to fundamental rights and other risks of personal or social damage to the individual. While appreciating the core principles of Directive 95/46/EC, IATA has contended that legal norms should be based on sound business practices and acceptable social norms, while ensuring a sound balance between the services of data bases and benefits to the airline industry as well as the passenger. European legal norms should also be consistent with international legal norms and competing legal and regulatory objectives.[13] With regard to IATA's position on data collection of passengers and European directives and regulations, Tony Tyler, Director General of IATA, acknowledging governments' legitimate interest (for safety and security purposes) in collecting passenger data, further elaborated: "we (airlines) follow the laws. We invest a lot of money and effort in developing IT systems that provide governments with the data they want. In return, we ask for the introduction of global standards on data collection. When a government asks for the data in a different format, it becomes a complicated and expensive process... we also want the authorities to actually use the data that we give them. It's absurd that airlines provide all this information in good time to immigration authorities, yet passengers are still all treated in exactly the same manner on arrival and there is no accelerated entry for passengers that have been pre-checked".[14]

The above discussion clearly underscores the fact that there are regulations, directives and court decisions on data processing and retention pertaining to airline passengers in Europe. As such, this issue must be analyzed with a great deal of caution. For one, rulemaking is not law making, where the latter is the exclusive remit of a State legislature. Another factor is that rulemaking has to be accomplished in accordance with demarcated principles to which due consideration is given. The third aspect is that the courts should not substitute their own views on a regulation, rule or law.

Rulemaking in air transport is a serious issue as it hinges on the safety of persons travelling by air without being exploited by commercial interests. The two key words in this context are *standardization* and *harmonization*. The first word means compliance of laws and regulations and the second word denotes consistency of application of rules in a seamless manner. As such legislatures cannot take a chance with rulemaking and at any cost should not relegate the task to the executive alone. This principle, although making eminent sense, carries with it a flaw that has to be addressed. While on the one hand, handing over rulemaking powers to governmental agencies would free the legislature to concentrate on more general policy issues, handing over rulemaking authority to agencies would mean that rules are then made by unelected civil servants, which defeats the philosophy of election and democracy

[13]See Response of the International Air Transport Association to The European Commission's Communication: "A Comprehensive Approach to Personal Data Protection in the European Union." http://ec.europa.eu/justice/news/consulting_public/0006/contributions/organisations/iata_en.pdf.

[14]IATA CEO: 'We need global standards on data collection' https://www.euractiv.com/section/transport/interview/iata-ceo-we-need-global-standards-on-data-collection/.

where the people elect their legislators to enact laws for them. The issue then would be, who would be the overall monitor of the rulemaking process in air transport? The answer lies squarely in the State, which has to ensure that rules.

Notwithstanding the above, it must be stated that the mere fact that an agency makes rules without having the power to do so does not make such rules invalid at law, particularly if the capacity to make such rules flow from a discretion granted to the agencies by the legislature. The criterion of validity lies in the judicial requirement that the rules are not too rigidly applied. An inflexible principle in this regard is that such rules should not bypass the legislature, precluding scrutiny by the legislature. Rules promulgated by the executive (or administration) must not be inconsistent with the parent legislation that they emanate from.

Another important factor in administrative rulemaking is that the rule must be promulgated by the person on whom discretion vests to make the rule. This principle is based on the maxim *delegatus non potest delegare* which essentially means that delegated power cannot be re-delegated. Thus a committee, which has been delegated the power by an executive (such as a minister or secretary) cannot delegate that power to an officer or group of officers to exercise such discretion.[15] Also, a judicial function—a function that bestows on a body to act judicially, taking decisions, cannot be delegated.[16]

Based on the above reasoning, rulemaking has to involve two vital factors, as the discussion in this book has reflected: public participation; and judicial review of administrative action. The former is left to the State (legislature) to set up. The latter is a matter for the courts, although the courts could not superimpose their stamp on the administration to the extent that would make the administration meaningless. As Lord Shaw said in *Local Government Board* v. *Arlidge*[17]: "[T]hat the judiciary should presume to impose its own methods on administrative or executive officers is a usurpation. And the assumption that the methods of natural justice are *ex necessitate* those of courts of justice is wholly unfounded".[18]

In the end, one is compelled to look for a balance between the guidelines of ICAO (as discussed at the outset of this article) and the various elements that form European laws, regulations, rules and *cursus curiae*.

3.2 Apps That Make Air Travel Easier

Contemporaneous to the KLM-Schipol initiative, Brussels Airlines launched a new app for iOS and Android which would enable passengers too book tickets, check-in, store mobile boarding passes and view real-time flight information. There would

[15]*Allingham* v. *Minister of Agriculture* [1948] 1 All. E. R. 780.

[16]*Barnard* v. *National Dock Labour Board* [1953] 2 Q.B. 18.

[17][1915] A.C. at 120.

[18]*Id.* 138.

also be provision in the app that would enable the passenger to have the choice of opting in for proactive updates.

Another similar initiative is that of Delta Airlines with its latest version of its Fly Delta app, which now includes access to detailed airport wayfinding maps, and the ability to access boarding pass and flight details, even when a reliable Wi-Fi or cellular connection is not available. In March 2017 Global IT provider SITA, in collaboration with Air New Zealand, launched its first trial of facial recognition technology at Brisbane Airport in Australia. The latest SITA Smart Path technology features "sophisticated biometrics that enable travellers to present their details at self-service kiosks during check-in".[19]

Delta's wayfinding tool features interactive maps for 20 major airports—including the airline's hubs—and guides customers with turn-by-turn directions to their gate, restaurants or baggage claim belt. Delta says it is now the only airline to give customers the ability to access airport maps on iPhone via their boarding pass by touching the departure city code, arrival city code or gate numbers, and through My Trips, Flight Status and the "More" section.

The QANTAS Bot (Concierge), which goes a step further is a Facebook Messenger bot that has been developed to give customers personalised travel inspiration, Qantas Concierge enables users to search for destination inspiration in a number of categories, including cities, beaches, culture and hotels. For instance, someone interested in flying to New York can read content about the best restaurants in New York City, while someone tempted by a trip to Bali can find information on the best spas on the Indonesian island. This in itself is a megatrend that encapsulates air transport with tourism, the largest industry combined. Tourism represents one quarter of all exports of services—40% with air transport revenues included. It is also noteworthy that the growth trend will continue, as according to a news release of 18 September 2007 issued by the International Civil Aviation Organization (ICAO), total world airline scheduled passenger traffic in terms of passenger-kilometers is expected to grow at an average annual rate of 4.6% up to the year 2025, half a % age point lower than the growth rate achieved over the period 1985–2005, according to forecasts prepared by ICAO. Total freight traffic growth over the same period is forecast to be stronger, at 6.6% per annum in terms of freight tonne-kilometers.

There can be particular benefits from tourism for the poorest economies, where international arrivals are growing at twice the rate in the industrialized States. Although they are still at a low level, the tourism receipts of the Least Developed Countries increased fivefold between 1990 and 2005, from 1 billion to 5 billion dollars. Tourism has become one of the largest sources of foreign exchange revenues for developing countries generally and for the 49 LDCs specifically,

[19]Brisbane Airport launches first Australian trial of SITA's Smart Path Technology, *Airport Technology.com,* 14 March 2017. See http://www.airport-technology.com/news/newsbrisbane-becomes-first-australian-airport-to-launch-sitas-smart-path-technology-trial-5761882?WT.mc_id=DN_News.

reducing their foreign debt and diversifying their economies. Tourism is often the principal service sector activity and it is a notably effective catalyst for gender equality, employment of young people, rural regeneration, cultural preservation and nature conservation.

Therefore WTO, which is the specialized agency of the United Nations with a central and decisive role in promoting the development of responsible, sustainable and universally accessible tourism, concludes that, for all these reasons, tourism can play a major role in improving the standard of living of disadvantaged populations and helping them lift themselves above the poverty threshold. Tourism can be a primary tool for achievement of the Millennium Development Goals of the United Nations, as long as a balance with climate change effects is maintained.

Tourism—business and leisure travel—is a significant global industry making positive contributions to growth, trade and development, with particular potential for poor countries. Tourism is both affected fundamentally by climate change and a contributor to the global emissions of greenhouse gases with air transport being a substantial contributor to total tourism emissions.

There is no doubt that tourism and air transport are symbiotic. Travel and tourism, the largest combination of industries and the largest creator of wealth, is estimated to generate $3.5 trillion a year in activity and potentially provides employment to 130 million people worldwide. This accounts for 10% of the world's GDP, 10.3% of the world's wages, 9.8% of the profits and 11.7% of indirect and direct taxes. The Annual Report of the World Tourism Organization for 2015 reflects that International tourist arrivals grew by 4.4% in 2015 to reach a total of 1184 million in 2015, marking the sixth consecutive year of above-average growth with international arrivals increasing by 4% or more every year since the post-crisis year of 2010. Some 50 million more tourists (overnight visitors) travelled to international destinations around the world in 2015 than in 2014.[20]

Demand remained strong overall, though with mixed results across individual destinations due to strong exchange rate fluctuations, increased safety and security concerns, and the drop in oil prices and other commodities, which increased disposable income in importing countries but weakened demand in exporters. Growth in advanced economy destinations (+5%) exceeded that of emerging economies (+4%), boosted by the solid results of Europe (+5%). By region, Europe, the Americas and Asia and the Pacific all recorded approximately 5% growth in 2015. Arrivals in the Middle East increased by 3% while data in Africa, albeit limited, pointed to an estimated 3% decrease largely due to weak results in North Africa, which accounts for over one third of arrivals in the region.

The above data strongly suggests that the initiatives of such innovators as Schiphol, KLM, Brussels Airport and Delta, along with QANTAS which links air transport with tourism have created more cohesive links of the travel chains bringing in apps and location based services. When taken together with the other digital tools and tech trends such as "Location-based Services" (LBS) which are a

[20]http://cf.cdn.unwto.org/sites/all/files/pdf/annual_report_2015_lr.pdf.

new generation of tracking devices and their applications,[21] these tech tools make it easy for the traveller and reduces the tedium of otherwise lengthy airport processes. However, at the same time any flaws in these systems may give rise to legal liability. LBS connect to a passenger's app to coordinate, advise and determine location and facilitate information that the passenger may need.

Of specific relevance to air transport is the Airport Terminal Beacon which is a device that provides by broadcast information that can be accessed by passengers through the use of their apps. Beacons can also give operations information, give access to web pages, and display advertisements in devices. A significant feature of an airport beacon is that it can provide information but cannot receive information. It is the provision of information that may give rise to legal liability, particularly of the designer of the beacon and manufacturer. Courts have decided, in analogous cases, for instance of a computer in a bank giving wrong information through a fault of its design, that caused clients monetary losses, that the designer of the computer as well as the user of the equipment (the bank) were liable.[22] This principle follows the 1932 Hooper Principle (arising from the 1932 case *T.J. Hooper v. Northern Barge*)[23] which dictates that as information technology becomes prolific, pervasive and sophisticated and their widespread use becomes more commonplace, negligence may arise from a failure to use computer systems which prevent damage and harm. Therefore, while on the one hand, airports would be expected to install tools such as *Ibeacons,* they are required to exercise a duty of care so as to not to negligently cause damage. In the 1947 Carroll Towing case[24] the court recognized the principle that if the cost of providing a facility or person to ensure that damage does not occur is not greater than the harm caused if such facility or person was not provided, the provider would be held liable in negligence.

The airport operator who provides information would have to ensure that accurate information is provided to the passenger using commercially available IT tools (if the operator has the resources to provide such) so that he could embark on his flight through the appropriate gate and at the time indicated in the display. A misstatement, particularly if negligently made, that misdirects the passenger leading to his missing his flight would entail legal liability for the airport operator. An airport is prima facie a business and a misstatement to a client would result in the airport's negligence.[25] Managers of airports have to bear in mind that principles of executive liability are now veering towards imposition of liability on a strict principle of implied or extended responsibility that would preclude denial of

[21]See Bennett and Crowe (2005).

[22]*Remfor Industries Ltd.* v. *Bank of Montreal* (1978) 90 D.L.R. (3d) 316 (Ont., C.A).

[23]60 F.2d 737 (1932).

[24]*United States* v. *Carroll Towing* 160 F.2d 482 (2d Cir. 1947).

[25]British Airports Authority (BAA) Airports Limited has the following disclaimer in its flight information web page: BAA Airports Limited does not verify the accuracy or completeness of this flight information and disclaims any implied warranties with regard to it. BAA Airports Limited shall have no liability for any loss or damage suffered as a result of relying on flight information on this site which may prove to be inaccurate or incomplete.

responsibility merely on the basis that the airport was just a conduit in conveying flight information to the passenger as provided by the airline. The information is a service provided by the airport inasmuch as the serving of food and beverages on board an aircraft is a service provided by the airline, even though the goods are provided by an outside caterer. In a case of food poisoning on board, the airline cannot hide itself behind a disclaimer. Neither should an airport be allowed to invoke a disclaimer as a defense where it conveys incorrect information to the passenger through its information unless there are compelling reasons.

In this context, tech megatrends such as the use of *Ibeacons* and other location based services bring with them, on the one hand an implied requirement of provision (if the airport concerned is capable of providing such services) and on the other hand entails liability if their designs are defective or if inferior services are provided. The decision in a 1986 American case—*United States Fire Insurance Co. v. United States*—affirmed the principles in *Hooper* and *Carroll Towing*, which directly addressed the failure to use a computerized system is. This case involved the use of a manual method by the Coast Guard instead of computer assistance which could have been available to locate a wreckage. As a result, warnings were misplaced and an accident ensued. The court found the government negligent for using the inferior manual method because, had it used the computer-based methodology, the wreckage would have been properly located and the damage would have been precluded.

Based on the above, it could be reasonably concluded that failure to incorporate into a system up-to-date features based on reasonably available technological advances, or to implement compensating controls, may lead to liability for negligence. In other words, the standard of care for any activity will rise as more sophisticated technology becomes available. One commentary says: "[Not] only does the use of a computer system not lower the standard of care (the third commandment), the existence and availability of computerized systems in the marketplace may actually have the effect of raising the standard of care for any given activity".[26]

The lack of emotional intelligence of a device would not be an acceptable defence. In *Pompeii Estates* v. *Con.Ed*[27]—a 1977 case which involved an action brought by a builder against a public utility for having terminated electricity to a house he was building and hence unoccupied, based on the public utility's erroneous computer records, The defence was that the computer used was incapable of using discretion of a human and therefore had routinely sent the electricity bill without knowing the circumstances of the case, and argument which the court rejected. POSNER, J. held: "The 'Dawn of the Age of Aquarius' has also ushered in the 'Age of the Computer'. There is no question that the modern computer is as indispensable to big business as the washing machine is to the American household. To ask the American housewife to go back to washing clothes by hand is as

---

[26]*Ten Commandments of Computerization*. 1992 Osler, Hoskin & Harcourt.

[27]91 Misc.2d 233 (1977).

unthinkable as asking Consolidated Edison to send out its monthly bills by any other method than the computer".

An airport operator or an airline must ensure that a new device is as efficient or better than a system already used. Therefore, what is relevant is that the system enables the provider of service to meet the duty of care and not necessarily that it is newer than ones that are used earlier. Thus, a provider of service must ensure that a new computer system is at least as effective and reliable as the system, be it manual or automated, that it replaces and cannot claim in defence that the device so installed was expected to run "reasonably well". Addy J held in the Canadian case of *87118 Canada Ltd. v. The Queen*[28]: "[W]here a service could obviously be performed properly by an individual and where that service has been computerized and has not been rendered properly, it is no answer, as the defendant has attempted to do in the case at bar, for the person who has chosen to install the computerized system to establish that it was efficient as a computerized service as could be reasonably furnished having regard to the state of the art at the time. Before installing such a service, or at least before relying on it in substitution for a previously existing manual one, then, failing full disclosure of the reduction of the quality of the service to be rendered or failing any valid legislation limiting or exempting liability, the person rendering it must satisfy the Court that the new automated service is as efficient as the previous existing manual one".[29]

3.3 Apps That Should Help the Authorities

E-tech megatrends such as the apps mentioned above could also be used to ensure security at airports and the safety of passengers. There are serious lapses that could be avoided through enhanced communications between authorities. An example is the unfortunate loss of lives in Florida in January 2017.

On 6 January the area proximate to the baggage terminal in Terminal 2 of Fort-Lauderdale Hollywood International Airport was the scene of a mass shooting perpetrated by a mentally deranged passenger who had arrived from Alaska. Five people were killed while six others were injured in the shooting. About 36 people sustained injuries in the ensuing panic. Reportedly the suspect was taken into custody after surrendering to responding police officers. The Federal Aviation Administration issued what is called a "ground stop" notice stopping all but emergency flights. 20,000 pieces of baggage and several hundred passengers were stranded, some of whom (perhaps with employees of the airport) were seen loitering on the tarmac for several hours—a rare sight in commercial aviation.

The killer clearly had a known history of mental disability of a grave nature. In November 2016 he had visited the field office of the Federal Bureau of

[28] 53 C.P.R. (2d) 177, rev'd (1981), 56 C.P.R. (3d) 209 (Fed.C.A.).

[29] See Sookman and Tetrault (1990).

Investigation (FBI) in Anchorage and informed of hearing voices in his head directing him to commit acts of violence. He had also reported that his mind was being controlled by the US Government which was making him watch videos by the Islamic State (ISIS) stating that the CIA was forcing him to join ISIS. The authorities had merely advised him to seek medical attention and notified the local police. The matter seemingly was dropped at that.

It is reported that the killer may have had the gun he used to kill during his rampage at Terminal 2 in his checked bag. This was apparently legal, where the regulations of the Transportation Security Administration allows a person within the United States to transport unloaded firearms in a locked hard-sided container as checked baggage only. He must declare the firearm and/or ammunition to the airline when checking his bag at the ticket counter. The container must completely secure the firearm from being accessed. Locked cases that can be easily opened are not permitted. Be aware that the container the firearm was in when purchased may not adequately secure the firearm when it is transported in checked baggage. This is all well and good as this right is protected by the 2nd Amendment to the United States Constitution which allows a person to bear arms.

The problem arises with the special circumstances of the case, where a known nut case, who certainly had a right to carry arms in his checked baggage, was not treated with caution, as a possible threat when he got off the aircraft and claimed his bag amidst the hundreds of passengers at the baggage carousel (this is of course assuming the gun used in the mass killings was the same as the weapon in the luggage). The essential ingredient in aviation security—anticipatory intelligence—seemed not to have worked. If there were a red flag—conveyed to the airport authorities in Fort Lauderdale—directed the authorities not to convey the bag to the assailant in the airport premises.

The fundamental premise of democratic government is that one must allow the government to control the governed, particularly to ensure the protection of the people. John Jay wrote that "[A]mong the many objects to which a wise and free people find it necessary to direct their attention, that of providing for their safety seems to be first". The US Supreme Court handed down in 2008 its decision in the case of *District of Columbia v. Heller*,[30] in which the Supreme Court held that the Second Amendment applied to protect an individual's right to possess firearm for traditionally lawful purposes, such as self-defense within the home. The Patriot Act of 2001 (the full title of which is Uniting and Strengthening America by Providing Appropriate Tools Required to Intercept and Obstruct Terrorism) adopted as a

[30]554.US 570 (2008), This was a seminal case in which the Supreme Court of The United States held in a 5-4 decision that the Second Amendment to the Constitution of The United States applies to federal enclaves and protects an individual's right to possess firearm for traditionally lawful purposes, such as self-defense within the home. The decision did not address the question of whether the Second Amendment extends beyond federal enclaves to the various states of the country which was addressed later by *McDonald* v. *Chicago* (2010). It was the first Supreme Court case to decide whether the Second Amendment protects an individual right to keep and bear arms for self-defense.

response to the attacks of 11 September of that year which covers all aspects of the surveillance of suspected terrorists, those suspected of engaging in computer fraud or abuse, and agents of a foreign power who are engaged in clandestine activities. President Bush in a 2005 speech explained that it is to protect the people and explained that The Patriot Act was essential to ensuring the protection of the American people against terrorists. The Act obviated the wall between law enforcement and intelligence officials so that they could share information and work together to help prevent attacks.

In 2016 under the Obama Administration was enacted Health Insurance Portability and Accountability Act (HIPAA) Privacy Rule and the National Instant Criminal Background Check System (NICS) which identities of individuals who are subject to a Federal "mental health *prohibitor* that disqualifies them from shipping, transporting, possessing, or receiving a firearm. All these seemingly bring to bear a certain lack of coordination and collaboration between all concerned—The FBI, medical authority who conducted (or ought to have conducted) an assessment of the mental state of the assailant.

The other mystery is why there were a couple of hundred people hanging around the tarmac. Who directed them there or ordered them there? Was this because of a particular threat? It has been reported that at least some passengers ran out the skyway and down stairs onto the tarmac, where they were told to drop their carry-on bags and dash out to the runway. They eventually were taken to a hangar and bused to Port Everglades. That's where they spent most of the night. Obviously these steps were taken out of necessity. It is noteworthy that there are specific measures recommended by the International Civil Aviation Organization: Annex 14 to the Chicago Convention in Chapter 9 carries provisions regarding emergency procedures. Also The Airport Services Manual, Part 7 as well as The Airport Emergency Planning have useful measures contained therein. Other documents are The Safety Management Manual on Emergency Response Planning. There is no doubt that Fort Lauderdale Airport was aware of these provisions and used them well.

To sum up, it seems advisable for those charged with ensuring security at airports to be provided with full information of potential offenders whether it concerns outgoing or incoming passengers or staff. It must be remembered that airports and airlines are intertwined and should improve their coordination and cooperation. With regard to damage caused to passengers, under international treaty (which will be discussed in the next chapter) the airline with whom the passenger has concluded the contract of carriage is liable for death or injury caused. However, in instances where airport services are involved the airport may be jointly or severally liable by the adjudicating court if the court finds that the airport was in the position of an agent of the airline.

3.4 Artificial Intelligence and the Flight Deck

At the time of writing, there was a report of an experiment called ALIAS (Aircrew Labor In-Cockpit Automation System) which was essentially a robot with spindly metal tubes and rods for arms and legs and a claw hand grasping the throttle, doing the flying. In the left seat, a human pilot tapped commands to his mute colleague using an electronic tablet.[31] The idea behind the experiment was to see how the robot could augment the human pilot by taking over a lot of the workload, thus freeing the human pilot—especially in emergencies and demanding situations—to think strategically. The super genius co-pilot concept and the reasons behind it are seemingly sensible and practical. However, if this concept or idea attains fruition, authorities would have to take all possible contingencies into account, such as the sudden death of the human pilot that would render the robot in command. Although the robot would surpass any human on the cockpit in terms of facts, data and trillions of algorithms,[32] air law is mostly based on ramifications and liabilities arising out of human actions and human conduct in response to contingencies and emergencies, and for instance a multi system failure which would require human expertise based on experience may not be an ideal; problem solving scenario for the robot.[33] The legal problems would arise when death or injury is caused to passengers and crew on board as a result of robotic malfunction where the defendant airline would be faced with having problems with its insurer (who ultimately pays) for problems arising out of the design and/or manufacture of the robot. The legal and insurance aspects of this particular issue will be discussed in some detail in the next chapter but suffice it to say that the various issues would be complex, requiring a carefully thought through consideration.

In October 2015 the pilot in command, aged 57, died while piloting American Airlines flight AA550 from Phoenix to Boston and the co-pilot landed the aircraft safely.[34] In 2009 on board a Continental Airlines flight the 60-year-old captain had died of a suspected heart attack and two co-pilots took over the controls. The 247 passengers aboard did not learn what had happened until the flight from

---

[31] Lowry (2016).

[32] An plethora of cameras enables the robot to see all the cockpit instruments and read the gauges in a phenomenally short time—a feat that cannot be matched by a human. It can recognize whether switches are in the on or off position, and can flip them to the desired position. And it learns not only from its experience flying the plane, but also from the entire history of flight in that type of plane.

[33] A commentator says: "an engine on a jumbo-sized Qantas airliner with 450 people on board blew up, firing shrapnel that damaged multiple other critical aircraft systems and the plane's landing gear. The plane's overloaded flight management system responded with a cascading series of emergency messages for which there was no time to respond. By chance, there were five experienced pilots on board—including three captains—who, working together, were able to land the plane. But it was a close call". See Lowry (2016).

[34] Botelho and Burn (2011).

Brussels landed safely and was met by fire trucks, emergency vehicles and dozens of reporters.

These are just two instances recorded and, although deaths of pilots in command are rare, nonetheless they have occurred several times, leaving the possibility open in the context of the use of artificial intelligence in the cockpit in the form of a first officer or support resource for the pilot in command. Another area of concern is pilot suicide—where the pilot deliberately crashes or attempts to crash an aircraft as a way to kill himself and sometimes passengers on board or people on the ground. Another instance was in 1982 on Japan Airlines Flight 350 where 35-year-old Captain Seiji Katagiri deliberately crashed his plane. It transpired later that the pilot had a history of mental illness, including indications of possible psychosis or sociopathy, The co-pilot and flight engineer fought captain Katagiri and regained control of the aircraft but failed in their attempt. Ultimately, the plane crashed into Tokyo Bay, killing 24 of the plane's 166 occupants. The Silk Air Flight 181 was another instance of pilot suicide where on December 19, 1997, flying in good, clear weather, the plane gently cruised 11,000 meters (35,000 ft) above Indonesia *en route* to Singapore Changi Airport. Then, without warning, the plane nosedived at supersonic speeds. When it hit the Musi River in the Indonesian city of Palembang, all 104 people onboard died instantly. The aircraft was new and did not show signs of any safety concerns.

The issue boils down to emotional intelligence and human experience of past contingencies which a robot's algorithms may not be able to cope with. Passenger deaths have also occurred on board where a programmed computer in command may not be able to handle. It was reported in January 2017 by a female cabin attendant who had noticed during flight an old female passenger silently weeping. When the cabin attendant asked the passenger if everything was alright the latter had said: "*my husband... he is gone*". In the next seat was her 70-year-old husband who had gently passed away. The cabin attendant placed the corpse in a resting position in his seat and placed a blanket over him which reached up to his neck. To all purposes he looked as though he were asleep. The attendant had then brought the grieving female passenger a hot cup of tea who then had held her hand and related to her endearing memories of the life she had spent with her husband. The cabin attendant had patiently listened.

Many (if not all) commercial airlines have practices that require their technical and cabin crews to treat medical emergencies and death on board with utmost care and afford every dignity to the passenger and his travelling companions in the event of a medical emergency or death. In January 2016 the International Air Transport Association (IATA)—which is the international association of airlines—issued rules where cabin crew should be trained to perform cardiopulmonary resuscitation (CPR) and should continue CPR until one of the following occurs: spontaneous breathing and circulation resume; or it becomes unsafe to continue CPR (e.g.in the event of heavy turbulence and/or forecasted difficult landing after liaising with the flight deck); or all rescuers are too exhausted to continue; or the aircraft has landed and care is transferred to emergency medical services; or the person is presumed dead. The rules add that if CPR has been continued for 30 min or longer with no signs of life within this period, and no shocks advised by an on board Automated External Defibrillator (AED), the person may be presumed dead, and resuscitation ceased. IATA adds that airlines may choose to specify additional criteria, depending upon the availability of ground to air medical support or an on board physician.

IATA also has a protocol for caring for passengers post mortem which requires the crew to advise the captain immediately as he/she will have to advise the destination airport using company protocol to make sure the proper authority meets the flight. Next, the crew has to move the corpse to a seat—if available, one with few other passengers nearby. If the aircraft is full, the corpse would have to be put back into his/her own seat, or at the crew's discretion, into another area not obstructing an aisle or exit, all this with the utmost care, diligence and gentleness required to honor the dead and consideration for companions and others. The corpse should be put in a body bag if such is available in the aircraft with the bag zipped up to the neck and restrained with a seat belt or other equipment.

Travelling companions of the dead passenger should be requested for any useful information. On arrival, passengers other than then dead passenger's relatives and/or companions should be disembarked first. The relatives and companions should stay with the body until ground staff arrive to render assistance. if a communicable disease is suspected, the applicable IATA communicable disease guidelines and Universal Precaution Kit (UPK) to handle the body should be followed.

Death on board an aircraft is sudden, instantaneous and without warning. One report says: "this type of loss can generate intense grief responses such as shock, anger, guilt, sudden depression, despair and hopelessness". All this, 30,000 ft up in the air, often in darkness and amidst loneliness, far away from loved ones, with only the air crew to comfort the aggrieved. Emotional intelligence would definitely be a sine qua non in such instances.

The final issue is the possible interaction between an unruly passenger and a robot controlling the aircraft.

An unruly passenger is both an ambivalent and an amorphous person, poorly defined by both ICAO and IATA which would leave a resolution of whether a person is unruly on board difficult for even a human to figure out. At the 39th Session of the ICAO Assembly in 2016, unruly passengers have been defined by some ICAO member States as:

> [P]assengers who behave in an undisciplined, unruly, or disruptive manner affect air services with their harmful acts of insubordinate behaviour on board aircraft. They pose a threat to on-board safety and disrupt operations, and their behaviour entails significant costs for airlines and airport operators. In order to deter such behaviour, Colombia decided to strengthen its framework of sanctions and impose administrative sanctions on disruptive passengers, thereby helping to protect operational safety, airport safety, and the sustainable development of air transport.[35]

[35]Sanctions for Unruly Passengers, A39-WP/2931 LE/12 5/8/16 WORKING PAPER, ASSEMBLY—39TH SESSION.

Annex 17 to the Chicago defines a disruptive passenger as: "[A] passenger who fails to respect the rules of conduct at an airport or on board an aircraft or to follow the instructions of the airport staff or crew members and thereby disturbs the good order and discipline at an airport or on board the aircraft." ICAO's Legal Commission described unruly passengers as:

> passengers who fail to respect the rules of conduct on board aircraft or to follow the instructions of crew members and thereby disturb the good order and discipline on board aircraft. In recent years, there has been an increase in the reported incidents involving such passengers.[36]

IATA defines an unruly passenger as "someone who, by action or stated intent, jeopardizes or might jeopardize the safety of the aircraft, persons or property therein or the accepted level of good order and discipline on board".[37] IATA has developed and promulgated a "non-exhaustive" list of examples of what is considered unruly or disruptive behavior whilst on board an aircraft. This list includes: illegal consumption of narcotics; refusal to comply with safety instructions (not following Cabin Crew requests such as direction to fasten a seat belt, to not smoke, to turn off a portable electronic device or by disrupting the safety announcements); verbal confrontation with crew members or other passengers; physical confrontation with crew members or other passengers; uncooperative passenger (examples include interfering with the crew's duties, refusing to follow instructions to board or leave the aircraft); making threats of any kind towards the crew, other passengers or the aircraft; sexual abuse/harassment; other type of riotous behavior (examples include: screaming, annoying behavior, kicking and banging heads on seat backs or tray tables).

Potentially unruly passengers can be identified through past records and data interchange. UN Security Council, in Resolution 2178 (2014), at paragraph 9, has called upon Member States "to require that airlines operating in their territories provide advance passenger information to the appropriate national authorities in order to detect the departure from their territories, or attempted entry into or transit through their territories, by means of civil aircraft, of individuals designated by the Committee established pursuant to resolutions 1267 (1999) and 1989 (2011) ("the Committee"), and further calls upon Member States to report any such departure from their territories, or such attempted entry into or transit through their territories, of such individuals to the Committee, as well as sharing this information with the

---

[36]Guidance Material on the Legal Aspects of Unruly/Disruptive Passengers, Cir 288, LE/1, June 2002, at 1. According to a survey conducted IATA to which 62 airlines responded, representing approximately 23% of the IATA member airlines worldwide, in 2001 there were 1132 reported cases of unruly passengers in 1994, 2036 cases in 1995, 3512 cases in 1996 and 5416 cases in 1997. In 2000, ICAO conducted a survey through a questionnaire, to which 62 Contracting States replied, representing some 80% of the total number of passengers carried worldwide in 1999 on scheduled services by the airlines of ICAO Contracting States. While many States have not yet established a reporting system, approximately 67% of the States replying to the questionnaire indicated that in recent years they had experienced an increase in the number of unruly passengers.

[37]Guidance on Unruly Passenger Prevention and Management Ist Edition: 2012, at 9.

State or residence or nationality, as appropriate and in accordance with domestic law and international obligations ICAO Resolution A39-20 (Consolidated statement of continuing ICAO policies related to facilitation), in its Appendix D urges States inter alia to call upon aircraft operators offering international air transport services to participate in electronic data interchange systems by providing advance passenger information in order to achieve maximum efficiency levels in the processing of passenger traffic at international terminals; and in the use of electronic data interchange systems, to ensure that the passenger data requirements conform to international standards adopted by relevant United Nations agencies for this purpose, and to ensure the security, fair processing and safeguarding of such data; and to assist and share best practices, as appropriate, with other Member States in the establishment of passenger data exchange systems.

It would be interesting to see how the element of "discretion" could be infused into a robotic programme that would enable a robotic first officer who has to take control of an aircraft in the unfortunate absence of the pilot in command, to determine what an uncooperative passenger would be, or what would constitute "verbal confrontation with crew members or other passengers".

In view of the above discussion, it is indeed difficult at the present time (in 2017) to envision a robot pilot. However, the concept of artificial intelligence as an analytics tool (such as IBM's Watson)[38] may greatly help in the flight deck providing instantaneous analysis to the flight crew.

References

Bennett C, Crowe L (2005) Location-based services and the surveillance of mobility: an analysis of privacy risks in Canada. June. http://www.colinbennett.ca/wp-content/uploads/2012/06/OPCREPORTFINAL.pdf

Botelho G, Burn P (2011) Pilot Michael Johnston dies during American Airlines flight. CNN. http://www.cnn.com/2015/10/05/us/american-airlines-pilot-death/

Lowry J (2016) That pilot in the cockpit may someday be a robot. 18 October 2016. https://phys.org/news/2016-10-cockpit-robot.html#jCp

Sookman BB, Tetrault M (1990.) Liability of geographic information systems provider in Contract and Tort. The Ontario Land Surveyor. http://krcmar.ca/sites/default/files/1990_Spring_Liability%20of%20Geographic%20Information%20Systems_1.pdf

[38]Watson is a cognitive technology that processes information much more like a smart human than a smart computer. Unlike typical computers, Watson can unlock the vast world of unstructured data that makes up as much as 80% of existing information. See *supra*, note 71 in Chap. 1.

Chapter 4
Effect of Megatrends on Airports

4.1 Congestion

A fundamental limb of enterprise governance, which is based on principles and processes of an enterprise that is calculated to move the enterprise toward a strategic direction, is predictive or anticipatory intelligence which could effectively preclude business disruption. A report released by *Booz, Allen, Hamilton* in August 2014 states: "[P]redictive intelligence combines tradecraft, big data and analytics, technology and workforce to help clients, anticipate, detect, prevent and respond to global threats and global opportunities with real time actionable insight about their environment – internally, externally, globally and socially – so that they can take action to be ready, to manage risks, to protect assets, and to thrive".[1] The necessity for corporate foresight stems from the continuing and rapid development of science and technology which are the drivers of social and economic change. Using these two knowledge-based and fact intensive fields, airports would be able to obtain a clear picture of challenges and opportunities confronting them. Airports are a complex, big business and their business environment is highly dynamic. Therefore, they need proactive measures to respond to the uncertainties of their business as well as a long term orientation to remain stable amidst imponderables. Airports need think tanks to mesh their technology trends and market trends to meet a growing demand for air travel. Foremost in this process is a far reaching and forward looking communications strategy as well as a good team of scientific and economic forecasters.

Predictive intelligence, or anticipatory intelligence is an essential factor in minimizing or eliminating the adverse effects of risks that threaten airports.

The first step to corporate foresight is to know what the future is going to be like by adopting a foresight-awareness culture. There are two aspects to the issue of

[1]https://www.boozallen.com/content/dam/boozallen/documents/2014/11/Predictive-Intelligence-Overview.pdf.

R. Abeyratne, *Megatrends and Air Transport*, DOI 10.1007/978-3-319-61124-2_4

preparedness for disruption to business at airports. The first is airport responsibility and the second is the need for corporate foresight. As regards corporate foresight, an airport has to start with a culture of corporate foresight. Emergency management is a dynamic process. Planning, though critical, is not the only component. Training, conducting drills, testing equipment and coordinating activities with the community are other important functions. More importantly, airports should work jointly, and in partnership with airlines and air navigation service providers in furthering their corporate foresight.

4.1.1 The American Example

The media reported on 8 August 2016 that at least 451 of Delta Airlines flights were stranded around the world, cancelled for nearly 6 h and nearly half a million passengers were facing delays on Delta Airlines flights due to what a spokesman for the airline called "a major systems collapse worldwide affecting passengers trying to check-in/board."[2] The disruptions came at an inopportune time when Delta Airlines was riding high with a sustained reputation of on time departures and a good chance of attracting more corporate and leisure customers. Worse still, Delta joined the band of carriers, including rivals Southwest Airlines Co and American Airlines Group Inc., that have suffered flight disruptions during the past year due to data system malfunctions.[3]

At the end of a 6-h delay, only some of the Delta Airlines flights had resumed. This occurrence, not being an act of God or weather related, carried with it implications of liability for Delta Airlines, both globally and regionally in Europe. From a global perspective, Delta Airlines, which is an American carrier (and member airline of SkyTeam[4]) comes under the Montreal Convention of 1999[5] which The United States has ratified, and which provides that the carrier is liable for damage occasioned by delay in the carriage by air of passengers, baggage or cargo. The carrier is exonerated and is devoid of liability for damage occasioned by delay if it proves that it and its servants and agents took all measures that could reasonably be required to avoid the damage or that it was impossible for it or them to take such measures.[6] In the case of damage caused by delay in the carriage of

[2]Delta computer system completely down. Flight operation at stillstand, *eTN Global Travel Industry News*, http://www.eturbonews.com/73542/delta-computer-system-completely-down-flight-operation-stillstan.

[3]See Dastin (2016).

[4]*SkyTeam* is an alliance of 20 member airlines which give its customers access to 1062 destinations worldwide.

[5]Convention for the Unification of Certain Rules for International Carriage by Air—Montreal, 28 May 1999.

[6]*Id.* Article 19.

persons, the liability of the carrier for each passenger is limited to 4150 Special Drawing Rights.[7]

4.1.2 The European Example

Regionally in the context of Europe, while the aforementioned treaty provision would apply for the airline with States in Europe it flew into which had also ratified the Montreal Convention, Regulation 261/2004[8] elaborates on Article 19 of the Montreal Convention and states at the outset in its Article 1 that the Regulation accords minimum rights to passengers when: they are denied boarding against their will; their flight is cancelled; or their flight is delayed. The Regulation applies to passengers departing from an airport located in the territory of a Member State to which the Treaty which establishes the European Community applies; and to passengers departing from an airport located in a third country to an airport situated in the territory of a Member State to which the Treaty applies, unless they received benefits or compensation and were given assistance in that third country, if the operating air carrier of the flight concerned is a Community carrier.

A pile up of passengers in an airport, whether it be due to a computer crash of the airlines serving that airport or the airport's inability to provide the facilities needed to move passengers in and out of that airport, brings to bear liability issues of the airport in responding to legal questions that might arise based on whether the airport was in breach of a duty of care to the passenger.

The Guardian of 17 December 2010 reported that heavy snow and ice threatened severe travel disruptions both in air transport and road transport in Britain, urging authorities to prepare for the upcoming chaos. *The Guardian* further reported that Gatwick Airport was monitoring the situation and if the snowfall was too severe, the runway would be closed.[9] On 19 December *The Guardian* reported: "Britain remained paralysed by snow today, with airport schedules heavily disrupted, trains delayed and roads coated in black ice as the government said it would ask its chief scientific adviser whether the country was experiencing a 'step change' in weather patterns. Heathrow said it would not be letting any flights land on its runway, with

---

[7] *Id.* Article 22. A Special Drawing Right (SDR) is a form of international money, created by the International Monetary Fund, and defined as a weighted average of various convertible currencies.

[8] The Regulation establishes, under the conditions specified therein, minimum rights for passengers when: they are denied boarding against their will; their flight is cancelled; or their flight is delayed. *REGULATION (EC) No 261/2004 OF THE EUROPEAN PARLIAMENT AND OF THE COUNCIL of 11 February 2004 establishing common rules on compensation and assistance to passengers in the event of denied boarding and of cancellation or long delay of flights, and repealing Regulation (EEC) No 295/91*. For a substantial discussion on Regulation 261/2004 see Verheyen (2015), pp. 659–677.

[9] Siddique and Milmo (2010).

only a 'handful' of departures taking place, piling on the misery for hundreds of stranded people who were forced to spend the night in terminals".[10]

From 17 December 2010 for a week or so, heavy snow and ice pounded Europe, grounding air travel across the continent and leaving thousands of passengers stranded as airports struggled to clear a backlog of flights cancelled or delayed by snowfalls. London's Heathrow, one of the world's busiest international airports, operated a limited schedule as one of its two runways was open and advised passengers not to travel to the airport unless their flight is confirmed. According to airport operator British Airports Authority (BAA) airlines worked to move aircraft and crew back to their normal positions as severe winter weather continued to cause disruption.

Airport operations are systemic and Heathrow's despair had a knock on effect on other European airports. Frankfurt airport, Germany's biggest, was clear of snow and ice but officials cancelled about 300 of 1340 flights because of problems elsewhere in Europe. During the period of crisis, French civil aviation authorities requested airlines to reduce their flights at the two main Paris airports by 30%. Thousands of travellers were stranded after about 400 flights in and out of Roissy-Charles de Gaulle were scrapped, with some 30,000 travellers' plans disrupted by the cancellations and delays. Throughout Europe hundreds of holiday flights were cancelled, as freezing rain and widespread snowfalls caused travel chaos. Repeated snowfalls stranded travellers in Ireland and Denmark and shut Dusseldorf airport in Germany for hours. Elsewhere, in the Netherlands and Spain the same problem ensued with numerous flights cancelled and passengers stranded. EUROCONTROL, Europe's air traffic supervisory body which supports its member States to achieve safe, efficient and environmentally-friendly air traffic operations across the whole of the European region, reported that approximately 3000 flights had been cancelled across Europe in a single day on 21 December.

4.1.3 The Vumbaca *Case*

In late December 2010, at John F. Kennedy International Airport, a severe snowfall effectively crippled equipment at Terminal One, which necessitated passengers on an Alitalia flight coming in from Rome to stay in the aircraft for 7 h with no food or drink as the aerobridge could not be connected to the aircraft. In the case of *Vumbaca* v. *Terminal One Group Association L.P*[11] decided in April 2012 by the United States District Court, E.D. New York. Vivian Vumbaca—the Plaintiff—an Italian citizen who was a permanent resident of the United States who arrived in New York during the snow storm of 26–27 December 2010 from Rome on the said Alitalia flight, alleged that she was kept locked in an aircraft on the ground without

[10]Davies (2010).

[11]859 F. Supp. 2d 343.

food, water, or adequate sanitary facilities for 7 h, suffering mental distress. She sued Terminal One Group Association, L.P. (TOGA), which operates Terminal One, and sought to represent similarly situated passengers claiming emotional harms resulting from negligence, false imprisonment, and intentional infliction of emotional distress under her contract of carriage on the ground that Terminal One Group Association did not afford her the facility of disembarking at her destination and kept her on board the aircraft for 7 h causing her mental distress.

What is important is to determine whether the court considered whether the defendant airport had used predictive intelligence as a basis to exculpate itself at law from possible liability. The Court *in limine* noted the contractual obligation of the defendant (Terminal One) under its lease obligations with the owner and operator of JFK, the Port Authority of New York and New Jersey (Port Authority), Terminal One "agree[d] to provide service at the premises for the benefit of the traveling public." It assumed "the entire responsibility for ... all repair, ... and maintenance whatsoever in the premises, whether such repair ... or maintenance be ordinary or extraordinary, [including] ... *remov[ing] all snow and ice* and perform[ing] all other activities and functions necessary or proper to make the premises ready for use".[12] The defendant had further agreed to "furnish all necessary or proper personnel, ... and facilities [and] ... furnish such services promptly, efficiently, and adequately to meet the demands therefor.".[13]

4.1.3.1 Terminal One

Terminal One had a snow plan which primarily allocated responsibility to various actors in the ground handling process and detailed the various procedures for clearing snow from terminal areas. The fundamental premise of the plan was that in the contingency of snow on the tarmac it would be necessary to coordinate with carrier maintenance representatives to move aircraft back from the gates with a view to facilitating the clearance process. The ground handling agent was expected to be aware of the possibility of a snowfall at that time of the year and have qualified push-back personnel available for immediate deployment. There were two elements that were critical to the efficient implementation of the plan that related to anticipatory or predictive intelligence in this context: close cooperation and information sharing without hindrance; and the freezing of leave of critical staff of the contractor or extension of their shifts to ensure fluid and safe operation of equipment to facilitate the unhindered movement of passengers from aircraft to the terminal. The court noted that, according to the contract the defendant had with the ground handling agent, the ground handling agent was not required under the snow plan to "freeze" its staffing during a snow event.

[12] *Id.*, at 354.

[13] *Ibid.*

According to the facts revealed at the hearing, the Port Authority, in view of g the severity of the oncoming storm and its potential impact on airport operations, declared on December 23, 2010, a snow emergency. The Port Authority brought in extra employees to prepare for this emergency and placed them in an airport hotel to ensure adequate staffing. The defendant, on 25 December, proceeded to advise air carriers which used Terminal One that all resources—both staff and equipment were prepared and ready for any exigency of a snowstorm. On 26 December, at 10.18 in the morning, snow started to fall. The airport was closed at 7:17 p.m. that evening.

The defendant's records (called the daily shift report) reflected that all flights which touched down at JFK airport on that day were requested to either consolidate flights, delay flights, or cancel them altogether that day. Nine incoming international flights to Terminal One were cancelled by airlines on December 26, 2010. The storm abated on December 27th at approximately 8:00 a.m. leaving over fifteen inches of snow on the ground. The airport reopened at 6:07 p.m. that day. At that time, all the gates at Terminal One were still occupied with aircraft that had been prepared for departure when the airport closed the previous night.

The court noted that the ground handling agent had sufficient staff at Terminal One on the morning shift of December 26th. While some employees stayed past the end of their shift, most had gone home. Presumably due to the difficulties caused to New York by the snowstorm, staff from subsequent shifts did not arrive.

The paucity of ground staff resulted in both departing and arriving aircraft experiencing delays in moving to and from the gates, resulting in the blocking of gates from between 24 h and 3 days, where aircraft could not be moved to fully clear the snow on the tarmac. Consequently, staff that were on duty were not sufficient enough to even accommodate us moving an aircraft off the gate in order for snow removal to be done.

The ground handling agent had in place mobile stairs and buses available to help disembark aircraft passengers at a remote location away from the terminal. However, this equipment could not be used because of uncleaned snow, ramp conditions, and a lack of staff to operate equipment.

According to the snow plan, the defendant usually contacts the local station managers of the airlines it services rather than to contact the headquarters of those airlines. However, local station managers do not have the authority to cancel flights that begin abroad. Accordingly, the defendants had made calls to the local station managers, advising the conditions that the terminal was in, the progress of the snow removal process, the staffing situation with the ground handler that the defendant was experiencing and the fact that there were no gates available for inbound flights, and to cancel flights.

The main problem appears to have been the inadequacy of ground staff which resulted in delays to aircraft in arriving at the gates as well as the dispatch of passengers from the aircraft to the gates. The court noted that between the afternoon of December 28th and the morning of December 29th, there were at least sixteen flights arriving at Terminal One with tarmac delays in excess of 4 h.

4.1.3.2 The Court's Findings

Although the main cause of action of the plaintiff, for delay in her carriage by air would have been against the carrier Alitalia, under the Montreal Convention of 1999,[14] the court held that Terminal One was an agent of the air carriers it serves[15] and thus covered by the Convention. The rationale for this reasoning was that, although Terminal One is not an international carrier but just a terminal operator, its operations are vital parts of carriage performed by the carrier—particularly those services that are necessary to get planes to and from the gates.

In the context of negligence of the airport, which could have been vitiated by adequate preventive intelligence exercised by the airport The court used a dictum in *Havas v. Victory Paper Stock Co.,*[16]: "[w]henever one person is by circumstances placed in such a position with regard to another that every one of ordinary sense who did think would at once recognize that if he did not use ordinary care and skill in his own conduct with regard to the circumstances he would cause danger of injury to the person or property of the other, a duty arises to use ordinary care and skill to avoid such danger".[17] Accordingly, the court held that the airport had a common law duty to ensure that passengers on arriving flights had safe and prompt access to the terminal on the basis that the airport is a necessary link in the chain of transportation, facilitating the conclusion of the contract of carriage that the carrier has with the passenger.

Going back to the computer problems faced by Delta Airlines in August 2016 as well as the problems faced by European airports in December 2010, the *Vumbaca* decision clearly established a link between the airline and the airport, thus making the airport liable for damage with regard to delays if airports are not properly equipped to handle passengers and, more importantly, if they do not have preconceived strategy or if they do not exercise predictive intelligence. The *Vumbaca* court opined: "The defendant's duty to passengers extends beyond merely ensuring that stairs are not slippery, or that gates are properly maintained. It must ensure that those stairs and gates are made available in a timely manner when needed for use by the passengers, and that adequate ground handling staff is present to facilitate access. TOGA (Terminal One) should have foreseen that a breach of this duty would cause passengers to remain trapped on their aircraft in cramped and increasingly unpleasant or dangerous conditions. Imposing on

[14]Article 19 of the Montreal Convention of 1999 provides that the carrier is liable for *damage occasioned by delay in the carriage by air of passengers, baggage* or cargo. Nevertheless, the carrier is not liable for damage occasioned by delay if it proves that it and its servants and agents took all measures that could reasonably be required to avoid the damage or that it was impossible for it or them to take such measures.

[15]Article 30 of the Montreal Convention stipulates that if an action is brought against a servant or agent of the carrier arising out of damage to which the Convention relates, such servant or agent, if they prove that they acted within the scope of their employment, shall be entitled to avail themselves of the conditions and limits of liability which the carrier itself is entitled to invoke.

[16]402 N.E.2d 1136 (1980).

[17]*Id.* 1138.

defendant this duty is neither novel nor undesirable as a matter of public policy".[18] Therefore, the court was of the view that if the plaintiff's injuries were recoverable under New York law, there would be a triable issue as to whether the defendant terminal: unreasonably failed to provide an adequate method of moving aircraft to and from the gates; or should have taken appropriate, available additional steps to prevent the arrival of additional aircraft at Terminal One once it became aware that those planes would not be able to access a gate in a timely manner.

It is submitted that airport liability in the context of cases and instances discussed in this article bring to bear the compelling importance for airports to practice prudent risk management, on the basis that airports should have a strategic direction where their predictive intelligence drives them toward either avoiding the risk involved; managing or minimizing the risk or shifting the risk on to another by strategizing and prioritizing.

4.1.4 Airports and Risk Management

A situation where massive delays at airports, whether they be caused by computer outages or natural disasters that preclude carriers from leaving on schedule could not only cause acute congestion in the terminal building but also may result in frustrated and irate passengers being unruly, causing injury and damage to persons and property. The courts, in a 1990 case held that if a policy included airport liability coverage it invariably would cover injury to passengers occurring in the airport's premises.[19] In *Mauriello v. Port Authority of N.Y. & N.J.*,[20]—a case where a passenger suffered injury as a result of tripping over a metal track just after picking up his bag from the baggage carousel on arrival, the court held that the terminal operator had a duty to safeguard passengers against the foreseeable risks created by its "concentration of allegedly unruly travelers around a congested baggage carousel". *Stagl* v. *Delta Airlines*[21] illustrated this danger well. After her arrival at the Delta Airlines Terminal, the defendant Ms. Stagl, who described the area near the baggage carousel as full of unruly fellow passengers, made her way to the "front rank" of the throng surrounding the baggage carousel with a view to retrieving her bag. She claimed that an unidentified man to one side of her reached across the conveyor belt, grabbed his satchel with great force, and unwittingly triggered a domino effect. His bag collided with another's suitcase, which, in turn, fell off the carousel",[22] toppling Mrs. Stagl, as a result of which Ms. Stagl sustained a broken hip.

---

[18]*Supra*, note 11 in this chapter at 372.

[19]*National Aviation Underwriters* v. *Augusta Aviation Corporation*, 1990 US Dist LEXIS 19768.

[20]779 N.Y.S.2d 199, 200-01 (1st Dep't 2004).

[21]52 F.3d 463 (1995).

[22]*Id.* 466.

The court was of the view that Delta Airlines, the owner and occupier of the terminal—owed a duty to take reasonable steps in maintaining the safety of its baggage retrieval area. Quoting an earlier decision[23] which held that "a landowner must act as a reasonable [person] in maintaining his property in a reasonably safe condition in view of all the circumstances, including the likelihood of injury to others, the seriousness of the injury, and the burden of avoiding the risk.",[24] the court in *Stagl* held that the duty was a broad one, which included the legal duty and obligation to take reasonable precautions to protect patrons from dangers which are foreseeable from the arrangement or use of the property.

A most useful tool that demonstrates predictive intelligence is risk management, which is primarily driven by the procurement of insurance. Airport insurance can be obtained in three headings—airport premises liability; product liability; and hangar keepers liability. Airport premises liability covers *inter alia* injury suffered by persons in the terminal building including any injury sustained as a result of the consumption of food or beverages at the airport's premises, irrespective of whether such premises were leased under concession. The policy may even cover areas adjacent to an airport which is under the control of the airport. In the 1991 case of *Dinocenzo* v. *Aitken*[25] the court held that if the premises policy covered any other area under the airport's aerial insurance policy, any injury incurred by a person within such premises would be covered for compensation under the policy.

Other essential elements in risk management are found in the principles of corporate governance. In addition to predictive or anticipatory intelligence, other aspects of corporate foresight hinge on the early identification of markets and technologies. However, it takes a long time to restructure a corresponding system along the lines of market forecasts and the development of technology, building competence to a level that would correspond to effective risk management. One commentator identifies a period of 10 years as preparatory for effective corporative foresight to be built.[26] Leadership is a critical feature in foresight which is linked inextricably to the quality of being reasonably prepared for a contingency that would occur based on reason and experience and not being surprised at any unexpected event or circumstance. This process will be usually driven by trade facts and knowledge and is the prompt identification of developments in the areas of science, technology and society that are likely to ensure future benefits both from a business and social perspective. Foresight has been categorized as (a) *predictive* or *anticipatory intelligence*, *i.e.* evaluation of factors that are calculated to lead to a probable event and providing background information and an early warning of recent developments; (b) *direction-setting*, *i.e.* establishing broad guidelines for the corporate strategy; (c) *determining priorities*, *i.e.* identifying the most desirable lines of R & D as a direct input into specific (funding) decisions; (d) *strategy formulation*, *i.e.* participating in the formulation and implementation of strategic

[23] *Basso v. Miller*, 40 N.Y. 2d. 233.

[24] *Id.* 243.

[25] 827 P.2d 478.

[26] Becker (2002), p. 8.

decisions; and (e) *innovation catalysing*, *i.e.* stimulating and supporting innovation processes between the different partners.

From an airport perspective, *predictive/anticipatory intelligence* should be extended to the various disaster scenarios that could be: (a) inability to accommodate flights due to frozen runways; (b) straining of infrastructure in accommodating a passenger influx greater than the airport could handle at any given time; (c) a possible security threat that would slow down traffic and clog the system; and (d) adverse weather systems (such as storms) that could halt ground handling systems. In this context, most problems that an airport could face are weather related. In *direction setting* the airport management should have a corporate strategy that would also be an adequate contingency plan. Such a plan should include adequate staff training for contingencies; providing back-up support staff who have pre-organized schedules for exigencies and adequately compensating staff who have to cope with a stressful situation and irate customers. The most important factor in such situations is an effective method of communicating with everyone and providing extra services. A major factor in *determining priorities*, is the assurance at all times, whether good or bad, of an effective and efficient safety and security system at the airport. *Strategy formulation* would include developing a range of alternative routes and timings and alternative means of transport; having adequate and additional accommodation ready to make customers comfortable; having joint plans with airlines for the provision of meals through ground handlers or other caterers at the airport; and ensuring that constant contact be maintained with the Consulates involved, and the local police.

Innovation catalyzing, which is arguably the most creative element of corporate foresight, has two aspects. The first is the need to conceptualize circumstances through best practices and the second is innovative planning. As for best practices, a community of practice of airport professionals would be helpful, an example of which is the IAPCOP (International Airport Professional Community of Practice) where the membership comprises graduates of the AMPAP diploma (Airport Management Professional Accreditation Programme conducted jointly by ICAO and ACI[27]). Through IAPCOP members can exchange best practices and their experiences of risk management and predictive intelligence. As for Planning, the starting point is to look at existing planning documentation. ICAO's *Airport Planning Manual* is geared to provide information and guidance to those responsible for airport planning,[28] where information on a comprehensive list of planning subjects such as sizes and types of projects[29] task identification,[30] preparation of manpower

[27]Airports Council International (ACI) is the only global trade representative of the world's airports. Established in 1991, ACI represents airports interests with Governments and international organizations such as ICAO, develops standards, policies and recommended practices for airports, and provides information and training opportunities to raise standards around the world.

[28]*Airport Planning Manual*, Doc 9184-AN/902, Part 3.

[29]*Id.* 1.3.1–1.3.5.

[30]*Id.* Chapter 2.2.1.

and cost budgets,[31] selection of consultants[32] and standard contract provisions[33] are given. With these guidelines each State can start its planning process. Regrettably, a study conducted on corporate foresight reflects that the transportation sector does not consider innovations as important in corporate foresight.[34] It is all the more reason that, as further action, corporate foresight in the airport industry needs an un-fragmented process of corporate development and strategic planning. An initiative could be taken by ACI to gather a team of forecasters, technical experts and airport planners to develop guidelines for disaster management.

It is incontrovertible that airports have a responsibility to persons adversely affected by cancellation of flights. Irrespective of the responsibility of a State with regard to airports within its territories, which is founded both at customary international law and at private law for liability incurred by airports, a privately run airport may incur tortuous liability on a private basis, as the occupier of the premises. In the instance of a privately managed airport where the entity charged with managing airport services is located within the airport premises, such an entity would be considered as a legal occupier for purposes of liability.[35]

There are three critical factors affecting modern day airport law and regulation. They are foresight; the synergy between airports and airlines; and governance. With regard to foresight, The weather crisis at European airports in the winter of 2010 brought to bear the fundamental reality that airport planners have to be sensitive towards the three broad areas of ecology, safety and infrastructural planning when planning and running an airport. Mr. Siim Kallas, Vice President of the European Commission urged the aviation industry to introduce a set of quality standards to obviate any future disruption to air travel similar to the crippling experience of the last few weeks of December 2010 which caused airlines to cancel 35,000 flights during the crisis.[36]

Mr. Kallas, expressed his views on the winter 2010 crisis at European airports by saying that clearly, contingency planning for snow at airports needed to be improved, and that the European Commission needed to ensure better co-operation between all those involved—in the air and on the ground and also to ensure the proper functioning of the airline hubs. He also stated that there was a need to provide better and more timely information about delays and rerouting. To achieve all this Mr. Kallas suggested that, to achieve all this, minimum service and quality requirements at airports for passengers was needed.[37] The chaos at

[31] *Id.* 2.4.

[32] *Id.* 3.1.

[33] *Id.* Appendix.

[34] Becker (2002), p. 7.

[35] For a discussion on this subject, See Abeyratne (2009), pp. 106–108. Abeyratne (2004), pp. 106–108.

[36] EU Transport Chief Kallas Wants Common Quality Standards, *Aviation Daily*, January 21, 2011 at 2.

[37] http://www.airtransportnews.aero/article.pl?mcateg=&id=27750.

European airports in the winter of 2010, particularly London Heathrow, wrought by pummelling snowstorms and ice, not only was caused by cancelled flights and stranded passengers but also resulted in the tremendous cost involved for the airport authorities. Airports operator BAA has released the figure of 24 million pounds sterling ($38 million) as the cost incurred by the Spanish owned firm which operates six airports in Britain. These costs included reduction in profit as a result of the decrease in passenger numbers by 11% over a few days.

The fundamental questions that arise are, should airports be held responsible for service failure brought about by a natural phenomenon; and should airports have had, what in modern business parlance is called "corporate foresight".[38] Firstly, in terms of responsibility, the question could be raised as to whether; irrespective of the business status of the airport (whether it is privatized, autonomous, commercialized or corporatized) the State in which the airport is situated should bear ultimate responsibility. This responsibility devolves upon the State *in limine* by virtue of Article 28 of the Chicago Convention which stipulates *inter alia* that each Contracting States to the Convention undertakes, so far as it may find practicable to provide, in its territory, airports, radio services, meteorological services and other air navigation facilities to facilitate international air navigation, in accordance with the standards and practices recommended or established from time to time, pursuant to the Convention. The provision also requires such a State to adopt and put into operation the appropriate standard systems of communications procedure, codes, markings, signals, lighting and other operational practices and rules which may be recommended or established from time to time, pursuant to this Convention. Obviously, the Convention, through an inarticulate premise requires in Article 28 that States provide *functional* airport services among other services prescribed in the provision. In his perspective, both the State and the airport should act in conjunction to ensure that adequate foresight and intelligence is applied through effective risk management.

[38]The functions and responsibilities of an airport will vary according to its size, type of traffic and areas of responsibility. For example, some airports are responsible for air traffic control as well as for meteorological services, while at most other airports such services are provided by separate government entities. Many airports are involved in security functions in varying degrees and in providing facilities for customs, immigration and health authorities. Ground-handling services for the airlines, including terminal handling or ramp handling, or both, are provided by some airports, while at others they are provided by the airlines or by specialized agents or companies. Certain airports also perform functions that exceed the scope of conventional airport activities, such as consultancy services, public works, construction, and real estate development. See *Airport Business Law*, *supra*, note 35 in this chapter at 13.

4.2 Communications: The Fort Lauderdale Case

On 6 January 2017 the area proximate to the baggage terminal in Terminal 2 of Fort-Lauderdale Hollywood International Airport was the scene of a mass shooting perpetrated by a mentally deranged passenger who had arrived from Alaska. Five people were killed while six others were injured in the shooting. About 36 people sustained injuries in the ensuing panic. Reportedly the suspect was taken into custody after surrendering to responding police officers. The Federal Aviation Administration issued what is called a "ground stop" notice stopping all but emergency flights. 20,000 pieces of baggage and several hundred passengers were stranded, some of whom (perhaps with employees of the airport) were seen loitering on the tarmac for several hours—a rare sight in commercial aviation.

The killer clearly had a known history of mental disability of a grave nature. In November 2016 he had visited the field office of the Federal Bureau of Investigation (FBI) in Anchorage and informed of hearing voices in his head directing him to commit acts of violence. He had also reported that his mind was being controlled by the US Government which was making him watch videos by the Islamic State (ISIS) stating that the CIA was forcing him to join ISIS. The authorities had merely advised him to seek medical attention and notified the local police. The matter seemingly was dropped at that.

It is reported that the killer may have had the gun he used to kill during his rampage at Terminal 2 in his checked bag. This was apparently legal, where the regulations of the Transportation Security Administration allows a person within the United States to transport unloaded firearms in a locked hard-sided container as checked baggage only. He must declare the firearm and/or ammunition to the airline when checking his bag at the ticket counter. The container must completely secure the firearm from being accessed. Locked cases that can be easily opened are not permitted. Authorities must be aware that the container the firearm was in when purchased may not adequately secure the firearm when it is transported in checked baggage. This is all well and good as this right is protected by the 2nd Amendment to the United States Constitution which allows a person to bear arms.

The problem arises with the special circumstances of the case, where a person with a known history of mental derangement, who although having a legal right to carry arms in his checked baggage, was not treated with caution as a possible threat when he got off the aircraft and claimed his bag amidst the hundreds of passengers at the baggage carousel (this is of course assuming the gun used in the mass killings was the same as the weapon in the luggage). The essential ingredient in aviation security—anticipatory intelligence—seemed not to have worked. Should there have been a red flag where the airport authorities would have been alerted? Or should the airline have taken the precaution of ensuring the safety of passengers on arrival?

The fundamental premise of democratic government is that one must allow the government to control the governed, particularly to ensure the protection of the people. John Jay wrote that "[A]mong the many objects to which a wise and free people find it necessary to direct their attention, that of providing for their safety seems to be first".[39] The US Supreme Court handed down in 2008 its decision in the case of *District of Columbia v. Heller*,[40] in which the Supreme Court held that the Second Amendment applied to protect an individual's right to possess firearm for traditionally lawful purposes, such as self-defense within the home. The Patriot Act of 2001 (the full title of which is Uniting and Strengthening America by Providing Appropriate Tools Required to Intercept and Obstruct Terrorism)[41] adopted as a response to the attacks of 11 September of that year which covers all aspects of the surveillance of suspected terrorists, those suspected of engaging in computer fraud or abuse, and agents of a foreign power who are engaged in clandestine activities. President Bush in a 2005 speech explained that it is to protect the people and explained that The Patriot Act was essential to ensuring the protection of the American people against terrorists. The Act obviated the wall between law enforcement and intelligence officials so that they could share information and work together to help prevent attacks.

The Health Insurance Portability and Accountability Act (HIPAA) Privacy Rule and the National Instant Criminal Background Check System (NICS) was enacted under the administration of the Clinton Presidency in 1996 which regulates the use and disclosure of protected health information held by "covered entities" (generally, health care clearinghouses, employer sponsored health plans, health insurers, and medical service providers that engage in certain transactions.[42] In 2016 under the Obama Administration was enacted Health Insurance Portability and Accountability Act (HIPAA) Privacy Rule and the National Instant Criminal Background Check System (NICS) which identities of individuals who are subject to a Federal "mental health *prohibitor* that disqualifies them from shipping, transporting, possessing, or receiving a firearm".[43] All these precautions, and their blatant lack of application in this instance seemingly bring to bear a certain lack of coordination and collaboration between all concerned—The FBI; the medical authority who conducted (or ought to have conducted) an assessment of the mental state of the assailant; the airline; and the airport.

The other mystery is why there were a couple of hundred people hanging around the tarmac. Who directed them there or ordered them there? Was this because of a particular threat? It has been reported that at least some passengers ran out the skyway and down stairs onto the tarmac, where they were told to drop their carry-on bags and dash out to the runway. They eventually were taken to a hangar and bused to Port Everglades. That's where they spent most of the night. Obviously these steps were taken out of necessity. It is noteworthy that there are specific measures

---

[39]Pestritto and West (2007), p. 253.

[40]554 U.S. 570 (2008).

[41]H.R. 3162, United States Government Publishing Office, https://www.gpo.gov/fdsys/pkg/BILLS-107hr3162enr/pdf/BILLS-107hr3162enr.pdf.

[42]See Terry (2009).

[43]Burrows and Geetter (2016).

recommended by the International Civil Aviation Organization: Annex 14 to the Chicago Convention in Chapter 9 carries provisions regarding emergency procedures. Also The Airport Services Manual, Part 7 as well as The Airport Emergency Planning have useful measures contained therein. Another document is the Safety Management Manual on Emergency Response Planning. Was the Fort Lauderdale Airport aware of these provisions and did the airport use them well?

To sum up, it seems advisable for those charged with ensuring security at airports to be provided with full information of potential offenders whether it concerns outgoing or incoming passengers or staff. It must be remembered that airports and airlines are intertwined and should improve their coordination and cooperation. With regard to damage caused to passengers, under international treaty the airline with whom the passenger has concluded the contract of carriage is liable for death or injury caused. However, in instances where airport services are involved the airport may be jointly or severally liable by the adjudicating court if the court finds that the airport was in the position of an agent of the airline. This article discusses law as an airport management tool against the circumstances of the Fort Lauderdale shootings and aspects of prudent airport management.

4.2.1 Interaction Between the Airport and Airline

The relationship between the airport and airline is integral to the air transport product as both are inextricable and intertwined. At the final stages of the air transport contract the airline delivers to the airport the passengers, baggage and cargo it carries and, during the period the three are in the airport premises there is joint accountability of both airline and airport in case something were to go wrong, whether it is injury or death caused to the passenger or damage to baggage or cargo. It is a generally accepted principle that in certain circumstances the airport can be considered an agent of the airline and can invoke principles of liability and limitations of liability accruing to the airline in support of the airport in case of liability.

A case in point is what happened at John F. Kennedy International Airport in late December 2010 when a severe snowfall effectively crippled equipment at Terminal One, which necessitated passengers on an Alitalia flight coming in from Rome to stay in the aircraft for 7 h with no food or drink as the aerobridge could not be connected to the aircraft. In the case of *Vumbaca* v. *Terminal One Group Association L.P*[44] decided in April 2012 by the United States District Court, E.D. New York. Vivian Vumbaca—the Plaintiff—an Italian citizen who was a permanent resident of the United States who arrived in New York during the snow storm of 26–27 December 2010 from Rome on the said Alitalia flight, alleged that she was kept locked in an aircraft on the ground without food, water, or adequate

[44]859 F. Supp. 2d 343.

sanitary facilities for 7 h, suffering mental distress. She sued Terminal One Group Association, L.P. (TOGA), which operates Terminal One, and sought to represent similarly situated passengers claiming emotional harms resulting from negligence, false imprisonment, and intentional infliction of emotional distress under her contract of carriage on the ground that Terminal One Group Association did not afford her the facility of disembarking at her destination and kept her on board the aircraft for 7 h causing her mental distress.

Although the main cause of action of the plaintiff, for delay in her carriage by air would have been against the carrier Alitalia, under the Montreal Convention of 1999,[45] the court held that Terminal One was an agent of the air carriers it serves[46] and thus covered by the Convention. The rationale for this reasoning was that, although Terminal One is not an international carrier but just a terminal operator, its operations are vital parts of carriage performed by the carrier—particularly those services that are necessary to get planes to and from the gates.

The plaintiff averred that her claim was based on Article 30 of the Montreal Convention which stipulates that if an action is brought against a servant or agent of the carrier arising out of damage to which the Convention relates, such servant or agent, if they prove that they acted within the scope of their employment, shall be entitled to avail themselves of the conditions and limits of liability which the carrier itself is entitled to invoke under this Convention. It was the contention of the plaintiff that Terminal One Group Association, L.P. (TOGA) was an agent of the carrier and therefore could be held liable under the Montreal Convention.

The Court found that the defendant TOGA had acted as an agent of the carrier. Despite the fact that TOGA was a terminal operator, its services were vital to the performance by the carrier of the contract of carriage with the plaintiff and therefore formed an integral part thereof and that TOGA had a common law duty to ensure that passengers on arriving flights had safe and prompt access to Terminal One. It provided a necessary link in the chain of transportation, facilitating the common carrier airline's service of its passengers. The defendant's duty to passengers extended beyond merely ensuring that stairs are not slippery, or that gates are properly maintained. It must ensure that those stairs and gates are made available in a timely manner when needed for use by the passengers, and that adequate ground handling staff is present to facilitate access. The Court further observed that TOGA should have foreseen that a breach of this duty would cause passengers to remain trapped on their aircraft in cramped and increasingly unpleasant or

---

[45]Article 19 of the Montreal Convention of 1999 provides that the carrier is liable for *damage occasioned by delay in the carriage by air of passengers, baggage* or cargo. Nevertheless, the carrier is not liable for damage occasioned by delay if it proves that it and its servants and agents took all measures that could reasonably be required to avoid the damage or that it was impossible for it or them to take such measures.

[46]Article 30 of the Montreal Convention stipulates that if an action is brought against a servant or agent of the carrier arising out of damage to which the Convention relates, such servant or agent, if they prove that they acted within the scope of their employment, shall be entitled to avail themselves of the conditions and limits of liability which the carrier itself is entitled to invoke.

dangerous conditions. Imposing on defendant this duty was neither novel nor undesirable as a matter of public policy.

In the context of negligence of the airport, which could have been vitiated by adequate preventive intelligence exercised by the airport, the court used a dictum in *Havas v. Victory Paper Stock Co.*,[47]: "[w]henever one person is by circumstances placed in such a position with regard to another that every one of ordinary sense who did think would at once recognize that if he did not use ordinary care and skill in his own conduct with regard to the circumstances he would cause danger of injury to the person or property of the other, a duty arises to use ordinary care and skill to avoid such danger".[48] Accordingly, the court held that the airport had a common law duty to ensure that passengers on arriving flights had safe and prompt access to the terminal on the basis that the airport is a necessary link in the chain of transportation, facilitating the conclusion of the contract of carriage that the carrier has with the passenger.

In the Fort Lauderdale incident, as already discussed, some of the persons killed by the assailant were in the process of collecting their bags from the carousel in the airport. Legally, the contract of carriage between the airline and the passenger ends only after the passenger collects his baggage. However, the liability of the airline is established only if the airline had, at the time of the damage, adequate control of the passenger, particularly at the airport. Therefore, current law on the subject seems to favour the test known as the *Day-Evangelinos* test which was developed as a consequence of a series of terrorist acts on passengers in airport departure lounges. This is a tripartite test which has three elements for consideration—the location of the passenger, the nature of his activity at the time of the accident and the degree of control exercised by the airline at the relevant time. A number of United States cases have accepted this test.[49] This test clearly establishes the fact that unless the passenger is under the control or direction of the airline at the terminal there is no liability for injury or death caused to the passenger under the provisions of the Montreal Convention. A case which brings out the significance of this test is *Adler v. Austrian Airlines* where a passenger slipped on some ice and fell between the terminal building and the aircraft when he was getting off the bus which transported him from the aircraft to the airport terminal building The bus was operated by the airport staff and not by the airline. A Brussels court, applying a test similar to the *Day-Evangelinos* test held that the passenger was not under the control of the airline and was thereby precluded from invoking the provisions of Article 17 of the Convention which details the circumstances under which a plaintiff can sue i.e., if the damage which caused the death or injury occurs on board or in the process of embarkation or disembarkation.

---

[47] 402 N.E.2d 1136 (1980).

[48] *Id.* 1138.

[49] *Day v. Trans World Airlines Inc.* 528 F 2d. 31 (2nd Circ. 1975); *Evangelinos v. Trans World Airlines Inc.*. 550 F2d 152 (2d. Circ. 1977); *Leppo v. Trans World Airlines Inc.*392 NYS 2d 660 (AD 1977); Rolnick v. *El Al Israel Airlines Ltd.551 Supp. 261 (EDNY 1982).*

The test itself obviates the need to painstakingly go through every possible exigency in the light of the requirement that the accident should occur during the process of embarkation or disembarkation. Prior to the adoption of this test there was no uniformity in the judicial reasoning behind the definition of embarkation and disembarkation. It was left to each individual court to determine whether a given situation would fall within the scope of chronology of these two extremities. Now, the tripartite test has made the task of the Courts much easier.

4.3 Regulatory Principles of Airport Management

At the 38th session of the Assembly of the International Civil Aviation Organization (ICAO) held in 2013, it was recognized that as a result of the exponential increase in the volume of air transport, a compelling need arose for a well-organized and comprehensive aviation system in member State for the safe and orderly development of international aviation. In this context the Assembly noted that efficient management of emergencies should be conducted in a comprehensive manner integrating the entire aviation system and such an approach to management was an absolute necessity.

Annex 14 (Aerodromes) to the Chicago Convention provides that an aerodrome emergency plan is an imperative establishment at an aerodrome, which should be commensurate with the aircraft operations and other activities conducted at the aerodrome. This emergency plan should provide for the coordination of the actions to be taken in an emergency occurring at an aerodrome or in its vicinity while, coordinating the response or participation of all existing agencies which, in the opinion of the appropriate authority, could be of assistance in responding to an emergency. Integrally linked to this provision is another provision in Annex 17 (Security) to the Convention which requires each Contracting State to ensure that contingency plans are developed and resources are made available to safeguard civil aviation against acts of unlawful interference. Furthermore, Annexes 3; 4; 6; 12; and 18 also require cooperation with related facilities in emergency or to preparation for such situations.

Annex 19 to the Convention (on safety management systems) calls for a framework for a Safety Management System (SMS), requiring service providers to ensure that an emergency response plan (ERP) is properly coordinated with the ERPs of those organizations that they must interface with during the provision of their products and services. The ICAO Safety Management Manual (Doc 9859) explains that ERP is a documented plan with actions to be taken by all responsible personnel during related emergencies focused on service providers. ERP is known by different terms to different service providers, such as contingency plan, crisis management plan and continuing airworthiness support plan. ERP is a plan to recover the failure of the SMS process. And as a follow-up action of the emergency, the responsible executives should reassess the risk and reflect the result to its SMS.

Regulatory management of airports also involves robust involvement of States. Annex 9 (Facilitation) to the Chicago Convention recommends that States establish measures for authorizing temporary entry for a passenger or crew member who does not possess the required entry visa prior to arrival, due to diversion or delay of a flight for reasons of force majeure. There is also a requirement in the Annex to establish measures whereby in-transit passengers who are unexpectedly delayed due to a flight cancellation or delay may be allowed to leave the airport for the purpose of taking accommodations. It is recommended that in emergency situations resulting from force majeure, States, aircraft operators and airport operators should give priority assistance to those passengers with medical needs, unaccompanied minors and persons with disabilities who have already commenced their journeys.

In 1991 The Supreme Court of Canada stringently applied the tortious concept of "occupier's liability" to a case where the appellants—occupiers of a farmhouse and driveway which they had neglected to clean the accumulated snow and ice which caused the respondent to slip, fall and grievously injure himself—appealed from a Court of Appeal decision[50] where they were found liable as occupiers of the premises. The Supreme Court endorsed the findings of the Court of Appeal. It is arguable whether this principle would apply to Fort Lauderdale airport as there was seemingly no negligence on the part of the airport as an occupier, although the fact that the airport is an occupier of premises and thus would come under the legal concept is not in doubt. The airport had not received a warning from the passenger's departure point (Alaska) nor from the airline that the passenger was carrying a deadly weapon.

On the issue of prudent airport management any determination of the conduct of Fort Lauderdale airport would be *post facto* as to what measures the airport took to cope with the emergency situation. As already discussed, questions arise: did the airport have an emergency plan as prescribed by Annex 14 to the Chicago Convention and a contingency plan as required by Annex 17 against unlawful interference? Was there an Emergency Response Plan as required by Annex 19 and was that put into action? Since the airport is an agent of the airline in the context of the contract of carriage, was there adequate communication between the airport and the airline with regard to the baggage and goods unloaded in the premises of the airport? Above all, did the airport excise a predictive management approach?

Prudent management starts with compliance of applicable laws and regulations but it does not end there. The ICAO Safety Management Manual calls for reactive, proactive and predictive (anticipatory) management in the context of safety but this principle is common to security as well. While the reactive method responds to events that have already happened, proactive management would look actively for the identification of safety risks through the analysis of the airport's activities. Arguably the most important of the three is predictive management which captures system performance as it happens in real-time normal operations to identify potential future problems.

[50] *Waldick v. Malcolm*, [1991] 2 S.C.R. 456, File No.: 21781, 1991: February 26; 1991: June 27.

The operative words here are "real time normal operations to identify future problems". Over the years, armed attacks inside terminal buildings have occurred with some regularity. The application of trends to possible scenarios would therefore logically lead one to address the possibility of an attack on a plane load of passengers who have just cleared their bags from the baggage carousel or are waiting to do so. What could be inside the bags? Should they be screened once again after arrival? The greatest danger in this scenario would be to let predictive management flow into reactive management. To avoid this catastrophic possibility airport should use certain management tools among which are compliance with regulations and laws; threat intelligence; threat modelling; event coding; and event detection. The application of these tools would involve logical and critical thinking involving forecasting and trend analysis as well as human judgment.

References

Abeyratne R (2004) Airport business law. Author house, pp 106–108

Abeyratne R (2009) Airport business law. Bloomington, Ind., pp 106–108.

Becker P (2002) Corporate foresight in Europe: a first overview. Institute of Science and Technology Studies, Germany, October 2002

Burrows VK, Geetter JS (2016) New HIPAA privacy rule permits disclosures to background check system. McDermott, Will and Emory, 13 January 2016. https://www.mwe.com/en/thought-leadership/publications/2016/01/new

Dastin J (2016) Power outage at Delta causes flight cancellations, delays. Reuters, 8 August 2016. http://www.reuters.com/article/us-delta-air-outages-idUSKCN10J0VP

Davies C (2010) Heathrow airport all but shut as snow hits Christmas travel plans. The Guardian, 19 December 2010. https://www.theguardian.com/uk/2010/dec/19/snow-weather-uk-heathrow-travel

Pestritto RJ, West TG (2007) Modern America and the legacy of founding. Lexington Books, New York, p 253

Siddique H, Milmo D (2010) Snow and ice bring travel chaos to UK. The Guardian, 17 December 2010. https://www.theguardian.com/uk/2010/dec/17/snow-ice-uk-weather

Terry K (2009) Patent privacy – the new threats. Phys Pract J 19(3). Access 2 July 2009

Verheyen W (2015) 10 years of 261/2004: any excuses left? Eur Transport Law L(6):659–677

Chapter 5
Artificial Intelligence and Air Transport

There is no doubt that artificial intelligence (AI) will play a prominent role in air transport, assisting professionals in the field in developing the industry to deliver even safer air transport while reducing its environmental impact. The term "artificial intelligence" has been challenged as connoting emotional intelligence that humans possess. Scientists cannot even imagine a time where computers would acquire emotional intelligence. IBM advocates terms such as "cognitive computing" or "augmented intelligence" to describe what is popularly known as AI for this reason. In this context, AI forms two broad categories: knowledge based intelligence delivered by knowledge based systems (KBS) and computational intelligence which involve neural networks fuzzy systems and evolutionary computing. The former is applied based on the reliance placed by information provided by a human (such as rules and algorithms) while the latter delivers through networks of computational systems. Air transport involves the use of qualitative and quantitative data but is primarily governed by human involvement, whether in maintenance, air traffic control or flight deck management. This factor makes it difficult to entirely rely upon mathematical computations or non emotive reasoning in air transport.

5.1 Technical Issues

Artificial intelligence has been applied to air traffic control with some success[1] and AI has been developed at The Lincoln Laboratory which has automated basic air traffic functions.[2] However, it has been recognized that general planning with AI does not easily rest with air traffic control:

---

[1]See Special Issue on FAA's Advanced Automated System, *Computer*, Vol 20:1987, at 25–31.
[2]Spencer (1989), pp. 537–554 at 537.

R. Abeyratne, *Megatrends and Air Transport*, DOI 10.1007/978-3-319-61124-2_5

> One difficulty in applying this method to ATC problems is that in ATC there exist no particular end states that need to be achieved. That is, in general a large number of possible future situations are acceptable. Another difficulty is that the use of logical assertions does not capture the continuous behavior of physical systems such as aircraft in flight. and it also introduces a number of artificial logical problems to the system.[3]

In other words, considering the large number of decisions to be taken and actions to be carried out in the process of providing air traffic control for the safe navigation of aircraft which involve the consideration of numerous factors such as the presence of other aircraft in the vicinity such as; severe weather conditions; simultaneous communications between multiple controller in different segments of airspace; the impossibility of directing an aircraft to climb further than the maximum altitude already reached; and the coordination of timing with the speed of ascent or descent, these factors could all be beyond the cognitive capacity of AI. However, this having been said, aviation could benefit largely from AI, particularly from neural networks. A neural network has been defined as:

> a distributed, adaptive, generally nonlinear learning machine built from interconnecting different processing elements[4]... The most commonly used architecture of NN is the multilayer perceptron (MLP). MLP is a static NN that has been extensively used in many transportation applications due to its simplicity and ability to perform nonlinear pattern classification and function approximation. It is, therefore, considered the most widely implemented network topology by many researchers[5]

DeepMind—a British AI company which Google bought in January 2014 pioneers research in AI and neural networks. The overall mission of the company is to create "multifunctional, general artificial intelligence that can think as broadly and effectively as a human".[6] IBM's Watson is another find, which consists of 10 racks of IBM POWER 750 servers running Linux, uses 15 terabytes of RAM and 2880 processor cores (equivalent to 6000 top-end home computers), and operates at 80 teraflops. Watson needed this amount of power to quickly scan its enormous database of information, including information from the Internet".[7] These technologies can substantially assist aviation in its many facets by providing correct information in a matter of seconds to assist humans involved in air navigation. The downside to this is that such marvels as Watson could also access questionable information available in the internet that could compromise its productivity and performance.

On the other side is the growing apprehension of "singularity" which is a concept that fears the uncontrollability of computers. Prominent figures such as physicist Stephen Hawking and Lord Rees, a former head of the Royal Society have

[3] *Id.* 541.

[4] Ishak and Trifiro (2000), pp. 17–32 at 17.

[5] *Id.* 18.

[6] Googles Hippocampus, *The Economist*, December 17th 2016 at 55.

[7] MIS 2016—Case Study 33—IBM's Watson: Can Computers Replace Humans, Top Ten, 15 July 2016. See http://toptenmba.com/mba-cases/54-mba-management-information-systems/854-mis-2016-case-study-33-ibm-s-watson-can-computers-replace-humans.

cautioned against computers turning evil, which has prompted billionaire Elon Musk to call for openness and transparency in the development of AI so that the world community could be reassured of safety. So far, the lack of consciousness of AI has allayed fears but in its actual use in transportation—particularly in air transport—could raise trepidation leading to its ultimate rejection.

Another danger in AI is classification where face recognition technologies such as Facebook's DeepFace could, while functioning at their most optimal, arrive at wrong or distorted conclusions. Ethical issues would also abound such as who a computer system would save in a crisis—the aircraft and the technical crew or the passengers on board. Then there are the legal implications, a discussion of which follows. Before discussing both ethical and legal issues, there is a contentious issue on the economic aspects of robots as they purportedly replace the human workforce. An Oxford Martin Study says that nearly half of jobs in The United States could be susceptible to computerization over the next two decades.[8] Bill Gates, Co-founder of Microsoft has proposed taxing robots on the principle that if the human they replace had paid income tax, so should the robot and the tax imposed would ease the vacuum as well as pay for finding jobs elsewhere for the humans so displaced. The flaw in this argument is that the robot would replace a human so that efficiency is improved and a tax on a robot would be a tax on efficiency.[9] Bloomberg says: "The fear isn't that *all* humans will become obsolete, but that automation will increase inequality among humans. Company owners and high-skilled workers – people who tell machines what to do – would be vastly enriched, while everyone else either works low-skilled jobs for meager wages or goes on welfare".[10]

5.2 Ethical Issues

With regard to the ethical issues that warrant discussion, a good place to start is Musk's suggestion of transparency as a moral basis for the use of artificial intelligence. For this discussion, one has to go all the way back to the seventeenth century philosophers who had their own conception of prudent human conduct which can be used as a basis for the standard to be included in a computer algorithm. If computers drive air transportation or play a major role in air navigation (such as what is happening in driverless cars) there would have to be a standardized system

---

[8]Oxford Martin School study shows nearly half of US jobs could be at risk of computerization, 18 Sep 2013. See. See http://www.oxfordmartin.ox.ac.uk/news/14-09-18-Jobs. http://fortune.com/2017/02/22/bill-gates-proposes-a-robot-tax/.

[9]Colvin and Derousseau (2017).

[10]Smith (2017). See https://www.bloomberg.com/view/articles/2017-02-28/what-s-wrong-with-bill-gates-robot-tax.

of preference for rules and sets of processes that would accord with acceptable moral philosophy.

The bottom line in this discussion would be "acceptable moral philosophy". This discussion should inevitably start with English philosopher Jeremy Bentham (1748–1832) who rejected the concept of natural rights and instead introduced the philosophy of utilitarianism which espoused the happiness of the most as the apex of his moral philosophy. In plain terms, Bentham's utilitarianism which is also called "consequentialism" when applied to an aircraft with its full complement of passengers that is plunging towards a sports stadium full of 10,000 spectators, could be could be shot down should there be a danger of it hitting the stadium and killing more than the number of person in the aircraft. One could also look at the other side of the coin and inquire whether the lives of the passengers on board the aircraft could be considered paramount as the primary and sacrosanct duty of the pilot is to ensure the safety of persons and property on board. Could he then land the aircraft in the stadium area which would carry the risk of killing more persons on the ground than those on board but at the same time ensuring with certainty that the passengers' lives would be saved?

This hypothetical issue can be infused with some reality with the recent debate in the automotive industry where the question was asked whether a driverless car should be programmed to save the driver when it was veering towards four persons on the sidewalk who could be killed with the maneuver to save the driver of the car. A typical example given is when a person is in a driverless car and a child suddenly darts across in front of your car. The car would be programmed to run over the child so as not to jeopardize the life of the passenger in the car. In a newspaper, this example was reported as follows: "the manager of driver-assistance systems at Mercedes-Benz, Christoph von Hugo, revealed that the company's future autonomous vehicles would always put the driver first. In other words, in the above dilemma, they will be programmed to run over the child every time".[11] A judicial analogy of this principle is *R* v. *Dudley and Stephens*[12] which involved a shipwreck and the defence of necessity. On May 19, 1884 the English yacht Mignonette set sail for Sydney, Australia from Southampton, England with a crew of four. The crew consisted of Tom Dudley, the captain; Edwin Stephens; Edmund Brooks; and Richard Parker, the cabin boy.

Owing to bad weather, the yacht sank off the Cape of Good Hope on May 19, 1884. The four crew mates were cast away, forcing them to abandon the ship and escape in an open boat that was in the yacht. Food and water were scarce, except for two tins of turnips that the captain saved before they abandoned ship. From the sea, they only caught a small turtle, which they had eaten by the twelfth day of their floating in the sea. Their diet, for 20 days adrift was only the turnips and the small turtle. Stephens and Dudley decided, without the consent of Brooks that

[11]Dodgson (2016). See http://www.businessinsider.de/mercedes-benz-self-driving-cars-programmed-save-driver-2016-10.

[12](1884) 14 QBD73.

they would kill and eat Parker. He was the youngest and weakest of them all. Parker did not consent to his killing, but he was too weak to resist. A few days later the three crew members were rescued by a passing ship just in time as they too were dying of starvation and dehydration.

Back in England, Dudley and Stevens were arraigned for murdaer on the ground that at English law where a private person, acting on his own judgment, takes the life of another, he is guilty of murder, unless his act can be justified by selfdefense. The defendants were not protecting themselves against any act of the hapless Parker. The verdict was that the two defendant's were guilty of murder. The court disagreed with Lord Bacon, who, in his commentary on the maxim, "necessitas inducit privilegium quoad jura privata," lays down the law as follows: "Necessity carrieth a privilege in itself. Necessity is of three sorts – necessity of conservation of life, necessity of obedience, and necessity of the act of God or of a stranger. First of conservation of life; if a man steal viands to satisfy his present hunger, this is no felony nor larceny. So if divers be in danger of drowning by the casting away of some boat or barge, and one of them get to some plank, or on the boat's side to keep himself above water, and another to save his life thrust him from it, whereby he is drowned, this is neither se defendendo nor by misadventure, but justifiable." Instead the Court held: "We are certainly not prepared to suggest that necessity should in every case be a justification. We are equally unprepared to, suggest that necessity should in no case be a defence; we judge it better to leave such questions to be dealt with when, if ever, they arise in practice by applying the principles of law to the circumstances of the particular case".[13]

Bentham's theory of utilitarianism—which is seemingly consistent with the position taken by the two defendants—can be considered as being opposed to the basic human rights phenomenon—that all human lives are equal and it is morally reprehensible to treat them as subjects of collective happiness. When this theory is applied to the aircraft descending on the sports arena, the credibility (or lack thereof) of Bentam's theory can be queried. An alternate dimension to human conduct in its moral setting is posited by German philosopher Immanuel Kant (1724–1804) who based his philosophy on human dignity and what he called the Categorical Imperative". Kant argued that Bentham's utilitarianism was fundamentally flawed because it left human rights vulnerable to desires which were of lesser importance, and that considering happiness as the primordial essence of human life is wrong. The categorical imperative stands for giving morality precedence over empirical considerations. Unlike Bentham's utilitarian theory and arguments that oppose it as reflected in the judicial decision of the *Dudley and Stephens* case which could be associated with a stochastic algorithm applicable to artificial intelligence in the context of air transport, at least in theory, it would be difficult to ascribe such an analogy to Kant's categorical imperative which appeals more to subjective reasoning and morality that leads to emotional intelligence—an area which scientists can only think of at the present time. The categorical imperative has, as its

[13]*Id.* 83.

base, a certain autonomy that we give ourselves to act according to a law we give ourselves. This is diametrically opposed to what Kant calls heteronomous determination, where, as in the utilitarian theory, we do something for the sake of something else.

5.3 Legal Issues

After the technical issues and ethical issues are considered, one is confronted with two questions: do we trust robots with our lives; and who is liable if anything were to go wrong. As for the first question, it will be for history to decide. In the mid-eighties, when the twin engine Boeing 767 was introduced, many airlines vowed that they would not use the aircraft as they could not place their trust on just two engines over the oceans. Now, one of the most prolifically used aircraft is the Boeing 777 which is a widely popular long range wide body aircraft used by airlines the world over. Clearly, it would be a matter of time where, if artificial intelligence attains a level of sophistication that would make people feel safe in its hands, this apprehension would disappear.

As for legal liability, matters are clearer at common law where judicial decisions on manufacturer's liability and user's liability for defective products offer a viable analogy in the context of artificial intelligence. There are three types of defects that entail liability: manufacturer's defects; design defects; and failures to warn. Manufacturer's defect goes on the basic principle that liability would not ensue if the manufacturer had followed and complied with regulations.[14] A design defect can be subject to liability if there is a foreseeable risk portended by the product when it was manufactured as intended and used for purposes that it was intended.

[14]*Jones* v. *W&M Manufacturing Inc*, 31 AD 3d 1099 (2007). The plaintiff was injured when he entered the area behind the safety fence, where the system was located, presumably through the modified sliding gate. Plaintiff was struck in the head by the gripper arms of the system and became pinned against the pedestal, thereby sustaining serious head injuries. Following an investigation, it was determined that the manufacturers violated the Occupational Safety and Health Administration regulations by installing the sliding gate without an interlock system and by allowing employees to work on the system within the safety fence while the system was operating, and the manufacturers were fined accordingly. However, in appeal the Supreme Court found that with respect to the negligence and strict products liability causes of action, the appealing defendants (manufacturers) met their initial burden by submitting expert evidence establishing that the system as originally designed and installed conformed to GM's "CPC Tonawanda MH-100 specifications" and was safe until GM modified it. see also *Amatulli* v. *Delhi Constr. Corp.*, 77 N.Y.2d 525, 532, 569 N.Y.S.2d 337, 571 N.E.2d 645; *Gian* v. *Cincinnati Inc.*, 17 A.D.3d 1014, 1015-1016, 794 N.Y.S.2d 215; *Wesp* v. *Carl Zeiss, Inc.*, 11 A.D.3d 965, 968, 783 N.Y.S.2d 439.

5.4 Manufacturer's Defects

In *Greenman* v. *Yuba Power Products Inc*[15]—1963 decision—which involved a case where the plaintiff, who bought a combination power tool was hit on the head by the product which dislodged itself from the main component the court upheld the plaintiff's claim on the basis of breach of warranty on the part of both the manufacturer and the retailer. In response to the defendant's claim of acceptance by the buyer the jury held that: "in the absence of express or implied agreement of the parties, acceptance of the goods by the buyer did not discharge the seller from liability in damages or other legal remedy for breach of any promise or warranty in the contract to sell or the sale. But, if, after acceptance of the goods, the buyer fails to give notice to the seller of the breach of any promise or warranty within a reasonable time after the buyer knows, or ought to know of such breach, the seller shall not be liable therefor".

The principle of manufacturer's responsibility was established in 1869 in the Canadian case of *George* v. *Skivington*[16]—a case where a woman was injured by a hair wash purchased at a sale, the court held that "there was a duty in the vendor to use ordinary care in compounding the article sold, and that this extended to the person for whose use he knew it was purchased, and this duty having been violated, and he, having failed to use reasonable care, was liable in an action at the suit of the third person". The court approved the earlier case of *France* v. *Cockrell*[17] where the plaintiff who was injured by the fall of a stand on a racecourse, for a seat in which he had paid, succeeded in his claim. The defendant was part proprietor of the stand and acted as receiver of the money. The stand had been negligently erected by a contractor, though the defendant was not aware of the defect. In *Heaven v Pender, Trading as West India Graving Dock Company*[18] where the plaintiff, a painter engaged to repaint a ship, and the defendant erected staging to support the work. The staging collapsed because one of the ropes was singed and weakened, injuring the plaintiff. Cotton L.J. held that:

> I in no way intimate any doubt as to the principle that anyone who leaves a dangerous instrument, as a gun, in such a way as to cause danger, or who without due warning supplies to others for use an instrument or thing which to his knowledge, from its construction or otherwise, is in such a condition as to cause danger, not necessarily incident to the use of such an instrument, or thing, is liable for injury caused to others by reason of his negligent act.

The *George* case was cited with approval in *Ross* v. *Dunstall* in 1922 where the court held that the principle of manufacturer's responsibility was entrenched in the law (of Quebec). The milestone on the subject of manufacturer's liability in negligence and the duty of care was in 1922 in the case of *Donoughue*

---

[15]59 Cal.2d 57.

[16](1869–70) L.R. 5 exch.8.

[17](1870) LR 5 QB 501.

[18](1883) 11 QBD 503.

v. *Stevenson*[19] where the appellant drank from a bottle of ginger beer manufactured by the defendant. She suffered injury when she found a half decomposed snail in the liquid. The glass was opaque and the snail could not be seen. The drink had been bought for her by a friend, so she was unable to rely upon any contract. The Court, which extended the principle of the *George* case (of ascribing liability of the manufacturer and retailer to a known user) to any consumer held:

> The English and the Scots law on the subject are identical. The pursuer was entitled to recover damages for negligence. The manufacturer intended that the contents be consumed without the opportunity first to examine them, and unless reasonable care was taken in the preparation a consumer may suffer injury. The cases of *George* v. *Skivington* and 'the dicta in *Heaven* v. *Pende*r 'should be buried so securely that their perturbed spirits shall no longer vex the law.

In *Hennigsen* v. *Bloomfield Motor Inc*[20]—a case decided in 1960—the court held:

> we hold that under modern marketing conditions, when a manufacturer puts a new auto in the stream of trade and promotes its purchase by the public, an implied warranty that it is reasonably suitable for use as such accompanies it into the hands of the ultimate consumer. Absence of agency between the manufacturer and the dealer who makes the ultimate sale is immaterial.

In all these cases the underlying principle is that the plaintiff must prove that the defendant was negligent in the three areas of liability discussed earlier—*i.e.* manufacturer's defects; design defects; and failures to warn. In *Butt* v. *Pepsi Cola*[21] the plaintiff was a victim of an accident when a bottle of Pepsi-Cola exploded, and he sued the bottling company on the ground that the glass used to manufacture the bottle was not strong enough as well as Pepsi-Cola Co. for bottling the liquid under improper and excessive gas pressure and without allowing for due regard to the dictates of public use and safety. The court held that in the absence of proof by the plaintiff of the alleged fault in either instance, liability could not be determined of both defendants merely because the accident occurred.

Although the above factors apply in the law of tort, the liability regime is different if the plaintiff were to sue under the laws of contract for breach of contract. Thus, in the case of a defective product of artificial intelligence, liability for damage caused by negligence in the context of defects or failure to warn would arise in the case of any victim who is injured (irrespective of whether the manufacturer knew the victim/plaintiff or not) under contract law there must be privity of contract to sue for breach of contract. In the 1965 case of *Terry* v. *Double Cola Bottling*[22] the court held:

---

[19]HL ([1932] AC 562, [1932] SC (HL) 31, [1932] ScLT 317.

[20](1960) 161 A 2d. 161.

[21](1939) 77 C.S. 108.

[22](1965) 138 S.E. 2d. 753. See also *Rabb* v. *Covington*, 215 N.C. 572, 2 S.E.2d 705; *Thomason* v. *Ballard & Ballard Co.*, 208 N.C. 1, 179 S.E. 30.

> A manufacturer is not liable to an ultimate consumer or subvendee upon a warrantee of quality or merchantability of goods which the ultimate consumer or subvendee had purchased from a retailer or dealer to whom the manufacturer had sold. for there is no contractual relationship between the manufacturer and such consumer or subvendee.... There is an exception to this rule where the warranty is addressed to the ultimate consumer, and this exception has been limited to cases involving sales of goods, intended for human consumption, in sealed packages prepared by the manufacturer and having labels with representations to consumers inscribed thereon.

In *Escola* v. *Coca Cola Bottling Co.*[23] where a waitress who was stacking bottles of coca cola was injured when one of the bottles exploded on her, the court held that absolute liability can be ascribed to a manufacturer when a defective article he produces and places on the market injures a person who places trust in the safety of the product and does not expect it to harm her. The court held that this principle should apply irrespective of privity of contract, and the manufacturer is responsible for an injury caused by an article, to any person who comes in lawful contact with it. The court further held: "even if there is no negligence, public policy demands that responsibility be placed where it will most effectively reduce the hazards of life and health inherent in defective products that reach the market. Those who suffer injury from defective products are unprepared to meet its consequences. The cost of an injury and the loss of time or health may be an overwhelming misfortune to the person injured, and a needless one, for the risk of injury can be insured by the manufacturer and distributed among the public as the cost of doing business. If public policy demands that a manufacturer of goods be responsible for its quality regardless of negligence, there is no reason not to fix that responsibility openly. The liability of the manufacturer to an immediate buyer injured by a defective product follows without proof of negligence from the implied warranty of safety attending the sale. Consumers will no longer need to be wary of products. The manufacturer's obligation to the consumer must keep pace with the changing relationship between them".[24]

It must be mentioned that liability of the manufacturer in all three categories of liability mentioned does not extend to consequential damages. This was pronounced in the 1982 case of *Mercer* v. *Long Manufacturing N.C. Inc.*,[25] which held that damages were not separable and would be restricted to actual pecuniary damage that occurred and would not be extended to personal or property damage that would be consequential to the actual damage.

In the air transport context the position of Jeppesen—a manufacturer of charts, maps and navigational aids—becomes relevant in the case of the Korean Air flight 007 disaster. Seven Plaintiffs alleged negligence, breach of implied and express warranties and strict liability against Jeppesen Sanderson, Inc. and contended that the Jeppesen charts did not contain a warning explicitly noting the possible consequences of straying over Soviet territory and that the absence of an explicit warning

---

[23]150 P.2d 436 (Cal. 1944).

[24]See Case Briefs at http://www.casebriefs.com/blog/law/torts/torts-keyed-to-epstein/products-liability/escola-v-coca-cola-bottling-co-of-fresno/2/.

[25]665 F.2d 61 (5th Cir. 1982).

was negligence, resulting in an "unreasonably dangerous" product being released into the stream of commerce. This was also a case of failure to warn by Jeppesen as the plaintiffs claimed that the area where KAL 007 was shot down should have been designated as a "Danger" or "Warning" area on the portion of the Jeppesen chart listing "Airspace Restricted Areas."

Jeppesen argued that the disaster occurred as a result of a supervening factor—that of the shooting down of the aircraft by the Russians and therefore there was no causal link between the company and the damage suffered by the plaintiffs. The court held that the plaintiffs could not, under any set of circumstances, demonstrate a causal link between what happened to KAL 007 and the claims that the Jeppesen warning was inadequately worded. The claim against Jeppesen was therefore rejected.[26]

5.5 Design Defects

Design defects as a head of liability has been regarded as arising from two situations: a product failing to meet consumer expectations or it does not meet risk-utility standards. In the 1990 case of *Lamkin* v. *Towner*[27] where a toddler fell through a screen at a window and suffered skull fracture among other injuries and an action brought by the mother of the injured child, the court held that a plaintiff may demonstrate that a product is defective in design, so as to subject a retailer and "a manufacturer to strict liability for resulting injuries, in one of two ways: (1) by introducing evidence that the product failed to perform as safely as an ordinary consumer would expect when used in an intended or reasonably foreseeable manner or (2) by introducing evidence that the product's design proximately caused his injury and the defendant fails to prove that on balance the benefits of the challenged design outweigh the risk of danger inherent in such designs".[28] The court held that the window screens were simply serving the purpose for which they were created when the accidents occurred. He court imputed to the plaintiff a degree of voluntary assumption of risk where she did not envision that the screen was not an absolute guarantee of safety of her child The court said: " even assuming that 'the ordinary [person]' may recognize the potential for a screen to restrict a fall from a window, we cannot conclude that, in the event a window screen fails to prevent the fall of a minor leaning against it, 'the ordinary [person]' would consider the screen dangerous beyond his original contemplation of the product. A consumer may rightfully expect a product to safely do the job for which it was built or for a foreseeable similar use, but neither a retailer nor a manufacturer can be held strictly liable for injuries resulting from the misuse of its product".

[26] *In Re Korean Air Lines Disaster of Sept. 1, 1983*, 597 F. Supp. 619 (D.D.C. 1984).

[27] 563 N.E. 2d 449. Also 138 Ill.2d 510, 150 Ill. Dec. 562, 563 N.E.2d 449.

[28] The court cited, in support of its findings, *Palmer* v. *Avco Distributing Corp.* (1980), 82 Ill.2d 211, 219–20, [45 Ill.Dec. 377, 412 N.

In some jurisdictions there is an attendant need for the plaintiff to show that an alternative design of the product could have obviated the risk if the manufacturer was able to produce the alternative design, if it was economically feasible and the manufacturer had the resources to introduce the alternative design and that the product would perform the function expected of it.

In *Bass* v. *Gen. Motors Corp*[29] plaintiff claimed that his head hit the car window during a collision due to a defectively designed seat belt mechanism which allowed too much slack to develop. The plaintiff claimed that a design that would have created more tension between the belt and the body of the plaintiff would have averted plaintiff's head injuries. The court held with the plaintiff. In a case[30] decided in 2006 the claim of the plaintiff was that the cruise-control mechanism of a 1993 Oldsmobile had caused the car to go out of control upheld. The plaintiff's case was supported by compelling expert testimony of alternative design of the cruise-control mechanism that would have avoided the accident. The court held with the plaintiff. In *Redfield* v. *Beverly Health & Rehab. Servs., Inc.,*[31] the manufacturer of a ventilator that failed causing death to plaintiff was held liable as the plaintiff introduced evidence that the ventilator was unreasonably dangerous because it did not have a redundant backup breathing system. In *Sappington* v. *Skyjack, Inc.*[32] defendant claimed that a "scissors lift" should have been designed with greater stability so that it would not tip over when the rear wheels dropped off a concrete floor into the hold the appeal court reversed the district court's grant of summary judgment and found that the plaintiff's position was acceptable since there was evidence that at the time the product was manufactured the technology existed to produce a more stable lift that would have avoided the plaintiffs death. In *Pritchett* v. *Cottrell, Inc.,*[33] court held that the plaintiff was not required to prove a reasonable alternative design, the plaintiffs' expert opinion set forth several practical alternative designs for ratchet mechanisms that were safer and would have avoided the plaintiffs' injuries.

In the case of Clements *Auto Co.* v. *Service Bureau Corp.,*[34] the product at issue was an automated accounting system designed to perform inventory control functions which the buyer had agreed to purchase from the Service Bureau Corporation (SBC). Consequent to the sale the system failed to operate properly and proved to be obsolete and overpriced with an input method so slow and expensive which made the accounting reports were too error-prone and voluminous to be of any use to the buyer. As a consequence, the buyer was compelled to assign two full-time executives to supervise the operation of the system. Among the buyer's action against the plaintiff seller were an application for rescission and reformation of the contract on the grounds of breach of

[29] 150 F.3d 842, 844–45, 851 (8th Cir. 1998).

[30] Peters v. Gen. Motors Corp., 200 S.W.3d 1, 17–20 (Mo. Ct. App. 2006).

[31] 42 S.W.3d 703, 710 (Mo. Ct. App. 2001).

[32] 512 F.3d 440 (8th Cir. 2007).

[33] 512 F.3d 1057 (8th Cir. 2008).

[34] 298 F. Supp. 115 (D. Minn. 1969).

implied warranty, breach of contract, and fraudulent misrepresentation. The court denied recovery on all grounds except the last, upon which it awarded the plaintiff for losses due to inventory obsolescence, executives' salaries, increased clerical costs, and rental costs and fees paid to SBC and other equipment suppliers. The court denied plaintiff's action for breach of implied warranty on the strength of a disclaimer by the seller which said that it made no warranties, expressed or implied, other than the express warranties contained in this agreement.

A product's design must meet minimum safety assumptions[35] whether the design is acceptable to experts on the subject or not. The plaintiff's case is strengthened if she could bring to the attention of the courts alternative designs that call to question the reliability of the defective product that caused injury or damage.[36] *United States* v. *Wegematic Corp*[37] was a case concerning contractual liability where the defendant contractor had submitted a bid to the Federal Reserve Board (FRB) to furnish an intermediate type, general purpose electronic digital computing system. The bid was in response to an invitation by the FRB The Federal Reserve Board which had invited proposals for the production of such a system at an early delivery date. The defendant's proposal was a much vaunted one touting a novel design, which it described as "a truly revolutionary system utilizing all of the latest technical advances", with a proposed delivery date within 9 months after the contract was awarded. On acceptance of this offer by the defendant FRB awarded a contract for $231,800, with a delivery date of June 30, 1957, and a liquidated damages clause requiring the defendant to pay $100 per day for delay. The defendant contractor accepted the offer accepting the conditions imposed by the Board. However, in mid-October 1957, the contractor sought annulment of the contract without penalty, citing impossibility of delivery due to engineering problems that had cropped up. The plaintiff sued the defendant contractor citing conditions of contract, after purchasing comparable equipment from another manufacturer. The trial court awarded the plaintiff damages of $235,806; $46,300 for delay under the liquidated damages clause, $179,450 for the excess cost of the replacement equipment, and $10,056 for wasted preparation expenses.

In a 1969 case—*Ford Motor Credit Co.* v. *Swarens,*[38] the court recognized that trust in the infallibility of a computer is hardly a defence, noting that under state law there must be evidence of "willful misconduct, malice, fraud, wantonness, or oppression, or that entire want of care which would raise the presumption of a conscious indifference to consequences" in order to impose punitive damages. The court opined that when the user of the computer fails to take "reasonable precautions to determine the accuracy of computer information, he may be not only liable for negligence, but also subject to exemplary damages for reliance upon computer information in reckless disregard of knowledge that it may not be accurate".

---

[35]*Soule* v. *General Motors Corp*, 573 P 2d. 876 at 878 (Ariz, 1985).

[36]*Potter* v. *Chicago Pneumatic Tool Co.*, 694 A. 2d 1319 at 1333 (Conn. 1997).

[37]360 F 2d 674 (2d Cir. 1966).

[38]447 S.W. 2d 53 (Ky. 1969).

Another issue that brings to bear liability in the realm of artificial intelligence is the action of a computerized system which keeps going after a contract has come to an end. Does the provider incur liability? The principles are enunciated in the 1972 case of *State Farm Mutual Automobile Insurance Co.* v. *Brockhorst.*[39] On 4 October 1969 the defendant was involved in an automobile accident about one and a half months after the defendant had defaulted on his premium payments and his insurance policy had lapsed. Immediately after the accident the defendant Brockhorst mailed a check for the amount owing on his policy and personally reported his actions to his agent. The insurer's computer erroneously reinstated his policy retroactively a few minutes prior to the accident where the policy had already lapsed. The insurer returned the premium to the defendant stating that his policy was no longer valid. The court held with the defendant on the ground that he was not guilty of non-disclosure and that the insurer had knowledge of the details of the accident. And the time the premium check was mailed. The court further held that the insurance company had waived its right to refuse reinstatement when the computer issued a new policy extending coverage prior to the time of the accident. The court held:

> A computer operates only in accordance with the information and directions supplied by its human programmers. If the computer does not think like a man, it is man's fault. The reinstatement of Brockhorst's policy was the direct result of the errors and oversights of State Farm's human agents and employees. The fact that the actual processing of the policy was carried out by an unimaginative mechanical device can have no effect on the company's responsibilities for those errors and oversights. State Farm's reinstatement of Brockhorst's policy while in full possession of information establishing its right to refuse reinstatement constituted a binding waiver, and the reinstated policy effectively extended coverage for the period during which Brockhorst's accident occurred.[40]

From an insurance perspective, there would be no prima facie liability in the case of damage caused to software in computers if there is an exclusion clause in the insurance policy regarding impaired property. This is because the data and software in a computer is not legally recognized as "property" to be brought under the head of property damage. Data or software are not tangible property as was held in the case of *America Online Inc.*, v. *Paul.*[41] The court held that

> Computer data, software, and systems do not have or possess physical form and are therefore not tangible property as understood by the Policy. ... Similar to the information written on a notepad, or the ideas recorded on a tape, or the design memorialized in a blueprint, computer data, software and systems are intangible items stored on a tangible vessel – the computer or a disk.[42]

If a computer causes damage to itself due to an imperfection in one of its components there is no cause for action either in tort or contract unless, in the case of the latter there was a breach of a contractual term that caused such damage.

---

[39] 453 F 2d 533 (10th Cir. 1972).

[40] *Id.* At 537.

[41] 207 F. Supp. 2d 459.

[42] *Id.* 462.

5.6 Failure to Warn

Failure to warn is a common cause of liability particularly in the context of defective products. One has only to read of the numerous instances of recalls by car manufacturers and manufacturers of other products which happen with monotonous regularity. In *Jones* v. *W&M Manufacturing Inc*[43] the court held that:

> With respect to the cause of action for failure to warn, we note that [t]here is no duty to warn of an open and obvious danger of which the product user is actually aware or should be aware as a result of ordinary observation or as a matter of common sense.[44]

Failure to warn comes into play as a separate head of liability when harm is caused to an unsuspecting user where the manufacturer, who becomes aware of the defect which causes the harm, fails to advise the victim. This essentially means that the manufacturer has a duty to research and exercise due care in the manufacturing process with a conscientious effort to ensure safety of his product. Failure to warn is not only limited to manufacturers. In *Daley v. U.S.*[45] an air traffic controller was found negligent when he failed to identify the location of an aircraft and advise it of its unsafe proximity to obstructions was the proximate cause of a crash and allowed recovery under the Federal Tort Claims Act (FTCA) of the United States. Similarly, in *Gill v. U.S.*[46] the court found the provider of weather information liable for an inaccurate and sketchy weather briefing which was found to be the proximate cause of an air crash and allowed recovery against the government under the FTCA.

In August 2016 Allstate Insurance Co. accused Electrolux Home Products Inc., of being aware that clothes dryers the latter sold had the real likelihood of sparking fires, a fact Electrolux know from the trial stage of the product. As insurer of clients' (homes) who bought the product Allstate claimed more than $728,000 in total damages to the insured homes. The claim was later settled out of court.[47] In early 2017 A commercial refrigeration manufacturer was sued by Philadelphia Indemnity Insurance Co. which claimed damages for alleged flaws with one of the manufacturer's freezers which caused a large fire that temporarily shuttered a Jewish Temple in Orange County. As Insurance co. had to pay out $3.75 million on the insurance claim. At the time of writing the case was *sub judice*.[48]

---

[43] *Supra*, note 14 in this chapter.

[44] See also *Lamb* v. *Kysor Indus. Corp.*, 305 A.D.2d 1083, 1084, 759 N.Y.S.2d 266, quoting *Felle* v. *W.W. Grainger, Inc.*, 302 A.D.2d 971, 972, 755 N.Y.S.2d 535).

[45] 792 F.2d 1081 (11th Cir. 1986).

[46] 429 F.2d 1072 (5th Cir. 1970).

[47] See Greene (2000).

[48] *Philadelphia Indemnity Insurance Co. et al.* v. *True Manufacturing et al.*, case number 8:17-cv-00401, in U.S. District Court for the Central District of California.

5.7 Artificial Intelligence and Treaty Law

The use of artificial intelligence would also have some effect on existing treaty law in the field of air transport. To begin with, Article 8 of the Chicago Convention[49] provides that no aircraft capable of being flown without a pilot shall be flown without a pilot over the territory of a contracting State without special authorization by that State and in accordance with the terms of such authorization. Each contracting State undertakes to insure that the flight of such aircraft without a pilot in regions open to civil aircraft shall be so controlled as to obviate danger to civil aircraft. On the face of it this 70-year-old provision is seemingly referring to artificial intelligence without human involvement. Today's drones mostly (whether civil or military) have a pilot somewhere on the ground and this brings to bear the need to discuss who a "pilot" may be. This subject has been addressed in detail by the author elsewhere.[50] Annex 1 to the Chicago Convention (Personnel licensing) defines the act of piloting as manipulating the flight controls of an aircraft during flight time.[51] The same annex defines the pilot-in-command as the pilot designated by the operator, or in the case of general aviation, the owner, as being in command and charged with the safe conduct of a flight. The First Officer—defined as the plot-in-command under supervision—is identified as the co-pilot performing, under the supervision of the pilot-in-command, the duties and functions of a pilot-in-command, in accordance with a method of supervision acceptable to the Licensing Authority. It is worthy of note that none of these definitions identify a human as a pilot.

5.7.1 Annex 1 to the Chicago Convention

Any significant role in the flight deck played by artificial intelligence in the future would involve cogent and rigid standardizing by ICAO. In this context Annex 1 (Personnel Licensing) to the Chicago Convention would be of analogical refer ence in considering some of the requirements that might be relevant. Under the Annex, licenses are issued (by the State of registration of aircraft as relevant) to the following categories: commercial pilot—aeroplane,[52] airship, helicopter or powered-lift;—multi-crew pilot—aeroplane;—airline transport pilot—aeroplane, helicopter or powered-lift—glider pilot;—free balloon pilot;—flight navigator;—flight engineer. (b) Other personnel—aircraft maintenance (technician/engineer/

[49] *Supra*, note 5 in Chap. 1.

[50] For an extensive discussion on pilotless aircraft see Abeyratne (2014), pp. 117–136.

[51] Chapter 1 Annex 1—Personnel Licensing, 1-5 17/11/11.

[52] Annex 1 defines "aeroplane" as a power-driven heavier-than-air aircraft, deriving its lift in flight chiefly from aerodynamic reactions on surfaces which remain fixed under given conditions of flight.

mechanic);—air traffic controller;—flight operations officer/flight dispatcher;—aeronautical station operator

—multi-crew pilot—aeroplane;—airline transport pilot—aeroplane, helicopter or powered-lift—glider pilot;—free balloon pilot;—flight navigator;—flight engineer.

Other personnel identifies are aircraft maintenance (technician/engineer/mechanic);—air traffic controller;—flight operations officer/flight dispatcher;—aeronautical station operator.

Competency is a key requirement for technical functions in the flight deck. Standard 1.2.5.1 of the Annex states that a Contracting State, having issued a license, shall ensure that the privileges granted by that license, or by related ratings, are not exercised unless the holder maintains competency and meets the requirements for recent experience established by that State. It is recommended under this Standard that a Contracting State establish maintenance of competency and recent experience requirements for pilot licenses and ratings based on a systematic approach to accident prevention and should include a risk assessment process and analysis of current operations, including accident and incident data appropriate to that State. Competency is standardized and common rated among ICAO member States. Standard 1.2.5.1.2 states that a Contracting State, having issued a license, is required to ensure that other Contracting States are enabled to be satisfied as to the validity of the license. The maintenance of competency of flight crew members, engaged in commercial air transport operations, may be satisfactorily established by demonstration of skill during proficiency flight checks completed in accordance with Annex 6 (Operation of Aircraft). Maintenance of competency may be satisfactorily recorded in the operator's records, or in the flight crew member's personal log book or license and flight crew members may, to the extent deemed feasible by the State of Registry, demonstrate their continuing competency in flight simulation training devices approved by that State.

Standard 1.2.9.1 would pose some logistical problems to artificial intelligence in that it requires aeroplane, airship, helicopter and powered-lift pilots and those flight navigators who are required to use the radio telephone aboard an aircraft to demonstrate the ability to speak and understand the language used for radiotelephony communications. Another aspect that calls for consideration is Standard 1.2.9.2 which refers to communications between the flight deck and air traffic controllers. The provision requires air traffic controllers and aeronautical station operators to demonstrate the ability to speak and understand the language used for radiotelephony communications. It is recommended that flight engineers, and glider and free balloon pilots should have the ability to speak and understand the language used for radiotelephony communications.

The Annex also requires that, as of 5 March 2008, aeroplane, airship, helicopter and powered-lift pilots, air traffic controllers and aeronautical station operators demonstrate the ability to speak and understand the language used for radiotelephony communications to the level specified in the language proficiency requirements in the Annex. Aeroplane, airship, helicopter and powered-lift pilots, flight navigators are required to use the radiotelephone aboard an aircraft, air traffic controllers and aeronautical station operators should demonstrate the ability to speak and understand the language used for radiotelephony communications to the level specified in the language proficiency requirements in Appendix 1.

Standard 1.2.9.6 sets out a chronological requirement to the effect that as of 5 March 2008, the language proficiency of aeroplane, airship, helicopter and powered-lift pilots, air traffic controllers and aeronautical station operators who demonstrate proficiency below the Expert Level (Level 6) shall be formally evaluated at intervals in accordance with an individual's demonstrated proficiency level. This also carries a recommendation that the language proficiency of aeroplane, airship, helicopter and powered-lift pilots, flight navigators required to use the radiotelephone aboard an aircraft, air traffic controllers and aeronautical station operators who demonstrate proficiency below the Expert Level (Level 6) should be formally evaluated at intervals in accordance with an individual's demonstrated proficiency level, as follows: (a) those demonstrating language proficiency at the Operational Level (Level 4) should be evaluated at least once every 3 years; and (b) those demonstrating language proficiency at the Extended Level (Level 5) should be evaluated at least once every 6 years.

The Annex requires that a person shall not act either as pilot-in-command or as co-pilot of an aircraft in any of the following categories unless that person is the holder of a pilot license issued in accordance with the provisions of the Annex for an aeroplane; an airship of a volume of more than 4600 cubic metres; a free balloon; a glider; a helicopter; or a powered-lift.

A Contracting State having issued a pilot license cannot permit the holder of such license to act either as pilot-in-command or as co-pilot of an aeroplane, an airship, a helicopter or a powered-lift unless the holder has received authorization as follows: (a) the appropriate class rating as specified in 2.1.3.1[53]; or (b) a type rating when required in accordance with the provisions of 2.1.3.2.[54] Standard 2.1.4.1.1 stipulates that, when a type rating is issued limiting the privileges to act as co-pilot, or limiting the privileges to act as pilot only during the cruise phase of the flight, such limitation shall be endorsed on the rating. Furthermore, Standard 2.1.4.2 provides that, for the purpose of training, testing, or specific special purpose non-revenue, non-passenger carrying flights, special authorization may be provided in writing to the license holder by the Licensing Authority in place of issuing the

[53]Standard 2.1.3.1 provides that class ratings shall be established for aeroplanes certificated for single-pilot operation and shall comprise: (a) single-engine, land; (b) single-engine, sea; (c) multi-engine, land; and (d) multi-engine, sea.

[54]Standard 2.1.3.2 stipulates that type ratings shall be established for: (a) aircraft certificated for operation with a minimum crew of at least two pilots; (b) helicopters and powered-lifts certificated for single-pilot operation except where a class rating has been issued under 2.1.3.1.1; and (c) any aircraft whenever considered necessary by the Licensing Authority. 2.1.3.1.1. recommends that Contracting States should consider establishing a class rating for those helicopters and powered-lifts certificated for single-pilot operations and which have comparable handling, performance and other characteristics.

class or type rating in accordance with 2.1.4.1.[55] This authorization shall be limited in validity to the time needed to complete the specific flight.

The above discussion on Annex 1 was meant to show that the use of artificial intelligence in the flight deck, if it comes to pass in the future, would require a technical metamorphosis of ultimate sophistication and imagination. Such a transition would clearly bring to bear the inexorable truth that, in addition to standardization and harmonization, the element of choice would be a key factor in the flight deck, as the following discussion on two key treaties clearly represents.

5.7.2 *The Tokyo Convention*

The Tokyo Convention of 1963[56] is arguably a significant multilateral treaty that could be affected by the use of artificial intelligence in the flight deck if the "super first officer" concept attains fruition one day. The Convention in Article 1 lays down certain powers of the command pilot which may be relevant both in the case of pilotless aircraft or in the case of debilitation of the human command pilot with a computerized version of a first officer in the flight deck. It applies in respect of: offences against penal law; and acts which, whether or not they are offences, may or do jeopardize the safety of the aircraft or of persons or property therein or which jeopardize good order and discipline on board. The Tokyo Convention also applies inter alia in respect of offences committed or acts done by a person on board any aircraft registered in a Contracting State, while that aircraft is in flight or on the surface of the high seas or of any other area outside the territory of any State. An aircraft is considered to be in flight from the moment when power is applied for the purpose of takeoff until the moment when the landing run ends.

Article 6 of the Convention is extremely relevant to the element of choice reposed in the pilot on the flight deck. It states that the aircraft commander may, when he has reasonable grounds to believe that a person has committed, or is about to commit, on board the aircraft, an offence or act contemplated in Article 1, impose upon such person reasonable measures including restraint which are necessary: (a) to protect the safety of the aircraft, or of persons or property therein; or (b) to maintain good order and discipline on board; or (c) to enable him to deliver such person to competent authorities or to disembark him in accordance with the provisions of the Convention. Article 6.2 stipulates that the aircraft commander may require or authorize the assistance of other crew members and may request or

[55]Standard 2.1.4.1. states that a Contracting State having issued a pilot licence shall not permit the holder of such licence to act either as pilot-in-command or as co-pilot of an aeroplane, an airship, a helicopter or a powered-lift unless the holder has received authorization as follows: (a) the appropriate class rating specified in 2.1.3.1; or (b) a type rating when required in accordance with the provisions of 2.1.3.2.

[56]Convention on Offences and Certain Other Acts Committed on Board Aircraft, signed at Tokyo on 14 December 1963. ICAO Doc 8364.

authorize, but not require, the assistance of passengers to restrain any person whom he is entitled to restrain. Any crew member or passenger may also take reasonable preventive measures without such authorization when he has reasonable grounds to believe that such action is immediately necessary to protect the safety of the aircraft, or of persons or property therein.

The powers entrusted to the commander in order to suppress any unlawful act that threatens the safety of the aircraft go as far as requiring the disembarking of any person in the territory of any State in which he lands and delivering him to its competent authorities.[57] The State is under an obligation to allow the disembarkation and to take delivery of the person so apprehended by the aircraft commander, but such custody may only be continued for such time as is reasonably necessary to enable the criminal extradition proceedings (if any) to be instituted. In the meantime, the State of landing should make a preliminary enquiry into the facts and notify the State of registration of the aircraft.[58] The operative question in this context which would challenge artificial intelligence would be, how would it have "reason to believe" that there is a "reasonable likelihood of harm being committed by a person who is unruly and disruptive[59] in the aircraft? Another challenge is posed by Article 7 of the Tokyo Convention which states that measures of restraint imposed upon a person in accordance with Article 6 shall not be continued beyond any point at which the aircraft lands unless: (a) such point is in the territory of a non-Contracting State and its authorities refuse to permit disembarkation of that person or those measures have been imposed in accordance with Article 6, paragraph 1(c) in order to enable his delivery to competent authorities; (b) the aircraft makes a forced landing and the aircraft commander is unable to deliver that person to competent authorities; or (c) that person agrees to onward carriage under restraint. The aircraft commander is required to, as soon as practicable, and if possible before landing in the territory of a State with a person on board who has been placed under restraint in accordance with the provisions of Article 6, notify the authorities of such State of the fact that a person on board is under restraint and of the reasons for such restraint.

Article 8 of the Convention addresses discretionary powers of the aircraft commander when it says that he/she may, in so far as it is necessary for the purpose of subparagraph (a) or (b) or paragraph 1 of Article 6, disembark in the territory of any State in which the aircraft lands any person who he has reasonable grounds to believe has committed, or is about to commit, on board the aircraft an act contemplated in Article 1, and the aircraft commander is required to report to the authorities of the State in which he disembarks any person pursuant to this Article, the fact

[57]Article 8 of the Tokyo Convention.

[58]See Articles 12 and 13 of the Tokyo Convention.

[59]Annex 17 to the Chicago Convention (Security) defines a disruptive passenger as "*A passenger who fails to respect the rules of conduct at an airport or on board an aircraft or to follow the instructions of the airport staff or crew members and thereby disturbs the good order and discipline at an airport or on board the aircraft.*"

of, and the reasons for, such disembarkation. Furthermore, Article 9 gives the discretion to the aircraft commander to deliver to the competent authorities of any Contracting State in the territory of which the aircraft lands any person who he has reasonable grounds to believe has committed on board the aircraft an act which, in his opinion, is a serious offence according to the penal law of the State of registration of the aircraft. In such circumstances the aircraft commander is required as soon as practicable and if possible before landing in the territory of a Contracting State with a person on board whom the aircraft commander intends to deliver in accordance with the preceding paragraph, notify the authorities of such State of his intention to deliver such person and the reasons therefor. The aircraft commander is also required to furnish the authorities to whom any suspected offender is delivered in accordance with the provisions of this Article with evidence and information which, under the law of the State of registration of the aircraft, are lawfully in his possession. Neither the aircraft commander, any other member of the crew, any passenger, the owner or operator of the aircraft, nor the person on whose behalf the flight was performed can be held responsible in any proceeding on account of the treatment undergone by the person against whom the actions were taken.

Article 11 of the Convention provides that when a person on board has unlawfully committed by force or threat thereof an act of interference, seizure, or other wrongful exercise of control of an aircraft in flight or when such an act is about to be committed, Contracting States shall take all appropriate measures to restore control of the aircraft to its lawful commander or to preserve his control of the aircraft. In the cases contemplated in the preceding circumstances, the Contracting State in which the aircraft lands is required to permit its passengers and crew to continue their journey as soon as practicable, and shall return the aircraft and its cargo to the persons lawfully entitled to possession.

5.7.3 The Inflight Security Officer as a Solution?

A question that was debated in ICAO in 2014[60] under the heading of a Protocol to the Tokyo Convention was whether the pilot in command's responsibilities should be supplemented (and perhaps removed in the area of security in the aircraft) by an IFSO (Inflight Security Officer). The Diplomatic Conference was presented with two options one of which had to be selected. The options were as follow:

[60]In June 2013, the ICAO Council decided to hold a Diplomatic Conference whereby ICAO member States would adopt a Protocol to the Tokyo Convention of 1963. This Conference was convened from 26 March to 4 April 2014.

Option 1

[The aircraft commander or in-flight security officer may, when he or she has reasonable grounds to believe that a person has committed, or is about to commit, on board the aircraft, an offence or act

contemplated in Article 1, paragraph 1, impose upon such person reasonable measures including restraint

which are necessary:

a) to protect the safety of the aircraft, or of persons or property therein; or
b) to maintain good order and discipline on board; or
c) to enable the aircraft commander to deliver such person to competent authorities or to

disembark him in accordance with the provisions of this Chapter.

2. The aircraft commander may require or authorize the assistance of other crew members and may request or authorize, but not require, the assistance of passengers to restrain any person whom he is

entitled to restrain. Any crew member or passenger may also take reasonable preventive measures without

such authorization when he has reasonable grounds to believe that such action is immediately necessary

to protect the safety of the aircraft, or of persons or property therein."].

Option 2

The aircraft commander may, when he has reasonable grounds to believe that a person has

committed, or is about to commit, on board the aircraft, an offence or act contemplated in Article 1,

paragraph 1, impose upon such person reasonable measures including restraint which are necessary:

a) to protect the safety of the aircraft, or of persons or property therein; or
b) to maintain good order and discipline on board; or
c) to enable him to deliver such person to competent authorities or to disembark him in accordance with the provisions of this Chapter.

2. The aircraft commander may require or authorize the assistance of other crew members and may

request or authorize, but not require, the assistance of passengers to restrain any person whom he is

entitled to restrain. Any crew member, in-flight security officer or passenger may also take reasonable

preventive measures without such authorization when he has reasonable grounds to believe that such

action is immediately necessary to protect the safety of the aircraft, or of persons or property therein."]

The problem with both these options is that they appeared redundant and repetitive in the context of Article 6.1 of the Tokyo Convention which has been retained. Article 6.1 provides:

The aircraft commander may, when he has reasonable grounds to believe that a person has committed, or is about to commit, on board the aircraft, an offence or act contemplated in Article 1, paragraph 1, impose upon such person reasonable measures including restraint which are necessary:

(a) to protect the safety of the aircraft, or of persons or property therein; or
(b) to maintain good order and discipline on board; or
(c) to enable him to deliver such person to competent authorities or to disembark him in accordance with the provisions of this Chapter.

What the draft Protocol proposed (erroneously) was reproduce the text of the existing articles 6.1 and 6.2 in its new provision while retaining the original Article 6.1, making confusion worse confounded. All this was to include the in-flight security officer in the new provision, which ultimately failed with the majority of the States participating rejecting the sharing of the pilot in command's overall prerogative and powers in the aircraft.

5.7.4 The Warsaw and Montreal Conventions

The Warsaw Convention of 1929[61] in Article 17 provides that the carrier is liable for damage sustained in the event of the death or wounding of a passenger or any other bodily injury suffered by a passenger, if the accident which caused the damage so sustained took place on board the aircraft or in the course of any of the operations of embarking or disembarking. The Montreal Convention of 1999[62] which replaced the Warsaw Convention states also in its Article 17 that the carrier is liable for damage sustained in case of death or bodily injury of a passenger upon condition only that the accident which caused the death or injury took place on board the aircraft or in the course of any of the operations of embarking or disembarking. Article 21 states that for damages arising under paragraph 1 of Article 17 not exceeding 100,000 Special Drawing Rights (SDRs) for each passenger, the carrier shall not be able to exclude or limit its liability. In other words, the carrier is strictly liable up to 100,000 SDRs. The carrier shall not be liable for damages arising under paragraph 1 of Article 17 to the extent that they exceed for each passenger 100,000 Special Drawing Rights if the carrier proves that: (a) such damage was not due to the negligence or other wrongful act or omission of the carrier or its servants or agents; or (b) such damage was solely due to the negligence or other wrongful act or omission of a third party. There are two issues in these provisions that would impact the involvement of artificial intelligence. The first is the word "accident" which brings to bear communications from the flight deck. The most common communication is the "fasten seat belts" sign which is lit at the discretion of the captain (pilot flying the aircraft). Would an erroneous signal generated by a computer in the flight deck be categorized or considered an act of negligence of the carrier? More importantly, would an omission by a computer

[61]Convention for the Unification of Certain Rules Relating to International Carriage By Air, Signed At Warsaw On 12 October 1929.

[62]Convention for the Unification of Certain Rules for International Carriage by Air, signed at Montreal on 28 May 1999. ICAO Doc 9740.

device in the flight deck which fails to advise the passengers of imminent turbulence that threatens their safety be negligence on the part of the carrier. For those States still under the Warsaw Convention (i.e. which have not ratified the Montreal Convention), Article 25 of the Warsaw Convention precludes the carrier from availing himself of the limitation of liability provisions of the Convention if the damage is caused by the carrier's wilful misconduct or by such default on his part as, in accordance with the law of the court to which the case is submitted, is considered to be equivalent to wilful misconduct. Similarly, the carrier is not able to seek the exclusions and limitations of liability under the Warsaw Convention if the damage is caused under the same circumstances by any agent of the carrier acting within the scope of his employment. Any action grounded on damages arising from delay in the carriage of passengers, however founded, can only be brought subject to the conditions and limits set out in the Convention.

It must be noted that under the Warsaw Regime, an important provision is Article 20(1) of the Warsaw Convention provides that the airline shall not be liable if it proves that the airline and its agents had taken all necessary measures to avoid the damage or that it was impossible for the airline and its agent to take such measures. An academic study has posited that the phrase "all necessary measures" is an unhappy one in that the mere happening of the passenger injury or death presupposes the fact that the airline or its agents had not in fact taken all necessary measures to prevent the occurrence.[63] The question is, would an airline be presumed to have taken all necessary measures by employing artificial intelligence (which could, like any other aspect of technology, can go wrong). To what extend would the test of prudence be extended in the case of artificial intelligence? The airline usually takes such precautions as making regular announcements to passengers on the status of a flight starting with instructions on security and safety measures that are available in the aircraft. These measures are taken by the airline to conform to the requirements of the Warsaw Convention that the airline has to take all necessary measures to prevent an accident in order that the presumption of liability is rebutted. Thus in the 1963 case of *Chisholm v. British European Airways*[64] the court held that a passenger who leaves her seat when the aircraft goes through turbulent atmosphere is barred from claiming under the Warsaw Convention for personal injury. Here it was held that an admonition of the airline that the passengers were to remain seated with their seat belts fastened during the time in question was proof of the airline having taken the necessary measures as envisaged in the Warsaw Convention.[65] This case also established the fact that all necessary measures was too wide in scope and that a proper interpretation of the intention of the Warsaw Convention would be to consider the airline to require taking all reasonably necessary measures. In a more recent case Chapman J imputed

---

[63] Shawcross & Beaumont, *Air Law*, Op Cit, VII (116).

[64] 1 LloydsRep. 626. Also *Grein v. Imperial Airways Ltd.* (1937) 1 KB 50 CA at 69–71 per Greer L.J.

[65] See *Chisholm v. British European Airways*, *op. cit.*

objectivity to the phrase reasonably necessary measures by declaring that such measures should be considered necessary by the reasonable man.[66] A similar approach was taken in a subsequent case where the court held that the airline should show more than the fact that it was not negligent in order to invoke Article 20 (1) of the Warsaw Convention.[67] The United States also follows this approach of objectivity. In *Manufacturers Hanover Trust Co. v. Alitalia Airlines*[68] it was emphasised that the airline must show that all reasonable measures had been taken from an objective standpoint in order that the benefit of the defence be accrued to the airline. What would the objective standpoint be in the case of artificial intelligence? Some French decisions have also approached this defence on similar lines and required a stringent test of generality in order that the criteria for allowing the defence by approved.[69] Again, how would "generality" be translated into the realm of artificial intelligence?

Finally, the exemption from liability contained in the Montreal Convention—that if the carrier can prove that the damage caused to the plaintiff was not due to the negligence of the carrier or its servant—would a computer, which is a capital investment and a commodity, be classified as a servant? Would the manufacturer of the computer be classified or recognized as an agent of the carrier?

One of the key concepts that would come into play in terms of the carrier's negligence in employing artificial intelligence would be negligent entrustment. On 5 July, a runaway train coupled to gas tanks containing hundreds of thousands of gallons of oil derailed in the small town of Lac Megantic, 216 miles east of Montreal, resulting in a series of horrific explosions and devastating fire which killed at least 20 persons (the death toll was rising as this piece was being written). Many are still missing, presumed dead.

Just a day later, a Boeing 777 ploughed into a runway on its attempt to land at San Francisco International Airport, totally destroying the hull of the aircraft in a ball of flame and ash. Two passengers died and over 150 were injured, some critically. The aircraft had successfully completed its 10 h flight from Seoul when it crash landed.

A statement issued on behalf of Montreal, Maine and Atlantic Railway which owned the train that ploughed into the tiny town of Lac Megantic with its 6000 inhabitants claimed that the accident was due to the engineer's not applying sufficient brakes after it had stopped earlier for a crew change.

A statement issued by Asiana Airlines claimed the engines of the ill-fated 777 were functioning normally. The weather was fine. It was revealed that the pilot was inexperienced with the 777 and had not landed at San Francisco before. The National Transportation and Safety Board of the United States, which is in

[66]*Goldman v. Thai Airways International Ltd.* (1981) 125 Sol Jo 413 (High Ct). Also in (1983) 1 All E.R. 693.

[67](1986) 2 All E.R. 188.

[68]429 F Supp. 964 (SDNY 1977).

[69]*Preyvel v. Cie Air France* (1973) 27 RFDA 198. Also *Riviere-Girret v. Ste-Aer-Inter* (1979) Uniform L.R. 173.

charge of the accident investigation stated that, whereas a fully loaded wide body aircraft such as the 777 could be evacuated in 90 s flat, it had taken the crew 90 s just to open the cabin doors to let the passengers down the emergency chutes.

Therefore, both these horrific accidents point to questionable crew conduct within the scope of their employment. In the Asiana case, one could question whether the responsibility, and indeed accountability, lay with the airline for negligently entrusting the aircraft and its 300 or more passengers to an inexperienced pilot. In the instance of the runaway train, the same question may asked of the senior management, in a different way, as to its legal liability for an act of its employee whether negligent or not.

Negligent entrustment is a civil wrong at common law grounding an action in tort which arises when one party is held liable for negligence because he negligently provided another party with an object that could cause harm to another and the latter caused injury to a third party with that object. The cause of action most frequently arises where one person allows another to drive his vehicle.

Negligent entrustment—a theory that dates back to the early nineteenth century—can, in its simplest form, be exemplified by the case of an owner of a pizza parlour who entrusts a vehicle for the purpose of delivery of his product to a person who does not possess a licence of competence to drive, whether or not the owner has knowledge of the absence of licence. Liability ensues when the person entrusted with the vehicle causes injury to a third party. One commentator identifies negligent entrustment as a general theory of recovery under which the plaintiff alleges that the defendant was negligent in entrusting a dangerous instrumentality to one incompetent to use it safely, when he know or should have known that the incompetent would injure a third party.

The American Second Restatement of Torts provides that one who supplies directly or through a third person a chattel for the use of another whom the supplier knows or has reason to know to be likely because of his youth, inexperience or otherwise, to use it in a manner involving unreasonable risk of physical harm to himself and others whom the supplier should expect to share in or be endangered by its use, is subject to liability for physical harm resulting to them. In the 2007 case of *Watrous* v. *Johnson et al.* involving a wrongful death action against the defendant who struck and killed the plaintiff's wife while she was walking on the street, the Court of Appeal of Tennessee held that the parents of the defendant could be held guilty of negligent entrustment if they knew or ought to have known that the defendant's use of a car was likely to injure a third party. The court held that even though the parents of the defendant had only purchased gasoline for the car and provided insurance and maintenance, there was a prima facie cause of action for the plaintiff on negligent entrustment. The Court therefore remanded the case to the trail court (which had earlier held that there was no case against the defendant's parents) for further hearing.

Foreseeability is a key issue in the determination of negligent entrustment as a separate head of liability. In the 1931 Minnesota case of *Clarine* v. *Addison*[70] which

[70]234 N.W. 295 (Minn. 1931).

involved liability of a parent who entrusted a firearm to his 19 year old son who then accidentally shot and fatally injured a minor, the plaintiff failed to prove that the defendant could have foreseen that his son would kill another person with his firearm, given that the son had not earlier conducted himself with recklessness or irresponsibility.

Contributory negligence is not a defence against acclaim in negligent entrustment in the event an entrusteee who is given in charge of a *res* (or thing) where the entrustor has violated a statute in so entrusting. Furthermore, an owner of a vehicle who knowingly entrusts that vehicle to an incompetent driver is liable for the consequences of damage in the drivers hands even if there is no statutory provision to that effect.

Common law countries apply the *The Corporate Manslaughter and Corporate Homicide Act* of 2007, which provides that an organization is guilty of an offence if the way in which its activities are managed or organized causes a person's death, and amounts to a gross breach of a relevant duty of care owed by the organization to the deceased. The Act applies *inter alia* to a corporation. The offence is termed "corporate manslaughter", in so far as it is an offence under the law of England and Wales or Northern Ireland; and "corporate homicide", in so far as it is an offence under the law of Scotland. An organization that is guilty of corporate manslaughter or corporate homicide is liable on conviction to a fine and the offence of corporate homicide is indictable only in the High Court of Justiciary.

The Act provides, *inter alia,* that the extent to which the evidence shows that there were attitudes, policies, systems or accepted practices within the Organization that were likely to have caused failures in the provision of services by the corporation could be taken into account in determining the culpability of that entity. The possible application of this legislation to air transport is a reality, as exemplified in the *Helios trial* which opened on 26 February 2009 in Cyprus. The trial pertained to the island's worst air tragedy, when 121 people perished on a charter plane that slammed into a Greek hillside nearly 4 years ago. According to reports, Helios Airways and four airline officials faced charges of manslaughter and reckless endangerment in one of the most complex and high-profile cases in the eastern Mediterranean island's legal history. Plaintiffs, who were relatives of the dead, called for criminal action against those deemed responsible when the Helios Airways Boeing 737-300 ran out of oxygen and crashed outside Athens in August 2005. It was also reported that, although the authorities did not initially name d those to be charged, the accused were known to be officials who held top management positions in the airline at the time of the crash.

The instances of corporate entities being found liable for injuring or causing death to persons on the increase. For example, in the field of environmental law, concerning a $333 million class action in 1999 which was successfully argued in court against a California utility for polluting the water supply of a local community, is a good indicator of corporate liability. In the area of hospitality there is the "hot coffee" paradigm of Macdonald's fame where two States in the United States went on for law reform after learning of the true facts of the case.

In so far as criminalizing corporate activity is concerned, this could set a dangerous trend against efforts by the air transport industry which are calculated to ensure safety. Negligent entrustment, unless in extreme cases of criminal negligence, in its classical sense is a tort and must be treated as such, with the damage being calculated in terms of monetary compensation. Any extension of the principles under this head of liability to criminal law would cast an undue burden on those involved in providing services that are usually given out by experts such as pilots and surgeons and their employers. They would be forced to concentrate on covering their tracks rather than ensuring the protection of those under their charge.

5.7.5 The Super Co-Pilot

This book has already addressed super computers such as IBM's Watson being considered "super co-Pilots" of the future. In this context t is relevant to aver to the real likelihood of the need for the co-pilot to intervene when the pilot in command is either dysfunctional or seriously incapacitated. Pace (P.A.C.E.—Probing. Alerting, Challenging, And Emergency Warning) is a system that provides for an effective takeover by the co-pilot when such an eventuality occurs.

One commentator says:

> Subordinate flight crew members will use the "P.A.C.E." hierarchy of inquiry and intervention strategies to successfully cope with the extremely rare but potentially lethal performance break down of the Captain. First Officers trained and rehearsed in the intervention progression will initiate "P.A.C.E." whenever there is an indication of upper level performance breakdown in airline cockpits. Creative ad-libbing, on the flight deck, will not be productive in life threatening situations. The commercial airline co-pilot needs a message equivalent to that used by the military fighter pilot; there is no misunderstanding, hesitation or mistake in the action to be taken when the wing man calls, "Blue Leader, Break hard left, now".[71]

PACE is a structured process based on intervention models that has to be infused into the co-pilot's mind set. This is a step by step process that strategize action through models that obviate immediate flight safety threats through sequential actions. This process should come with an inherent guarantee against failure. The co-pilot under PACE should be able to immediately alert the captain if something were to go wrong or is likely to go wrong due to the captain's error or indiscretion. What is interesting is the inquiry into how a super computer would be able to accomplish the task of intervention. For one, the super computer would lack the emotional intelligence to reason with the captain. The other difficulty would be the impossibility of physical intervention by a computer in instances of extreme urgency with an uncooperative captain. Although it may well be that a super co-pilot would be able to track and identify a captain's "blind spots" it is quite

[71]Besco [(Capt. AAL, Ret.) President, PPI] (2000). See http://www.picma.org.uk/sites/default/files/Documents/Background/Besco%20Co-pilots%20dilemma.PDF.

another matter as to how the super computer taking the place of a human co-pilot would handle the situation in either convincing the captain that he is going off a cliff or physically taking over controls of the aircraft.

References

Abeyratne R (2014) Convention on International Civil Aviation: a commentary. Springer, Heidelberg, pp 117–136

Besco RO (2000) To intervene or not to intervene? The co-pilot's Catch 22. P.A.C.E. Probing. Alerting, challenging, and emergency warning; the integration of crew resource management with operational procedures

Colvin G, Derousseau R (2017) Bill Gates proposes a Robot Tax. Fortune, 22 February 2017

Dodgson L (2016) Why Mercedes plans to let its self-driving cars kill pedestrians in dicey situations. Business Insider Deutchland International, 12 October 2016

Greene K (2000) Allstate Says Electrolux Knew About Dryer Fires Before Sales, Law 360. https://www.law360.com/articles/826031?scroll=1

Ishak S, Trifiro F (2000) Neural networks. *Transportation Research Circular E-C 113*: Artificial Intelligence in Transportation, p 17

Smith N (2017) What's wrong with Bill Gates' Robot Tax. Bloomberg Views, 28 February 2017

Spencer DA (1989) Applying artificial intelligence techniques to air traffic control automation. Lincoln Laboratory J 2(3):537

Chapter 6
Millennials and Disruptive Innovation

Another megatrend that was identified in the Preface of this book is the *Global Code* that will be the domain of millennials of Generation Y (25–35 year olds) which would constitute 34% of global population in 2020. They are now identified as The Global Tribe who would be in constant travel across the globe in the years to come. Millennials are the largest generation with a population of 79 million in the United States. (also known as the Gypsy Tribe or Satellite Tribe) are the tech savvy young who are plugged in throughout the day to social media and the internet. They relentlessly need connectivity. In 2036 they could amount to 81.1 million, according to the Pew Research Centre.[1] They are the ones who mostly use the travel apps discussed in a previous chapter. They have income to spare and treat travel almost as a daily part of their lives. Millennials travel patterns have been identified as follow: "85% of millennials check multiple sites before booking their travel to get the best deal possible; 46% book travel through a smartphone or tablet; 60% will upgrade their travel experience by purchasing in-flight wi-fi, early deplaning, etc. They WILL post their experiences on social media. In fact, 97% will post while traveling, and 75% will post once a day. That's a lot of social activity. 68% will remain loyal to a program that offers them the most rewards; Cash/Freebies'; Upgrades; Discounts".[2]

Boeing's Dreamliner 787 has followed this trend in the best traditions of disruptive innovation—which means the discovery of a new market and tailoring the product for that market—where the aircraft, being smaller than its rival the Airbus A380 and being able to operate sustainable long distances, reduces the need for connections and layover times at airports. From the millennials airports perspective of time lags in airports, aircraft manufacturers are already planning aircraft with vertical take offs that would bring the landing of an aircraft closer to the cities—another factor favoring the millennials choices. This trend would adversely

[1]Fry (2016).

[2]Hospitalitynet (2017).

R. Abeyratne, *Megatrends and Air Transport*, DOI 10.1007/978-3-319-61124-2_6

affect many countries, such as India, China and certain South East Asian countries which are involved in long term planning and building new airports.

Clotaire Rapaille, an expert on global trends gives an anecdotal example of the Global Tribes' preferences:

> Fish do not occasionally swim. Likewise, members of the Satellite Tribe do not occasionally travel. They are migrating in flocks. . .They do not travel solely for work or to visit family: rather, they follow the migration patterns of the tribe.[3]

Millennials will be largely in what author Steve Case calls the "Third Wave" which will be defined by the "Internet of Everything"—in other words, where everything is interconnected.[4] According to Case, we have already seen the First Wave—which was when we got connected to the internet with rudimentary computers—and the Second Wave; when there was a surge in the use of the internet and smart phones as well as the introduction of social media such as Facebook. The first step for airlines seeking to cash in on disruptive innovation with the millennial market would be to be up there with apps and connecting tools that could boast of having the internet of things involved in the product they offer this new market. The third wave could disrupt every competitor unless they step up to the Third Wave. One of the key strategies in the internet of everything is forming partnerships with the "connectors". For instance, an airline which wins the new market of millennials would have to be in partnership with the providers of up to date inflight entertainment systems.

The above discussion brings to bear the compelling need for airlines to think systemically so that all the dots are connected in the internet of everything. The interconnection of all elements that makes the air transport product attractive to the millennial would require looking at parallel scenarios; being flexible in the context of being able to adapt to changing trends; a certain amount of risk taking; and seeking new partnerships. Domestically, airlines should review their employment policies and mindset to gain the maximum benefit from their employees in terms of their creativity. Demands of the millennials must be matched with their own creativity within the work force. The *Harvard Business Review* incorporated in its October 2016 issue a series of interviews, opinions and views of Francesca Gino, professor of business administration at Harvard Business School, who has: "conducted ground breaking research and found that whether consciously or unconsciously, organizations pressure employees, including leaders, to save their real, authentic, nonconforming selves for outside of work". Her research concludes that there are benefits to encouraging "constructive nonconformity." The fundamental question is how one could deviate from the dogmatic, restrictive and undue curbing of a worker's creativity at the workplace by the imposition of authoritarian rules that prohibit the publication of original and creative research that would in fact help the workplace. The *Harvard Business Review* observes: "most of us learn to

---

[3]Rapaille (2015), p. 86.

[4]Case (2016), pp. 42–43.

conform throughout our careers-to fit into the status quo, to align with the opinions and behaviors of others, and to seek out information that supports our views. This pressure to conform can have a significant negative impact on our engagement, productivity, and ability to innovate. In turn, our organizations suffer".

Taking on from this discussion, it is submitted that with new professional involvement in the effects of megatrends on the aviation industry (which includes the air transport, airport, air navigation services and manufacturing industries), an airline should embark upon new forms of contextual awareness, built upon strong conceptual and strategic thinking capabilities. When megatrends are analyzed against developments in aviation a proactive airline would need to conceptualize change in an unprecedented manner, based on conceptual and strategic thinking, taking into consideration global technical, political, economic, legal and demographic trends. The airline's projected leadership in this area would require exposure to new forms of intellectual openness and curiosity, and, above all, an enduring capacity to identify and analyze the effects of such trends on aviation. Megatrends and aviation would essentially entail a palpable transition from best practices to strategic analysis in the context of the new global business order and global risks facing global trends. This paper offers no more than a conceptualized view of megatrends and aviation and ways and means that the airline may approach the subject as an initiative. In order to provide an exclusive offering on megatrends and aviation, an airline would have to develop a two pronged approach: be up to date in political, economic, technological and business intelligence and translate the knowledge and information gained into analysis from an aviation perspective. This in turn would have to be communicated efficiently and strategically to the aviation community through a credible medium. The meaning and purpose of this initiative would be to: increase the airline's profile; and to generate possible income streams in terms of the sale of publications and offer of services within personalised seminars and workshops.

Communication on megatrends should essentially be based on strategic analysis on how to overcome challenges posed to aviation by megatrends. In this sense "strategy" is defined as per *The Harvard Business Review* as "*the creation of a unique and valuable position, involving a different set of activities from your competitors*". A Strategic Plan is a dynamic process, not a one-time event. This process will become an integral part of the way ASI does business and lead the company.

The "different set of activities" for an airline would involve incisive analysis of megatrends as they impact on aviation. This could be achieved both by publications and the offer of services. The absence of other players in this area makes such an approach attractive. However, strategy should not be about competition nor should it be about planning. It should not be about tactics nor achieving goals but be based on uplifting ASIs profile as a specialist in the area.

To find and sustain a new market an airline's strategy should be a collaborative effort based on trust and commitment by its network of experts and specialists. The strategy should be based on the following elements: *Rethink* the airline's look at the world: this initiative may need a fresh look at the world that is an extension of the airline's current focus on training and offering consultancy services. This would be followed by an in depth look at the playing field, meaning a comprehensive look at what is out there; *Redefine* the airline's ambition: the airline's purpose explains why it exists. A determination of redefining would bring to bear the nature of ASI and whether its approach should change with the involvement in megatrends. This might involve transcending best practices and going into strategic analysis and innovation; *Reshape* the business model: This would need a look at what the airline wants to achieve in its involvement in megatrends—elevation of profile or profit making or both.

The airline should: reinforce organizational system; create a dedicated team; evaluate possible impact on aviation community; develop a strategy; strengthen research and policy development through activities and membership of expert groups; increase public engagement; connect with the aviation community; develop new brand and marketing campaign, including focus on social media; become hub of megatrends and aviation policy and analysis by building leadership capacity and commitment; and advance its leadership role.

The curbing of creativity, original thinking and innovation is personified by what is called *The Mushroom Theory* where a penetrating mind in the workplace is considered in analogy to a mushroom in a mushroom farm where "*they keep you in the dark, cover you with bullshit and if you grow too much, they cut your head off*". Constructive non conformity is encouraged at face value by many employers including international organizations. The personnel instructions of one such organization provides: "outside activities may, of course, be beneficial both to staff members and to the Organization. [The Organization] should allow, encourage and facilitate the participation of international civil servants in professional activities that foster contacts with private and public bodies and thus serve to maintain and enhance their professional and technical competencies". This turns out to be mere hogwash as elsewhere in its staff rules this same organization gives the antithesis of constructive non conformity by stating peremptorily that lectures shall not be given by a staff member, nor articles and books written by staff on the subjects dealt with by that organization, except with the permission or agreement of his supervisors.

On the face of it, this requirement seems fair—that a supervisor with superior knowledge could embellish an article or even infuse it with diplomacy and impartiality. The problem is that the supervisor is often less qualified than the writer and in most cases oblivious to the subject matter. It is often the case that appointments are mere opportunities given to one through political influence or patronage, frequently with complete disregard to merit. Publications, on the other hand and lectures delivered are achievements and this distinction is deliberately blurred as a result of ineptitude or pure jealousy, as a result of which, an article submitted to a supervisor gets buried under a pile of obsolete files on the supervisor's desk and never sees the light of day.

Creativity should be generated in the workplace. Michael Poh, in his article *6 Ways to Unleash Creativity in the Workplace* says: "Some of you may think that creativity is an inborn trait rather than something that can be learned and developed. This may be so, but without a conducive environment for creativity to be expressed, how can we expect to see ideas arising from creative employees"? Poh suggests that creativity should be supported and rewarded, not punished and subverted.[5] Barbara Dyer in her article: "*Why Creativity is Absolutely Crucial in the Workplace*" published in the *Fortune Magazine* says: "all organizations have creative people and they should be encouraged. But there is an important distinction between welcoming the occasional out-of-the-box idea and cultivating creativity as an approach to doing business. Promoting a culture of creativity requires honing the skills observation and invention". Nancy Brown, CEO of the American Heart Foundation in her article "*Why Do Organizations Absolutely Need Creative People*" writes to *Fortune*: "However, creative thinking holds little value if people don't feel free to share their thoughts. It's important to foster a culture of open and ongoing communication. If you have an idea, we want to hear about it and explore its potential. Likewise, if you have a question, you should not hesitate to ask it. Whether it's a one-on-one meeting with your manager, a department-level meeting or an organization-wide conference, people should feel free to say what's on their mind. That's the only way to solve problems and develop solutions".

Another factor which stultifies creativity in the workplace is that creativity is perceived as threatening the status quo. Such an approach is the antithesis of the fundamental truth that organizations are made of people and it is their minds that would ultimately contribute to the progress of that organization. Michael Sloane, in this article *Does Encouraging Creativity in the Workplace Improve Innovation*?[6] quotes Teresa Amabile who says in her 1988 book, *A model of Creativity and Innovation in Organizations*[7] that there are seven factors for facilitating creativity in the workplace: *Organizational motivation* which is based on four items: the level of the firm's forward facing strategy towards the future, the extent that the firm follows opportunities rather than maintaining the status quo, the extent that the firm encourages its employees toward creative attitude, and the level of flexibility in the management systems to accommodate the desired behavior: *Resources* which include all resources necessary for achieving innovation. Here five items are measured: availability of time to explore new ideas, expertise of employees to handle problems creatively, availability of material and information resources, and training opportunities: *the need to challenge* by measuring the extent to which employees are emotionally involved in their tasks. The goal is to measure how well employees' capabilities match with task requirements so that employees feel intellectually challenged; *Freedom* which relates to the freedom of employees to plan their work and choose their own means to accomplish an assigned task; *idea support* which indicates how supportive and constructive the management is for idea generation and development. It also measures how much support the firm

[5]http://www.hongkiat.com/blog/unleash-creativity-workplace/.

[6]http://www.innovationmanagement.se/2012/11/09/does-encouraging-creativity-in-the-workplace-improve-innovation/.

[7]http://web.mit.edu/curhan/www/docs/Articles/15341_Readings/Group_Performance/Amabile_A_Model_of_CreativityOrg.Beh_v10_pp123-167.pdf.

receives from its employees for the initiatives taken to assess the dynamism in the firm; *proactiveness* which refers to the attitude of the firm towards risks and opportunities in contrast to conservatism; how experimental and tolerant towards ambiguity the firm is, and how fast decisions are made to avoid missing opportunities; and finally, *idea time* which refers to the extent to which employees use time provided as a resource to work on new ideas, test spontaneous new opportunities, and deal with a heavy and complex workload. The variable captures the actual usage of time rather than the availability (availability is measured in the resources variable).

If staff rules prohibiting creativity do not work, some organizations take other measures of discouragement, such as demolishing the library which has served the workplace for decades; refusing to promote a person with constructive non conformity to a higher grade even if the person who is so endowed is entitled to a promotion by merit and his superior credentials; humiliating the staff member by locating him away from the branch office he works in; and generally ignoring him.

In the above context the *Harvard Business Review* initiative for October 2016 should open the eyes of those who promote a myopic status quo to appease external influences that could be determinative factors in their own interests.

However, this alone is not sufficient as the involvement of States is crucial for its airlines to succeed and face megatrends. Firstly, States should be mindful of the contribution of aviation to the global economy as well as to their national economy. The aviation industry supports $2.7 trillion (3.5%) of the world's gross domestic product (GDP). Aviation Benefits Beyond Borders, a think tank, states that:

> The world's airlines carry over three billion passengers a year and 50 million tonnes of freight. Providing these services generates 9.9 million direct jobs within the air transport industry and contributes $664.4 billion to global GDP.
>
> Compared with the GDP contribution of other sectors, the global air transport industry is larger than the automotive industry, which accounts for 1.2% of global GDP and chemicals manufacturing (2.1%). It is more than half the size of the global financial services industry, which accounts for 6.2% of GDP. In fact, if air transport were a country, its GDP would rank it 21st in the world, similar to that of Switzerland or Sweden.[8]

The current annual carriage of 3.3 billion passengers would double in 15 years' time and the increase would comprise a sizeable n umber of millennials who would be living in large hubs. Progressive States would therefore look at their air transport systems through the eyes of hubs. With global unity crumbling and hyper connectivity advancing, the air transport product should be geared to adapting to cultural integration and absolute freedom of movement of airlines without restraint. In order to do this States, need to move their mindset from pure commercial interests to national interests. In other words, not exclusively how and in their countries. Millennials as a new market contribute much to this equation. A report by Standard & Poor's U.S. chief economist Beth Ann Bovino states that the millennials, born

[8]http://aviationbenefits.org/economic-growth/value-to-the-economy/.

from 1981 to 1997, numbers 80 million and that they spend an annual $600 billion. By 2020, they could account for $1.4 trillion in spending, or 30% of total retail sales.[9]

The millennial equation has to be take a step further to State policy in air transport to ensure that supply meets demand. Bilateral relations between States become important in terms of air transport. International relations are first and foremost a political tight rope walk. A State involved in obtaining traffic rights for its airline should wholeheartedly support the airline from a holistic point of view and not only from the airline's profitability point of view. In other words, a State, unlike an airline, must think of what the airline will contribute at the economy of the country. The United Arab Emirates and Qatar are good examples. The global tribe looks for quick connections with good inflight service and in and out of airports which have a good service quality. For them, connectivity comes first. Connectivity is intrinsically linked to fair and equal opportunity. States must ensure that their airlines have fair and equal opportunity to compete.

In a statement issued by Emirates (Airlines) the airline stated: "'fair and equal opportunity to compete' simply means that there must be non discriminatory treatment of all carriers. Different countries have different rules in place with regard to many things, such as advertising, taxes and consumer protection. There is no obligation that countries harmonise their laws. What the 'fair and equal' clause means is that those rules should apply to all carriers doing business there and not just to some. Equal treatment is not 'unfair' just because the rules are different from another country. In recent times concern regarding fair competition in international air services has focused on the issue of subsidy. The EU has strict rules in place about the grant of subsidies to ailing business, because a grant given to one business can affect all other businesses in the same industry. It is unfair in the Single Market for one state to bail out an airline when airlines from other states cannot be given the same grant. Concern about the effect of state aid to non-EU airlines led to Regulation 868, which allows the Commission to take action where a subsidised foreign carrier is seriously threatening the airlines of the European Community. The EU and its Member States, as well as countries such as the US and Canada, have asked for provisions on the treatment of subsidies to be included in Air Services Agreements with third countries.

Emirates has no issue with fair competition clauses per se, and some third country proposals to date seem fair and reasonable. But other third country clauses are clearly a sham: a political exercise proposing the absurd and impossible so that any reasonable rejection of biased terms can be painted as demonstration of guilt".[10]

---

[9]Shin (2015). see https://www.forbes.com/sites/laurashin/2015/04/30/how-the-millennial-generation-could-affect-the-economy-over-the-next-five-years/#549bf8132e15.

[10]Emirates Response—Our Position, http://content.emirates.com/downloads/ek/pdfs/openskies_rebuttal/EK_Response_Main.pdfat, p. 12.

In the long run, airlines would depend on their State of nationality to ensure that they have a fair and equal stab at disruptive innovation and to supply services commensurate with the demands of a new market such as the millennials, which is the largest generation alive, with over 79 million in the United States alone. For their part States have to link air transport to their development and one important aspect would be to consider the emergence of important cities in their territories and the potential they offer in terms of air transport connectivity. There are some States where the disparity between the major (capital) city and the second largest city is quite substantial. Thailand is an example where Bangkok's population and commercial importance is ten times that of Chiang Mai, its second largest city. India is also an example where the commercial importance between big cities such as New Delhi and Mumbai are secondary cities is quite significant. This not only gives rise to rural dissatisfaction and in some cases revolt against the government establishment, but it greatly stultifies growth. In turn this would stultify connectivity with the outside word and leads to the inability to engage in disruptive innovation by not being able to attract new markets and retrogression in air transport in the country. Ruchir Sharma, in his book *The Rise and Fall of Nations*[11] says:

> To make the most of any geographical advantage, leaders also have to bring their own most backward provinces into the global provincial flow... the ten-million plus population of central Bangkok is more than ten times larger that the population of Thailand's second largest city...A ratio that lopsided is abnormal in any country with a sizeable population... A look at twenty of the major midsize emerging nations shows that in most, the population of the largest city outnumbers that of the second city by that of three to one...ranging from Poland; Turkey, Colombia, and Saudi Arabia to Kenya Morocco, Vietnam and Iran.[12]

Sharma says that the rise of cities at the center of various industries and the rise of cities along trade routes go hand in hand, by which it can be inferred that the millennials, who are primarily service oriented could be a market that gives further credibility to this phenomenon. Despite the internet, which was originally thought—in the first phase when it was introduced—would make geography irrelevant, the opposite has happened where face to face meetings, which make travel and the importance of locations matter more than ever before, are increasing. Some countries have cottoned on to this trend of which India is one. It is worthwhile in this discussion to discuss India's new aviation policy in this context.

6.1 The Indian Case Study

Many millennials, particularly from the tech sector come from India and therefore one could envision their travel to and from the country. India—one of the largest economies in the world—therefore forms a good case study to consider the

[11] Sharma (2016).
[12] *Id.* 189–190.

millennial trend in air transport further. The aviation market size of India is US$16 billion, making it the ninth largest civil aviation market in the world. It is envisioned that in 2020 it will be the third largest, next to the United States and China, and in 2030 it would surpass the two giants to take first place. *Airbus Industrie* has forecast that by 2020 India will need 1600 new aircraft. 71 of the 430 airports and airstrips are currently functioning and India plans to develop and modernize 50 new airports/airstrips over the next few years. This would, among other positive improvements to the domestic air transport scene, enable the number of airports which generate more than a million passengers a year to triple in just a few years.

India plans to increase its carriage of domestic passengers to 500 million per year and its international passengers to at least 200 million per annum. From April 2015 to January 2016 the carriage of international passengers grew by 7.6% to 45.4 million and domestic carriage grew by 20.6% over the same period.

India has been gearing up and preparing for its giant leap with a few measures of its own that it adopted from 2008. For one, low cost carriers such as Air Daccan, Spicejet, Indigo and GoAir made strides while a considerable degree of airport modernization took place. Recently, restrictions on foreign direct investment (FDI), giving greater access to foreign carriers and more liberalization of international air services saw restrictions hitherto imposed, considerably relaxed. This is indeed a positive sign, taking into consideration the fact that India has been doling out US$1 billion each year in subsidies to ensure the sustenance of its national carrier.

Yet, India has a few shortcomings to focus attention on. For one, India has so far not taken effective and positive measures to capitalize on its geographic location of a hub between the east and the west and, above all, not embarked on a programme that would adequately train aviation managers. Infrastructure development has been slow and professionals have not been adequately rewarded. This has given more impetus to robust and energized middle east carriers such as Emirates, Etihad and Qatar Airways to capitalize on their geographic locations; obtain the active involvement of their governments in proactive decision making in the development of air transport in their countries as hubs between the west and the east; and above all, attract Indian professionals to leave India and work for them.

Improvements in the carriage of cargo out of India is a compelling need to bring the "Make in India" objective into fruition. Currently only 2.5 million tonnes are carried out of India from all the Indian airports which contrasts with, say, Hong Kong, which carried 4.4 million tonnes last year all by itself. Added to that has been the anomalous and contentious 5/20 rule which effectively precludes a new airline from being entitled to start international operations until and unless it was at least 5 years in domestic service and had 20 aircraft in the minimum to offer such services.

With this glaring dichotomy in place and the leaps and bounds growth India is experiencing that requires air transport to be a primary engine of growth in the country, it is not surprising that, on 15 June this year, India adopted a wide ranging and comprehensive aviation policy. The key "slogan" of the policy seems to be "taking flights to the masses". With the vast middle class that is emerging with expendable financial resources for travel, and the surge toward travel and connectivity both domestically and internationally, the new aviation policy embarks on an ambitious but achievable domestic connectivity scheme which introduces a "Regional Connectivity Fund" made up of a new levy on domestic flights. The fund would enable airlines to bid for financial aid from the fund to boost services to and from underserved points in India. On the benefits side, the policy aims at capping the price of an airline ticket at Rs. 2500 (about US$37) to give more affordable access to air travel for those wishing to travel within India. There is also the measure of lowering sales taxes to 1% and waiving off landing charges for airlines who serve these airports. The 5/20 rule would be extended to the deployment of aircraft to domestic flights.

With regard to airport development, the key word is "modernization" where the Public Private Partnership (PPP) concept has been endorsed with a view to its wide application throughout the country. 20% of non-aeronautical revenue earned at airports would be involved in supplementing aeronautical charges.

The liberalization of the FDI rules under the policy will see 100% of foreign equity in the hands of new airlines, where equity beyond a 49% threshold will have to be approved by the government. Foreign airlines could own 49% of equity and the balance 51% could be tied up with foreign enterprises that carry out businesses of a non-aviation nature. There are many proactive measures introduced by the new policy, on passenger facilitation, such as the automation of check in procedures and the establishment of data interchange processes throughout the country.

With regard to ground handling, carriers are allowed to self handle under the policy. The airport operator is required to ensure that there will be three ground handling agencies including the subsidiary of Air India at all major airports.

India will enter into an Open Skies agreement with all countries of the South Asian Association for Regional Cooperation (SAARC) and other countries situated beyond a 5000 km radius from New Delhi, its capital. This would of course exclude from the purview of open skies the middle east carriers, and carriers of certain South East Asian countries. As for countries within the 5000 km radius, India will enter into bilateral air services agreements (BASAs) where carriers of India have not fully utilized 80% of their capacity entitlements. As for foreign carriers that have utilized their rights under the BASAs with India, modalities and principles will be suggested by a Committee headed by the Indian Cabinet Secretary. In instances where Indian carriers have utilized 80% or more of their capacity, and seek more capacity, this would be settled under new BASAs to be negotiated. Also liberalized are domestic code share principles where Indian carriers will be free to enter into domestic code share agreements with any foreign carriers at any point in India.

Last but not least is aviation education and training, which is a must if India is to ensure its third place in 2020 and first place in 2030. The Policy acknowledges that the growth of civil aviation in the country has been hamstrung by the shortage of appropriate skills required in different sectors of civil aviation. This is not only in the area of trained pilots but also aircraft engineers and technicians, cabin crew, ground handling staff, cargo handling staff, administrative and sale staff, et al. The

Government plans to create the necessary eco system and architecture for ensuring full utilisation of the skill development capacities of the institutes under the control of Government/Public Sector Undertaking, and will expedite the commencement of courses by the National Aviation University (NAU) in the financial 2016–17 after due consultations with Stakeholders.

It is hoped that this proactive policy will boost connectivity; *Make in India* stronger, and achieve the aims and objectives of the government in the area of air transport through a policy which enables and is driven by a sound legal and regulatory policy.

6.2 Comment

The millennial equation is a triangle made up of the Y Generation (which is another name for the satellite of millennium generation), the proactive airline whose conduct and strategy should be as discussed above and the State which has to rethink its strategy to meet this particular megatrend. Location is the key issue here where emerging examples, such as Gdansk, Krakow and Wroclaw in Poland show compelling potential with global manufacturing and service industries that are starting to boom. Air transport should be looked at an engine of growth that can promote domestic consumption; investment in fixed assets and foreign trade—the three most important elements for growth in a nation.

References

Case S (2016) The third wave. Simon & Schuster, New York, pp 42–43

Fry R (2016) Millennials overtake Baby Boomers as America's largest generation. 26 April 2016. http://www.pewresearch.org/fact-tank/2016/04/25/millennials-overtake-baby-boomers/

Hospitalitynet (2017) Millennial travel trends: a look at the largest generations' habits. HighTech Amsterdam, Talking Hospitality Tech, 28–30 March 2017. http://www.hospitalitynet.org/news/4075929.html

Rapaille C (2015) The global code: how a new culture of universal values is reshaping business and marketing. St. Martins Press, New Your, p 86

Sharma R (2016) The rise and fall of nations: forces of change in the post-crisis world. W.W. Norton and Company, New York

Shin L (2015) How the millennial generation could affect the economy over the next five years. Women@Forbes, 30 April 2015

Chapter 7
The Internet of Everything

The Internet of Everything is the last of the three waves of the internet as discussed, the first wave being the building of the internet infrastructure with its foundations such as AOL, HP, Cisco systems; the second being the entry of social media such as Facebook and search engines such as Google and Yahoo and Google's Android and Apple's IPhone. This phase started at the beginning of this century. The third phase—which is a logical corollary to the second—would see a shift between the ownership of the internet in internet companies and the total involvement of the internet in all important aspects of our lives. The Internet of Everything (IoE) is known to be the intelligent connection of people, process, data and things while the Internet of Things (IoT) involved communications exclusively between machines. Needless to say, the internet of everything will have a bearing on air transport, with interesting ramifications for its legal aspects which will be discussed below. According to Cisco IoE is "a $19 trillion global opportunity over the next decade: Private-sector firms can create as much as $14.4 trillion of value while cities, governments and other public-sector organizations can create $4.6 trillion".[1] Cisco goes on to say that "(IoT) brings together people, process, data and things to make networked connections more relevant and valuable than ever before – turning information into actions that create new capabilities, richer experiences and unprecedented economic opportunity for businesses, individuals and countries".[2]

One commentator says:

> The Internet of Everything has become a catch-all phrase to describe adding connectivity and intelligence to just about every device in order to give them special functions...The IOE focus on health is quite interesting... [S]ome of these devices, such as connected blood pressure kits and connected blood glucose testing kits can even send the data they collect to your healthcare provider so that he or she can monitor your progress.[3]

[1] http://ioeassessment.cisco.com/.

[2] http://ioeassessment.cisco.com/learn/ioe-faq.

[3] Bajarin (2014).

R. Abeyratne, *Megatrends and Air Transport*, DOI 10.1007/978-3-319-61124-2_7

IoE will get rid of paper medical records and fax machines and connect medical conditions of a patient to one another, enabling medical professionals to come to diagnoses as well as treatment programmes easier, and more importantly, much quicker. In the third wave diagnosis could be taken over by Apps which could do the job much quicker than a human. However, IoE requires much work to get it functional as all systems must be synchronized. As the commentator concluded: "All industries will still have to deal with issues like security, privacy, hardware compatibility, software compatibility, synchronization, wired infrastructure, wireless infrastructure, data mining, data analysis and dozens of other things that will make IOE really work all over the world. While IOE is the next big trend, the next step will be to work on these major issues if IOE is to meet its full potential".[4]

7.1 Medical Issues

As already discussed in preceding chapters, IoE could make it easier in the context of the overall air travel experience with apps covering check in; security clearance; information in the terminal and boarding. Particularly, IoE could be indispensable for technical and cabin crew of an aircraft when an illness occurs on board. One in every 604 flights is reported to have a medical emergency. This translates to the fact that for every one million passengers, 16 will have a serious medical problem while on a plane, which amounts to the disconcerting fact that medical emergencies on board would affect about 44,000 people a year globally.[5] In such eventualities IoE could greatly assist the crew on board in treating the indisposed passenger. The other side of the coin is that, given the nature of liability of an airline with its curious departure from general principles of civil liability in other instances, IoE could present a different picture.

As already discussed under the head of artificial intelligence, Article 17 of the Montreal Convention of 1999[6] provides that the carrier is liable for damage sustained in case of death or bodily injury of a passenger upon condition only that the accident which caused the death or injury took place on board the aircraft or in the course of any of the operations of embarking or disembarking. The operative words are "accident"; "death" and "bodily injury". In the case of *Olympic Airways v. Husain*[7] where a passenger died of a cardiac asthma attack on board as a result of

---

[4]*Ibid.*

[5]Picard (2014). See http://www.theglobeandmail.com/life/health-and-fitness/health/when-passengersfall-ill-at-30000-feet/article18593303/.

[6]*Supra* note 62 in Chap. 5.

[7]540 U.S. 644 (2004). On January 4, 1998, 52 year-old Dr. Abid M. Hanson died while a passenger on Olympic Flight 417 between Athens, Greece and New York City. His death occurred after he suffered complications when he was exposed to ambient second-hand smoke while seated in the airplane's non-smoking section three rows in front of the smoking section. The plane had clearly demarcated sections for seating, one for smokers and one for non-smokers, though no partition

inhalation of cigarette smoke coming from the smoking compartment which was in close proximity to the seat occupied by the deceased, the issue was whether the airline could have assigned the passenger a seat away from the smoking section of the aircraft which the airline refused to do, resulting in the death of the passenger. The Supreme Court of the United States held that that an airline's mere inaction can constitute an "accident" within the meaning of the applicable treaty which was the Warsaw Convention of 1929 at that time, Article 17 of which bore similar wording as the corresponding provision in the successor Montreal Convention. The Court derived this principle from an earlier case *Air France* v. *Saks*[8] which held that an accident is "an unexpected or unusual event or happening that is external to the passenger." The Court in *Husain* held that this definition encompasses failures to act like the flight attendant's refusal to reseat the deceased in the face of a request for assistance. In the *Saks* case the Court with which the appeal was remanded was of the view that liability under Article 17 of the Warsaw Convention arises only if a passenger's injury is caused by an unexpected or unusual event or happening that is external to the passenger. This definition should be flexibly applied after assessment of all the circumstances surrounding a passenger's injuries.

The Court in Husain distinguished the decision in the case of *Abramson* v. *Japan Airlines Co.*,[9] where the plaintiff, who had suffered from a pre-existing paraesophageal hiatal hernia for which he had been undergoing treatment for 6 years and been hospitalized for the condition in June 1981 and been informed that he should have elective surgery to alleviate the condition, did not disclose that fact to the defendant airline. He had been on a Japan Airlines' flight in August 1982, during which the plaintiff's condition had been aggravated. When the plaintiff's wife had asked that he be able to lie down across multiple seats to apply a self-help remedy to relieve the pain, a flight attendant told her there were no empty seats. It was later determined through discovery in the case that nine first class seats were open. The plaintiff alleged that the flight attendant's refusal to allow him to lie down caused his condition to worsen, ultimately leading to his hospitalization. The district court entered summary judgment in favor of Japan Airlines finding that

separated the two. Dr. Hanson's wife, Rubina Husain, had asked Olympic's employees on multiple occasions with increasing urgency to move Dr. Hanson to another seat away from the smoking section. She explained the critical reasons Dr. Hanson had to move and made her concerns known about the consequences of leaving him exposed to the offensive smoke. Ms. Husain's requests were ignored, primarily by the flight attendant. Dr. Hanson died from a severe asthma attack caused by the smoke exposure.

[8]470 U.S. 392 (1985). On November 16, 1980, respondent Valerie Saks boarded an Air France jetliner in Paris for a 12-hour flight to Los Angeles. The flight went smoothly in all respects until, as the aircraft descended to Los Angeles, Saks felt severe pressure and pain in her left ear. The pain continued after the plane landed, but Saks disembarked without informing any Air France crew member or employee of her ailment. Five days later, Saks consulted a doctor who concluded that she had become permanently deaf in her left ear. Saks filed suit against Air France in California state court, alleging that her hearing loss was caused by negligent maintenance and operation of the jetliner's pressurization system.

[9]739 F.2d 130, 131 (3d Cir.1984).

Abramson's injuries were not the result of an accident. The Third Circuit affirmed the district court, finding that an aggravation of an existing injury during a routine flight, absent "proof of abnormal external factors," was not an unusual or unexpected event.

The court in *Husain* considered the Australian case of *Qantas Ltd.* v. *Povey*[10] where Ormiston, J. A. opined:

> The allegations in substance do no more than state a failure to do something, and this cannot be characterised as an event or happening, whatever be the concomitant background to that failure to warn or advise. That is not to say that a failure to take a specific required step in the course of flying an aircraft, or in picking up or setting down passengers, cannot lead to an event or happening of the requisite unusual or unexpected kind and thus be an accident for the purpose of the article. A failure by a pilot to use some device in the expected and correct manner, such as a failure to let down the landing wheels or a chance omission to adjust the level of pressurisation, may lead, as has been held, to an accident contemplated by Article 17, but I would venture to suggest that it is not the failure to take the step which is properly to be characterised as an accident but rather its immediate and disastrous consequence whether that be the dangerous landing on the belly of the aircraft or an immediate unexpected and dangerous drop in pressurisation.[11]

The Supreme Court observed in the *Husain* case that if it is established that the passenger's death would not have occurred, or his injury would not have been as severe, but for the flight crew's "unexpected or unusual" response to his medical condition, the death or bodily injury would not have "resulted from the passenger's own internal reaction to the usual, normal, and expected operation of the aircraft" but instead from an aberration in the aircraft's operation.

With the advent of IoE airlines would face a more stringent standard of liability under the Montreal Convention. For instance, when Article 21 of the Montreal Convention *inter alia* exempts the carrier of liability over the strict liability limit of SDR 100,000 if the carrier were not negligent, IoE could make it more difficult for the carrier than under usual circumstances to prove that it was not negligent purely because of the plethora of information that IoE enables to flow between data, processes, information and humans. For example, in the *Husain* case, IoE could have forewarned the airline of the possible fatal consequences of placing the passenger, given his known pre-existing condition, in close proximity to the smoking section, given the passenger's history.

7.2 Mental Injury

One of the important features of IoE would be its potential to assist the judiciary in advancing its knowledge on "physical" injury as mentioned in Article 17 of the Montreal Convention. The insistence of the courts in refusing to entertain "mental

[10][2003] VSCA 227, 17, 2003 WL 23000692 (Dec. 23, 2003).

[11]*Id* 242.

injury" as a purely separate injury from physical injury in this context has been on a somewhat pretentious assumption on the art of the courts that they are the arbiters of what constitutes physical injury and what constitutes mental injury and that they know, without consulting medical evidence, that there is no co-relation between the two. IoE could enlighten the legal fraternity including the judiciary with the help of such tools as IBM's Watson as to the current medical conclusions on whether mental injury could conclusively be considered a physical injury.

The issue of compensation for injury caused as a result of an aircraft accident is not one for judicial naiveté, nor is it one for judicial ineptitude and feckless insouciance. For over 83 years, courts have vacillated between a gross disregard for finding the true nature of mental injury, mostly by ignoring its relevance to recovery as a separate head of liability, and claims to pretention that mental injury is something completely comprehensible to the judicial mind as a "non-bodily injury". It is arguable that, both in their interpretation of the Montreal Convention's Article 17; its intent, and their gross disregard of medical science, the courts have got their act upside down, and that it is time for a paradigm shift with regard to recovery for mental injury, which should be spearheaded by the judiciary as well as legal and medical experts. In this context one commentator has said:

> Although the 1999 Montreal Convention retained "bodily injury" language, a close study of the treaty's history and more importantly, the negotiations among the signatories' delegates suggests that the great majority of nations intended to broaden allowable recovery beyond strict bodily injury and that many had already interpreted the phrase to include mental injury. As a result, courts interpreting "bodily injury" under the new treaty should closely review the intent of the signatories before adopting the previous treaty's precedent.[12]

For the reason that the judiciary has not abandoned its pretentious and opinionated view that, although being destitute of medical expertise and knowledge on the subject, it has the ability to determine that mental injury is not part of physical injury, the judiciary has vacillated to and fro on the subject. On the positive side, in the 1999 case of *Weaver* v. *Delta Airlines Inc.*[13] where the plaintiff experienced terror and felt physical manifestations of that terror during an emergency landing, which necessitated her seeking medical treatment for emotional and physical problems attributable to her flight experiences, and she was diagnosed with, and received treatment for post-traumatic stress disorder, the court held that no floodgates of litigation will be opened by allowing for claims such as the plaintiff's, which are based on a definite diagnosis of a disorder that arises from a physical injury that is medically verifiable. The court held that fright alone is not compensable, but brain injury from fright is.

On the negative side, and this has been the prevalent judicial trend, in the case of *In re Crash at Little Rock, Arkansas on 1 June 1999*[14] although the trial judge held that from the evidence presented, it could be accepted that post-traumatic stress

[12]Cunningham (2008).

[13](1999) 56F Supp 2d 1190.

[14](2000) 27 Avi 18,428.

disorder is a biological/physical as well as psychological injury, this contention was rejected at the appellate level on the basis that the evidence was not sufficient to establish a physical change to the plaintiff's brain.

The glaring neglect of the judiciary in ascribing to itself the status of expert on mental injury on the presumption that mental injury is simplistically an injury of the mind which is devoid of and completely separate from bodily injury, leaves the question unanswered as to whether a more enlightened approach is called for, if only to involve the medical fraternity in the determination of this issue. This article will attempt to address this issue as well. In the 1991 case of *Eastern Airlines Inc.* v. *Floyd et al.,*[15] the United States Supreme Court concluded that there must at least be physical manifestation of injury, if not death or physical injury, in order for a claimant to successfully sue an air carrier under Article 17. The court, however, did not address the issue as to whether mental injury accompanied by physical injury was a compensable element. The *Floyd* decision is consistent with its precursor—the 1974 case of *Rosman (and Herman)* v. *Trans World Airlines*[16] which related to a hijacking incident—holding that there have to be palpable, objective bodily injuries, including those caused by psychic trauma related to the incident, and for the damage flowing from the bodily injuries and not from the trauma *per se*. The *Rosman* decision followed in the wake of a 1973 decision[17] which held the same.

The inclination of the courts to insist on pure physical injury as an essential element of compensability is arguably due to the reason that courts took refuge in the original French terminology of the Convention which was "*lésion corporelle*" which means in the French language "physical wound " as against "*lésion mentale*" which means "mental wound".[18]

A diametrically opposed view emerged in a *cursus curiae* which ignored the connotations of the French language and visited the original intention of the drafters of the Convention. In *Husserl* v. *Swiss Air Co. Ltd.,*[19] also a case concerning the hijacking of an aircraft, the court observed the lacuna relating to the absence of reference to emotional injury in Article 17 and deemed fit to construe the provision broadly, to include injuries other than pure physical injury But the question is, is it arguable that mental injury could indeed be construed as bodily injury? How would the Courts interpret Article 17? Would there be, on the other hand separate compensation for mental injury that follows a bodily or physical injury?

Let us first take the issue of the interpretation by the Courts of Article 17. Starting with the exclusivity of bodily injury, the courts would have to bring in mental injury as a bodily injury or as the result of physical injury resulting from an accident. The first issue therefore is "is mental injury a bodily injury?

[15] 17 April 1991, 23 *Avi.* 17,367.

[16] 358 *N.Y.S.* 2d 97 (1974), 13 *Avi.* 17,231.

[17] 368 *F Supp.* 1152 (1973), 12 *Avi* 18,405.

[18] For a detailed discussion on this subject see Desbiens (1992), p. 153 at pp. 159–166.

[19] (D.C.N.Y. 1972) 351 F. Supp. 702.

Psychosomatic injury is an accepted category of injury by the medical profession, and has been for long. It is defined as: "pertaining to mind-body relationship' having bodily symptoms of psychic, emotional or mental origin".[20] In an aircraft accident, although a passenger in the aircraft may not suffer physical injury at all, he could suffer what is medically identified as *Somatoform Autonomic Dysfunction* (SAD) which the World Health Organization describes as follows:

> Symptoms are presented by the patient as if they were due to a physical disorder of a system or organ that is largely or completely under autonomic innervations and control, i.e. the cardiovascular, gastrointestinal, respiratory and urogenital systems. The symptoms are usually two types, neither of which indicates a physical disorder of the organ or system concerned. First, there are complaints based upon objective signs of autonomic arousal such as palpitations, sweating, flushing, tremor, and expression of fear and distress about the possibility of a physical disorder. Second, there are subjective complaints of a non-specific or changing nature such as fleeting aches and pains, sensations of burning, heaviness, tightness, and feelings of being bloated or distended, which are referred by the patient to a specific organ or system.[21]

SAD is a system where a mental condition brought about by stress may result in palpable physical discomfort and disease, and which could well result from an aircraft accident. WHO lists some of the physical diseases that could result from SAD as cardiac neurosis, gastric neurosis, neurocirculatory asthenia, and psychogenic forms of aerophagy, cough, diarrhoea, dyspepsia and irritable bowel syndrome.[22]

The WHO also lists *Persistent Somatoform Pain Disorder* which is a predominant complaint of severe, persistent and distressing pain which cannot be explained fully by a physiological process or a physical disorder, and which occurs in association with emotional conflict or psychosocial problems that are sufficient to allow the conclusion that that they are the main causative influences. The result is a marked increase in personal or medical attention given to the patient.[23]

Another glaring fact of judicial inadequacy in the determination of the nature of "injury" under firstly the Warsaw Convention of 1929—which had the exact provision as the Montreal Convention's Article 17—and then the Montreal Convention, is blatant in that the judiciary has gone on the theoretical definition of "bodily injury which is "damage to the body" which seemingly has been relegated by the judiciary to tissue damage. This theoretical definition cannot be applied to mental injury in judicial parlance. However, this is where the legal and medical synergy should occur. As some authors correctly point out:

> ...a sexual assault which results in no tissue damage but from which the victim experiences severe depression, will only be covered by the theoretical definition if the scope of bodily damage is broadened to include psychological damage. There would seem to be a case for such harm to be included in a theoretical definition given that significant numbers of those

[20]Dorland (2007), p. 1573.

[21]ICD-10 (1992), p. 349.

[22]*Ibid.*

[23]ICD-10 (1992), p. 350.

in injury research and practice consider this a legitimate area of concern for the field. Moreover in New Zealand (population of 4 million) at least the agency, Accident Compensation Corporation, which has the primary mandate for injury prevention, rehabilitation and compensation, compensates victims who suffer such harm.[24]

One way of reaching a reasonable outcome to this inept judicial approach is for both the judicial and medical fraternities to put their heads together when a case comes up for adjudication. In doing so, they could consider the relevance of "accident neurosis"—also called compensation or litigation neurosis- which is essentially a disabling subjective functional nervous disorder that sometimes occurs without physical injury of any kind.[25] Miller states of accident neurosis:

> Symptomatology is described with a wealth of superlatives and often with a palpable determination to emphasize the seriousness of disablement. Headache, dizziness, irritability, loss of memory, anxiety, easy startling, bouts of depression,[26] blackouts, and nightmares about the accident...loss of interest and an unshakable conviction of unfitness for work usually comprise the picture.[27]

Miller also inquires into the possibility of schizophrenia being caused by accident neurosis without any attendant physical injury. He states:

> Schizophrenia is rarely provoked by head injury and here the paramount role of constituent factors cannot be doubted. In a personal case the traumatic delirium of a severe injury shaded imperceptibly into a frankly schizophrenic illness which persists several years later- a development that was strikingly clarified when I discovered that the patient's elder brother had already spent several years in hospital with a schizophrenic illness unassociated with any injury.[28]

Sarah B. Rasool, in her doctoral thesis in 2007 stated:

> Research in the field of trauma has shown that accidents can lead to the onset of an array of psychiatric disorders, not only PTSD and acute stress disorder (ASD). Depression, anxiety and specific phobias, substance misuse, and insomnia have all been implicated in the psychological aftermath of Road Traffic Accidents (RTAs).[29]
>
> The concept of psychological trauma has evolved over the 20th century. From a psychodynamic perspective, a traumatic event is one that breaks through, or overrides the mind's filtering process and floods the mind with a degree of stimulation that it cannot manage. There is a colossal disruption in functioning, amounting to a kind of breakdown of the defence organisation, leaving individuals vulnerable to intense overwhelming anxieties from internal sources which have been provoked by an external event. The associated treatment guided by this conceptual model is long term psychotherapy. The aim of which is

[24]Langley and Brenner (2004).

[25]Miller (1966), p. 258.

[26]Accident neurosis must be distinguished from examples of true depressive illness of endogenous pattern beginning shortly after cerebral trauma.

[27]*Ibid.*

[28]*Ibid.*

[29]Rassool (2007), p. 113. Also at www.kellyconnor.com/research/f/phd_thesis.pdf.

> to make the unconscious conscious and resolve conflicts that the current trauma may have unearthed.[30]

One way of evaluating the extent of mental injury is to follow the New Zealand model of assigning external cause codes to cover mental health outcomes where psychological injury could be ascertained through injury events which can in turn be paired with particular mental disorders. This system could be implemented through the maintenance of hospital records that assign codes at discharge from the hospital even if there is no linking physical damage. IoE could step in to facilitate this process and establish the necessary connections between data, processes and humans. An operational physical and mental injury through established medical research and findings. A thorough revision should be undertaken pertaining to hitherto acceptable theoretical and operational definitions that are arrived at without basis or appropriate scientific and legal considerations. Injury statistics should be carefully considered at an international platform and ICAO medico-legal expertise should be utilized to make appropriate recommendations to the international civil aviation community.

The ICAO Council also has the opportunity, under Article 55 d) of the Chicago Convention to study any matters affecting ICAO and the operation of international air transport. Taking into consideration the above discussion, and given ICAO's new role in air transport—that of fostering the development of the civil aviation system—one is encouraged that the Organization's impetus will be increased and more guidance could be forthcoming in air transport law and economics. For instance, in accordance with the permissive functions of the Council, which provides that the Council may conduct research into all aspects of air transport which are of international importance,[31] such studies, taking into account trends such as those discussed at the commencement of this chapter, could analyse global legal trends affecting air transport and their effects on ICAO's aim to ensure the safe, regular, efficient and economical air transport. Although this approach is highly desirable, it might not be deemed by ICAO to be practical or even worthwhile. However, such an approach could largely embellish the current role of ICAO as a leader which provides expertise in matters of law and economics, rather than just being the global forum for air transport, technically, economically and legally.

The most logical step in this process would be to make the paradigm shift from bodily injury to mental injury that could result in mental injury being accepted as a compensable element and determine the inextricable link between the two, in interpreting the term "bodily injury" under the Montreal Convention. IoE could greatly help in this exercise and ICAO could do a great service by the international aviation community if further study is undertaken through the Legal Committee of its Council.

[30] *Id.* 117–118.

[31] Chicago Convention, *id.*, Article 55 c).

7.3 Safety Issues

There are just two (out of several) examples that illustrate the inextricable link between IoE and safety. The first is the *Air Asia* Flight QZ 8501 crash into the ocean and the second is the suicide by the co-pilot of the *Germanwings* flight. In the former instance, *AirAsia* Flight QZ8501 operated by an Airbus A320-200 from Surabaya in Indonesia to Singapore crashed into the Java Sea off Borneo shortly after take-off (40 min into the flight) on 28 December 2014. All 162 people on board perished. An accident investigation report issued in December 2015 debunked the initial blame for the crash which was entirely placed on prevailing bad weather and instead revealed that a faulty component and crew action were contributing causes. Of course bad weather was a red flag, which could have been more apparent prior to the take off if IoE had been involved. Modelling of weather prevailing patters as well as the coordination of all information links pertaining to the flight would have given the flight crew clearer indications of the real threats involved in the operation of the flight. A fortiori, those involved in dispatching the flight could have also had more insight into the threat and risk faced by Flight QZ 8501.

In the context of the malfunction, the report revealed that there were multiple contributory factors: a component malfunction which led to a miscommunication between the pilot and the co-pilot. Firstly, there was a repeated technical problem with the Rudder Travel Limiter (RTL), requiring the complete attention of the pilot in command, leaving the co-pilot to take control of the plane. Electrical interruption to the RTL happened three times in the space of 13 min, eventually causing the autopilot to disengage. The loss of the autopilot function left the co-pilot to manually operate the flight. It was at that point that the miscommunication occurred between the captain and co-pilot. Information contained in both the cockpit voice recorder and data recorder revealed that the pilot instructed the co-pilot to "pull down", by which the pilot meant "go down" but was taken literally by the co-pilot to pull down on the gear control which automatically led the aircraft to rise rapidly to 38,000 ft. More standardized terminology, which could have been easily transmitted by a system subscribing to IoE may been safer.

Alec Scot, in his article *8 ways the Internet of things will change the way we live and work* says:

> Airplanes have long been equipped with sensors that collect data on fuel efficiency, altitude, location and maintenance issues. But that data has typically only been processed after the aircraft lands. With advances in connectivity and data processing software, there's no reason it can't be sent off and parsed mid-flight... But change is coming, slowly. Sensors in an aircraft's engines can now detect and isolate developing problems—in part by measuring the temperature of a jet engine's exhaust—and communicate those to both pilots and ground crews while the plane is still in the air.[32]

[32]http://www.theglobeandmail.com/report-on-business/rob-magazine/the-future-is-smart/article24586994/.

Communications in the flight deck is a critical element which has contributed to human error which has been recognized to have caused 70–80% of civil and military aviation accidents. Of these many have been due to improper communications either between cockpit crew or between cockpit crew and air traffic control. Inadequate communications between technical crew and air traffic control and between members of technical crew have led to serious accidents. In 1977, the worst aviation disaster occurred at Tenerife in the Canary Islands, caused by heavy accents and improper terminology among a Dutch KLM crew, an American Pan Am crew and a Spanish air traffic controller. 583 passengers perished.

Traditionally, industrial accidents have gone through three phases of causation. The first phase involved regular instances of technical malfunctions or system failures. This phase was followed, after technological development had reached a reasonable level of sophistication, by the second phase dominated by human error. The third phase was known as the sociotechnical period which involved human interaction with technology, which in turn led to the phase we are in at the present time which one commentator[33] calls the "organizational culture period" wherein operators perform as a coordinated team according to a particular safety culture instilled in them by their employers. This evolutionary pattern also applies to the air transport industry.

The need for operators to perform as a coordinated team has become increasingly apparent with globalization, where pilots of differing ethnic backgrounds are thrown together to fly an aircraft. Members of different cultures have not only been found to differ in their styles and attitudes towards leadership but also to exhibit distinct conversational norms.[34] *A fortiori*, culture influences how juniors relate to their seniors. Therefore, a multinational, multicultural crew has to mesh their communications coherently, and, above all, transcend ethnic and cultural inhibitions in the cockpit.

Malcolm Gladwell, in his book *Outliers—The Story of Success*[35] has a chapter which he has entitled *The Ethnic Theory of Plane Crashes*.[36] Gladwell suggests that the ethnicity of the pilots and first officers in the cockpit of an aircraft may have an impact on the safety of flight and cites the famous example (among others) of the crash of the Colombian airliner Avianca flight 052 in January 1990. Here the first officer, in his communications with the air traffic controller had indulged in what was called "mitigated speech" which downplayed or sugar coated critical information that was needed both by the pilot and by the air traffic controller. Gladwell quotes an expert, Earl Weener, a former chief engineer for safety at Boeing who said:

> The whole flight deck design is intended to be operated by two people, and that operation works best when you have one person checking the other, or both people willing to

[33]Amin (1999).

[34]Merritt and Helmreich (1996), pp. 5–24.

[35]Gladwell (2008).

[36]*Id.* Chapter Seven, at 177–223.

> participate. Airplanes are very unforgiving if you don't do things right. And for a long time it's been clear that if you have two people operating the airplane cooperatively, you will have a safer operation than if you have a single person who is simply there to take over if the pilot is incapacitated.[37]

Let us analyse what happened to the Avianca flight. The aircraft was dangerously low on fuel and needed immediate landing. The Captain instructed the first officer to tell air traffic control "We are in an emergency". The First Officer relayed the following message: "That's right to one-eight-zero on the heading and, ah, we'll try once again. We are running out of fuel".[38] This does not, by any means, tell ground control that the aircraft had an emergency. The phrase "running out of fuel" does not convey the grave emergency at all. After a period of silence in the cockpit (which was extremely unusual for an emergency) the aircraft slammed into an estate in Long Island town of Oyster Bay, New York. Seventy three passengers perished.

The first officer mitigated his communication to the air traffic controller because he wanted to be polite, presumably because he held the controller in high esteem. Another aspect to the disaster was that Klotz (the first officer) who was Colombian, expected his pilot to take the decisions Gladwell says:

> Klotz sees himself as a subordinate. It's not his job to solve the crisis. It's the captain's. Then there's the domineering air traffic controllers at Kennedy Airport ordering planes around. Klotz is trying to tell him he's in trouble. But he is using his own cultural language, speaking as a subordinate would be, to a superior. The controllers though, aren't Colombian. They are low-power distance New Yorkers. They don't see any hierarchical gap between themselves and the pilots in the air. To them, mitigated speech from a pilot doesn't mean the speaker is being appropriately deferential to a superior. *It means the pilot doesn't have a problem.*[39]

The first measure which should be taken in ensuring team work is to create a positive work environment where each employee feels valued. Listening to one another and honouring the other's point of view is the most effective way to have a common base of equality in a team. In the Avianca instance the first officer, due to his ethnic and cultural background, did not expect his captain to seek his point of view. There did not exist in the cockpit environment a feeling of respect for every individual.

The second measure is to build mutual trust. Inasmuch as trust is the basic tenet for all relationships, it should not be on a one-way basis, as was in the case of Klotz who trusted his captain to take the decisions, thereby relinquishing his own responsibilities of saving the aircraft and passengers. Trust is about doing what you say you are going to do and being who you say you are. It's about showing one's peers and team mates in everything one does that one is reliable, responsible and

[37] *Id*, 185.
[38] *Id* 193.
[39] *Id*. 207.

accountable, and that they can rely on that person for consistency. That was certainly not what Klotz did with his captain.

As for the captain of the Avianca flight, what he did not do was to make his first officer feel that the latter played an important role. The captain did not encourage an environment of cooperation. Rather, he created an environment of competition where Klotz felt he was the inferior and weaker member of crew. The effective leader lets each member of staff know he is a valued part of the team, and that will create a work environment where staff members will respect each other for their unique contributions. This essentially requires the leader to create team spirit by demonstrating that he is open to communication from everyone.

The Avianca example resonates with the aviation community a similar trend that existed in civil aviation in Korea until recently. The strongly hierarchical nature of Korean culture[40] was often instrumental in blocking a second in command in the cockpit of a Korean airliner from advising the captain when he knew that the captain was taking wrong action during the flight. This resulted in a high crash rate, until Korean Air trained its flying crew not to behave hierarchically in the cockpit.[41]

Another example that has been cited is that of China Air, the national carrier of Taiwan, which had one of the worst accident records from 1986 to 1998 which reported 561 fatalities.[42] Donald Davis, an expert who carried out a 3 year study commissioned by the National Aeronautics and Space Administration (NASA) of the United States on how differing styles impede or otherwise adversely affect cockpit communication and coordination has reportedly said of Air China during the period in question:

> a reasonable inference is that the autocratic decision-making style preferred by Air China pilots, most of whom received their training in the Taiwanese Air Force, can be counter-productive during times of crisis. Compared to pilots of other nations, the Taiwanese place the greatest emphasis on rules, order, strict time limits and a preference for finding a single correct answer to any problem. Chinese subordinates are unlikely to question or challenge their superiors, even if they are aware of situation-critical information that senior pilots are not.[43]

In discussing an accident involving an aircraft which was operated by Filipino crew one commentator has observed that, during the final moments before the impact the pilot's foremost thoughts, as reflected in his expostulations recorded in the black box, focussed on his family and creator, not on battling the defects that were bringing his aircraft down. The commentator mentions that Filipinos bend

---

[40]Culture is the behaviour, customs, values, language and beliefs of a social group. See Tam and Duley (2005).

[41]Korean Airline Pilots, Arrogant Physicians, and Life-or-Death Decision Making, December 13, 2008 at http://physioprof.wordpress.com/2008/12/13/korean-airline-pilots-arrogant-physicians-and-life-or-death-decisionmaking/.

[42]Schultz (2002).

[43]*Ibid.*

towards spirituality and messianic self sacrifice as a response to stress.[44] In contrast, American and Australian pilots are lone men braving the elements and tend to fix problems in the cockpit by themselves.[45]

One of the reasons ascribed to the breakdown of communications between the captain and his subordinate crew is that the former is generally considered an elite, confident and competent professional in the aircraft who is often unwilling to admit impairment of judgement or failure. The captain is a self-sufficient hero who does not make a mistake.[46] This brings to bear the gender issue and the question as to whether a male pilot generally conducts himself and functions differently from his female counterpart. Although a study has concluded that there is no difference between pilot error accident rates attributed to male and female pilots,[47] male pilots have been reported to be more task-oriented and exude more confidence than women pilots, whereas women pilots naturally are reported to be more sensitive towards the needs of the passengers and be better at communicating.[48]

A significant aspect of good communication and leadership in the work place is approachability, where the boss demonstrates that he is available to hear any point of view and give credit for success of staff. Above all, the boss should always take responsibility. For example, it could be argued that in the case of the Avianca disaster, the captain should have taken over if he was not satisfied that the gravity of the emergency was not being relayed appropriately by the first officer to ground control.

At the end of the day there is no established magic formula for effective communication except for best practices as discussed. However, it is prudent to shed inhibitive cultural nuances if crew members are to perform at their optimum, particularly in the face of potential disasters.

Inadequate communications between technical crew and air traffic control and between members of technical crew have led to serious accidents. In 1977, the worst aviation disaster occurred at Tenerife in the Canary Islands, caused by heavy accents and improper terminology among a Dutch KLM crew, an American Pan Am crew and a Spanish air traffic controller. 583 passengers perished. In 1980, another Spanish air traffic controller at Tenerife gave a holding pattern clearance to a Dan Air flight by saying "turn to the left" when he should have said "turns to the left"—resulting in the aircraft making a single left turn rather than making circles using left turns. The jet hit a mountain killing 146 people. As already mentioned, In 1990, Colombian Avianca pilots in a holding pattern over Kennedy Airport told controllers that their 707 was low on fuel. The crew should have stated they had a "fuel emergency," which would have given them immediate clearance to land. Instead, the crew declared a "minimum fuel" condition and the plane ran out of fuel,

[44] Lima (2000), pp. 85–89 at 86.

[45] *Ibid.*

[46] Amin (1999), *ibid.*

[47] Mcfadden (1996), pp. 443–450.

[48] Turney (1995), pp. 262–268.

crashing and killing 72 people. Three years later Chinese pilots flying a U.S.-made MD-80 were attempting to land in northwest China. They just did not understand a simple instruction in English which caused them to crash their aircraft. The pilots were baffled by an audio alarm from the plane's ground proximity warning system. A cockpit recorder picked up the pilot's last words: "What does 'pull up' mean?" In 1995, an American Airlines jet crashed into a mountain in Colombia after the captain instructed the autopilot to steer towards the wrong beacon. A controller later stated that he suspected from the pilot's communications that the jet was in trouble, but that the controller's English was not sufficient for him to understand and articulate the problem. Another glaring example of failed communications occurred in New Delhi, India on November 13, 1996, when a Saudi Arabian airliner and a Kazakhstan plane collided in mid-air. All indications were that the Kazak pilot may not have been sufficiently fluent in English and was consequently unable to understand an Indian controller giving instructions in English.

On 22 May 2010 a Boeing 737-888 operated by Air India Express between Mangalore and India, carrying 160 passengers on board, four of whom were infants, approached the runway too high, crossing the runway threshold at almost 200 ft whereas the normal approach would be 50 ft. The aircraft broke through the boundary fence, plunged into the steeply wooded gorge beyond it, where it broke into three and caught fire. Eight passengers escaped through gaps in the fuselage. All others on board died. The Captain was Serbian and the First Officer and four other cabin crew were Indian. It has been reported that:

> Apart from the captain's numerous procedural violations during approach, cultural factors played a role in the development of this accident. The captain and the first officer did not communicate adequately with each. When the captain continued the approach in an unstabilized condition, despite the fact that it was not in accordance with standard procedures, and then failed to take corrective action, the first officer did not assert himself.[49]

The accidents cited above are symptomatic of a lack of aircrew coordination or crew resource management (CRM)[50] which were the most common determinants and causal factors.[51] Applebaum and Fewster hold the following view:

> Research has long shown that accidents and poor service quality are rooted primarily in sociotechnical human factors, not technology per se. Sub-optimisation, or poor quality with

[49]Job (2011), pp. 62–65. ICAO Document 9683 states that Human Factors is multidisciplinary in nature. human error. For example, information is drawn from psychology to understand how people process information and make decisions. From psychology and physiology comes an understanding of sensory processes as the means of detecting and transmitting information on the world about us. See *Human Factors Training Manual* Doc 9683-AN/950 First Edition—1998 at 1.2.5.

[50]Crew Resource Management is the species of the genus Human Resource Management which has been defined as: "a set of processes, which – through the recruitment, training, motivation, appraisal, reward, and development of individuals, and through the effective handling of industrial relations – translates strategy into action. See Holloway (1998), cited in Applebaum and Fewster (1999), p. 70.

[51]Yavacone (1999), pp. 392–395.

regard to management, decision-making, teamwork, employee motivation or communication, can translate into loss of customers, loss of market share, loss of organization assets and, above all, loss of life.[52]

The Tenerife disaster personifies this statement. The crash involved two Boeing 747 aircraft, one belonging to PAN-AM which was taxing on the runway on which the other aircraft, operated by KLM was taking off in thick fog where visibility was minimal. The KLM captain was the most experienced in the airline' fleet, with 1100 flying hours' experience. The Accident Investigation Report reflects:

Conclusions from all of this it may be ascertained that the KLM 4805 captain, as soon as he heard the ATC (altitude) clearance, decided to takeoff.

The fundamental cause of this accident was the fact that the KLM captain: 1. Took off without clearance (to take off). 2. Did not obey the "stand by for take-off" from the tower. 3. Did not interrupt take-off when Pan Am reported that they were still on the runway. 4. In reply to the flight engineer's query as to whether the Pan Am airplane had already left the runway, replied emphatically in the affirmative...

The report records the following additional causative factor *inter alia*:

Inadequate language. When the KLM co-pilot repeated the ATC clearance, he ended with the words, "we are now at take-off". The controller, who had not been asked for take-off clearance, and who consequently had not granted it, did not understand that they were taking off. The "O.K." from the tower, which preceded the "stand by for take-off" was likewise incorrect – although irrelevant in this case because take-off had already started about six and a half seconds before.[53]

The Report made just three recommendations: placing of great emphasis on the importance of exact compliance with instructions and clearances; use of standard, concise and unequivocal aeronautical language; avoidance of the word "take off" in the ATC clearance; and adequate time separation between the air traffic control clearance and the take-off clearance.[54]

ICAO recognizes that the interface between liveware and hardware (human and machine) is a frequent source of error: knobs and levers which are poorly located or lack of proper coding create mismatches at this interface. In the liveware-software interface, delays and errors may occur while seeking vital information from confusing, misleading or excessively cluttered documentation and charts. Environment interface are caused by environ- mental factors (noise, heat. lighting and vibration) and by the disturbance of biological rhythms in long-range flying resulting from irregular working/sleeping patterns.—In the liveware-liveware interface. the focus is on the interaction between people because this process affects crew effectiveness.

[52] Applebaum and Fewster (1999), p. 70.

[53] Secretary of Aviation Report On Tenerife Crash: KLM, B-747, PH-BUF and Pan Am B-747 N736 collision at Tenerife Airport Spain on 27 March 1977. Report dated October 1978 released by the Secretary of Civil Aviation, Spain. *Aircraft Accident Digest* (ICAO Circular 153-AN/56), pp. 22–68.

[54] *Ibid.*

This inter- action also includes leadership and command. and shortcomings at this interface reduce operational efficiency and cause misunderstanding.[55]

Difficulties in interpreting messages can be obviated by communications by machines such as IBM's Watson. ICAO document 9683 states that before a person can react to information. it must first be sensed; there is a potential for error here, because the sensory systems function on& within narrow ranges. Once information is sensed. it makes its way to the brain, where it is processed. and a conclusion is drawn about the nature and meaning of the message received. This interpretative activity is called perception and is a breeding ground for errors. Expectation. experience. attitude, motivation and arousal all have a definite influence on perception and are possible sources of errors.[56]

An integral part of a person's culture is his language and the expressions he uses. This is particularly relevant in many countries where English is the second language, the usage of which has changed over the years and been mixed with cultural expressions and nuances of those countries. The use of standardized phraseology in aeronautical communications has been a critical issue addressed by the international aviation community for several years. The surging growth in aviation involving numerous pilots of various nationalities whose first language would differ from those countries they fly over, brings to bear the need for a common level of English to allow for safe and efficient air traffic management. Global enforcement of language proficiency regulation is an essential pre requisite in this endeavour, since variations in teaching methods around the world could only result in confusion in the skies. Arguably the most dangerous factor in this equation could be the presumption of a pilot who is conversant in the English language as required by international standards, that the personnel in the tower directing him have the same degree of proficiency in language as he does.

Exponential growth in air traffic, involving longer flights operated by ultra-long range aircraft crossing several territorial boundaries in a given flight could cause crew fatigue, leading the pilot to misunderstand instructions, particularly if he is unfamiliar with the language of communication with the tower.

Such failures in communication bring to bear the compelling need for a standardized aviation language that all those who are involved in the technical operation of a flight could speak and understand. The unique challenges posed by communications in air transport are also due to the fact that the protagonists are in two different places. In this regard, there has been a suggestion from a seasoned air traffic controller that controllers should have "familiarization" privileges of riding in the cockpit up to eight times a year, so that they could learn what goes on in the flight deck during landing and take-off.[57] Conversely, pilots would have the opportunity to ask questions as to how the tower works.

---

[55]*Human Factors Training Manual*, supra note 49 in this chapter, at 1.4.2.

[56]*Id.* 1.4.3.

[57]This practice was, in fact in place before the events of 11 September 2001 in the United States. See Richards (2007), p. 343.

Ironically, new developments and the use of electronic communications may be adding to the problem. Prior to the introduction of paperless cockpits and MFD[58] and FMS[59] displays, which replaced the hard copy paper manuals, the crew could highlight and annotate on the paper documents, which enabled them to familiarize themselves with unfamiliar terminology. These two display systems are essentially visual and, without the appropriate language background, a pilot could find it difficult to decipher the visuals.

ICAO has, throughout its many years of serving the international aviation community, carried out sustained efforts at harmonizing language requirements for aeronautical communications. These efforts to address language proficiency for pilots and air traffic controllers is long standing and was first made by the 32nd Session of the Assembly[60] in September 1998. At that session, ICAO member States adopted Resolution A 32-16 on the subject of proficiency in the English language for radio telephony communications which was adopted as a direct response to an accident that cost the lives of 349 persons, as well as previous fatal accidents where the lack of proficiency in English was a causal factor. This resolution acknowledged the fact that recent major accident investigations had indicated lack of proficiency and comprehension of the English language by flight crews and air traffic controllers as a contributing factor and that in order to prevent such accidents, it was essential that ICAO devise ways and means to ensure that all member States take steps to ensure that air traffic control personnel and flight crew involved in flight operations in air space where the use of the English language is required, are proficient in conducting and comprehending radiotelephony communications in the English language.

Accordingly, Resolution A32-16 urged the ICAO Council[61] to direct the Air Navigation Commission—a subordinate body of the Council- to consider the matter

[58]The MFD (Multi Function Device) is a big, multicolour GPS moving map on the screen of the dashboard. The MFD is a small screen in an aircraft surrounded by multiple buttons that can be used to display information to the pilot in numerous configurable ways. Often an MFD will be used in concert with a PFD (Primary Flight Display). MFDs are part of the digital era of modern planes or helicopter. The first MFDs were introduced by air forces. The advantage of an MFD over analog display is that an MFD does not consume much space in the cockpit.

[59]A flight management system or FMS is a computerized avionics component installed in most commercial and business aircraft to assist pilots in navigation, flight planning, and aircraft control functions. FMS is composed of three major components: FMC—Flight Management Computer; AFS—Auto Flight System, and Navigation System including IRS—Internal Reference System and the Global Positioning System—GPS.

[60]The ICAO Assembly, comprised of the Organization's 191 Member States, meets once every 3 years. An extraordinary meeting of the Assembly may be convened by the Council at any time. The powers and duties of the Assembly are stated in Article 49 of the Chicago Convention.

[61]The ICAO Council is a permanent body responsible to the Assembly. It is composed of 36 Member States elected by the Assembly. In electing the members of the Council, the Assembly gives adequate representation to States of chief importance to air transport; States not otherwise included which make the largest contribution to the provision of facilities for international air navigation; and States not otherwise included whose designation will ensure that all the major geographic areas of the world are represented on the Council. The mandatory and permissive

with a high level of priority. Subsequently, and in response to action taken by the Council, the Air Navigation Commission initiated the development of language provisions in the following Annexes to the Chicago Convention: Annex 1—*Personnel Licensing*, Annex 6—*Operation of Aircraft*, Annex 10—*Aeronautical Telecommunications*, and Annex 11—*Air Traffic Services*. On 5 March 2003, the Council adopted Amendment 164 to Annex 1.[62] As of 5 March 2008, the ability to speak and understand the language used for radiotelephony that is currently required for pilots and air traffic controllers will have to be demonstrated based on the ICAO holistic descriptors and language proficiency rating scale (at Level 4 or above). Additionally, since November 2003, Annex 10 to the Convention on International Civil Aviation has required the availability of English language at all stations on the ground serving designated airports and routes used by international air services.

Since 2003, several steps have been taken to assist States with the implementation of these requirements. The first edition of the *Manual on the Implementation of ICAO Language Proficiency Requirements*[63] and the training aid entitled *ICAO Language Proficiency Requirements—Rated Speech Samples* were produced. The second edition of Document 9835 is presently under development. To date, eleven regional seminars have been conducted. Two ICAO Aviation Language Symposia were conducted in September 2004 and in May 2007 respectively.

These symposia have been popular and well attended. The Second ICAO Aviation Language Symposium was attended by 221 participants from sixty-two States and eight international organizations. While some participants were from State authorities, many of the participants were from air operators, air navigation service providers and language training and testing entities. During the Symposium, concerns were expressed to suggest that some Member States were encountering difficulties in implementing the language proficiency requirements including the establishment of language training and testing capabilities. Some support was expressed for ICAO to establish a system for the endorsement of language testing as a means to identify testing services that meet harmonized ICAO criteria. Several participants also requested clarification on the steps States should take if they did not implement the requirements by 5 March 2008.

During its deliberations in June 2007, the Council recognized that a single, universally applicable aviation language proficiency test, although desirable, would be inappropriate. However, the Council supported the development of

functions of the Council are stipulated in Articles 54 and 55 of the Convention on International Civil Aviation respectively. The Council has its genesis in the Interim Council of the Provisional International Civil Aviation Organization (PICAO). PICAO occupied such legal capacity as may have been necessary for the performance of its functions and was recognised as having full juridical personality wherever compatible with the Constitution and the laws of the State concerned. See Interim Agreement on International Civil Aviation, opened for signature at Chicago, December 7 1944, Article 3. Also in Hudson (1942–1945), p. 159.

[62]See C-DEC 168/9.

[63]Doc 9835, AN/453, First Edition 2004.

globally harmonized language testing criteria. The implementation of such criteria could effectively be achieved through the establishment of an ICAO endorsement mechanism for aviation language testing. The Council recognized, however, that budgetary resources would be required to establish an ICAO endorsement mechanism for aviation language testing.

ICAO advised its member States at the 36th Session of its Assembly (Montreal: September 18–28, 2007) that it was widely recognized that implementation of the language provisions is resource intensive. Since the language provisions have become effective, several States have invested considerable resources and efforts to comply with the provisions by 5 March 2008. While some States may not be compliant by March 2008, the applicability date established a milestone that would help to retain the focus required to implement the safety Standards related to language proficiency as soon as practicable.

The Assembly was also advised that understanding the consequence of non-compliance was important in order to take appropriate action. A negative impact on safety would be considered the most serious consequence of non-compliance. In addition, the multilateral recognition of pilots' licences provided for under Article 33[64] of the Chicago Convention could also be impacted when a State is unable to meet the minimum Standards prescribed in *Annex 1* to the Convention. Transparency and regular communications among Member States would be the best means of mitigating the potential impact. It should be noted that the Convention provides for the means to deal with such situations and to ensure the continuity of international civil aviation. In the case of flight crew licences, and in application of Articles 33, 39[65] and 40[66] of the Convention, those pilots that do not meet the operational Level 4 requirements would require permission from other States to operate in the airspace under their jurisdiction.

[64]Article 33 is on the subject of Recognition of certificates and licenses. It provides that certificates of airworthiness and certificates of competency and licenses issued or rendered valid by the member State in which the aircraft is registered, shall be recognized as valid by the other member States, provided that the requirements under which such certificates or licences were issued or rendered valid are equal to or above the minimum standards which may be established from time to time pursuant to this Convention.

[65]Article 39 is on the subject of endorsement of certificates and licenses. It provides: (*a*) that any aircraft or part thereof with respect to which there exists an international standard of airworthiness or performance, and which failed in any respect to satisfy that standard at the time of its certification, shall have endorsed on or attached to its airworthiness certificate a complete enumeration of the details in respect of which it so failed; and (*b*) that any person holding a license who does not satisfy in full the conditions laid down in the international standard relating to the class of license or certificate which he holds shall have endorsed on or attached to his license a complete enumeration of the particulars in which he does not satisfy such conditions.

[66]Article 40 concerns the *validity of endorsed certificates and licenses* and provides that No aircraft or personnel having certificates or licenses so endorsed shall participate in international navigation, except with the permission of the State or States whose territory is entered. The registration or use of any such aircraft, or of any certificated aircraft part, in any State other than that in which it was originally certificated shall be at the discretion of the State into which the aircraft or part is imported.

ICAO also recommended that, in all cases, including those of States where air traffic controllers are not yet compliant, States should notify ICAO of the differences in accordance with Article 38[67] of the Convention and ensure that these differences are indicated in their Aeronautical Information Publication (AIP). They will also have to endorse the personnel licences in accordance with Article 39 of the Convention.

States that may not be in a position to comply with the language proficiency requirement by the applicability date should also provide information on their implementation plans and interim measures taken to mitigate risk. It is important for safety purposes that each State has sufficient information to make a proper risk analysis. This analysis will be required in order to allow an aircraft with pilots who may not meet the language proficiency requirement to fly in the airspace under the jurisdiction of another State. This analysis will also be required for States to authorize their operators to fly in the airspace under the jurisdiction or responsibility of another State that may not be compliant. The purpose of the risk analysis is to ensure that the lack of language proficiency is minimized as a potential causal factor of incidents and accidents. This step will not only help to eliminate or mitigate risk, but to actually strengthen a Standard that could otherwise be ignored by some States.

To this end ICAO planned to provide guidance on the development of implementation plans by the end of October 2007 and to conduct seminars in each ICAO Region as soon as practicable. At the time this article was being written, work on the guidance material was being finalized by ICAO.

In response to the recommendations of the ICAO Council, ICAO member States, at the 36th Session of the Assembly convened in September 2007, adopted Assembly Resolution A 36-11[68] (Proficiency in the English Language used for radiotelephony) which superseded the earlier resolution A32-16 on the same subject. This resolution, while recognizing ICAO's work in introducing language provisions to ensure that air traffic personnel and pilots are proficient in conducting and comprehending radiotelephony communications in the English language, including

[67]Article 38 concerns departures from international standards and procedures and provides that any State which finds it impracticable to comply in all respects with any such international standard or procedure, or to bring its own regulations or practices into full accord with any international standard or procedure after amendment of the latter, or which deems it necessary to adopt regulations or practices differing in any particular respect from those established by an international standard, shall give immediate notification to the International Civil Aviation Organization of the differences between its own practice and that established by the international standard. In the case of amendments to international standards, any State which does not make the appropriate amendments to its own regulations or practices shall give notice to the Council within 60 days of the adoption of the amendment to the international standard, or indicate the action which it proposes to take. In any such case, the Council shall make immediate notification to all other states of the difference which exists between one or more features of an international standard and the corresponding national practice of that State.

[68]This Resolution was transmitted to all the 190 ICAO member States by the Secretary General of ICAO per State Letter *AN 12/44.6-07/68* dated 26 October 2007.

requirements that the English language shall be available on request at all stations on the ground serving designated airports and routes used by international air services; acknowledged that the language provisions reinforce the requirement to use ICAO standardized phraseology in all situations for which it has been specified. The Assembly gave due recognition to the fact that ICAO member States had made substantial efforts to comply with the language proficiency requirements by 5 March 2008. However, some States still encounter considerable difficulties in implementing the language proficiency requirements including the establishment of language training and testing capabilities. Furthermore, some member States will require additional time to implement the language proficiency provisions beyond the applicability date.

There was also the reality according to Resolution A36-11 that some States were finding it impracticable to comply in all respects with any international standard or procedure but were obliged to give immediate notification of a deviation from a Standard in an Annex to ICAO *in* accordance with Article 38 of the Convention. The Resolution makes mention of the requirements in Articles 39 and 40 which have been already referred to in this article and urges the member States to use ICAO standardized phraseology in all situations for which it has been specified. It also directs the Council to support Member States in their implementation of the language proficiency requirements by establishing globally harmonized language testing criteria and urges member States that are not in a position to comply with the language proficiency A-2 requirement by the applicability date to post their language proficiency implementation plans including their interim measures to mitigate risk, as required, for pilots, air traffic controllers and aeronautical station operators involved in international operations on the ICAO website as outlined in accordance with the practices recommended by ICAO together with ICAO guidance material. Finally, the Resolution directs the Council to provide guidelines to States on the development of implementation plans, including an explanation of the risk mitigation measures so as to enable Member States to post their plans as soon as practicable, but prior to 5 March 2008.

The Resolution also calls upon the member States to waive the permission requirement under Article 40 of the Convention, in the airspace under their jurisdiction for pilots who do not yet meet the ICAO language proficiency requirements, for a period not exceeding 3 years after the applicability date of 5 March 2008, provided that the States which issued or rendered valid the licences have made their implementation plans available to all other Member States. States are also requested *not* to restrict their operators, conducting commercial or general aviation operations, from entering the airspace under the jurisdiction or responsibility of other States where air traffic controllers or radio station operators do not yet meet the language proficiency requirements for a period not exceeding 3 years after the applicability date of 5 March 2008, provided that those States have made their implementation plans available to all other Member States.

Member States were required, in accordance with Resolution A36-11, provide data concerning their level of implementation of the Language Proficiency Requirements when requested by ICAO.

At the 37th Assembly (Montreal, 18 September–8 October 2010) Resolution A 36-11 was superseded by Resolution A 37-10 (proficiency in the English language used for radiotelephony communications) which recognized *inter alia* that language provisions introduced ICAO helps in preventing accidents and ensuring that air traffic personnel and pilots are proficient in conducting and comprehending radiotelephony communications in the English language, including requirements that the English language shall be available on request at all stations on the ground serving designated airports and routes used by international air services. The resolution also recognized that the language provisions reinforce the requirement to use ICAO standardized phraseology in all situations for which it has been specified and that some Contracting States encountered considerable difficulties in implementing the language proficiency requirements including the establishment of language training and testing capabilities. It was also noted by the Assembly that some Contracting States required additional time to implement the language proficiency provisions beyond the applicability date.

Resolution A 37-10 urged the Contracting States to use ICAO standardized phraseology in all situations for which it has been specified to assist each other in their implementation of the language proficiency requirements. It also urged ICAO member States that have not complied with the language proficiency requirement by the applicability date to post their language proficiency implementation plans including their interim measures to mitigate risk, as required, for pilots, air traffic controllers and aeronautical station operators involved in international operations on the ICAO website as outlined in accordance with the associated practices below and ICAO guidance material. The Resolution directed the ICAO Council to continue to support Contracting States in their implementation of the language proficiency requirements.

It also called upon Contracting States to waive the permission requirement under Article 40 of the Chicago Convention,[69] in the airspace under their jurisdiction for pilots who do not yet meet the ICAO Language Proficiency Requirements, for a period not exceeding 3 years after the applicability date of 5 March 2008, provided that the States which issued or rendered valid the licences have made their implementation plans available to all other Contracting States and have notified ICAO of the differences pertaining to language provisions. The Resolution furthermore urged Contracting States to take a flexible approach after 5 March 2011 towards States that do not yet meet the Language Proficiency Requirements, yet are making progress as evidenced in their implementation plans. It is a requirement under the Resolution that decisions concerning operations should be made on a non-discriminatory basis and not be made for the purpose of gaining economic advantage and directed the Council to monitor the status of implementation of the

[69] Article 40 provides that no aircraft or personnel having certificates or licenses so endorsed shall participate in international navigation, except with the permission of the State or States whose territory is entered. The registration or use of any such aircraft, or of any certificated aircraft part, in any State other than that in which it was originally certificated shall be at the discretion of the State into which the aircraft or part is imported.

Language Proficiency Requirements and take necessary actions to advance safety and maintain the regularity of international civil aviation;

7.4 Crew Resource Management (CRM)

The essence of good airmanship is situational awareness and good decision making particularly in stressful situations.[70] Communications act as an integral link between these two essentials.

It is evident that effective communication between crew members is an essential prerequisite for good CRM. Research has shown that in addition to its most widely perceived function of transferring information, the communication process in an aircraft fulfils several other important functions as well. It not only helps the crew to develop a shared mental model of the problems which need to be resolved in the course of the flight, thereby enhancing situational awareness, but it also allows problem solving to be shared amongst crew members by enabling individual crew members to contribute appropriately and effectively to the decision-making process. Most importantly, it establishes the interpersonal climate between crew members and is therefore a key element in setting the tone for the management of the flight.

The starting point for CRM is incontrovertibly Annex 6 to the Chicago Convention which addresses aeronautical aspects of the operations of aircraft. Prudent operation of aircraft is vital in avoiding accidents and incidents. The essence of Annex 6, simply put, is that the operation of aircraft engaged in international air transport must be as standardized as possible to ensure the highest levels of safety and efficiency. In 1948 the Council first adopted Standards and Recommended Practices for the operation of aircraft engaged in international commercial air transport. They were based on recommendations of States attending the first session of the Operations Divisional Meeting held in 1946, and are the basis of Part I of Annex 6.

In order to keep pace with a new and vital industry, the original provisions have been and are being constantly reviewed. For instance, a second part to Annex

[70]Stress is a factor which can quickly undermine the emotional climate in which the crew is operating is stress—defined as a state of highly unpleasant emotional arousal associated variously with overload, fear, anxiety, anger and hostility—all of which threaten both individual performance and teamwork. Stress often arises as a result of a perceived gap between the demands of a situation and an individual's ability to cope with these demands. As stress involves the processes of perception and evaluation, it impinges directly on the cognitive and interpersonal skills which form the basis of good CRM. Both arousal and alertness are necessary to enable each individual to achieve optimum performance in CRM-related skills, but too much or too little arousal will have a significantly adverse impact on the ability of the crew to function effectively as a team. It is therefore important for crew members not only to be aware of the symptoms of stress in themselves and others, but also to understand the effects which stress can have on CRM, and to mitigate these effects where possible by taking measures to counter them.

6, dealing exclusively with international general aviation, became applicable in September 1969. Similarly, a third part to Annex 6, dealing with all international helicopter operations, became applicable in November 1986. Part III originally addressed only helicopter flight recorders, but an amendment completing the coverage of helicopter operations in the same comprehensive manner as aeroplane operations covered in Parts I and II was adopted for applicability in November 1990.

It would be impractical to provide one international set of operational rules and regulations for the wide variety of aircraft which exist today. Aircraft range from commercial airliners to the one-seat glider, all of which cross national boundaries into adjacent States. In the course of a single operation, a long-range jet may fly over many international borders. Each aircraft has unique handling characteristics relative to its type and, under varying environmental conditions, may have specific operational limitations. The very international nature of commercial aviation, and of general aviation to a lesser degree, requires pilots and operators to conform to a wide variety of national rules and regulations.

However, it is certainly possible to provide one international set of rules on CRM. In 1994, the Air Navigation Commission (ANC) of ICAO adopted a proposal to include a Standard in Annex 6, pursuant to a review of the Annex, pertaining to the initial and recurrent human performance training for flight crews. The Standard, promulgated through Amendment 21 to the Annex became applicable in November 1995. The new Standard, which appears as 9.3.1 in Chapter 9 Part 1 of the Annex provides that performance training for flight crews shall also include training in knowledge and skills related to human performance and that such training will be given on a recurrent basis as determined by the State of the operator of the aircraft. A further review by the ANC of Annex 6 resulted in Amendment 23 to the Annex which brought out in Chapter 8, Standard 8.7.5.4. which provides that the training programme established by the maintenance organization shall include training in knowledge and skills[71] related to human performance, including coordination with other maintenance and flight crew. This provision established the clear requirement to mesh coordination among crew members through knowledge and skills. In Chapter 10 this requirement is extended to the flight operations officer and flight dispatcher.

Communication skills essentially involve the need to be conversant with and apply as polite assertiveness and participation, active listening and feedback. Communication skills also ensure clear and effective use of language and responsiveness to feedback.[72] Ambiguities in communication are the antithesis of good

[71]A CRM skill is a goal-directed, well-organized behaviour that is acquired through practice and performed with economy of effort. See Proctor and Dutta (1995), p. 18.

[72]Colloquialisms should be avoided at all cost. There is a recorded instance of an air traffic controller in an airport in the United States deciding to ignore the standard rules governing Federal Aviation Administration (FAA) radio phraseology in communications to cockpits. He strongly exhorted more hustle on the part of pilots taxiing in a line of planes waiting to take off in the narrow gaps of airspace between planes landing on the same runway. As a result, the airport's

communication skills. Communications are improved by taking into account cultural influences as well as factors such as rank, age and crew position, all of which can create barriers to communication in the cockpit. Polite assertiveness is a skill frequently ignored in communications training but vital to a healthy cockpit. A pilot-in-command may be open to communication but temporarily unable to receive and comprehend. As the disasters of Avianca and Teneriffe showed, other crewmembers must be aware of the importance of the information they hold and have a strong feeling of self-value and a single hesitant attempt to communicate important information and data constitutes a failure to discharge individual responsibility. Pilots-in-command must constantly strive to emphasize this responsibility in their team-building efforts. There must be created in the cockpit environment a legitimate window of dissent and disagreement so that a clear line of unequivocal communication exists between the captain and other flight crew members.

Situational awareness is complete knowledge and understanding of a situation and environment through one's ability to accurately perceive what is going on in the cockpit and outside the aircraft. It also involves the instant planning and the ability to execute one or more of several responses to any emergency situation that could occur in the immediate future. Awareness of one's situation could be a complex process that is driven by the appreciation that one's perception of reality may differ from reality itself. Therefore, to remain within the realm of reality it is necessary to indulge in ongoing questioning, cross-checking and refinement of one's perception. A tenaciously constant and conscious monitoring of the situation is also required.

These three areas are integrally linked and interrelated. The accepted fact among accident investigators is that an accident is an ultimate cause of a concatenation of errors and that the resolving of one error may break the chain and prevent the accident. Therefore problem solving is necessary to tackle an overall cycle of events beginning with information input and ending with pilot judgment in making a final decision. A danger in the information receiving phase of problem solving is that several interpretations of information and conflicting points of view may be represented. Skills in resolving conflict are therefore especially appropriate at this time. The pilot in command is in charge of making a decision[73] with the agreement of others. At least there must be a clear understanding among the crew that no crew member has a radically different view from that of the captain.

To exercise leadership is to use appropriate authority to ensure focus on task and crew member concerns. Therefore the role of the captain carries a special responsibility, where although other members of the crew are engaged in carrying out their

---

hourly rate of flights improved. The controller's "hurry-up" attitude led to what is known as the "Pete Rose departure," a reference to the former Cincinnati Reds baseball star nicknamed "Charlie Hustle." Richards (2007), pp. 136–137.

[73]The responsibility of the pilot in command under rules of the air is both critical and grave. Standard 2.4 of Annex 2 to the Chicago Convention (Rules of the Air) states that the pilot-in-command of an aircraft shall have final authority as to the disposition of the aircraft while in command. It is therefore quite obvious that irresponsible conduct that would lead to an accident or incident would bring to bear negligence of the part of the pilot in command.

own responsibilities, it is for the captain to be responsible for supervising the overall management of the flight. His authority and command must be acknowledged at all times. Recognition and acceptance of the captain's cannot be assumed by position alone. The credibility of a leader is built over time and must be accomplished through conscious effort. Similarly, every non-command crewmember is responsible for actively contributing to the team effort, for monitoring changes in the situation and for being assertive when necessary. This last aspect is extremely relevant, as was shown in the instance of the First officer's reticence to differ with the Captain in the Avianca instance.

The crew must be vigilant at all times and consciously avoid complacency during the flight. In some cultures, there is no emphasis on readiness for anticipated risk. CRM training must inculcate in the crew member the need for him to keep watch over system and environment changes and inform other crew members of potential threats and errors.

Crew members must be trained to establish prioritization of tasks and appropriate utilization of resources within the flight deck. The purpose of Annex 6 is to contribute to the safety of international air navigation by providing criteria for safe operating practices, and to contribute to the efficiency and regularity of international air navigation by encouraging ICAO's Contracting States to facilitate the passage over their territories of commercial aircraft belonging to other countries that operate in conformity with these criteria. ICAO Standards do not preclude the development of national standards which may be more stringent than those contained in the Annex. In this context it becomes essential that States establish a safety culture that espouses a non-punitive response to operational error so that they could identify errors that lead to incidents and accidents.[74]

The organizational culture period calls for a particular mind-set in the safety culture of States and of airlines. It is a common feature of globalization that we tend to interpret the world through our individual cultural lens or worldview. However, it must be remembered that aviation is a multicultural domain and crew members should go through a rigid CRM system that would enable them to shed their cultural roots in the flight deck and adapt themselves to a common culture of communicating clearly and assertively, putting their point across to both fellow crew members and air traffic and ground traffic controllers, irrespective of rank.

The most important is for pilots to have the comfort, irrespective of their misjudgement or inhibition brought about by their cultural origin, of knowing that they are operating under a non-punitive corporate culture which would not criminalize their actions unless they are guilty of negligence. A critical provision in Annex 13 to the Chicago Convention (Accident Investigation) is Standard 3.1 which provides that the sole objective of the investigation of an accident or incident shall be the prevention of accidents and incidents and that it is not the purpose of that activity to apportion blame or liability.

---

[74]*Human Factors Training Manual,* ICAO Doc 9683-AN/950, ICAO: Montreal First Edition—1998, at 2-2-7.

Two significant provisions in Annex 13 in this context are a Standard and Recommended Practice. Standard 5.4 provides that the accident investigation authority shall have independence in the conduct of the investigation and have unrestricted authority over its conduct, consistent with the provisions of the Annex. The investigation would include: (a) the gathering, recording and analysis of all available information on that accident or incident; (b) if appropriate, the issuance of safety recommendations; (c) if possible, the determination of the causes; and (d) the completion of the final report. When possible, it required that the scene of the accident be visited, the wreckage examined and statements taken from witnesses. Recommendation 5.4.1 suggests that any judicial or administrative proceedings to apportion blame or liability should be separate from any investigation conducted under the provisions of this Annex.[75]

It is a serious issue that in accident investigations persons with knowledge of the circumstances that lead to an accident are reluctant to come forward to give evidence in fear of criminal prosecutions against them. This anomaly has serious connotations in instances where cultural differences may have caused miscommunication among the crew or between the crew and air traffic control which leads to an accident. In the absence of clear evidence given by the crew involved investigators could find it difficult to obtain valuable information, particularly when judicial proceedings are launched at the same time as the safety investigation. EUROCONTROL suggests a "just culture" which has been defined as

> a culture in which front line operators or others are not punished for actions, omissions or decisions taken by them that are commensurate with their experience and training, but where gross negligence, wilful violations and destructive acts are not tolerated. This is important in aviation, because we know we can learn a lot from the so-called honest mistakes[76]

The just culture as suggested by EUROCONTROL draws a delicate balance between protection of the public from errors of such persons as pilots and air traffic controllers and the protection of such professionals from being arbitrarily prosecuted for mistakes that are not grounded by negligence or gross negligence. The idea is for a just culture to protect people against being blamed for honest mistakes, but also to lay them open for prosecution for their reprehensible conduct. The idea

---

[75]5 Standard 5.12 of Annex 13 provides that the State conducting the investigation of an accident or incident shall not make the following records available for purposes other than accident or incident investigation, unless the appropriate authority for the administration of justice in that State determines that their disclosure outweighs the adverse domestic and international impact such action may have on that or any future investigations: (a) all statements taken from persons by the investigation authorities in the course of their investigation; (b) all communications between persons having been involved in the operation of the aircraft; (c) medical or private information regarding persons involved in the accident or incident; (d) cockpit voice recordings and transcripts from such recordings; and (e) opinions expressed in the analysis of information, including flight recorder information.

[76]Just Culture Guidance Material for Interfacing with the Judicial System, Edition date: 11.02.2008 Reference nr: 08/02/06-07.

is neither to create a list of offences nor is it to label certain conduct as culpable. The idea is to determine the extent of accountability and responsibility exhibited by the person concerned and to draw the line in each case. The role of the judiciary in determining these factors becomes vital. Judicial action as a driver of this determination has a dichotomy of a balance between two fundamental societal interests that go to the importance of serving the interest of the public through the maximising of safety (through incident and accident investigation and reporting) and the maximising of justice (through the application of laws). The two can well conflict with each other and the prudent approach would be to establish a reasonable balance between the two while not prejudicing the interest of the professional who acts within the parameters of good employment.

Finally, there must be a sustained environment of trust between the flight crew and their employer. The critical issue is whether crew members would usually volunteer information regarding their decisions and actions taken in the flight deck that could be ascribed to the cause of an incident or accident. The answer is, as long as the crew member suspects or has reason to believe that such disclosure would result in punitive measures or loss of pay (which could even lead to loss of career) he/she would not usually volunteer information even if such decisions or actions may have jeopardized the safety of the flight. Such is human nature. One approach to this question would lie in the triumvirate of regulator, operator and crew member reaching a cohesive relationship of trust that would obviate jeopardising the interests of the pilot's career and more importantly the interests of safety. Attitudes should change, resulting in a culture change. The regulator must ensure that there are regulations in place that would protect both the operator and crew member. The following elements are critical to this process: shared responsibility; acknowledgment of the complexity of stress and cultural diversity in the flight deck as a risk factor that can never be totally eliminated; multiple solutions for multiple problems; scientific progress; and continuous evaluation of CRM with a view to enhancing guidance.

7.5 Germanwings Flight 9525

The second example—*Germanwings* Flight 9525—was a scheduled international passenger flight operated with Airbus A320-211 on 24 March 2015 from Barcelona–El Prat Airport in Spain to Düsseldorf Airport in Germany. While the co-pilot was at the controls alone in the flight deck (the captain had gone out of the flight deck to answer a call of nature) the co-pilot crashed the aircraft 100 km (62 miles) north-west of Nice in the French Alps after a constant descent that began one minute after the last routine contact with air traffic control and shortly after it had reached its assigned cruising altitude. All 144 passengers and six crew members were killed. Conceptually, IoE could prevent such man-made disasters. Scot says:

> But the fact that the technology to prevent tragedies like the *Germanwings* crash—in which a disturbed co-pilot locked out the captain and deliberately flew into the French Alps—already exists makes it all the more senseless... That same technology could also be used to override the pilots in crisis situations like *Germanwings*, or to up-load each plane's location more frequently—which would have helped greatly in the search for Malaysia Airlines Flight 370, another recent aviation tragedy.[77]

IoE can also help in making the co-existence of civil and military aviation safer. Coordination of information and their exchange through information and data retrieval. The question as to whether civil aviation and military aviation have demarcated operational regimes or whether they can still function in symbiosis has become an argumentative one, in view of developments in the air transport industry which have occurred over the years. At its incipient stage, civil aviation held closer ties with military aviation since both were the protégés of government, and were controlled by instrumentalities of State. In recent times, however, governments are increasingly ceasing to be the principal actors of commercial aviation, thereby making at least a cosmetic deviation from civil aviation and recognizing the aspects of private enterprise (which often control civil aviation) as the real protagonists in matters pertaining to civilian air transport.

Security against aggression was naturally the paramount consideration at the end of World War II. It is therefore incontrovertible that considerations regarding a post-war civil aviation regime would have been bifurcated between civil and military aviation when the Chicago Convention was being drafted.[78] Article 3 of the Convention, which provides that the Convention shall apply only to civil aircraft, explicitly excludes state aircraft such as aircraft used for military, customs and police purposes from the jurisdiction of the Convention. Furthermore, the Convention expressly prohibits aircraft of a Contracting State which are used for military purposes (on the basis that aircraft used for military purposes are "state aircraft") from flying over the territory of another State or landing thereon without authorization or by special agreement or otherwise. Under Article 3 (d) of the Convention, Contracting States undertake to have due regard for the safety of navigation of civil aircraft when issuing regulations for the use or application of State aircraft.

Annex 2 to the Chicago Convention—pertaining to Rules of the Air—which was adopted on 15 April 1945, further protects civil aircraft by providing that interception of civil aircraft shall be governed by appropriate regulations and administrative directives issued by Contracting States in compliance with Article 3(d) of the Chicago Convention.

Perhaps the most fundamental difference between the operation of civil and military aircraft lay in the fact that, although they were expected to share the same skies, the procedures by which they did this varied greatly. Civil aircraft depended entirely on predetermined flight paths and codes of commercial conduct which

---

[77] *Ibid.*

[78] Sochor (1991), p. 86.

varied depending on aircraft type and types of traffic carried, whereas military aircraft operated in line with the exigency of a situation and were not necessarily always guided by predetermined flight paths. For example, The Democratic Peoples' Republic of Korea (DPRK)—otherwise known as North Korea—has a history of launching missiles that have been deemed to jeopardize paths used by civil aircraft.[79] North Korea in 1997 permitted civil aircraft to fly over its airspace. However, there was no guarantee that all foreign civil aircraft would be safe as there was no accurate method of coordinating information that could guarantee safety. As a response the Federal Aviation Administration (FAA) of the United States issued Special Federal Aviation Regulation number 79 (SFAR 79) stating that "immediate action is necessary to prohibit certain flight operations within DPRK airspace. The DPRK air defense system includes modern surface-to-air missile systems and interceptor aircraft capable of engaging aircraft at cruising altitudes," the notice said. The FAA has been unable to determine the current level of coordination and cooperation between civil air traffic authorities and air defense commanders for civil aircraft overflights, including military rules of engagement if an aircraft strays from its assigned flight route. Any "lack of coordination presents a risk that civil aircraft operating in the Pyongyang FIR west of 132 degrees' east longitude could be misidentified as a threat by the DPRK."[80]

In March 2017 North Korea launched four ballistic missiles three of which fell into Japan's exclusive economic zone (EEZ) after flying some 1000 km (620 miles). They were fired from the Tongchang-ri region, near the North's border with China. The type of missile is unclear but the North is banned from any missile or nuclear tests by the UN. When internet of everything reaches sufficient maturity, not only could preparatory activities be tracked but with the use of sensors tracking airborne objects could be much easier.

References

Amin H (1999) Promoting a safety culture in aviation. http://harisamin.hubpages.com/hub/Safety-Culture-in-Aviation

Applebaum SH, Fewster BM (1999) Human resource management strategy in the global airline industry – a focus on organizational development. Business Briefing: Aviation Strategies: Challenges and Opportunities of Liberalization, p 70

Bajarin T (2014) The next big thing for tech: the internet of everything. 13 January 2014, Time/Tech. http://time.com/539/the-next-big-thing-for-tech-the-internet-of-everything/

[79]North Korean airspace extends well beyond the land borders of the country to include a large portion of the Sea of Japan (East Sea) and, to a lesser extent, a region over the Yellow Sea (West Sea).

[80]Martyn Williams, What's going on with North Korean airspace? North Korea Tech, July 25 2014, http://www.northkoreatech.org/2014/07/25/whats-going-on-with-north-korean-airspace/.

Cunningham M (2008) The Montreal Convention: can passengers finally recover for mental injuries? Phoenix School of Law, From Selected Works of McKay Cunningham, January 2008. http://works.bepress.com/mckay_cunningham/1
Desbiens C (1992) Air Carrier's liability for emotional distress under Article 17 of the Warsaw Convention: can it still be invoked? Ann Air Space Law XVII, Part II:153
Dorland WAN (2007) Dorland's Illustrated Medical Dictionary, 31st edn. Elsevier, Saunders, p 1573
Gladwell M (2008) Outliers – the story of success. Little Brown and Company, New York
Holloway S (1998) Changing planes: a strategic management perspective on industry in transition, vol 1: Situation analysis. Ashgate, Aldershot
ICD (1992) ICD-10, International Statistical Classification of Diseases and Related Health Problems (Tenth Revision), vol 1. World Health Organization, Geneva, p 349
Job M (2011) Falling off the mountain. Flightsafety, Sept–Oct 2011, (82):62–65
Langley J, Brenner R (2004) What is an injury? – a clear definition is needed. Inj Prev. http://www.ncbi.nlm.nih.gov/pmc/articles/PMC1730061/
Lima EP (2000) Paradigm shift in the cockpit. Air Transport World 37(11):86
Mcfadden KL (1996) Comparing pilot-error accident rate of male and female airline pilots. Omega Int J Manag Sci 24:443–450
Merritt AC, Helmreich RL (1996) Human factors on the flight deck: the influence of national culture. J Cross Cult Psychol 27:5–24
Miller H (1966) Mental after effects of head injury. Proc R Soc Med 59:258
Picard A (2014) When passengers fall ill at 30,000 feet: how medical emergencies are handled in the air. The Globe and Mail, 11 May 2014
Proctor RW, Dutta A (1995) Skill acquisition and human performance. Sage, Thousand Oaks, p 18
Rassool SB (2007) Psychological trauma and road traffic accidents. Doctoral thesis on clinical psychology, University of Hertfordshire, Chapter Four, Literary Review: 9 November 2007, p 113
Richards B (2007) Secrets from the tower. Ithaca Press, New York, p 343
Schultz J (2002) Hear what they are saying: the influence of culture on cockpit communication. http://www.odu.edu/ao/instadv/quest/CockpitCommun.html
Sochor E (1991) The politics of international aviation. Macmillan Press, London, p 86
Tam L, Duley J (2005) Beyond the west: cultural gaps in aviation human factors research. In: Proceedings of the Mini-Conference on Human Factors in Complex Sociotechnical Systems – 2005 1-1 to 1-5. www.sjhfes.org/miniconference/PDFs/01-Tam.pdf
Turney MA (1995) Womens' learning and leadership styles: impact on CRM, applications of psychology to the aviation system. In: McDonald N, Johnston N, Fuller R (eds) Proceedings of the 21st conference of the European Association for Aviation Psychology (EAAP), vol 1. Ashgate, Aldershot, pp 262–268
Yavacone D (1999) Mishap trends and cause factors in naval aviation: a review of naval safety centre data, 1986–1990. Aviat Space Environ Med 64:392–395

Chapter 8
Conclusion

An OECD Report states that by the mid-twenty-first century the world population will reach 10 billion and will continue to grow. Africa will be the biggest contributor more than half of this growth, which will generate significant young demographic surges that would, in the author's views, resemble the global tribe. Ageing of populations will continue and, by 2050, 10% of the population will be over the age of 80. This could result in the work force being depleted, resulting in a threat to existing living standards. To balance this trend, technologies that enhance physical and cognitive capacities could enable older people to work longer, and the exponential development of automation will greatly diminish the demand for human labor. 90% of the growth will occur in Asia and Africa. Urban living could be greatly advanced in terms of better access to electricity, water and sanitation. There will be smart cities in developed regions which connect utility and transport networks and systems efficiently enabling these cities to manage resources more sustainably.[1]

The Report also opines that one of the primary drivers over the next 15 years would be digital technologies that will continue to have major impacts on economies and societies. Business entities over that period would rely heavily on digitized technology that would impact product design, manufacturing and delivery processes to be highly integrated and efficient. In keeping with economies of scale, costs of equipment and computing machinery would fall, but the business community will continue to grow with the drastic advantages afforded by the development in automation.

A distant possibility is the ultimate extension of artificial intelligence called quantum computing which could establish quantum technology that could unravel indecipherable and unshakable communication links. Although this is still a distant

[1]*An OECD Horizon Scan of Megatrends And Technology Trends In The Context Of Future Research Policy*, Danish Agency for Science, Technology and Innovation, 2016, http://ufm.dk/en/publications/2016/files/an-oecd-horizon-scan-of-megatrends-and-technology-trends-in-the-context-of-future-research-policy.pdf.

R. Abeyratne, *Megatrends and Air Transport*, DOI 10.1007/978-3-319-61124-2_8

theoretical possibility in terms of its practical application, quantum computing which would introduce what is called a "contractor" could make even the most unfathomable measurement decipherable. The possibilities this technology would present to biometric identification and scanning as well as record handling would be extremely important to future air transport. It could also bring to bear new criteria of liability of airlines and airports on the basis that with such technology a greater degree of care would be expected of the providers of goods and services.

Megatrends and their effect on air transport have to be viewed in the current context of the drastic diversion of the business culture that existed a few years ago—that business leaders' thinking was focused on making money for their shareholders at any cost. The 2016–2017 crisis *Volkswagen* (the leading car maker) was caught up in a global scandal where the firm falsified the diesel emission standards of its vehicles is a good example. In March 2017 the car manufacturer was expected to plead guilty on to three felony counts in the United States' Justice Department's emissions investigation. The German automaker agreed to sweeping reforms, new audits and oversight by an independent monitor for 3 years after it admitting to installing secret software in vehicles to enable it to beat emissions tests over a 6-year period. Furthermore, *Volkswagen* pledged to change the way it operates in the United States and other countries under the settlement of charges that it installed secret software in 580,000 U.S. vehicles to allow them to emit up to 40 times the amount of legally permitted pollution. The precursor to this trend where company directors were held liable was the famous *Enron* case[2] where corporate executives, who were in a comfort zone of their own, and believing they had only to act in the best interests of their employer by increasing the profits of their company, altered the books of the company where the reported financial condition of the company was sustained mostly by institutionalized, systematic, and creatively planned accounting fraud. The *Enron* case highlighted the fact that an executive could be exposed for corporate misdeeds and for personal liability for such misdeeds.

The lawsuit against *Enron*'s directors, following the scandal, was notable in that the directors settled the suit by paying very significant amounts of money personally. Executives have a personal liability to their shareholders, employees, creditors and other stakeholders. This is not only applicable to the private sector but also apples to government departments and instrumentalities of States. The corporate veil that shielded executives from personal liability has now been lifted, often compelling executives to take precautionary measures before they act, particularly by seeking legal counsel. This practice is morally and ethically wrong and is frowned upon both judicially and socially. Society views companies (including

---

[2]In January 2002, the United States Justice Department confirmed that it had begun a criminal investigation of *Enron*, following the events of the company in October 2001 when Enron reported a $638 million third-quarter loss and disclosed a $1.2 billion reduction in shareholder equity, partly related to partnerships run by its Finance Chief that hid huge amounts of debt as well as write downs in money-losing broadband and water trading ventures. *Enron* went bankrupt on 2 December 2001, putting all its employees out of employment.

airports and airlines) as morally responsible. It is no longer enough to conduct business while avoiding breaking the rules. Companies have to benefit society. In this sense, air transport should use the megatrends that affect it to the benefit of the people using the air transport product. *eGovernance*; *eCitizens*; and smart transportation are the main headings of megatrends in air transport.

The entire air transport industry would have to redefine its purpose. A paradigm shift from pure company profits to serving the travelling public using the shifting trends is what is called for. Connectivity, improved facilitation of air transport using technology and other trends as well as corporate responsibility have to be meshed together to redefine the industry.

Megatrends connects everything—data, processes and humans—and geo political instability and volatility, coupled with cyber deceit would make it easier for cyber hackers to engage in duplicitous practices to the detriment of airlines and airports. Cyber breaches will increase and destructive techniques will improve. Therefore, megatrends will have to be developed with technology that could reduce cybersecurity risks associated with both insider and external threats. "Cyber savvy companies and their boards are demanding more information about the specific threats they face, evaluating their resources, bolstering protection for critical assets, and preparing for incursions by advanced threat actors".[3]

If air transport were to ease into the megatrends as discussed in this book the aviation community (that includes air transport; airport; air navigation service providers; manufacturers) and regulators would have to come together under the umbrella of the only international organization—ICAO which is permitted by its constitutional document—the Chicago Convention—to convene studies in collaboration with its partners IATA, ACI and CANSO that would show a distinct link between where the industry is and where the industry would be in the future in serving the global community that uses air transport to connect itself with the world. Serious consideration may have to be given for a review of the constraints that exist in market access fuelled by protectionism. The trends facing environmental factors would also have to be studied. Legal ramifications of privacy issues that would emerge from technological advancement would have to be studied. Airlines would have to focus on the most practical way to achieve optimisation and efficiency. For manufacturers the key words would be size and speed. China, Canada, Russia and Brazil. Who are in the aircraft manufacturing business will intensify their competitive strategies, resulting in many new dynamics to the air transport sector and to the aerospace industry. Things could get complicated particularly in air traffic management, as there will be a greater variety of technologies to interoperate.

Technological development has had a significant impact on the economics of air travel. Each technological development has enabled aircraft to travel faster and further with better fuel efficiency and comfort. New information technology has

[3]EY identifies top fraud and corruption trends for 2016 New York, 14 December 2015, EY Building a better world, at http://www.ey.com/us/en/newsroom/news-releases/news-ey-identifies-top-fraud-and-corruption-trends-for-2016.

automated many things, not only improving comfort and operational efficiency, but also contributing greatly to safety For States the operative criterion would be the evolution of air transport in their territories that would benefit society within and the travelling public. Competition would be a key issue for all players in the megatrends equation. Going with the flow would of course be the main driver but not the only one. Innovation, finding new markets and supplying to their demand would be factors that megatrends would benefit.

Adaptation to shifting trends would also be an important factor. Diversification by both airlines and airports of their business models and their products to shifting demographic trends as well as geo-political developments would be a factor for consideration. Low-fare carriers would also have to diversify their products and offer services that remain attractive at reasonable prices. The emergence of Very Light Jets (VLJ), which are manufactured at low cost and carry 40–50 passengers on a air taxi basis could proliferate in the skies. Unmanned aircraft systems (UAS) will also proliferate and will use automation to a level that would require coordination at an advanced level in terms of air traffic control. Also from a legal perspective, lawyers would have to be imaginative in the context of looking differently at air carrier liability and possible stringent standards that might be imposed by the courts for damage caused to passengers for death or injury. The last frontier would be the interest of the user—the passenger—who would be attracted to the competitor that would offer the most number of apps to make her journey a better one that competitor airlines would offer.

Index

R. Abeyratne, *Megatrends and Air Transport*, DOI 10.1007/978-3-319-61124-2

MIX
Papier aus verantwortungsvollen Quellen
Paper from responsible sources
FSC® C105338

If you have any concerns about our products,
you can contact us on
ProductSafety@springernature.com

In case Publisher is established outside the EU,
the EU authorized representative is:
Springer Nature Customer Service Center GmbH
Europaplatz 3, 69115 Heidelberg, Germany

Printed by Libri Plureos GmbH
in Hamburg, Germany